The Death and Life of Malcolm X

Also by Peter Goldman

Report from Black America

Civil Rights: The Challenge of the Fourteenth Amendment
(For young people)

The Death and Life of Malcolm X

PETER GOLDMAN

Harper & Row, Publishers

NEW YORK

EVANSTON

SAN FRANCISCO

LONDON

FIRST EDITION

STANDARD BOOK NUMBER: 06–011582–3

LIBRARY OF CONGRESS CATALOG CARD NUMBER: 70–138726

Designed by Sidney Feinberg

For Helen

Contents

PART II. The Hour of the Knife

PART III. A Detective Story

PART IV. Every Goodbye Ain't Gone

Illustrations

Photographs appear after page 170 and page 266.

A diagram of the Audubon Ballroom appears on page 272.

Being from America made me intensely sensitive
to matters of color.

—*The Autobiography of Malcolm X*

Foreword

This is a white book about Malcolm X. That makes it an anomaly by the politics and aesthetics of color in our time; one ought accordingly to say it before anything else, so that those who believe a white writer incapable of dealing honestly or compassionately with a black hero can tune out immediately. Obviously, I disagree with this proposition, but a lot of black people do believe it, and they have persuaded a lot of white people that it is so. The distance between our two Americas is so wide now that I had to explain myself to practically everybody, black and white, in interviews for this book and even in casual social conversation about it. My answers in the space of more than three years working on the project got quite unspontaneous. The first thing black people asked me was why I wanted to write about a black saint; my answer was because I was interested and. The first thing white people asked was whether it wasn't, well—*difficult* nowadays; my answer was yes but.

The reason for this book, really, is Malcolm. I knew him; I was not his friend or confidant, but we did meet between 1962 and 1964, usually for those marathon two- and three-hour interviews he granted too generously, and we exchanged letters when I was a newspaperman in St. Louis. I hope that I earned some small degree of his trust; my only evidence for thinking so is that our meetings got progressively more like conversations, and after the last one, in 1964, one of his people telephoned to say that Malcolm had considered my ensuing *Newsweek* piece about him "fair." I do know that he had enormous impact on me, quite beyond the fact that I liked and admired him. I was covering the race beat in those days, first as a sort of subspecialty at the St. Louis *Globe-Democrat,* later more or less full-time for *Newsweek;* the media simply did not have black reporters then, and the few who were around covered the story like the rest of us, which is to say from a liberal, integrationist point of view. Malcolm was a revelation for many of us. He was for me; he could be outrageous at moments, but he spoke with enormous personal authority, and he showed us another black America that most of us didn't know existed. Malcolm changed me, and I suppose that is why I wanted to write about him.

I approached him here quite consciously from a white perspective. Or a double perspective, really: I have tried to see him both out of our innocence of the early 1960s, at the romantic crest of the civil-rights revolt, and out of the burned-out vision of the early 1970s, after some of his uglier prophecies had come true. I have not tried to pre-empt the field—as if one book could. I have considerable sympathy for the notion that the black experience is unique and that black people therefore ought to define black heroes; I hope black writers will do shelves of books about Malcolm and his time. But Malcolm addressed himself to white people, too, and was therefore part of the white experience; one had, that is, to respond to him, and Malcolm seems to me large enough to survive being seen and written about from a white as well as a black point of view.

It would be disingenuous to say that I have not tried to define Malcolm. Every work of biography, even an entry in *Who's Who* or a two-paragraph newspaper obituary, is an attempt at definition. But I have tried to define him minimally—to resist the temptation to crowd him into some neat little box and label him nationalist, or socialist, or militant, or hatemonger, or any of the other names in which we have tried in the past to contain his protean life and intelligence. My "definition" of Malcolm, to the extent I have one, is that he was neither saint nor sinner but a good and gifted man struggling imperfectly toward daylight; I believe that his past killed him just as he was triumphing over it. Beyond that, I think, he quite resists definition. The difficulties are clear in some of the existing Malcolm literature. He can be as unrecognizable in his eulogies as he was in his old media caricature as the apostle of hate and violence.

One might also note that Malcolm has left us all, black and white, a substantial body of written and recorded material defining himself. His *Autobiography* is a great American life, a compelling and irreplaceable book, and there are now several volumes or parts of volumes of Malcolm's speeches and several LP recordings as well; Malcolm was not without weaknesses, but he was and he remains entirely able to speak for himself. I have attempted here as best I can to pick up where the available literature leaves off. This book greatly foreshortens Malcolm's early life and focuses heavily on his last years—the period of his progressive estrangement from the Nation of Islam (the Black Muslims, to most of us) and his single year on his own, trying to create a new politics of blackness in America and Africa. Alex Haley, Malcolm's collaborator on the *Autobiography,* had diminishing access to him during that last year, and the Malcolm of that period has always seemed to me tantalizingly just out of reach. Malcolm is gone now, but I have tried to reconstruct that time as nearly as I could out of the reminiscences of dozens of his friends and associates and out of his own words in speeches, interviews and talk shows, some already in print, some quoted here for the first time. Another major section of the book examines Malcolm's assassination and the ensuing investigation and murder trial; there is considerable folklore as to who killed him and why, but almost nothing serious in print about how the official verdict was arrived at and what its strengths and weaknesses really are. And finally there are some observations about the Malcolm Phenomenon—

his transfiguration since his death, by blacks and not a few whites, into a kind of plaster sainthood in which some of his rich humanity and his real contributions have got lost.

A few people—surprisingly few, in retrospect—did decline to be interviewed for this book. One of these, to my regret, was Malcolm's widow, Mrs. Betty Shabazz; this book is in that sense what jacket writers call an Unauthorized Biography. She communicated her reluctance in the course of two long conversations. She is a bright, lively woman, reminiscent in subtle ways of Malcolm. I liked her and in fact rather sympathized with her suspicions; in the end I could not overcome them. The Organization of Afro-American Unity twice made appointments for me with Malcolm's half-sister, Mrs. Ella Collins, who took over the organization after his death. She did not appear either time. I made repeated further attempts to reach her by phone and letter, without success. Two of Malcolm's followers did refuse to see me; a third, whom I wanted very badly to interview, had disappeared since Malcolm's death and was out of reach by mail, message or that most pervasive of communications media in Harlem, The Wire; at least two others were in prison and inaccessible.

But others of his friends and associates were most generous with their time and reminiscences, and I am greatly indebted to all of them. Nearly one hundred interviews went into the making of this book, most of them conducted by me, several others by *Newsweek* colleagues and stringers in Europe and Africa. Many of the interviewees are identified clearly in the text; many others, though not quoted directly, have influenced my feelings about Malcolm in ways they will recognize. There is no point attempting to list all of them here. I would like to express my particular thanks to Benjamin Goodman and Charles Kenyatta, both of whom worked bravely and well with Malcolm in the Nation of Islam and beyond. I want also to absolve them, with more than the usual energy, of any responsibility for my conclusions about Malcolm and his assassination. The judgments, and the mistakes, are mine alone.

It is customary in forewords to place one's wife last ("but not least") in one's list of acknowledgments and to credit her principally with the virtue of patience and the capacity for silent suffering. My wife, Helen Dudar, belongs first, and her contributions were considerably larger than her ability to endure. She knew Malcolm, for one thing, at least as well as I; we met him together in 1962, and she later wrote a number of stories about him for the New York *Post,* including a series that Malcolm himself (see the *Autobiography* at page 397) admired. Her recollections about and perceptions of Malcolm were extremely helpful; so were the notes assembled by her and various *Post* colleagues, including Al Ellenberg and Ted Poston. She not only suffered my progressively more monomaniacal conversation about Malcolm but participated in it. And she read the manuscript in installments, like some incomprehensibly long-running newspaper serial, making unfailingly useful editorial suggestions along the way.

One's further debts proliferate over three years. Claude Lewis, an old friend and colleague, lent me a richly evocative taped interview from Malcolm's last months. Peter L. F. Sabbatino let me haunt his law office and read his set of the murder trial minutes, *People* v. *Thomas Hagan et al.* The Schomburg Collection in Harlem is a marvelous mother lode of black history; I used their files on Malcolm, the Muslims and Marcus Garvey. *The Militant,* the only paper outside Harlem to cover Malcolm regularly in his last year, kindly allowed me to use their bound files. The morgues at *Newsweek,* the Washington *Post* and the London *Daily Express* were all helpful. Mary Doris of the *Newsweek* London bureau did a particularly useful interview for me; so did Ahmed Shawki in Cairo and Segun Osoba in Nigeria. Kermit Lansner, the editor of *Newsweek,* generously granted me a leave of absence to write this book. Other past and present *Newsweek* colleagues—among them Ed Cumberbatch, Joseph B. Cumming, Jr., Lenore Jenkins, Don Johnson, James Jones, Nicholas Profitt and Peter Webb—helped me locate people or knot up unraveled ends. Mary Hood and James Buell typed the manuscript. Jeannette Hopkins edited it.

Lisa Katz and Susan Tyler Hitchcock worried it through the system. I am grateful to them all.

And last (but not least) my thanks to the management and staff of the Gramercy Park Hotel for The Crow's Nest. It is a splendid place to write a book.

New York City
April, 1972

The Death and Life of Malcolm X

PART I

Matters of Color

. . . I felt an easily identifiable flood mounting out of the countless facets of my being. I was about to be angry. The fire was long since out, and once more the nigger was trembling.

"Look how handsome that Negro is! . . ."
"Kiss the handsome Negro's ass, madame!"
—FRANTZ FANON, *Black Skins, White Masks*

1. The Death of Malcolm X

At the end, death was closing on him, and everybody saw it. The police saw it: two weeks before the event, the top command received an intelligence estimate that he was in imminent danger and offered him round-the-clock protection, knowing he could never accept. His friends saw it: they begged him to get out of town for a while—to Africa, to Europe, to California, anywhere away from Harlem and the most visible of his enemies. And Malcolm X saw it. He told people that he didn't care really, not for himself, but he lived out his last weeks and months jumping at street sounds and flinching at shadows, and at the end some of the brothers worried that he might be cracking. "He really got strung out," one of them told me. "He wanted to die. Malcolm *wanted* to die." One could not easily imagine a man so alive embracing death. Yet the desperation of those days finally did seem to push him past caring, and if he did not want to die, he was too spent to run from death any longer.

And so he managed to get himself uptown to the Audubon Ballroom that winter Sunday in 1965 to meet his followers; there was nowhere else for him to go. He came in early and sat in a dressing room offstage, taut, jangled and growling at friends. *Strung out.* He was harried and broke. He had been bombed out of his home, then run out of the ruins a step ahead of the eviction papers. His infant organization was coming unglued. His Sunday afternoon crowds had shrunk to a point where sometimes the buckets had to be passed twice just to raise the $125 rent on the hall. He had promised to announce his program for the liberation of the blacks that day, but the committee assigned to put it together for him hadn't finished yet, not to his satisfaction, and he wasn't sure what he was going to say. He had invited several guests to share the platform with him, but none of them showed up; Malcolm, waiting to go on, could see the row of chairs stretching empty beyond the plywood lectern. He sometimes thought he had the gift, or the curse, of second sight, and something troubled him about that afternoon. "I just don't *feel* right," he told the brothers in the room.

Finally it was time; he could hear Brother Benjamin finishing the introduction ("And now . . . a man who would give his life for you"), and then he was out on stage, alone and terribly vulnerable. He had always insisted on the right of black people to defend themselves *by any means necessary* against physical attack. But Malcolm's defenses that afternoon consisted of a rather uncertain corps of bodyguards; his personal armament, a tear-gas pen in his own breast pocket. Malcolm, or somebody speaking in his name, had directed that nobody be searched coming into the meeting; had told the brothers on guard duty to leave their guns at home, though a few disobeyed; and had asked the police kindly to take most of their twenty-man guard detail off the sidewalk in front of the Audubon and deploy them out of sight across the street. There was a case of sorts to be made for all of this at the time: Malcolm had begun worrying that the talk of death and the martial aura of policemen and armed guards and body-searches were frightening people away from his meetings. But the result was to lay him wide open to the men who had been hunting him. He stood there in the pallid February sunlight filling the room, and it was almost as if he were delivering himself to his assassins.

The police tape-recorded the meeting as a matter of routine, Malcolm's speeches having been deemed a potential threat to the peace and good order of New York City. Later they played their tape, hoping it would help them reconstruct what had happened.

You could hear Brother Benjamin's introduction, then the clatter of applause and the exchange of greetings. *As-salaam alaikum.* Peace be unto you. *Wa-alaikum salaam.* And unto you be peace. A shout, a stirring in the audience, Malcolm saying "Hold it, hold it—" A sudden roar—*blaaam!* And then dead silence; the first shotgun blast had splintered the plywood and cut the microphone wires dangling in front of Malcolm's chest.

2. A Conversation at the Shabazz Frosti Kreem

He was the messenger who brought us the bad news, and nobody wanted to hear it. I didn't—not the day we first met in the early spring of 1962 at the Shabazz Frosti Kreem, a scrubbed-down little Black Muslim luncheonette in the North Side ghetto of St. Louis. Malcolm and the Muslims and the notion that whites as a race might have incurred—might in fact have earned—the undifferentiated loathing of black people had then only just begun intruding on the American liberal consciousness. I had done a newspaper series on the Muslims in St. Louis and had discovered—happily, I remember—that they had fared badly there; the nightly television newscasts in those days were full of young blacks and whites singing that they would overcome someday, and I still wanted to believe them. I knew from my own encounters with the Lost-Found Nation of Islam in the Wilderness of North America—the people we called the Black Muslims—that I was, in the eyes of some fraction of the ghettoed black masses, a white devil. But it seemed rather an abstract and distant proposition until that afternoon. Malcolm made it real, and the reality was numbing.

He came late. My wife, Helen Dudar, who is also a journalist, and I were waiting outside the luncheonette when Clyde X, the local minister, chauffeured Malcolm to the door. I remember him unfolding out of the car; he was a tall, coppery man, six-feet-three and long-muscled, with close-cut hair, cool gray-green eyes and the straight-up bearing of a soldier, or a priest. He led us all inside and left us at a table briefly while he studied the jukebox and dropped in a coin. In a moment, we heard the pop-popping of a bongo drum and a voice singing, ". . . So my friends, it's easy to tell—a white man's heaven is a black man's hell." Malcolm sat down smiling. He signaled for coffee, and the baleful young black man behind the counter brought over four cups. Malcolm stirred some cream into his and smiled again. "Coffee," he said, "is the only thing I like integrated."

It was one of his stock lines; Malcolm had by then heard all the questions and rehearsed all the answers. Over the next three hours—an interview with Malcolm almost always ran two or three hours—he told us perfectly pleasantly that whites were inherently the enemies of Negroes; that integration was impossible without great bloodletting and was undesirable anyway; that nonviolence—"this mealy-mouth, beg-in, wait-in, plead-in kind of action"—was only a device for disarming the blacks and, worse still, unmanning them; that everything we had heard to the contrary from the Martin Luther Kings and the Roy Wilkinses and the Whitney Youngs was a deadly dangerous pack of lies. "That's etiquette," he said. "Etiquette means to blend in with society. They're being polite. The average Negro doesn't even let another *Negro* know what he thinks, he's so mistrusting. He's an acrobat. He had to be to survive in this civilization. But by me being a Muslim, I'm black first—my sympathies are black, my allegiance is black, my whole objectives are black. By me being a Muslim, I'm not interested in being American, because America has never been interested in me."

One had the feeling of having strayed into another country; in the Lost-Found Nation, all the white racist stereotypes and the white liberal sentimentalisms spun dizzyingly upside down. Black blood, we learned, is stronger than white—"A person can have a teaspoon of black blood in him, and that makes him black." Black genes, too—"Black can't come from white, but white can come from black. That means black was first. If black is first, black is supreme, and white is dependent on black. Genetically, white is recessive. 'Recessive' has the same Latin root as 'recess'; it means 'retreat,' or 'minus.' If you were in France, for 'white' you'd say *blanc*. In Spanish, *blanco*. The English equivalent of *blanc* or *blanco* is not 'white' but 'blank.' The white people constitute a race that is blank—that has lost its pigmentation."

We found ourselves on his ground, protesting that the chemical composition of black and white cells is basically the same. "To withdraw pigmentation," Malcolm answered, "changes the chemical composition. It has a weakening effect. Like the cream in this coffee." The dazzling smile again, working according to its own independent thermodynamics: where the words chilled, the smile somehow warmed. "An example: music. Music involves vibration, or life itself. It has a different effect on whites than on blacks—as much a difference as night and day—because the so-called Negro has this vibration." I remember thinking: *He's saying they're naturally rhythmic.* "We don't hate. The white man has a guilt complex—he knows he's done wrong. He knows that if he had undergone at our hands what we have undergone at his, he would hate us. But it's easier for a white man to hate than a black man. The black man is naturally happy-go-lucky." Wait, Helen managed—isn't that the white stereotype? "The Negro intellectual *you* come into contact with doesn't want to be identified with stereotypes. He doesn't want to be identified with something different from what America represents, because he wants to open that door and get in. So he'll dispute that. But it's true."

"I wouldn't think of Minister Clyde here as happy-go-lucky," I said. Clyde X, like most of the middle management of the Nation of Islam, was not a very spontaneous man; he had sat through the conversation glowering silently, smiling only when Malcolm smiled first. "Or you either."

"That's because we're discussing serious matters here."

We smiled together only once, near the end. Helen asked what would happen if all the little businesses the Muslims were starting got successful—wouldn't their people go bourgeois and defect to the NAACP? Malcolm started a serious answer; Helen assured him she was only kidding; then he chuckled and said it couldn't happen. Mostly, we did discuss serious matters. I remember saying at one point that our best hope lay not in the separation of the races, as he and the Muslims proposed, but in a single society in which color no longer made a critical difference. I suppose I believe that still, though no longer with very much faith that it will happen. Malcolm began my re-education that day at the Shabazz Frosti Kreem. "You're dealing in fantasy," he said sharply. "You've got to deal in facts."

3. Malcolm

He saw his life as combat, and words as his weapon. It has been said of him that he brought no pursuable strategy, no concrete program, to the struggle of the blacks in white America—that he stood talking on the sidelines through the most momentous years in our race relations since the Civil War. He was denouncing intermarriage on a radio talk show the night James Meredith and five thousand soldiers "integrated" the University of Mississippi; he watched the police dogs and fire hoses of Birmingham on television in New York; he was off in Cairo pursuing a dream alliance with black Africa when the first of the big-city ghetto insurrections exploded out of the alleys of Harlem. He was always somewhere else, it was said, with a lavaliere mike or a little knot of reporters, hooting, heckling, scolding, accusing, but never participating. He never got anybody a job or decent housing, Whitney Young once complained in a moment of private bitterness, but you could find his name in the *TV Guide* program listings more times than Johnny Carson's.

All of it was true, and probably beside the point. Malcolm's life was itself an accusation—a passage to the ninth circle of that black man's hell and back—and the real meaning of his ministry, in and out of the Nation of Islam, was to deliver that accusation to us. If he lived at the margins of our national life, he was rarely out of sight. He was a dark presence, angry, cynical, implacable; a man whose good will or forgiveness or even pity we could neither earn nor buy. He meant to haunt us—to play on our fears and quicken our guilts and deflate our dreams that everything was getting better—and he did. "America's problem is *us,*" he said. Others had been telling us that politely for years, and now we have the judgment of a Presidential commission that we are a society decisively shaped by our racism. The difference was that most of the others offered us the hope that matters could be put right with application and conscience and money. Malcolm did not. He did not believe that America had a conscience; he offered as proof the tragic past of the blacks beginning the day the first trader took the first slave out of Africa. He therefore did not accept the formulation that there is an American Dilemma—a constant tension between the ideals of the American Creed and the realities of caste and color. Our Creed and our Constitution were never meant to include black people, Malcolm told us, and if we argued that the sins of the past ought not to be visited on us, he replied: "Your father isn't here to pay his debts. My father isn't here to collect. But I'm here to collect, and you're here to pay."

Malcolm may never really have hated all white people with that pure wrath he preached during his dozen years in the service of Elijah Muhammad, the Last Messenger of Allah, and his little Lost-Found Nation in the Wilderness. Whites who encountered Malcolm even in those days and who could see past his press reputation as a hatemonger found him unfailingly civil and occasionally friendly, in a distant way. Later, during the year between his break with Muhammad and his death, he absolved us of the blanket judgment that we were all devils and announced that he would thereafter hold us accountable only for our behavior, not for our color or our genes. Whereupon we missed the point again and made too much of our absolution; it seemed somehow terribly important to us, as Ivanhoe Donaldson of the old Student Nonviolent Coordinating Committee put it sourly, "that this man shouldn't have the audacity to go to his grave saying that all white folks are full of shit."

He didn't—but neither did he alter the fundamental terms of the indictment: that American whites collectively remain the enemy of the blacks collectively until their behavior proves otherwise. "He was always challenging the white man, always debunking the white man," said his friend C. Eric Lincoln, whose book *The Black Muslims in America* helped bring Malcolm and the Nation to public light. "I don't think he was ever under any illusion that a powerless black minority could mount a physical challenge to a powerful white majority and survive. But they could mount a psychological challenge, and if they were persistent, they might at least produce some erosion in the attitudes and the strategies by which the white man has always protected himself and his interests. His challenge was to prove that you are as great as you say you are, that you are as moral as you say you are, that you are as kind as you say you are, that you are as loving as you say you are, that you are as altruistic as you say you are, that you are as *superior* as you say you are." One after another of Malcolm's friends, Lincoln among them, felt obliged to assure me that this never really changed—that Malcolm never softened on whitey. Maybe they were afraid I would try to make him an integrationist; maybe they were suspicious of a white writer even raising the question. I remember meeting John Oliver Killens, the novelist, one afternoon in a midtown Manhattan bar, an overwhelmingly white place with twittering birds and syrupy violins. Killens, who had befriended Malcolm before it was fashionable or even respectable to do so, was particularly insistent: sure, Malcolm saw some White Muslims on his pilgrimage to Mecca, but he knew when he came home that America was still the same white-supremacist society he had left. We had two or three rounds, and then Killens got up to leave. "Malcolm," he said, "knew what color he was."

Malcolm did reach some whites, probably more than he imagined, and far more after his death and the publication of his posthumous *Autobiography* than during his lifetime. But the redemption of whites was of secondary interest to him, and then only because we had the power, not because he thought we deserved redeeming. "His main message," said Killens, "was to the black grass roots. If white folks dug what he was saying, fine. If not, shame *on* them." His more urgent business was the retrieval of black people from what he saw as the worst crime white America had done them: we had taught them to hate themselves.

Malcolm himself had been dragged low by self-hatred; had pimped and hustled and sniffed coke and flashed his white women and had finally done time for burglary; had even in the Black Muslim days occasionally tripped over one of his stock formulations and said he hated every drop of black blood—uh, *white* blood—in his body. His self-esteem was purchased first at the cost of indenturing his mind and soul to Mr. Muhammad and the mysteries of the Lost-Found Nation; only later did he find it in his own manhood. He achieved it, out of the ashes of his old life, by creating a totally new one. He determined that his past was ours, a part of our landscape of ruins, and he declared his independence of it, and of us. He became in his own eyes neither a Negro nor an American—"I'm not going to sit at your table," he told us, "and watch you eat, with nothing on my plate, and call myself a diner"—but a spiritual DP, an African Muslim in forced exile in the mother country. Melvin Van Peebles, now a successful moviemaker, once trailed Malcolm around Paris for a free-lance French newspaper piece and asked him routinely what he thought had been the most significant event of the year just passing. That was November 1964; Khrushchev had fallen; Lyndon Johnson had delivered the Republic from a Goldwater Presidency and, so we thought, a widening Vietnam war; the Civil Rights Bill had passed; the first of the riot summers was just behind us. But Malcolm without hesitation chose the successful detonation of China's first primitive nuclear bomb. Van Peebles was surprised, and impressed. "The cat," he said, "had a decolonized mind."

Malcolm understood decolonization to be his work in black America. Whatever one made of the particulars of his argument, he delivered it with a personal authority that few other pretenders to leadership could claim, since he had lived so much of the black experience himself. "Malcolm," said Killens, "was all of us." Having experienced the degradation of the blacks, he was appalled by it, and even more by their acquiescence in it. He understood what Charles Silberman, a white writer he respected, has called "the black man's Negro problem"—the demoralization and the anomie of the ghetto. The original sin in his eyes was the white man's—he had severed the blacks from their past and reduced them to property—but the responsibility for the salvation of the blacks, Malcolm always insisted, was their own. This meant getting up out of the mud, out from under the white man's charity as well as his tyranny. It meant forgetting about integration, which was only a further denial of the worth of black people, and about nonviolence, which was only a newer, subtler form of humiliation before the slavemaster. It meant embracing the African past, till then a source of shame; it meant identifying not with the white majority in America and the West but with the dark majority of the world. It meant the discovery of what Eric Lincoln terms "a negotiable identity" as black men and women, deserving of the world's respect and their own.

And it meant standing up to The Man. One of the worst humiliations of all, in Malcolm's eyes, was that paralytic silence, that head-bobbing surrender, that seemed to him to afflict so many blacks in the presence of white people. The ghetto had been cursing whitey for years, in its own parlors and chicken shacks and street-corner rallies, but seldom to his face; so seldom, indeed, that a black man who did so seemed to whites presumptively insane—a crazy nigger—and so was accorded a kind of gingerly safe-conduct against reprisal. Malcolm was the crazy nigger gone public: he undertook to carry Harlem's fury downtown, to tell white people to their faces, in their own mass media, what ordinary blacks had been saying about them backstairs for all those years. Malcolm didn't teach hate, or need to; he exploited a vein of hate that was there already and to which few black Americans were totally immune. "Malcolm was saying what people wanted to say themselves and couldn't," said Charles Kenyatta, who followed him in the Nation of Islam and beyond. "He relieved them. They have to walk around all the time with everything stored up inside. Malcolm was the beginning of putting some backbone into this black child." Malcolm believed that their rage, once surfaced, could be a liberating force for black people—could disabuse them of that stifling terror and move them to action. He saw the equal possibility that it might explode, at catastrophic cost, and he was prepared to run the risk. "Like Samson," he once said, "I am ready to pull down the white man's temple, knowing full well that I will be destroyed by the falling rubble."

He meant it. He was, as he saw himself, waging war—a war of words, maybe, but a war nevertheless—and in a war anything goes. "There were two Malcolms, really," said M. S. Handler of the *New York Times,* one of the very few white journalists Malcolm allowed closer than arm's length. "There was the private Malcolm, a man of ineffable charm and courtesy; a born aristocrat. And there was the public Malcolm, Malcolm in combat, whose job it was to frighten the white man out of his shoes." He was a generously gifted leader, but his talents lay not nearly so much in organizing or programming as in that pitiless vision and that flailing tongue. His genius was attack. He often rationalized that you had to waken people first—that you couldn't give them a program until they knew they needed one. But the fact was that he loved the war; loved hearing the quick, sharp bursts of applause and seeing the white faces flush pink when he scored a point; loved outraging an enemy to whom black people could not otherwise cause pain.

Malcolm, as a consequence, could not resist a platform, or an interview, or even an audience of two or three in a hotel lobby in Jedda or on a street corner in Harlem. In his war, improvisation became a strategy. He discovered his art in a prison debating society and never lost the debater's faith in the quickness of his tongue and his mother wit; he did his cerebrating on his feet, in the heat of battle. Combat excited him, quickened his pulse, set his long fingers flying and jabbing the air, brought a red glow rising in his own face. Some of the brothers despaired of the time he gave the media, knowing as he did that the stories would usually come out Malcolm-the-man-of-hate. "It really destroyed him," one of them said. "He got drunk off it. He used to sit by the TV set and watch himself, and you could see how much he liked it." He could rarely bring himself to say no. His intuitive public-relations sense told him that the message, however badly refracted by the medium, would reach some black people who would listen—who would in fact be the more receptive precisely because the press put him down. There was thus a dividend in Malcolm's extempore war. He probably would have fought it anyway. Combat made him reckless of his time, his agenda and his reputation. It was at once his vice and his soul.

He could be quite conscienceless in a fight. He believed (and once defended in a debate at Oxford) the Goldwater homily that moderation in the pursuit of justice is no virtue, and, because he believed it, he quite literally didn't care what he said. "This is the thing—whatever I say, I'm justified," he ventured once, late in his life. "If I say that Negroes should get out here right tomorrow and go to war, I'm justified. Really. I may sound extreme, but you can't say that they wouldn't be justified." He saw nothing but the comfort of white people to be served by lowering one's voice and being "responsible." Once, in a debate at New York's Community Church, Bayard Rustin accused him of engaging in emotionalism. It stung. "When a man is hanging on a tree and he cries out," Malcolm retorted, his voice rising, "should he cry out unemotionally? When a man is sitting on a hot stove and he tells you how it feels to be there, is he supposed to speak without emotion? This is what you tell black people in this country when they begin to cry out against the injustices that they're suffering. As long as they describe these injustices in a way that makes you believe you have another hundred years to rectify the situation, then you don't call that emotion. But when a man is on a hot stove, he says, 'I'm coming up. I'm getting up. Violently or nonviolently doesn't even enter into the picture—I'm coming up, do you understand?' "

The end justified anything, even transient cruelties. Once, at a Harlem rally just after his break with Muhammad, someone in the question-and-answer period mentioned the six million Jews sent to the ovens in the Third Reich. "Everybody talks about the six million Jews," Malcolm said. "But I was reading a book the other day that showed that one hundred million of us were kidnaped and brought to this country—*one hundred million.* Now everybody's wet-eyed over a handful of Jews who brought it on themselves. What about our one hundred million?" The line got a good hand; the Jews Harlem sees tend to be landlords, storekeepers and welfare workers, and nobody gets wet-eyed about them. Waiting for the applause to quiet, Malcolm glanced down at the row of reporters up front—the only whites in the house—and noticed one of them, Al Ellenberg of the New York *Post,* noting down his words. "Now there's a reporter who hasn't taken a note in half an hour," he said, "but as soon as I start talking about the Jews, he's busy taking notes to prove that I'm anti-Semitic."

"Kill the bastard," a voice behind the reporters growled. "Kill them all."

Ellenberg, who actually had been taking notes throughout the speech, smiled unhappily. "Look at him laugh," Malcolm gibed. "He's not really laughing. He's just laughing with his teeth"—Malcolm grimaced in imitation of a laugh—"but look at his eyes and you'll see he's not laughing." The mood started turning palpably nasty—whereupon, as expertly as he had started it, Malcolm ended the game. "The white man doesn't know how to laugh," he said. "He just shows his teeth. But we know how to laugh—we laugh deep down, from the bottom up." He laughed; so did the crowd, and the tension wound down. It was a graceless performance, and Malcolm knew it. When Ellenberg chanced to call him a few days later for an interview, Malcolm half-apologized for having tormented him. "When I'm talking, I use everything that's around," he said. "It doesn't mean anything."

In debate, Malcolm could cut (he addressed any well-spoken black opponent as "doctor" to set him apart as an accredited and therefore co-opted Negro) and he could bludgeon: once, on the mildest provocation, he called a luckless NAACP spokesman a "well-dressed, fat, pompous Negro . . . satisfied to get crumbs from the master's table" and then charged *him* with getting personal.

Malcolm nearly always won these encounters, or at least the crowds who attended them, partly because he was so brilliant at it, partly because he was unconstrained by the conventional niceties of debate, and partly because he pre-empted a kind of moral high ground for himself. It was Malcolm who carried the indictment against white America for the historic wrong done the blacks, and he prosecuted it with a bleak moral fury. To answer that he overstated the case was to quibble with details; the condition of the blacks in America was proof enough of his basic claims. To oppose him by arguing the necessity of alliances and programs was to throw in with the enemy, since programs and alliances implied the good will or at least the tractability of whites. And to contend that there had after all been some progress was to deny the continuing pain of the great masses of blacks. "You don't stick a knife in a man's back nine inches and then pull it out six inches and say you're making progress," Malcolm said. "It's dangerous to even make the white man *think* we're making progress while the knife is still in our backs, or while the wound is still there, or while even the intention that he had is still there."

Malcolm's war challenged the leaders and the orthodoxies of the civil-rights movement in the midst of its glory days, and he paid for it; the cost was a kind of quarantine that lifted only with his death. Alive, he made the elders of the movement uncomfortable. They thought him a genuine danger to the cause of racial comity; they resented his running attacks on them; they envied his easy access to radio and television; they were embarrassed by his claim to the allegiance of a ghetto lumpenproletariat they had talked about but never reached. A few were willing to debate him—Rustin, for one, and the late writer Louis Lomax, for another; and James Farmer of CORE, until he and Malcolm finally agreed between themselves to quit putting on black family quarrels for the amusement of white people. But King wouldn't meet him (he once threatened to cancel out of a David Susskind television panel if Malcolm was invited), and neither would Roy Wilkins or Whitney Young. The two of them tried unsuccessfully to talk Farmer out of one TV confrontation with Malcolm; Young argued that the only black he had ever seen hold his own against Malcolm was the ultraconservative columnist George Schuyler, which proved that you couldn't be moderate or liberal or even conventionally militant and hope to win.

So Malcolm found himself in isolation from the front-line struggle, even after he had broken with Mr. Muhammad and wanted to join it. He was isolated from respect as well. Now that he is dead and buried and beatified, a saint whom all must praise, one easily forgets how little the recognized Negro leadership of the day—even the militant leadership—wanted to have to do with him, at least in public. His commitment to the liberation of the blacks from bondage, body and soul, was total and consuming. "My hobby is stirring up Negroes," he liked to say, and he gave it eighteen or twenty hours a day every day. Yet for the mainstream leaders, he was never a comrade-in-arms, only a hobgoblin they could hold up to whites for a certain scare effect: look who's waiting in the wings if you don't deal with us. They placed him in moral Coventry, and it wounded Malcolm; something in him wanted acceptance, though never at the price he would have had to pay. "He really hungered to be recognized as a national leader," one friend said. "It hurt him when first Kennedy and then Johnson would call King, Wilkins, Young and Farmer to the White House. He wanted it to be a fivesome instead of a foursome." King's celebrity particularly rankled him, built as it was on a philosophy and a style of action Malcolm found degrading. Harlem put on a rally for King in late 1964, to celebrate his Nobel Peace Prize. It wasn't Malcolm's party, but he and a few followers showed up anyway and watched in heavy silence from a back row. "He got the peace prize, we got the problem," he told a black writer bitterly a few days later. "I don't want the white man giving me medals. If I'm following a general, and he's leading me into battle, and the enemy tends to give him rewards, or awards, I get suspicious of him. Especially if he gets a peace award before the war is over."

His bad press ultimately wounded him, too, particularly after he left the Nation of Islam with its iron black-and-white certitude and entered on the extraordinary personal transformations of the last months of his life. He couldn't make us see those changes; he remained, in print, a cartoon Black Muslim urging our otherwise affectionate black masses to hatred and violence against whites. Malcolm came to understand that he shared the blame for this with the media—that he had after all been too obliging with his time and his hot rhetoric. He had been our Frantz Fanon; the natives in America have neither the numbers nor the guns to do whites that gratifying violence that Fanon identified at the heart of the Algerian terror, but, at least for a time in the 1960s, they could make whites jump when they said *Woof!* and that was something. It was Malcolm, really, who discovered this—discovered how close the specter of the black revenge lies to the surface of the white American consciousness—and, having discovered it, he could rarely resist its pleasures.

At his press conference formally declaring his independence of Mr. Muhammad, he argued that black people ought to get guns and organize to use them in their own defense wherever the government failed in its duty to protect them. It was not an unreasonable position, given the run of unpunished and unrequited acts of violence against blacks in the South, and it was in any case only one of several themes Malcolm struck that morning. But the call to arms produced more questions at the news conference than any other point, and Malcolm responded with what seemed to me at the time an almost palpable relish. I saw him that afternoon in Harlem; I remember suggesting that he had anticipated the response to the business about guns and had actually enjoyed it. He grinned widely. "I bet they pass a bill to outlaw the sale of rifles," he said, "and it won't be filibustered either." But in his last days he began to have second thoughts—to wonder whether that kick-ass audacity that had made his reputation hadn't been a trap for him as well. His press image, he said, "was created by them and by me. . . . They were looking for sensationalism, for something that would sell papers, and I gave it to them."

People who met him privately—particularly black people—were baffled by the caricature; the Malcolm they knew was too complicated a man to fit the labels the rest of us attached to him. He had, given his feral reputation, a surprisingly formal look—a look of reserve heightened by his half-rimmed glasses, his high-polished shoes and his three-button, three-piece suits. The style went with an inner austerity, a final distance imposed by his role as a leader and his sense of what a leader ought to be. Malcolm achieved, by will and later by habit, a sort of contained calm that was part of his mastery of people and situations. Benjamin Goodman, who as Benjamin 2X was Malcolm's assistant minister in the Nation of Islam and a trusted deputy afterward, remembered that extraordinary discipline: "He was the kind of man that, if you came up and said there's a bomb in here, he'd say, 'Now sit down, brother, let's be cool, let's figure this out.'" Goodman remembered the distance as well. "Nobody was close to him—nobody. Some of these brothers now saying they were close to him—no, they weren't close. He used to send me out of town, and I'd come back and go to his house maybe at one in the morning and we'd talk. But we didn't get close. Not in the buddy sense. He was always in *command.* You didn't get close, that wasn't his way."

Malcolm was an ascetic man as well. The Nation of Islam holds its true believers to a very nearly monkish code of conduct: no drinking, no smoking, no drugs, no sexual license or even dating, no dances or ballgames or movies, no sleeping late, no more than one meal a day. Malcolm practiced it all scrupulously in the Nation; he wouldn't even go to his friend Ossie Davis's Broadway play, *Purlie Victorious,* without a dispensation from Mr. Muhammad. When he left, he brought the Muslims' morality with him, exacting it of himself even after he quit asking it of his followers. The code was particularly severe about sex. Malcolm was developing a considerable reputation in the Nation as a misogynist until he finally married Betty Shabazz in 1958, when he was nearly thirty-three. There were, particularly after the break with Mr. Muhammad, the usual rumors of dalliances that attach to public people—particularly to public men as masculine and as attractive as Malcolm. Some of the tales were promoted by the Nation once Malcolm began publicly to question Mr. Muhammad's own moral behavior. Most of his acquaintances simply refused to believe the talk. "It doesn't fit," one woman friend told me. "Anything amoral or immoral from Malcolm just would not follow. He loved Betty and he loved those children. And women never threw themselves at him. There was something about him that forbade—what's the word—vulgarity? Or intimacy?" I offered "intrusion." "Intrusion. Exactly."

Yet the distance was never forbidding, the morality never chilling. Malcolm could be a man of contagious warmth, which whites infrequently saw because he rarely squandered it on them. Black people, by contrast, found his presence transforming. "He could make you see things," his lawyer, Percy Sutton, recalled. "Malcolm undressed you, put you in front of the mirror and let you smile at yourself and say, 'I've got to change that.' " He loved gossip and celebrities and parties, though his drink was usually orange juice or coffee, or tea late at night, and his small talk was almost all about The Problem. He commanded any room he was in. "You'd walk in and look around and see a crowd," Killens said, "and there'd be that tall man standing in the middle of it. When he would come over to my house, there would be people there whom other people ask for autographs. And they would ask for *his.*" Malcolm was oddly shy about his own celebrity, almost as if it so defied credibility that he couldn't quite believe it himself, and his diffidence made him the more attractive. "He didn't reach for power," Mike Handler said. "Power came to him."

Away from the crowds and the microphones, Malcolm was rather a gentle man. His purposefulness never quit, but the jugular impulse did, and instead of the chance cruelties of the platform, there were the small kindnesses that people remembered. James Farmer's white wife went to the March on Washington alone—Farmer was in jail for demonstrating in Louisiana—and she happened into a hotel lobby where Malcolm was declaiming to a little clump of marchers about, among other things, his theory that most prominent black integrationists liked integration mainly because they had married white. Mrs. Farmer edged close and introduced herself. "That's exactly what I was talking about—"

Malcolm started, turning back to his audience. But something checked him; he missed a beat, then went on: "Farmer's in jail and Kennedy isn't doing anything about it." Everyone sensed what he had begun to say, and was grateful that he hadn't.

Men with power over people are not always afflicted by conscience, but Malcolm was, much as his public role prevented him from displaying it. Some of his conversions to Black Islam caused him pain later; there were others he couldn't even bring himself to attempt. Kenneth Clark, the black psychologist, has never forgotten the days in the early 1960s when his son Hilton, then a freshman at Columbia, became "very taken with Malcolm. . . . He saw us on TV together, and I suppose he always felt that Malcolm came out on top. He began spending some time around the Muslim mosque in Harlem. He was *fascinated.* I suspected this, but I didn't know it, until one day I was down there and Malcolm took me aside."

"You know," said Malcolm, "Hilton has been around here rather frequently."

"Really?" Clark answered guardedly.

"Don't worry," Malcolm said.

"I won't," Clark replied. He understood Malcolm to be saying he wouldn't proselytize Hilton; Malcolm didn't, and, though they crossed paths often, they never discussed the subject again.

Malcolm was a man of rich, bubbling humor. Offstage, in the family, it was race humor, dependent not so much on wordplay or memorable laugh-lines as on styles of speech—he could do wicked imitations of the national civil-rights leaders—and shadings of voice. "A lot of black American humor is based on tonal inflection," Maya Angelou, the novelist and poet, remarked. "Malcolm could talk for an hour and a half at a meeting, and then on the way to the car, he'd say something like 'Was I *bad*' "—her voice tripped high—" 'or was I *baaad?*' "—this time drawly and low. "Not those words exactly, but something like it, and he'd break you up. A minute before, he was showing you the pits of hell and the possible pinnacles of heaven, and then, between leaving the meeting and getting into the car, you'd be laughing."

On the platform, particularly before black audiences, Malcolm's bantery streak turned into authentic black comedy, all parody and self-deprecation. In a black crowd, the inflection would broaden, the correct mixed-company English would go slurred and slangy and the smiles would turn inward, lancing at black fears and black vanities. "And you gonna get nonviolent with this man—why, you out of your mind." It was a humor that could dissipate tensions. At street-corner rallies in Harlem, Malcolm would harangue the police unmercifully for their brutalities and corruptions, but never the particular policeman assigned to stand guard. "Maybe some of these blue-eyed devils in blue uniforms here are really black," he would say. "If any of them smiles, it's 'cause he knows he's a brother." Some cops would invariably grin, the crowd would laugh, and nobody would get hurt, which was precisely the object.

Comedy, for Malcolm, served the ends of war; his speeches mixed wit with a high, deadly seriousness. "During slavery," he would say in one of his set routines, "there were two kinds of Negroes—the field Negro and the house Negro. The house Negro was near Boss. He had Boss's ear. His job was to tell Boss what was going on in the field, among the field Negroes. He ate better. He dressed better. He had better housing. If you went to Uncle Tom and said, 'Let's go' "—this was during the Black Muslim days when Malcolm was still arguing for the separation of the races—"he said, 'Where'm I goin'? I'm livin' good. I've got a good house. I'm near my boss.' And when he would be talking to his master, he'd say, '*We* have good food. *We* have a fine home. *We* have fine clothes.' Every time the master would say 'we,' the house Negro would say 'we'—he identified himself with his master. When his master got sick, he'd say, 'What's the matter, Boss? We sick?' If the master's house caught fire, he would fight even harder to put out the flames than the master himself.

"There were also the field Negroes. They were in the majority. They were the masses. If you went to them and said, 'Let's separate,' they wouldn't ask, 'Where we goin'?' They wouldn't even be interested. They were suffering. They were the downtrodden. They were the oppressed. If the master got sick, the field Negro would pray that he died. If the house caught on fire, the field Negro would pray that a heavy wind would come along and burn the house down."

"I am a field Negro," he would always wind up. That finally was the source of his authority. The recognized civil-rights leaders of his day were preoccupied with the desegregation of the South and were not in any case at home in the ghetto; Malcolm never left it, not during working hours. "He spoke like a poor man," Dick Gregory observed, "and walked like a king." He liked to move on the back streets and talk with the bloods on the corners, the nodding kids, the maids waiting at the bus stops, the winos bibbing muscat out of bottles wrapped in brown paper bags. He spoke to them in their language; Malcolm, one friend told me dryly, was condescending only to white people.

Harlem is a cynical, street-wise place, and it had its quarrels with Malcolm from time to time, mainly over its brooding suspicion that he liked going on television too well and that he was all talk and no action. But Harlem knew, long before Malcolm died broke, that he couldn't be bought. One Harlem civic figure told me how, in the days before the poverty program regularized the practice of purchasing the good will of militants, you could go around doling out $100 or so to this or that black nationalist to guarantee peace at some public occasion. "But not Malcolm," he said. "You never approached him with money. You made it a matter of community pride." Nor could Harlem, even when it questioned his wisdom, doubt Malcolm's love. It was a passion that left neither time nor energy for any of the ordinary pleasures. Nobody remembers Malcolm watching a television show other than the news, going to a play other than *Purlie Victorious,* seeing a movie other than *Nothing But a Man*—the story of a young black couple fighting for air in Alabama. He read greedily but never as an escape; *Uncle Tom's Cabin* was the only novel he permitted himself after taking the vows as a Muslim. He plowed through books with a single utilitarian purpose. One of his favorites—one he quoted constantly—was Dwight Lowell Dumond's *Antislavery.* Dumond, a white scholar, saw his materials as the record of the heroism of the largely white abolition movement, achieving, in his words, "this country's greatest victory for democracy." But Malcolm read it not for its heroics, only for its proofs of the savagery of the slavemasters, and, by implication, their children. Being from America, he was indeed intensely sensitive to matters of color, and the victories of our democracy didn't impress him. "When I speak," he said, "I speak as a *victim* of America's so-called democracy."

"Malcolm," Charles Kenyatta thinks, "was the reincarnation of Nat Turner, Denmark Vesey and Gabriel Prosser. Lot of people don't know that, but he was. Stokely Carmichael, Rap Brown, LeRoi Jones—they can't identify with the masses. They went to the best schools. Came from middle-income-class homes. They can't talk about hardship and really know what it is. Me, I lived my life; I didn't get as good an education as Malcolm, even. But we lived in the streets and we knew the streets. Like Nat Turner, Denmark Vesey and Gabriel Prosser. They were field Negroes. They all identified with the masses." A moment slid by. Kenyatta looked wanly out the window of his uptown housing project, down into the streets he and Malcolm knew. "Course," he added softly, "they was destroyed by the masses, too."

So it was with Malcolm; the cruelest irony of the doom-haunted last months of his life was that he no longer felt he could walk the streets of Harlem safely after dark. People who knew him find it painful remembering the Malcolm of those days, his certainties shattered, his attention fragmented, his days a paranoid nightmare come to life. Even his rippling humor took on a corrosive bitterness. He talked about it one day with Claude Lewis, a black journalist, over coffee at 22 West, a little Harlem luncheonette he favored. "Anything that's paradoxical has to have some humor in it," he said, "or it'll crack you up. You know that? You put hot water in a cold glass, it'll crack. Because it's a contrast, a paradox. And America is such a paradoxical society, hypocritically paradoxical, that if you don't have some humor, you'll crack up. If you can't turn it into a joke, why, you'll crack up." He laughed, shortly and joylessly. "Imagine Adlai Stevenson standing up in the UN and saying, 'America needs no credentials for freedom'—I said, why, good God, this man is a joke, you know; and they had just turned loose twenty-one assassins in the South that had murdered three civil-rights workers. They didn't murder three criminals—they murdered three civil-rights workers. Naw. So that's a joke. And you have to laugh at it. You have to be able to laugh to stand up and sing, 'My country 'tis of thee, sweet land of liberty.' *That's* a joke. And if you don't laugh at it, it'll crack you up. I mean it's a *joke.* 'Sweet land of liberty'—that's a *joke."* The short laugh again. "If you don't laugh at it, you'll crack up."

Years later, I met Benjamin Goodman at 22 West; we sat near the back, at a table Malcolm had liked because you could watch for your friends—or, in the last days, your enemies—coming in from 135th Street. Those days had been difficult ones for Benjamin, a time of estrangement from Malcolm after years at his side, and he spoke carefully about them. Black people, he said, sing in the churches about a wall so high you can't get over it, so low you can't get under it, so wide you can't get around it—you've got to go in at the door. Black leaders come up against a wall like that, Benjamin said, and when they get to the door, they see death. He thought it had been that way with Malcolm; he had come to the wall, had been to the door and had seen death. His own.

Yet, having seen death, Malcolm didn't run; he stood there and met it, with that certain audacity of bearing, that certain icy clarity of vision that are his enduring legacies today. We found that audacity frightening, that vision canted and unreasonable; we were innocent then, and he was the one who brought us the bad news. "The servant sees the master," he told us, "but the master doesn't see the servant. The servant sees the master eat, but the master doesn't see the servant eat. The servant sees the master sleep, but the master doesn't see the servant sleep. The servant sees the master angry, but the master never sees the servant angry. The master doesn't really see the servant at all." Malcolm was persuaded that that had to change—that we had not only to see the servant but to see him as potentially our enemy, aggressive, demanding, dangerous and quite beyond our logic, our reason and our compromises. We did glimpse him in Malcolm X, many of us for the first time.

Near the end of his personal journey, Malcolm did arrive at a wall he couldn't get over, under or around—not in the time he had left. At moments he himself began to wonder whether his real contribution to the struggle of the blacks wasn't in his role as bogeyman after all. It was sad that he should have thought so, even fleetingly. Malcolm helped to alter the style and the thought of the black revolt of the 1960s, even when it denied him a place in its certified leadership. He left another, more lasting bequest as well —the example of that unchained, unbowed black manhood. "Like somebody said," one of Malcolm's movement friends told me, "I never heard nobody call Malcolm X 'nigger.' " That was a considerable bequest to servant and master alike, and neither has been quite the same since.

4. Malcolm Descending

One morning in March 1964, when Malcolm was fresh out of the Nation of Islam and preoccupied with starting up his own Muslim Mosque, Inc., a Swedish television interviewer cornered him in his new headquarters in Harlem and asked him: What was the first day you were hurt because of segregation? Liberals were forever asking him that, rather as if his anger could be explained by isolating some single, identifiable trauma at its source; it is our virus theory of militancy. That morning, Malcolm answered irritably, "When I was born. I was born in a segregated hospital of a segregated mother and a segregated father." But the reporter kept pressing, and Malcolm said: "The first was when we were living in Lansing, Michigan, in an integrated neighborhood. One night I woke up and found the house on fire. The good Christians of the neighborhood had come out and set the house afire. The second was when my father was found under a streetcar where he had been thrown by the good Christians—that's my second." He grinned impiously into the camera. "You want my third and fourth and fifth and sixth and seventh?"

It was an accurate statement of his beginnings. He was born Malcolm Little in Omaha on May 19, 1925, the fourth of eight children of the Rev. Earl Little, a huge, tar-black Baptist preacher from country Georgia, and his wife, Louise, a fragile West Indian woman who was light-skinned enough to pass for white. Her first legacy to Malcolm was his own light color, a reddish-brown somewhere between copper and *café au lait;* black people call the shade "mariny" (pronounced "ma-*rye*-nee") and, in those days particularly, valued it as a sign of white lineage and so a badge of status. Malcolm wore it that way through his early years, until his conversion to Black Islam made it a mark of shame—the evidence that, as he believed, his mother's mother had been raped by a white man. He would tell the brothers then that if the whites ever attacked them, his own head would get whipped first precisely because of his light color. "I make the white man feel his guilt," he would say. "When he looks at this mariny face of mine, he knows what he did to my grandmother."

Earl Little's bequest to him was the beginning of rage, a primer schooling in the way the world was for black people and who made it that way. Little was a Baptist on Sundays, but he made his daily devotions to the first of Harlem's great black nationalists, Marcus Garvey, President General of the Universal Negro Improvement Association and, by his own ordination, Provisional President of Africa. Garvey had come up out of Jamaica, a furious black gnome afire with the humiliation of the Negroes and with dreams of grandeur for them. "I asked," he once wrote, " 'Where is the black man's Government?' 'Where is his King, and his kingdom?' 'Where is his President, his country, and his ambassador, his army, his navy, his men of big affairs?' I could not find them, and then I declared, 'I will help to make them.' "

He tried. In a Harlem only lately gone black, teeming with refugees from the poverty, travail and nearly daily lynchings of the American South, Garvey dreamed a nation into being, with its own flag of red, black and green; its own president, government and state religion, the African Orthodox Church; its own uniformed militia, the African Legion, and its corps of Black Cross nurses; its own press and foreign policy; and, at its zenith, its own little Black Star steamship line, the beginning of a fleet that was to repatriate the children of the slaves to Mother Africa. He did it all with dazzling éclat, with gold braid and touring cars and splendid parades; though the responsible Negro leaders of his day, men like W. E. B. DuBois and A. Philip Randolph, opposed him, hundreds of thousands—possibly even millions—of ordinary black people paid him dues. But the Garvey nation foundered, under its own mismanagement and the opposition of the government and the Negro establishment. The year Malcolm X was born, Marcus Garvey went to prison for mail fraud. "After my enemies are satisfied," he wrote bravely from the Federal penitentiary in Atlanta,

> in life or death I shall come back to you to serve even as I have served before. In life I shall be the same; in death I shall be a terror to the foes of Negro liberty. . . . When I am dead wrap the mantle of the Red, Black and Green around me, for in the new life I shall rise with God's grace and blessing to lead the millions up the heights of triumph with the colors that you well know. Look for me in the whirlwind or the storm, look for me all around you, for, with God's grace, I shall come and bring with me countless millions of black slaves who have died in America and the West Indies and the millions in Africa to aid you in the fight for Liberty, Freedom and Life.

It was all over then, really—Garvey over the next fifteen years went from prison to exile and from exile to his death—but nobody told Earl Little that the dream had died in the Atlanta pen, and he and a thousand men like him labored to keep it alive. Earl, like Malcolm after him, was a crazy nigger, and he paid for it. White vigilantes—"the good Christians"—harried the Littles out of Omaha, burned their home in Lansing, and finally (or so black Lansing suspected) beat Earl nearly to death, then finished him off by throwing him under the back wheels of a trolley. Malcolm was six then. His boyhood memories thereafter were of poverty and days dizzy with hunger; of boiled dandelion greens for dinner and orange peels for dessert when you could beg them from the neighbors; of the family finally disintegrating—or being disintegrated, Malcolm always thought—by the clumsy cruelties of the welfare bureaucracy. Louise Little, hurt and cornered, wound up in a mental hospital, the other children in various foster homes—and Malcolm, stormy and rebellious, in detention in Mason, Michigan, awaiting transfer to reform school. He never went. "I was nice," he told me once, "and the white lady who ran the home let me stay with them. I was like a pet, a mascot, a little Chihuahua. White people in those days thought so little of the basic intelligence of Negroes that they didn't hesitate to discuss anything in front of them. They'd talk about niggers—anything." *The servant sees the master, but the master doesn't see the servant.* "I learned things I never forgot."

His records have disappeared with time from the Mason school files; we have his recollection that he did exceedingly well—straight A's, the debating club, the seventh-grade presidency, a place near the head of the class. But in the eighth grade, he collided with the fact that none of it mattered, that the black children of Middle America then did not dare risk having ambitions or dreams. "They didn't have too many Negro doctors or lawyers, especially where I grew up," he said once. "They didn't even have any Negro firemen when I was a youth. When I was a youth, the only thing you could dream about becoming was a good waiter or a good busboy or a good shoeshine man. I mean, that's the American Dream. Back when I was a youth, that's the way it was, and I didn't grow up in Mississippi either—I grew up in Michigan." One day, a teacher he rather liked asked him what he wanted to be, and Malcolm offhandedly said a lawyer. The teacher said something, no doubt kindly intended, to the effect that niggers don't get to be lawyers, so why not plan on something more *practical,* like being a mechanic or a carpenter? "I just gave up," Malcolm remembered years later; as soon as he finished the eighth grade, he started running.

His life thereafter was, as he put it in the *Autobiography*, "a chronology of changes"—a series of provisional identities that he never lived to complete. He lit in Boston, moved in with his half-sister Ella (Earl Little had had three children in a first marriage) and shortly acquired a zoot suit, a head of hair conked straight with lye, a diddybop walk, a Lindy step and a white Beacon Hill chick with looks, money and a car; a new persona that denied his past and its wounds. Maybe white folks saw him then, popping a shoeshine rag and hustling condoms in the men's room at the Roseland State Ballroom, clearing away the dinner dishes at the Parker House, selling sandwiches on the Boston–New York train. Maybe, that is, he passed within eyeshot, white-jacketed and grinning, a part of the furniture too familiar to notice. He thought he loved white people in those days; rather, he envied them across that distance between his invisibility and their obtrusive affluence and power. "I loved the devil," he said. "I was trying as hard as I could to be white."

Invisibility did not suit him very long. Malcolm, still in his middle teens but gangly-tall and brassy enough to pass for a man, dropped out of our service and drifted to Harlem and a succession of hustles—selling reefers, running numbers slips and bootleg whiskey, steering johns to brothels, sticking up stores and discovering the pleasant sense of power a gun gave him. The dudes in the life called him Detroit Red then—nobody ever heard of Lansing—or, later, Big Red. He was a bad-ass cat, a murder-mouthing blood with an evil temper and a piece jammed in his belt to back it up; a manchild who loved white people, and believed himself to be imitating them, bopping around the back reaches of our promised land.

Malcolm may at times have exaggerated his past in the retelling —may have added a few bills to his bankroll, a few employees to his private staff, a few degrees extra to the prestige of his clientele and to his own status in the world of the Harlem hustle. His police record, given the energy and variety of his criminal life, stayed remarkably clean: it shows arrests for larceny in Michigan and burglary in Massachusetts, but none at all—not even a traffic ticket

—in New York. ("The cops in Harlem," Malcolm once explained, "take money faster than cops anyplace else in the country.") I tried through intermediaries in Harlem to reach some of Malcolm's old street crowd, with no luck. Ted Poston, the veteran black journalist, made a similar effort years earlier, while Malcolm was still alive, with almost equally disappointing results. Poston, in an unpublished memorandum, reported that most of his contacts in the Harlem demimonde professed never to have heard of Malcolm—not the old Malcolm, anyway. A veteran bookie and numbers man guessed that his real base of operations must have been Boston. An old-time doorman at the Apollo Theater insisted that Malcolm "didn't ever crush a crumb at Ma's"—a breakfast nook where all the hustlers ate. A policy banker recalled only one Big Red around Harlem and that was somebody else—a junkie strong-arm man. Poston found just one senior racketeer who remembered Malcolm at all, and that not very gloriously. "He was a john-walker. He worked for so-and-so, who ran a pretty good whorehouse on West 144th Street. He opened the doors, ran errands, moved the cars, made himself handy. It was a second-floor apartment, and this cat used to walk johns in from the sidewalk or the door, or if he saw some ofay guys walking through 144th Street, he might hustle them up to the joint. But he never got nowhere. Big Red, hell—he was just a john-walker."

The search was not definitive; in any event, whatever his professional standing, there can be no overstating the depths of Malcolm's degradation. He may or may not have been medically an addict, but he stayed high for days on end on a whole pharmacopoeia of drugs—"opium, hashish, reefers, cocaine, all that stuff I used." He plunged on the numbers and never hit. His life of the mind consisted of pulp Western novels and Humphrey Bogart movies; his vocabulary, a few hundred words of the hip lingua franca of back-alley Harlem. He was full of nameless mad furies: he played crazy to talk himself out of the draft and World War II but later came to fear that the act was coming true. He was becoming, by his own measure, an animal—a beast of prey in a jungle full of predators. He finally had to get out of Harlem, a jump ahead of the cops and his enemies in the streets. "Things were getting too hot for me in New York," he once reminisced, "and it wasn't summer." He slipped back to Boston, looked up his old Beacon Hill girl and involved her, her sister and two black pals in a biracial burglary gang. They apparently did well for a time, though once again there are dissenting accounts; the Nation of Islam, trying everything to deflate Malcolm in the bitter days following his departure, floated the story that he wasn't even good at burglary—that he was a small-timer who got caught trying to hock a stolen portable radio for $7.

Malcolm said it was a gold watch. It hardly mattered. He was arrested along with the rest of his gang. There was never any question of his guilt—"The cops," he acknowledged years afterward, "caught us with the evidence." What seemed to offend the Commonwealth of Massachusetts more than the crime, as Malcolm remembered it, was the company he kept. "The judge told me to my face, 'This will teach you to stay away from white girls.' " A first burglary offense was normally a two-year fall. The girls got one to five years. Malcolm got eight to ten. He had then lived a hustler's lifetime. He was not quite twenty-one years old.

5. The Devil in the Flesh

Malcolm reformed in prison, or, rather, in spite of it. He served seventy-seven months in three Massachusetts penitentiaries, the first a stinking, century-old fortress at Charlestown with no running water, no plumbing and no notion of rehabilitation more advanced than keeping men locked in cells twenty hours a day. Malcolm quickly discovered the local currency, cigarettes, and what it could buy. "You can get anything in prison that you can get in the streets if you know how to operate," he told an interviewer once, and Malcolm, knowing how to operate, got liquor, nutmeg, reefers, bennies and a dependably steady high. The prison authorities typed him early on as "arrogant" and "uncooperative," which seems rather to have understated the case. Detroit Red, lately of the Apollo and the Savoy and Small's Paradise Café, was known inside the walls as Satan—an incorrigible hard-timer, with his mind, as he later put it, in a "fog bag" and his gut in a state of permanent mutinous rage.

His rehabilitation was begun not by the penitentiary but by a fellow impenitent, a convicted burglar called Bimbi whose homemade education and gift of gab Malcolm noticed in the yard and envied. Bimbi interested Malcolm in books and in correspondence courses in English, Latin and German. Malcolm was always, in surprising ways, deeply American, even after his spiritual secession from us; being American, he was pragmatic to the bone, and being a pragmatist, he saw learning not as a pleasure or an end but as an instrument. At first, it had no larger purpose for him than the little cachet it gave him on the tier.

A purpose, and a calling, soon followed. I corresponded briefly with Malcolm, after our meeting in St. Louis, and once asked him how he had come into the Lost-Found Nation. It had been—as Malcolm often told it—a classically Pauline conversion, a blinding, shattering transformation, only instead of a flash of light and a vision of Jesus, there had been a nod of the head from his kid brother Reginald and a glimpse of Satan. *Them. White people are the devil.* Reginald, Malcolm wrote me, had this on the authority of the Honorable Elijah Muhammad, who learned it from Allah Himself, and he was "able to convert me in five minutes. Despite my many experiences with whites, the fact that I had grown up with whites and was reared by whites and had socialized with whites in every form of their life, and even though I was in prison, I still respected whites. But when my brother told me that God had taught Mr. Elijah Muhammad that the white race was a race of Devils, my eyes came open on the spot."

Them. It was an authentic religious illumination, the innermost mystery of the Nation of the Lost-Founds, the first source of its authority over the faithful and its influence on countless blacks outside its immediate sway. Muslims and ex-Muslims I have met tend invariably to minimize the importance of the devil theory; white journalists have too often misunderstood it, have taken it as a personal affront rather than as an organizing principle akin in force, say, to the divinity of Christ or the labor theory of value. The faithful are therefore guarded when speaking about it to strangers. "People thought we were just talking about the white man is the devil," Benjamin Goodman told me. "No. It was men getting together and talking about everything—biology, chemistry, astronomy, world events, everything." The common formulation to outsiders is that the Muslims are not antiwhite but problack—that their first concern is to get black people to forget about whites and love themselves. This is surely true and yet only half the truth. For some part of black America, the possibility that white people are Satan incarnate has the force not only of religious metaphor but of empirical truth—a hypothesis by which one can at least explain why one lives in a rat-ridden slum and works, if at all, carrying the white man's baggage and diapering the white man's babies. It may be difficult to love oneself otherwise, given the circumstances of black life in America. A man may not be able to liberate himself from his condition by knowing who the devil is. But he may retrieve some part of his *amour-propre* if he understands how he got in that condition. He may even be able to recreate himself, as Malcolm did, so as no longer to pay the devil his dues.

The discovery of the devil was, in the language of the Lost-Founds, the beginning of Malcolm's resurrection from the grave, and he spent his remaining years in prison struggling to complete it. His conversion had taken seconds; his accession to the faith was like some long Essene labor, an endless passage of days copying out the dictionary word by word onto grade-school writing tablets and nights reading himself astigmatic by the half-light of prison corridors. First his family, then Mr. Muhammad himself tutored him by mail in the sacraments of Black Islam. He read black history, what bleached and broken fragments of it he could scratch out of the prison library. He drove himself through the Greeks and the *Rubaiyat,* Hegel and Kant, Shakespeare and Schopenhauer and Nietzsche, philosophy and philology and etymology, searching in all of it for wisdom and for evidence against white folks. Language seduced him—became, as he later told a man from *Ebony*, "an obsession with me. I began to realize the meaning and power of words." He went out for debating. He learned to pray. He made a cedar chest in the shop and sent it to the Muslims in Chicago to sell for him, so he would have a little coming-out money. He quit all his vices and most of his pleasures. He severed himself totally from his past; Big Red, born in our casbah, died in our penitentiary. Malcolm became, by any measure, a model prisoner; his remaining problem thereafter, as he told it in later years, was that he couldn't tell whether the prison authorities despised him more before or after his transformation.

What they or any other white people thought no longer mattered to Malcolm; in the eyes of the born-again Muslim, their authority even in prison is a temporary thing, an accident of history, a trial to be endured in the service of Allah. One insomniac night, Malcolm told the brothers long afterward, a man appeared in his cell—a smallish man with light skin and faintly Eurasian features. He stayed for a time, Malcolm said, and then left—vanished, really—without having spoken a word. Malcolm didn't dare guess at what the apparition meant, he told the brothers, until he got out of prison in 1952, went to visit Mr. Muhammad in Chicago and saw a picture of the man, a tinted photo hanging heavily framed on the wall. Malcolm wondered about it. Mr. Muhammad told him that it was a photograph of God.

6. Allah in Paradise Valley

God, it is written, appeared to the black people of Detroit's Paradise Valley slums on July 4, 1930, in the person of a peddler of clothing and silks known variously as Wallace D. Fard, W. Fard

Muhammad, F. Muhammad Ali, Wali Farrad or simply Mr. Farrad. His coloring was fair, His hair oily black, His antecedents uncertain. A fair guess is that He was an Arab immigrant; His own word was that He came from Mecca, the son of a jet-black man, the Hidden Imam, first among twenty-four black scientists who manage Allah's creation, and a platinum-blonde Armenian woman—the devil. Mr. Farrad was versed in the Bible and the Holy Qur'an, in history and mathematics and astronomy, and on his door-to-door rounds He acquired a little circle of followers who met secretly in musty tenement basements and were transfixed by His stories of their lost grandeur in "the East." He seems to have been received first as a teacher, or a minister—nothing more. But one day, the oldest Muslims say, He called for a glass of water, gathered a few of the believers around and made them see an image in it—the figure of a man praying. Another time, it is said, He plucked a single hair from His head, dipped it into water and pulled it out; ten thousand hairs had sprouted from it. Just so easily, Mr. Farrad said, could He destroy white America.

One of the circle said to have witnessed this was the man known now as Elijah Muhammad but then as Elijah (or possibly Robert) Poole, a tiny Georgia sharecropper's son come North in the great black diaspora of the 1920s to the auto factories and later the relief rolls of Detroit. Poole, then in his middle thirties, was an inconspicuous sort, fragile as an eggshell and pale as beige, but his sleepy eyes and his faltering speech masked a keen native wit and a certain genius for the main chance. He and the little silk peddler were drawn together, and one day, it is written, Poole asked Him: "Who are you, and what is your real name?"

"I am the one the world has been expecting for the past two thousand years," Mr. Farrad replied.

"What is your name?" Poole asked again.

"My name is Mahdi; I am God. I came to guide you into the right path that you may be successful and see the hereafter."

God, it is said, dwelled four years in Paradise Valley, developed a flock of perhaps eight thousand and then vanished; His disappearance, at a time of internal division in His little Nation, is often called mysterious by outsiders, but the faithful accept that He returned to Mecca to await the end of the world.* During His residence in America, He disclosed to Poole that He was indeed Allah, the All-Perfect One—not the God who created the universe but the latest, perhaps the last, in a succession of Gods who appear as men at 25,000-year intervals and who, once having transacted their business on earth, die in their fleshly person. His mixed parentage in this incarnation, He said, was partly to enable Him to move easily in either the black or white world, partly to establish a more perfect balance, or justice, within Him. He said He had come this time to waken his "Uncle," the spiritually dead black Lost-Founds in America—and to bring judgment against their white slavemasters. He took Poole under His patronage, replaced his slave surname with a succession of "Original" names (first Karriem, finally Muhammad) and designated him His Last Messenger. Having thus raised Elijah in the wilderness, Mr. Farrad gave him the keys to divine wisdom, including a secret syllabus of 104 books and a set of allegorical mathematical puzzles still labored over by the believers. Their tutorials, it is said, ran night after night until dawn. Elijah would nod off; Mr. Farrad would shake him awake and dose him with black coffee. Elijah began to wonder if Mr. Farrad ever slept. Once, curious, he left the room on a pretext and peeked back in through the keyhole to see if Mr.

*Benjamin Goodman told me that a light-skinned, "Eastern-looking" stranger who called himself The Master appeared among the brothers in Harlem in 1963, during Malcolm's last months in the Nation of Islam, and stayed until 1965, after Malcolm's death. According to Goodman, the stranger could work difficult mathematical problems at computer speed; could narrate history "as if he had lived it"; could speak not only English but Spanish, Chinese, Swahili and other languages fluently and accentlessly; could shatter objects at a touch; could flick cigarette tobacco into the air and cause it to ignite spontaneously. The Master, Goodman said, made the brothers edgy—some even suspected he was a CIA agent—but none of them ever asked him who he was. I wondered whether they hadn't thought the name unusual. "It's like somebody calling himself Big Man," Goodman said. "If that's what you want to call yourself, people accept it." I asked if they had thought The Master might have been Mr. Farrad returned to the wilderness. Goodman did not answer directly. He said that The Master did not look like Mr. Farrad—was bigger, for one thing—but he believed that it would have been within Mr. Farrad's powers of mind to alter his size and appearance.

Farrad was napping. It seemed to him that Mr. Farrad was staring back at him. Through the door.

Mr. Farrad taught Mr. Muhammad that the God who created the universe was not the "spook" or "mystery god" worshiped by the Christians but a black man like Himself. All of it—the sun, the stars, the planets—was His work; even light itself was the projection of a black idea. The Adam of the Bible was not the first man at all but the first white man, which is to say the first devil. God created men black, in His own corporeal image, 66 (or 72) trillion years ago and thereafter entrusted operational control of the universe to twenty-four of them, twelve major and twelve minor Imams, or scientists, each of whom was allotted 25,000 years to effect his own ideas. The Imams stay constantly tuned in to one another's thought; they are also empowered to read men's minds and to penetrate secret meetings. ("There *are* no secret meetings," a Muslim assured me.) At the end of each 25,000-year cycle, the Hidden Imam calls the others together to look down the Wheel of Time and to compose the "history" of the 25,000 years just beginning.

Mr. Farrad taught Mr. Muhammad that, for most of those trillions of years, high black civilization reigned unchallenged on earth. (Even Mars was indirectly under black hegemony. Mr. Farrad taught that Mars is peopled with men seven to nine feet tall and "sort of skinny" and was able to tune them in so Mr. Muhammad could hear them. These men, Mr. Farrad taught, worship one of their own as God, but their God worships a man on earth—a black man.) The whole earth, in earliest times, was called Asia; Malcolm X's draft card listed his race as "Asiatic." Black scientists made the animals, raised the mountains, even created (or, as the faithful say, "deported") the moon by sinking explosives down a shaft to the core of the earth and blowing nearly a third of its mass into orbit. The craters of the moon are the scars of this explosion: they exactly match the islands of the Pacific. There were occasionally divisions in the perfect harmony of black man, but never wars; dissidents, instead of doing battle, split into tribes and peaceably went their separate ways.

But paradise was not to last. Mr. Farrad taught Mr. Muhammad that black men were destined for enslavement and that, because they were then too delicate for the ordeal, a scientist named Shabazz led a tribe of them into the jungles of Africa fifty thousand years ago to toughen them up. (This was the tribe from which the so-called American Negroes were descended—and from which Malcolm X ultimately got his own "Original" name, Malik Shabazz.) The tribe succeeded in mastering the jungle and the jungle beasts and in recreating a civilization; but a "jungle civilization," not the old glory. Africa did toughen them, and changed them; made their hair hard and kinky, for example. "Before then, Mr. Farrad said, our hair was like our eyebrows," an ex-Muslim who had not entirely lost faith told me. He bent forward and let me touch his eyebrows; they were fine and silky. He seemed oddly, and sadly, rueful, given the pride of the Muslims in their blackness. "We weren't the same then," he said, "as we are now."

At the core of the faith is Yacub's History—the story of the creation of the devil. Mr. Farrad taught Mr. Muhammad that Yacub, a dissident black genius known as "the big-head scientist," was exiled during the present 25,000-year cycle to the Island of Patmos, where he set about the manufacture of the white race out of the recessive genes, or "germs," of the black. He did this by a process Mr. Farrad called birth control but which more nearly resembled genocide: the butchery over generations of black, then brown, then red, then yellow babies until all that remained on Patmos was a weak, blue-eyed, blond-haired mutant species devoid of color, character or human feeling; a bleached-out parody of man.

Mr. Farrad taught Mr. Muhammad that this devil race was granted dominion over the world for six thousand years down to our own time. So depraved were the whites that their reign was late getting started; they were run out of the society of black people and into the caves of Europe, where they lived on all fours—and where their women kissed and coupled with dogs—while the blacks were wearing silk and building pyramids and tracking the stars. Their ascent to power was predestined, but they were too weak and too corrupt to come into it honestly. They achieved it instead by murder, rapine, robbery, sedition and "tricknology." Jesus himself was their victim: he was not the white Son of God but a black prophet, a Muslim actually named Isa, and he was stabbed to death, not crucified, by white Roman cops while preaching in front of "the Jew's store."

But the greatest of all the devil's crimes befell the children of the Tribe of Shabazz, the people known in Scripture as the lost sheep or the lost tribe or the dry bones in the valley. Mr. Farrad taught Mr. Muhammad that, beginning with a blue-eyed slaver named John Hawkins and a slave ship named *Jesus*, the devil tore the blacks out of Africa, carried them into slavery, tricked and brutalized them out of their own language, culture and religion, corrupted them with the white man's spook gods and the white man's morals and so murdered them mentally and spiritually. Their bondage was to last four hundred years; then, in fulfillment of the ancient promise given to Abraham, God would deliver them, and would bring their slavemaster to a terrible judgment. The devil's day was up in 1914 but was extended, possibly till as late as 1984, not as a beneficence to white people but to permit Allah and His Last Messenger time to resurrect the dead and bring them safely out of Babylon to some separate land of their own.

All of this Mr. Farrad taught to Mr. Muhammad; all of this Mr. Muhammad taught to his own star pupil, Malcolm X. Mr. Farrad taught that we are living now in the Last Day—that the end of the devil's time is at hand and that repentance and atonement are not in him. "I have come," Mr. Farrad told Mr. Muhammad, "to destroy the world." He meant our world. America first.

7. The History of the End of the World

It will not do to smile at the lessons of Allah to the Lost-Founds, or to forget that Malcolm believed them quite literally for much of his adult life. The theology of the Muslims, as James Baldwin once wrote, is "no more indigestible than the more familiar brand asserting that there is a curse on the sons of Ham." Some of it strikes outsiders as quaint, even those outsiders who accept on faith the parting of the Red Sea or the miracle of the loaves and fishes. But the mysteries of the Nation may not seem so farfetched to a black person, whose religious options otherwise are to accept his color and his caste as a divine judgment against him or to give up on God altogether. The third possibility, raised by the ministry of Martin Luther King, Jr.—the Christian church militant in the cause of temporal justice—was not open to Malcolm when he embraced Black Islam. There was no church militant then, and its style would not have suited Malcolm in any case. For the sons of Ham in those days, the only choices were, or seemed to be, acquiescence on one hand or atheism on the other. Malcolm had passed through both when Allah's Last Messenger found him in prison and told him that he need be neither criminal nor slave—that he was the lost-found son of a race of black princes and scholars and that his condition now was a judgment not upon him but upon the devil.

The theology that amused or frightened us was the agency of Malcolm's liberation from shame and the instrument he used to liberate thousands of others. The cost to one's sensibilities hardly counted as against the restoration of one's ruined ego. Malcolm, when he received the faith, was hardly more than a child, a half-literate blood off the block, tripped out on drugs and undirected rage. He was street-sharp and cynical but not yet sophisticated. He had spent his young manhood encapsulated in the ghetto and then in prison; he had seen the white man's sins and power at first hand but not yet his ambiguities and confusions. Faith, for him, preceded learning and guided it: in a sense, he read everything from *Othello* to *The World Almanac* for confirmation of the duplicity of Yacub and his children toward Allah and His. We were accustomed to the public Malcolm, worldly and well read, a self-made social critic debating the intentions and the public policies of white America in university auditoriums and on Sunday afternoon TV. We did not see him in the mosque, calling the black dead to the shelter of the Sun, Moon and Stars of Islam, flinging down the Christian Bible and stomping on it, announcing as revealed truth that white people have vestigial tails and that the blacks are the chosen of God. We saw Malcolm as a politician, not as a priest.

We saw him incompletely. Malcolm was, for the last dozen years of his life, a clergyman, and for most of that time a doomsday fundamentalist—a religious militant who abstained from the secular struggle of the blacks, even when his gut said fight, because he believed that Allah would do his fighting for him. The dream of the oppressed is the death of the oppressor. King, who was almost precisely Malcolm's contemporary, denied this dream. Malcolm embraced it, and preached it as religion.

"The first lesson I ever heard him teach," a former Muslim told me one evening in Harlem, "was The History of the End of the World. We called it history, but it was more like prehistory—something that's written before the thing takes place. He said that Allah had told Mr. Muhammad about another planet that is man-made, called 'The Mother Ship' or 'The Mother Plane.' It's in the shape of a great wheel, a half-mile by a half-mile. It's the wheel Ezekiel in the Bible saw. You can see it twice a week even now. The stock-market crash in 1929 was caused by some rich men who saw a UFO rising out of the Pacific—the Mother Plane. They panicked and sold all their stocks. The Mother Plane has fifteen hundred baby planes. Each one of them is also wheel-shaped and each one has three two-ton bombs made of the same powerful explosive that was used to raise the mountains. The baby planes are flown by pilots who have been raised from the age of six to fly them; they've never known a woman, and they have never smiled. The Mother Plane is commanded by Mr. Farrad.

"For twelve months before the end of the world, America will be hit by natural disasters. Winds, earthquakes, hailstorms, blizzards, tornadoes, hurricanes, everything. Eight or ten days before the end, one plane will fly over by itself dropping leaflets in English and Arabic, warning the Negroes to join onto our own kind and leave. There will be people to tell us where to go. Then another plane will appear and make a fearful sound—the trumpet call of prophecy. There will be a war in Asia and two-thirds of the American armed forces will be destroyed, and another war between East and West Germany. There will be great tidal waves on both coasts; they'll drive people inland and bunch them together to be slaughtered.

"Then, on the Last Day, the Mother Plane will drop the fifteen hundred babies—we called that 'letting go its burden.' Each one will drop its bombs from twelve miles high, but they won't be visible until they descend to nine miles and by then it will be too late to do anything. The bombs will burrow a mile deep in the earth and explode with enough force to raise mountains a mile high. Each of the bombs will give off poison gas, which will destroy life for fifty miles around. Our atmosphere is polluted, not just by chemicals but by thoughts. Allah will short-circuit it on the Last Day and set it afire. The atmosphere will burn for 310 years, and then it will take 690 more years to cool off, and it will never sustain life again. At the end of that thousand years, the children of the Original People will be brought back to see it, to witness the total destruction and purification."

This is accepted by the faithful not as religious metaphor but as literal fact; another former Muslim told me later about how you would be riding along Lenox Avenue with some of the brothers and suddenly everybody would pile out of the car and point at the night sky and yell, "There it go! There it go!" I asked my ex-Muslim friend when our destruction was supposed to happen. He said 1970. It was then the early autumn of 1969; we had just had

Hurricane Camille and a devastating tornado in Lubbock, Texas, and from the headlong way my friend recited the history, I guessed that he wouldn't be surprised if it had begun coming true. I said as much. "No," he answered. "I wouldn't be surprised."

I remember sitting there for a long moment, not saying anything, with my pad full of notes toward a political biography of Malcolm X heavy in my coat pocket. In that silence, I was hearing Lotte Lenya singing the Pirate Jenny song in *The Threepenny Opera*—the chambermaid's dream of a black freighter pulling into the harbor and the men pouring off and the town shelled flat, all but the one cheap joint where she worked. "In that quiet of death . . . they'll pile up the bodies, and I'll say, 'That'll learn ya. . . .' " A black freighter; a Mother Plane. My friend may have thought I was smiling to myself. "Some of it sounds like science fiction, I know," he said. "But this is what we were taught." Another moment passed. "This is what Malcolm taught us," he said.

8. Malcolm Redux

In 1952, when Malcolm left Charlestown State Prison with his parole, his coming-out suit and his head freshly skinned in the Muslim style, the belief that Allah would deliver the blacks was at least as reasonable on its face as the expectation that white people meant even to try. The case of *Oliver Brown* v. *Board of Education of Topeka, Kansas,* was only just making its way up to the Supreme Court, and the nine white men who sat there were sorely divided over whether they could or even ought to attempt to end the Federally sanctioned segregation of possibly 40 percent of America's schoolchildren. Both political parties wrote some pro forma civil-rights pieties into their platforms that summer, but neither they nor their Presidential candidates, Dwight Eisenhower and Adlai Stevenson, ever raised the subject seriously again. The recognized civil-rights movement consisted mainly of the NAACP worrying its lawsuits through the courts and the Urban League nagging for jobs for underemployed middle-class blacks. Martin Luther King was a Ph.D. candidate at Boston University, Whitney Young an Urban Leaguer getting restless in the sticks, Stokely Carmichael a schoolchild in Trinidad, CORE a small and largely white gadfly organization sitting in and picketing in New York, St. Louis and a few other cities.

The little Kingdom of Allah in the wilderness wasn't much to look at either—a communion of possibly four hundred souls scattered among storefront mosques and front-parlor missions in Detroit, Chicago, Washington, Harlem and possibly a half-dozen other places—but Malcolm rushed to its embrace like the prodigal come home. He found it in stasis. Allah and His Last Apostle had had some initial successes—had got going what one Detroit newspaper of the day described unhappily as "an Asiatic trend among Negro dole recipients." After God's departure, however, Mr. Muhammad's claim to the apostolic throne was disputed within the Nation, and he was forced to take flight from city to city through the 1930s. This gave him an opportunity to scatter the seeds of Islam and, so he told the believers later, to hunt down the books on Mr. Farrad's syllabus in the nethermost stacks of the Library of Congress, where the devil keeps them hidden from the Original People. But his best holdings in Detroit, where the Nation began, and in Chicago, to which the Messenger had moved its headquarters, languished during his long hegira and, later, during three and a half years he spent in Federal prison for failing to register for the draft in World War II. (The Muslims, as the draft case against Muhammad Ali reminded us nearly three decades later, count themselves conscientious objectors to war, or in any event to the white man's wars.) The seat of the Nation in Chicago was a renovated dog-and-cat hospital, and the fold to which Malcolm came home, in Detroit, was stagnating; Paradise Valley had all but forgotten that God had ever been there.

Malcolm, being an American by habit of mind if no longer by national allegiance, shared our belief that nothing fails like failure

—that whether you win or lose does after all count more than how you played the game. From the beginning, he played it passionately, with a convert's zeal and a drummer's instinct for packaging and promotion, and he played it to win. He sealed his own commitment the day he abandoned the name "Little," laboriously copying out a required form letter to God ("Dear Savior Allah . . . I bear witness that there is no God but Thee and, that Muhammad is Thy Servant and Apostle. . . . Please give me my Original Name") and receiving in due course his provisional "X." "The Honorable Elijah Muhammad teaches us," Malcolm once explained, "that if a Chinese person were to come in here calling himself Patrick Murphy, he'd look and sound ridiculous, because Murphy is an Irish name, an Irishman is a white man and a yellow man looks out of place with a white man's name. And if a yellow man looks out of place with a white man's name, a black man looks even more out of place. These so-called Negroes in this country who have these names like Johnson, Jones, Smith, Powell and Bunche and names of this sort actually are wearing the names of their slavemasters, not the names of their forefathers." But for the born-again Muslim, there is more to the change than merely correcting history. To take one's "X" is to take on a certain mystery, a certain possibility of power in the eyes of one's peers and one's enemies; it is to annul one's past and to assert that one has a future. The "X," said Malcolm, announced what you had been and what you had become: "Ex-smoker. Ex-drinker. Ex-Christian. Ex-slave."

Malcolm thereupon plunged into the business of Nation-building, testifying in the temple, fishing for souls in the streets, graduating quickly to assistant minister in Detroit and then minister in Boston and Philadelphia, where he organized the eleventh and twelfth temples of Islam in a matter of months. After Malcolm split with Muhammad and bad blood came between them, the Nation felt it necessary—through its tabloid newspaper *Muhammad Speaks*—to belittle Malcolm's achievements even in these first, nearly forgotten assignments. Malcolm, according to a revisionist history written by two of his oldest Muslim associates, had only accepted Islam in the first place to get out of prison faster. Having achieved this, the account went on, he went to Detroit, immediately began subverting the incumbent leadership of Temple No. 1 there and soon created a "Malcolm cult" of misguided admirers who started promoting him for minister. It didn't work: the older temple people "rebelled against this young upstart" and forced him to skip to Boston, "to help the Messenger," he said. There, he shortly got in hot water again for his "high-handed and unMuslim-like manner" with the believers and had to be bailed out by a rescue mission from Detroit. "He thanked us, adding: 'Whenever you find me wrong, pull my coat,' " the revisionists said. "In later years, however, he not only refused to permit you to pull his coat, he wouldn't let you come near it." This version makes interesting Muslimology but unpersuasive history: Malcolm's penalty for these supposed early disasters was his appointment to the ministry of Mosque No. 7 in Harlem—the most important pastorate, after Chicago, in the whole Lost-Found Nation.

The Nation found it necessary as well, after the split, to assert that Mr. Muhammad had known all along that Malcolm would betray him—that he had accepted Malcolm knowing this just as Jesus knowingly accepted Judas as his disciple. If so, the Messenger kept his prophetic vision secret from everybody, possibly including himself. The relationship that flowered between the old man and his young novitiate over a decade was, by every other account, one of deep and demonstrative love. "I sat in Elijah Muhammad's home one Saturday morning while he was lecturing a group of ministers," a mutual friend recounted. "The doorbell rang, and a servant came in and announced that Malcolm had come. Elijah's eyes lit up as if the prodigal son was home. He leaped up from his seat, and when Malcolm appeared they embraced and kissed. Seeing this could not have left room to doubt their affection for each other." Mr. Muhammad himself once said in a speech in Philadelphia that anyone trying to kill him would have to get past Malcolm first, a former Muslim told me. "And it was true. He would have died for Mr. Muhammad."

It was, for Malcolm, the love of the son for the father. He had hardly tasted it as a boy: he had been too young, and Earl Little too full of fury, during the few years they had together. He was a ruin, a ravaged kid in a cage, when Muhammad found him. "This man sort of *rebirthed* Malcolm," John Killens said. "Brought him back from the lower depths." Malcolm never forgot it. The Messenger was always "the Honorable Elijah Muhammad" to him, in public speech or private conversation; he said it so often it turned into incantation and "Honorable" sometimes came out "Honorbubble." Malcolm sought the Messenger's blessings for his marriage to Betty in 1958 and named the third of his six daughters Ilyasah, Arabic for Elijah, after him. Friends outside the movement twitted him for his blind allegiance to the old man and probed in private for soft places in it. "We spent time together," said one. "He visited my home. We laughed and joked, and he let his hair down about many things. Those of us who enjoyed his confidence tried every way we knew how, subtle and unsubtle, to find a crack in his dedication. There was none. He would say, 'I was nothing when the Honorable Elijah Muhammad picked me up. I may not have much money, but he gave me the ability to respect myself.' It was comparable to the black church experience—'He picked me up and He cleaned me up.' Muhammad made him feel himself to be a person of dignity and worth."

Malcolm in turn undertook his Harlem ministry as though it were a debt to be repaid. He was a very human man, with his own needs and vanities, but he never failed in his obeisances to his patron. "I am not the author of anything I say," he would insist. "I'm only repeating that which has been taught to me by the Honorable Elijah Muhammad." Even in the mosque, among brothers whom he had brought to the faith and who revered him at least as much as they did Mr. Muhammad, he would say: "I'm just a little Charlie McCarthy who's sitting on the Messenger's knee." The Muslims, believing themselves to be the Chosen of God, are forever hunting for themselves in Scripture, and they found a parallel for Mr. Muhammad and Malcolm in the story of Moses and his brother Aaron. When God first came to Moses and commissioned him to separate his people from their masters, Moses protested, "O my Lord, I am not eloquent . . . but I am slow of speech, and of a slow tongue"; and God replied: "Is not Aaron the Levite thy brother? I know that he can speak well. . . . And thou shalt speak unto him, and put words in his mouth: and I will be with thy mouth, and with his mouth, and will teach you what ye shall do. And he shall be thy spokesman unto the people: and . . . he shall be to thee instead of a mouth, and thou shalt be to him instead of God." The inarticulate Messenger of God, the eloquent spokesman for the Messenger—it all seemed to fit. Malcolm himself was drawn to the analogy, Charles Kenyatta told me. "He really believed he were Aaron."

So did the brothers, Kenyatta said; and when Malcolm left the Nation, a lot of them went back to their Bibles to check out which man had died first, Aaron or Moses. It turned out to have been Aaron.

9. Harlem

"Wherever a black man goes," Malcolm X used to say, "that's Harlem." Harlem is another country for most white people. Our subways go under it, our commuter trains over it, our expressways around it; our politicians bemoan it, our policemen contain it, our children romanticize it, our pop culture imitates it, our social scientists quantify and requantify its pain until the figures swim and columns blur; and still we seem never to see it. We do not see it partly because we are calloused to it and partly because we are afraid of it, but also because it shames us. Harlem is the symbol of our failure, and of the terrible cost that failure exacts of black people merely to survive.

Harlem is a place where the Great Depression of the 1930s was interrupted by World War II but has never ended; where probably one man in three is either unemployed or employed at less than subsistence pay; where fathers vanish and families collapse and lines of welfare women overflow the banks into the streets on "Mother's Day," when the checks come in; where roughly one person in six is a junkie and children disappear, or die; where demoralized and frightened cops walk double, triple and quadruple and never seem to stop anything; where the leading cause of death among young men under thirty is violence; where whole streets hide behind drawn shades and Fox-locked steel doors after dark; where there are blocks so hopelessly overcrowded that, at similar rates of density, the whole population of America could be crammed into three of New York's five boroughs; where people pay exorbitant rents for tenement rooms not appreciably better or better served than what squatters find free in abandoned buildings; where the American Dream is merchandised to people who can't afford it on usuriously E-Z terms; where Afro hairdos announce a renascent pride in blackness and rows of sidewalk merchants peddling straight-haired blond, brunette and redheaded wigs along 125th Street deny it; where teachers who too commonly doubt the educability of black children bump them cynically along from grade to grade anyway until they graduate half-literate or flounder and drop out; where there is more capital in black churches than in black businesses and where, as Benjamin Goodman dourly noted, the bars look better than the houses; where people subsisting on chicken-necks and hog-jowls witness our affluence daily from our kitchens or on our television programs; where white tourists and their money once were welcome but now are greeted with hostility or, much more often, wonder; where even the rackets belong to whitey but kids like Malcolm Little still dream about growing up to be pimps like Detroit Red 'cause the pimp got the walk and the cloze and the bread and pimpin' beat pushin' a truck on Seventh Avenue; where periodic riots are only an acute expression of a chronic, depressive rage; where Malcolm X grew to manhood and preached and felt more at home than anywhere else in the world but would not keep his wife or raise his children.

The bad news Malcolm brought the rest of us wasn't news to Harlem. Harlem already knew its poverty and desperation; had heard it anatomized and catechized and railed at from a tho front stoops and soapboxes; had heard it all so often that the there assure you to this day that Malcolm was really only Detroit Red with a new hustle, merchandising the old uptown complaints in downtown, media-age wrappings. Harlem was stirred by the civil-rights revolt then wakening out of the Montgomery, Alabama, bus boycott—there are more pictures of Martin Luther King than of Malcolm X on its walls even now—but at a vast distance: the style of the revolt was Southern and churchly and the goal of desegregation abstract for people who saw no way out of the ghetto anyway. ("The black cat in Harlem," says Livingston Wingate of the New York Urban League, "wasn't worried about no damn bus—he'd been riding the bus for fifty years. What he didn't have was the fare.") Some fraction of the ghetto has always despaired of ever finding that way out and so has sought it in dreams. Harlem has been home to the dreamers since Marcus Garvey got off the boat in 1916 and has witnessed an unending train of refugees in spiritual flight from our midst—American Negroes turned Moor or Muslim or Black Jew or Copt or Yoruba or Ras Tafarian because to be American Negroes was no longer supportable for them.

So Malcolm was a face in the crowd when he arrived in June 1954 to take over his tiny storefront mosque, then situated in a section so drowning in misery that the older, better-off blacks further uptown called it a "nigger neighborhood." The locus of Harlem nationalism then lay at 125th Street and Seventh Avenue, where the street speakers harangued their crowds on the corners and where an ancient impish Garveyite named "Professer" Lewis Michaux presided over the National African Memorial Bookstore —"The House of Common Sense and Home of Proper Propaganda." Michaux, when I looked him up in the late 1960s, had been forced by the vicissitudes of urban renewal to move to a smaller shop further along on 125th but had recreated the pyramiding jumble of books, records, placards (THE WHITE MAN'S DREAM OF BEING SUPREME HAS TURNED TO SOUR CREAM), posters and fading photographs I remembered from the old place. "I don't know how I got in this business," Michaux, then eighty, told me; sitting there in his basement storeroom, in a space just big enough for a tiny desk and our two chairs, one imagined it having simply piled up around him.

Michaux called the old store "the gateway to Harlem's problems"; it was, for Malcolm and the younger nationalists, a point of entry to the Garvey past as well. Malcolm got to be a regular in the back room, where the Professer kept his Black Hall of Fame (with portraits of Dwight Eisenhower and Douglas MacArthur hanging unaccountably among the American race heroes and the African heads of state) and where he pieced out the tradition to its heirs. "I had the Back-to-Africa movement, and Malcolm had the Muslims, and we'd sit in the back and talk," Michaux told me. "He was a very fine fellow to meet, very agreeable. He was fortunate enough not to have enough education to be tamed. A *trained* Negro is a *tamed* Negro—he's tamed to say soft, *intellectual* things. But Malcolm learned by experience. He learned the way of poverty, he learned the way of trickery, he learned the way of *white* people to keep *other* people in their place." Michaux smiled a lemony, mischievous smile; he told me that white people turn red when you sting them, and he watched me closely to see if I would. "I used to talk with him. A Negro is not a nationality of people. I speak English, but I'm no damn *English*man. I belong to the man who lent me his tongue." I realized he had slipped into what must have been a soliloquy of those days, or a reasonably reliable memory of one. "*Negro* can't speak anything else. He's lost. He don't have a God—this man Jesus with straight hair, he's the *white* man's God. When a Negro gets the white man's religion, he won't even kill a *chinch.* If a chinch bites him, he gets out of bed and prays for the chinch. The white man would give you a Sunday-school card when you were a kid. It'd say, 'Thou shalt not steal'—that mean don't steal from *him.* 'Thou shalt not kill'—that mean don't kill *him.* 'Love your enemy.' Then why don't *he* hug *China?* . . ." Malcolm would listen, and grin; occasionally, Michaux said, he would tug out the little notebook he always carried, and his red ball-point pen, and would note something down. He remembered once having said something about America's chickens coming home to roost, and out came the notebook and the pen; long afterward, Malcolm got in trouble with Mr. Muhammad for using the phrase to describe John Kennedy's assassination, and Michaux has always wondered whether the words if not the sentiment that caused the trouble came from his back room.

Malcolm also made himself a regular at the corner of 125th and Seventh, where from spring to fall the sidewalk nationalists with hip-pocket organizations rain abuse on whitey and anyone of whatever color who serves him. Malcolm's own sidewalk rallies, when he began holding them, were rather more formal affairs, dressed up with bunting, placards and platform guests and wired for sound. The more common sight at 125th and Seventh is a lone man on a wobbly pine platform or a ladder, with an American flag incongruously next to him because the ordinance requires it at public meetings, squalling at little crowds of black people who tend to get bored and drift on unless you raise some hell. The language of the street speakers accordingly tends to be more direct than the Muslim eschatology of blue-eyed devils and mother planes. You can hear them still when the weather is fine, with their changeless angry litany:

". . . Why, with all the hell you caught for the past four hundred years, you haven't got *time* to talk about good white folks, is that right? [*Right!*] You haven't got *time* to say, 'Well, this white man and that white man was a liberal, so let's don't kill him.' 'Cause when killin' day comes, *you gonna have to kill 'em all!* I'm reminded of Dessalines in Haiti, when he had an argument with Toussaint about going to Paris to meet Napoleon. Toussaint told Dessalines, 'I'm goin' to Paris to negotiate an honorable peace.' Dessalines says, 'I don't trust 'em. I don't trust *no* white man. Don't go to Paris, 'cause you won't come back.' Toussaint says, 'No, Napoleon is a man of honor, and I'm goin' over there.' You know the story—he went to Paris and he never returned to Haiti, is that right? [*Right!*] When Dessalines had drove out all the white folks, that was against the wishes of the black folks who fought in the struggle to free themselves in Haiti. So some black folks told Dessalines, 'Invite the white folks back. *We got a job to complete.'* So fifteen thousand Frenchmen went back to Haiti. And Dessalines says, 'Bring them to the auction block, where the slaves used to be sold.' So all these white folks came there, and Dessalines got up and said, 'You know, I'm very proud that you came back.' Said, 'You know, my folks told me to invite you back 'cause they had something that hadn't been completed.' Then he took off his shirt and turned his back to the white folks and told 'em, said, 'You see them stripes? That was put on me during slavery.' Then he told all those black folks to take off their shirts, and they disrobed themselves, and he said, 'Now, of course, you know it's not up to me. Far as I'm concerned, you can live. But it's not left up to me to make the decision. The people must decide whether you're to live, according to what you done to them.' *And the verdict of the people was—DEATH!* And they killed *every white man there,* is that right? [*Right!*] So you see when this thing start to rollin' . . ."

Malcolm listened and learned, and with his fishers-for-souls worked the edges of other people's crowds for converts to his struggling temple. They worked the church doors as well, and the carry-out shops and poolrooms and back streets—anywhere black peope were—and gradually, inchmeal, built the communion of the Original People in Harlem from a few dozen to a few hundred regular followers.

Malcolm worked Harlem, but he never came back there to live —not even during those first uncertain days when he was single and scuffling by on whatever came back in the collection buckets. As a hustler years before, he had lived downtown when he could, bunking for a time with "a friend" on Park Avenue ("I had to go through the service entrance," he remembered wryly, "and make believe I was a delivery boy") and for another period in his own pad in Greenwich Village. When he returned as a Muslim, something held him back from that last symbolic commitment of the pastor to his parish. Perhaps it was the sensibility of the Nation, perhaps Malcolm's own upwardly mobile reach for respect; in any case, he took a furnished room in the black inner suburbs, in a brother Muslim's house in East Elmhurst, Long Island. Increasing prosperity eventually regularized his income: the temple put him on a base allowance of $125 (and later $150) a week* plus anything more he needed for traveling and propagating the faith. Prosperity upgraded his housing, too; he moved out of his single room to three rooms in a two-family flat—and later, after he married and began having children, to a seven-room home of his own. But Malcolm never left East Elmhurst; he was a commuter to Harlem until the day he died.

Neither did Harlem come to Muhammad. Those early years were a Sisyphean labor for Malcolm, begging and badgering Allah's lost children to hear the word of God. "You can't organize Harlem," one of the brothers told me. "Harlem got too many people with too many ways to destroy you." He said this in sad retrospect, five years after Malcolm had been hunted down and murdered by black men. It may have seemed true to Malcolm, too, during his first years preaching in Harlem, when he was bursting with his new truths and unable to get more than a handful of people at a time to listen to them. Harlem has destroyed men and organizations, less out of malevolence or envy or even its deep corroded cynicism than out of despair. Harlem destroys because there has been so much destruction there already.

10. The Parable of Hinton Johnson

What Harlem wanted from Malcolm and the Muslims was proof that they were as big and bad as they claimed to be. One April evening in 1957, chance, or providence, handed Malcolm the

*For tax purposes, the money was always styled "expenses" and was always paid in cash. It is said that the Internal Revenue Service was investigating both Malcolm and the Nation late in his life, but his drawing-account arrangement apparently was never formally questioned.

opportunity to furnish it. The vessel for Allah's will was a Muslim brother named Hinton Johnson, who happened upon a couple of white policemen billy-whipping a black suspect on a Harlem street corner and protested, "You're not in Alabama—this is New York!" For this impertinence, the police told Johnson to go away, then—when he refused—clubbed him down and arrested him. The incident was unremarkable enough, given the constant low-grade tension between Harlem and its police garrisons, but somebody ran and told the Muslims, and Malcolm decided the time had come for a show of strength. At his order, a few score of the faithful were rounded up by chain telephone calls—Kenyatta remembers having tumbled out of bed and into the street in his pajamas—and assembled for a march on the police.

What followed became an authentic Harlem parable—a folk story that stretched and grew and blurred in the retelling until the precise detail was lost and only the lesson of Allah's authority remained. Not even Malcolm himself remembered the events exactly: he scrambled Johnson's name in the *Autobiography* (it came out Johnson Hinton) and misplaced the episode in time by two years. I heard several versions, no two alike. James Hicks, who was there as the editor of Harlem's weekly newspaper, the *Amsterdam News,* and as a mediator between the police and the Muslims, told it this way:

"I was chairman of the 28th Precinct Community Council at the time, and at two in the morning, I got a call from the 28th to come over to my office. I went there and I met Inspector McGowen, Deputy Commissioner Walter Arm and Deputy Inspector Robert J. Mangum, who's black. McGowen said, 'I had a normal arrest, he was resisting, he got beat up and he's over there in the 28th Precinct now.' He said, 'They've got two thousand people out there.' He said, 'You know Malcolm X?' I said, 'Yeah, I know him' —we were pretty good friends by that time. Got to be lunch buddies at the Chock Full O' Nuts at 125th and Seventh. McGowen said, 'You think you can get him up here?' I said, 'Yeah, give me a little time. Where is he?' He said, 'Over at the 28th.'

"So I got over, and there he is with his people—with them and the bystanders they must have had 2,600 people lining the sidewalks between Seventh and Eighth avenues on 123rd Street. I said, 'Hey, Malcolm, Jesus. What's going on?' He told me one of their people was inside, he'd been beaten and needed medical attention. He said, 'We're going to stay right here, Brother Hicks.' I asked him if he'd come back to my office and talk to the police people. He said, 'If you think anything can be accomplished, I'll go. But only on your word.' So we went back and walked up to my office at the *Amsterdam News*—it was on the fourth floor.

"When we got there, Walter Arm started talking. He was in charge of public relations; he'd been a police reporter, and a good one, but he was white. He said, 'My presence here, and Inspector McGowen's, and Deputy Inspector Mangum's, indicates how much concern the police department has for this situation. However, I'd like to say that the police of the city of New York can handle any situation that arises in Harlem, and we're not here to ask anybody's help.'

"Well, Malcolm sat there and listened, and then he got up and put on that camel's-hair coat of his—he'd been a hustler and he always dressed sharp—and he told them, 'There's nothing more to be said.' Just like that. And suddenly he was striding out the door of my office. I can still hear his steps—clump-clump-clump—going into that gloomy city room. All the lights were out; my office was in the back at the end of the corridor, and he walked out into the darkness. Someone said, 'Where's he going?' And I said, 'He's leaving.'

"I followed him out. I said, 'Wait a minute, Mr. X.' He stopped out in the darkness there. He said, 'Brother Hicks, I'm only here 'cause you said something could be accomplished.' He said, 'They don't need me. They say they can handle it. Well, let them handle it.'

"I said, 'Wait a minute.'

"I went back to the room. Mangum said, 'Tell him there must be *some* level we can get together on if he'll only come back.' I went back out and told it to Malcolm, and he came back. He said,

'I only came back because I respect Brother Hicks.' And I said, 'Have a seat.'

"This time, Arm shut up. Malcolm said, 'I have no respect for you'—Arm—'or the police department.' He may have said something to Mangum, too. [What he told Mangum, according to a police source, was: "I don't talk with white man's niggers." Mangum, this source said, was "very hurt."] Malcolm said, 'One of our brothers has been beaten, and all we are asking is that we be allowed to go in there and see him and determine if he is in need of hospitalization. The evidence we have now is that he should be in the hospital. If we find that he doesn't need hospitalization, you can go on with your case. If he does, we want him hospitalized.' So Mangum and Arm agreed. They hadn't even seen the man themselves. They said, 'All right, let's take a look. If he does need hospitalization, we'll give it to him. Would that be satisfactory to you?' Malcolm said yes. They said, 'Will you then get your people out of the block?' Malcolm said, 'This is all we asked for and this is all we want.'

"In effect, the police were saying, 'We *can't* handle it without you.' Nobody got down on his knees. But they bowed.

"So we walked the three blocks back to the station, and Malcolm's people were still there. The men were standing in the gutter with their arms folded. Immobile. The women were on the sidewalk behind them with white kerchiefs on their heads. And nobody said a word. The light in the stationhouse was the only light in the block. I remember thinking, 'Where did they all *come* from?'—a movement like that growing up right under your nose. When we got to the station, there was a black sergeant on the door. I heard him saying, 'Goddamn Muslims—who the hell are they anyway? Turn me loose with this club and I'll clear this block.' John X, who was with Malcolm, turned and just stared at him, and I said to McGowen, 'You better get that sergeant off the door.'

"We went on in and saw the man, and they had torn his head off—he eventually won $70,000 from the city. One look and McGowen said, 'Get him to the hospital.' He said, 'Mr. X, he's going to be sent to Harlem Hospital—is that all right?' Malcolm said, 'That's all we asked.' McGowen said, 'Would you take the responsibility of sending your people home?' Malcolm said, 'I'll do that.'

"And then, in that dim light, Malcolm stood up and waved his hand, and all those people just disappeared. *Disappeared.* One of the police people said to me, 'Did you see what I just saw?' I said, 'Yeah.' He said, 'This is too much power for one man to have.' He meant one black man. I'll never forget that."

Nor did Harlem. For white New Yorkers, those who heard of the confrontation at all, it was a chilling glimpse of a world we didn't know existed; a world of unblinking, unforgiving black men and women who weren't afraid of our police or our guns or death itself; an army, one black writer told me, of people nobody wanted. But what chilled us thrilled Harlem, partly for the sheer nerve of it, even more because it was black people standing together in defense of one of their own. "You know," a black journalist friend who started going to Muslim meetings years later told me, "we live all our lives feeling that we're subject to sudden and arbitrary violence. I don't know if that's reasonable or not, but we do. There's a kind of peace at those meetings that you don't feel anywhere else. They give you an hour or two of *shelter,* and that's something." I imagined that some kindred feeling must have got around Harlem that April, among people who saw the facedown on 123rd Street or read about it in the *Amsterdam.*

Benjamin Goodman, for one. He was in his middle twenties then, a tall, angular young man trained in radar in the Air Force but working in a record-company shipping room in New York—"building maintenance work, I guess you'd call it"—because airports weren't hiring black radarmen in those days. "I guess I was born dissatisfied," he said. He had grown up in Virginia; had gone to schools where they told him to be a good boy and churches where they told him to fear God; had rooted for the crooks in the movies—there were no black people to identify with—and had even taken a correspondence course in gambling for a while. He had an unhappy time in the service (except for a tour in Japan, where color didn't count as much) and an unhappier time in New

York afterward, discovering that it counts plenty in the promised land. "The white man is the same everywhere you go. It's like Brother Malcolm said. 'When you buy a box of crackers, the crackers on the top are the same as the crackers on the bottom.' " He was bumping aimlessly around Harlem and Harlem's lesser vices when he heard the parable of Hinton Johnson—"how this man Malcolm X was out front protesting against that act and how the Muslim brothers and sisters reacted. The brotherhood was what attracted me. The unity. How a Muslim goes to the aid of a brother when he is mistreated. It seemed like unity and brotherhood and —*love.* So I went there to seek out the Muslims."

Others did, too, and while most of them were put off by Muslim mythology or Muslim morality, some few, like Goodman, stayed and labored over their letters to God and received the faith. The Hinton Johnson affair established the Nation in Harlem and launched it on a period of growing membership and rising prosperity. The few hundred signed-up believers became two thousand or so, with a presence and an impact far larger than their actual number. The collection buckets started coming back full, and, since Malcolm was assumed by the temple people to be more trustworthy than the white man's banks, his home for a time became "the vault"—the cache for the tithes of the faithful and the collection point for the men with dispatch cases from Chicago. Temples sprang up in other cities along the Eastern seaboard and far beyond, most of them called to life by Malcolm and his deputies. "We organized by talking," Goodman said. "You'd move into a town and call a meeting; Malcolm's name would draw a crowd; then you'd work with those who came back to the next meeting. You could start a mosque with five people. Or two, even—they'd bring others." Malcolm claimed years later to have been in on organizing every temple after No. 10 in Atlantic City. The temple numbers ran to 35 by the time he left the Nation, and the writ of Allah ran from Boston to Miami to South Bend to Fresno.

With growth, slowly, came public attention. Malcolm had to beg it at first; he protested to Hicks one day that the *Amsterdam* wasn't paying the Nation enough attention, and Hicks, sensing a good thing, offered him a column. "I remember the very first one teed off on the 'chicken-eaters'—that's what he called the black preachers," Hicks told me. "He just *devastated* the Christian church. Called it the slaveowners' church. So, first thing, I got a delegation. Some preachers came down, said, 'Brother Hicks, what the hell is this? This is our community paper and he's cutting the ground out from under us.' Well, the bulk of our circulation was in the black church, and the publisher got nervous, and I finally told 'em, 'The man's got a point of view. I'll give you equal space—run your column side by side with his—and you can refute what Malcolm said." Hicks half-hopefully nominated Adam Clayton Powell, but the churchmen chose someone less controversial, and the duel began. It was no contest. "By the third week," said Hicks, "it was apparent that, by having a target, Malcolm was even more devastating. Malcolm *murdered* the man. It got so the rebuttal column would be mostly quoting the Bible. You know—'Malcolm says this and this and this, but the Book of Matthew says . . .' And Malcolm was wailing away."

The column was a great popular success for Malcolm—so great that word got back to Chicago and caused what may have been the first premonitory stabs of jealousy there. Malcolm asked Hicks one day if he would agree to let Mr. Muhammad take over the column. "My reaction was why do I need Muhammad?" Hicks said. "He finally admitted to me that Muhammad wanted to write it. He saw that Malcolm was becoming the biggest thing in New York blackwise. So Malcolm said, 'Beginning next week, the Honorable Elijah Muhammad will write the column.' " He did, and Hicks ran it for a few weeks, but Muhammad's rambly pieces—whatever their worth as revelation—made pallid copy as against Malcolm's bang-bang topicality. "After a while," Hicks remembered, "the ministers weren't worried any more." The column slid out of the paper and was forgotten. Malcolm never complained. He learned enough newspapering to give the Nation a line of media of its own, first worrying together a few one-shot publications, later—with technical advice from the late black journalist Louis Lomax—launching the tabloid *Muhammad Speaks* out of his own basement. Malcolm himself produced much of the copy and took most of the pictures for the early editions, with his own and his temple's activities extensively covered. Once again he incurred Chicago's displeasure, and the newspaper was taken away from him, too. Malcolm never complained about that either—not until his relations with the Messenger had deteriorated nearly to the breaking point.

Heightened visibility in the ghetto brought heightened exposure downtown. Eric Lincoln, who coined the nickname "Black Muslims" and can be said to have discovered the Nation of Islam to the nation of America, was a divinity student working a summer job on a black Atlanta daily when Malcolm wandered in one day and struck up a conversation. "I remember it," Lincoln said, "mainly for his eagerness to argue, to attack all the established acceptances of black people—about themselves, about the world at large, about the white man. He stood at my desk and we argued for the better part of an hour. He was not trying to convert me to Islam—he was trying to liberate me from the bonds of myth, the bonds of taboo, the bonds of fairy tale he assumed I was under." The acquaintance blossomed into a mutually rewarding friendship. Lincoln brought Malcolm to the Boston University human-relations center—"the first time he appeared in public"—and arranged several other early speaking dates in our nation; Malcolm in turn opened doors in his when Lincoln was researching a doctoral dissertation on the Muslims. Said Lincoln: "We coached one another."

His dissertation became the first book about the Nation. Others followed, one by a Nigerian scholar, E. U. Essien-Udom, whose interest seemed to flatter Chicago and who was accordingly given access to a great deal of inside detail; and later another, by Lomax, whom Malcolm liked for his energy and his endless line of black gossip. Mike Wallace put the Muslims on TV, with a week-long documentary series reported largely by Lomax and co-starring Malcolm, who encouraged the project, with Mr. Muhammad, who had to be talked into it. Magazines and newspapers put the Nation on public view. So did the radio and TV talk shows, and, to Malcolm's enormous pleasure, the university lecture bureaus. I remember him, at our first meeting, happily rattling off his recent campus dates (". . . Harvard four times, Wellesley, Simmons, Boston University, Wesleyan, Rutgers, all the New York colleges . . .") faster than I could note them all down; one easily forgot, in the face of his marvelous self-assurance, what those invitations must have meant to a black man with an eighth-grade diploma and a homemade prison education.

The exposure was a mighty boon to the Nation, at least in the short run, but a mixed blessing for Malcolm. A lot of it cast him in the most simplistic terms as a hatemonger and a demagogue. He used to rationalize this as inevitable ("Anybody who's effective among the masses usually is considered extremist, subversive, seditious and—you know—*irresponsible*") and even as useful, given that some indeterminate number of black people will respond warmly to any man so characterized by whites. But the image ultimately hurt the Nation and haunted Malcolm after he left it. The publicity, moreover, tended to focus on Malcolm, not the Messenger. The two of them managed for several years to postpone the inevitable difficulties over this, partly because Malcolm assiduously mentioned Mr. Muhammad's name at least once a minute, by his own accurate count, in any speech or interview. But the imbalance of attention was to haunt him, too. Much of America came to believe that Malcolm *was* the Muslims.

In many respects, he was. Muhammad had met God, but Malcolm knew the devil—understood not only his guilts and his anxieties but how to tease them to a point where white people would deliver his message for him. "You [media] people are masochists," Whitney Young once told me. "You made Malcolm X." We didn't, not really; Malcolm created himself. But we did find him irresistible, and, through us and our media, he reached that other country called Black America.

How deeply he reached it was a question beyond quantification by polls, head counts or any of our accustomed measures of success and failure. Malcolm always ducked questions about the Nation's signed-up membership; his favorite formulation was that those who know don't say and those who say don't know. I remember pestering him about it once, over a table at Mosque No. 7's luncheonette in Harlem, till he finally told me: "Nobody really knows. But if I came out of Lincoln Tunnel into the city and said *'As-salaam alaikum'* to the first Negro I saw, he'd answer, *'Wa-alaikum salaam.'* " He was less reticent after he had quit and his reputation had come under challenge; he claimed then to have been instrumental in increasing the Nation's population a hundredfold, from four hundred to forty thousand. Ten thousand was probably nearer the peak registered membership in his day, something over two thousand of them in Harlem, but the numbers game that we of the media played—and that Malcolm obliquely encouraged, being as much the prisoner of our conventions of judgment as we—was surely a waste of time. That the census was "only" ten or even forty thousand was a false comfort: it didn't tell us about the concentric circles of sympathizers and admirers-from-a-distance and just plain street people who were touched and influenced and who talked the Muslim talk even when they couldn't manage the total Muslim submission to Allah. Once, in St. Louis, a bewildered cop told me that even the hookers and boosters were calling him a blue-eyed devil and would only talk to his black partner, not to him. "People don't need to sign up," Malcolm always insisted. "The most effective part of the tree is the roots. They're signed up with the tree, but you don't ever see them. They're always beneath the ground."

What Malcolm sensed was that he could touch some responsive nerve in black people however distant from the ghetto, however aloof from the struggle, however resistant to the embrace of Allah. The confrontation over Hinton Johnson gave him a chance to prove it—to reach black people to whom the Nation, if the name rang a bell at all, had previously been only another of those storefront utopias so common in the ghettos. It gave Malcolm a certain mystery, a certain authority as well. The wonder of the episode was that he had only had to get his people out and have them stand in 123rd Street for a few hours, nothing more—and that, having done so, he didn't have to turn them out again for five more years.

Malcolm understood this quite clearly; he knew the psychology of crowds, black and white, and the values of symbolic action. "If you have a cocked fist," he said once, "you don't have to throw it." He was talking about the values of abstaining in elections, but he was too keen a man to miss the equal utility of the cocked fist in the politics of the street. It is easy now to forget how fearsome the Muslims seemed to us in those days. I think a lot of us, black and white, suspected that Malcolm could start Armageddon if he wanted to. When people believe that of a man, he hardly needs to try.

11. What Mr. Muhammad Told Dr. King

Was there really a bit of Malcolm X in every black man? Martin Luther King is said to have confessed to a friend once that, yes, even he felt an empathic twinge of hatred when he saw Malcolm railing at white folks on television. I tried this out on a close associate of King's; he doubted that it was so. But later in the same conversation, he told me that King had visited Mr. Muhammad in Chicago one day and had, during the course of a "very friendly" conversation, asked the Messenger: "Do you really believe that *all* white folks are devils? I know a lot of white people have a lot of devil in them, but are you going to say that *all* of them are devils?" Mr. Muhammad smiled. "Dr. King," he said, "you and me both grew up in Georgia, and we know there are many different kind of snakes. The rattlesnake was poisonous and the king snake was friendly. But they both snakes, Dr. King." And the two of them, the Messenger of Allah and the apostle of Christian love, had a hearty laugh.

12. Strangers in a Strange Land

In those days, when Malcolm and the Muslims had reached their zenith and white people wondered why, Bayard Rustin used to say, "You push a man into a corner, and there's no light and he begins to act desperate. And then you say, 'How desperate you are.' " Some of Malcolm's spontaneity eroded during the Black Muslim years, most of his positions having been either revealed to him by God through Mr. Muhammad or rehearsed by him in a hundred speeches and interviews, but his voice never lost that desperation. He came to us in a time when our television screens were full of God-fearing, hymn-singing, abstract Negroes in daily confrontation with the billy-mauling, nigger-baiting, equally abstract defenders of the old white order in the South. For liberal whites, it seemed a distant contest between something called segregation and something called integration—between barbarity and common decency—and one imagined that, however slowly and incrementally, common decency was winning. We hardly heard that voice out of a lightless corner telling us that we were lying, to ourselves no less than to the blacks; that the problem was not somewhere else but at our own doorstep, in our own festering ghettos, and that it was not soluble by jobs or lawsuits or piecemeal integration or Brotherhood Week luncheons or any other measure we had yet imagined. "What you don't realize," Malcolm told white America, "is that black people today don't think it is any victory to live next to you or enter your society. This is what you have to learn—that the black man has finally reached the point where he doesn't see what you have to offer. Today you haven't *got* anything to offer. Your own time has run out, your own ship is sinking, the seas are stormy, and now that your boat is rocking and on its way down, you're offering the black man a chance to integrate into your doomed society. And those Uncle Tom, brainwashed, white-minded Negroes who *love* you may do it, but the masses of black people want a society of their own in a land of their own."

Malcolm considered white folks incorrigible. In the shelter of the mosque, he taught the absolute evil of whites as a matter of pure-and-simple revelation. "These aren't white people," he told the believers. "You're not using the right language when you say the white man. You call it the devil. When you call him the devil, you're calling him by his name, and he's got another name—Satan; another name—serpent; another name—snake; another name—beast. All these names are in the Bible for the white man. Another name—Pharaoh; another name—Caesar; another name—France; French; Frenchman; Englishman; American; all these are just names for the devil." In the presence of white people, he was somewhat more fastidious about using that particular name—surprisingly so considering how little he cared for their feelings. But, while his language turned political and historical, his message was no less harsh. Muslims, he said, didn't have to judge white people on their color—only on their intentions and their conscious behavior. "Historically, I think," he offered mildly, "the weight of the evidence is against them if you're looking for angelic deeds."

Liberal whites kept trying, out of some inner urgency, to get him to relent; to exempt somebody—anybody—white from the blood-guilt he laid to them. In their debate in 1962 at New York's Community Church, Bayard Rustin protested gently that the whites in the gallery—his own white friends among them—were applauding Malcolm longer and louder than the blacks were. "May I explain the process," said Rustin. "It is, my friends, that many white people love to hear their kind damned to high water while they sit saying, 'Isn't it wonderful that that nice black man gives *those* white people hell? But he couldn't be talking about *me*—I'm the liberal.' " Malcolm was talking about *all* whites; there were no exemptions, try as one might to place names in nomination. A television panel moderator once offered the freedom riders. "We don't think," Malcolm replied tartly, "that any whites who went down and joined freedom rides did any good for our people because no problem has been solved." Or the sit-in kids? "In my opinion, sir, any white who went down into the South to get Negroes the opportunity to drink an integrated cup of coffee, they couldn't have had the welfare of those people at stake." Was there nobody, then? "We don't take a microscope," Malcolm answered, "and run around here trying to find some whites out of a 170 million population who mean well or who are doing well. We're not even concerned with the white man."

Malcolm was not quite so rigorous in his own daily dealings with whites. He saw more of them than most Muslims did, and as white people became less abstract to him, they surely became less formidable than Satan, if not more lovable in the mass. Malcolm glimpsed their humanity, and privately, in measured ways, responded to it. "I doubt very much that he ever really hated anybody," Eric Lincoln ventured. "Malcolm said what he felt—he was outspoken—and sometimes he overstated his case for emphasis. The rhetoric was intended to produce certain kinds of responses both in his black constituency—Malcolm wanted them to understand that the white man was human and that being human he was vulnerable—and among the 'blue-eyed devils' he loved so much to annoy." But if he did not hate, neither would he retreat from hatred as a legitimate political position for black people in white America: Malcolm could not ask them, as King did, to hate the lynching and love the lyncher. Once, before a mixed audience of his Muslims and the Rev. Representative Adam Clayton Powell's Baptists at Powell's church in Harlem, someone raised the hate issue, and Malcolm shouted hoarsely: "How can anybody ask us do we hate the white man who kidnapped us four hundred years ago, brought us here and stripped us of our history, stripped us of our culture, stripped us of our language, stripped us of everything you could have used today to prove that you're a part of the human family, bring you down to the level of an animal, sell you from plantation to plantation like a sack of wheat, sell you like a sack of potatoes, sell you like a horse and a plow, and then hung you up

from one end of the country to the other, and then you as
I hate him?" In the exploding applause of the mingled Musl
and Christians, you could hardly hear his reply: "Why, your question is worthless!"

Malcolm recognized no statute of limitations on those historic wrongs, and he could not forgive white people for them. "You can't solve a problem by dealing with the current situation," he said. "You have to go into the roots as to how that racial mythology developed." Black people, he believed, had been dragged down by whites from an old splendor that may have been partly Mr. Farrad's fancy but was also partly fact. Black scientists who deported the moon and created the devil dwelled in Malcolm's lost Africa, but so did black engineers who raised the pyramids, black scholars who built a great university at Timbuktu, black kings who created vast ordered empires below the Sahara, black soldiers who defeated the Crusaders and spread Islam by the sword into Southern Europe. He conceded offstage that he was laying on an "overdose" of black culture and was quite unabashed about it; he was, in the vocabulary of the Nation, trying to bring the dead to life, and he used whatever medicine he thought necessary. "Before Negroes came here, they weren't drunkards," he said. "They weren't dope addicts. They weren't fornicators and adulterers. They were living in palaces, wearing silks in Africa, eating cooked and seasoned foods, highly civilized, when people up in Europe were falling into caves. Still eating raw meat. Still eating up their mothers and their fathers as cannibals."

White men, Malcolm said, had brought black men low; had colonized Africa and reduced the Africans to servants in their own land and slaves in ours; had suppressed their language and religion by brute force and substituted our tongue and our spook gods; had imprisoned them not only with shackles and slave codes but with the very name we gave them—Negro. Malcolm was a man of words, and he imputed almost magical powers to them; he believed that the liberation of the Negroes—they were always the "so-called Negroes" to the Muslims—would begin the day they started calling themselves black men and women.* "Negro," according to our etymology, derives from the Latin *niger*, or "black," but according to Malcolm's and Mr. Farrad's, it came from the Greek *nekros*, meaning "corpse"; this more accurately described not only the condition of the people who bore the name but the intentions of the people who gave it to them. "The only way we could be made slaves," Malcolm said in a sermon to the believers, "we first had to be made dumb. We first had to be placed in darkness. We first had to be placed in the graves of ignorance. And after the white man had destroyed our mind and destroyed our soul and destroyed our culture, destroyed our memory, destroyed our past, then he turned around and told the whole world we were animals. . . . It's the same as taking a horse and putting him in a cage and putting another horse outside the cage and then expect that horse that's *in* the cage to run as fast or as far as the horse that's outside the cage. That's what the white man has done to the black man here in America—he has stripped you and me of everything that it takes for a man to walk or a man to move, and after he has made us helpless, he stands up and tells the world we can't walk as fast as he. We can't walk on the same level as he. We can't *think* on the same level as he, and he knows that he is the one who has destroyed our minds."

Malcolm saw us from the ruins, not as our fellow citizen but as our victim. He could not therefore accept that we would do anything serious to retrieve the damage we had wrought. "Usually," he said, "the criminal who has committed the crime is never the one to whom you look for a solution." He could be quite pitiless in the application of this rule. There were no "liberals" or "con-

*This has been a recurring dream down to our own day, when—since Malcolm's death—the old shame word "black" has at last been rehabilitated and brought into vogue. The dream has endured despite the doubts of men more worldly than the Garveyites and the Lost-Found Nation. "Suppose," W. E. B. DuBois wrote a half-century ago, "we arose tomorrow morning and lo! instead of being 'Negroes,' all the world called us 'Cheiropolidi'—do you really think this would make a vast and momentous difference to you and me?" But the dream has powerful psychic meaning; one guesses that it will even survive the evidence around us that, at least in a material sense, DuBois was right.

servatives" for Malcolm, no Northern good guys and Southern villains; only, in his Aesopian terms, foxes and wolves. He used to tell the story of the white coed who had come to the Muslim restaurant one day asking whether there wasn't some way she could help; he had said no, and she had run out in tears. Malcolm came to regret his answer; he had developed a small soft spot for white students even then—they seemed to him capable of listening—and, in his last year, he began to imagine that some few of them might be some small help after all. But in the Muslim days, he could not admit this possibility even to himself. To see whites singly was to compromise the faith and the wintry purity of vision and purpose it gave him. There would be no microscopes for Malcolm. "When you begin to think of it in terms of an individual basis," he said once, "you lose sight of the whole question. It's collective."

Neither would he accept that America was anything more than a prison to the blacks—a latter-day house of bondage from which the children of God had to be delivered. "If you'll notice," Malcolm said, "whenever I refer to America, I don't say *we.* I don't say *I* or *our.* I say *you.* This is *yours,* it's not *me* or *mine.* And you'll find that this thinking is increasing among black people today. They don't say *our* government, *our* President, *our* Senate, *our* Congress, nor do they say *our* troubles. They say *your* President, *your* Congress, *your* Senate—and *your* troubles." America, he contended, was "founded by white Europeans for white Europeans" and had never intended citizenship for the blacks. "The founding fathers—the ones who said 'liberty or death' and all those pretty-sounding speeches—were slaveowners themselves. When they said 'liberty,' they didn't mean the black man, they meant the white people. When Lincoln said 'of the people, by the people and for the people,' Lincoln meant 'of white people, by white people and for white people.' " If it were otherwise—if the American Creed was meant for black people—a dozen or so Southern states wouldn't be able to tie up the appropriate legislation in Congress; legislation wouldn't even be needed. No, it was all a game, a shuck, in which the fox was equally culpable with the wolf. "You got a gorilla on your back," Malcolm told a street crowd in Harlem one summer Saturday in 1962. "A great big white gorilla named Uncle Sam."

The attempt to integrate blacks into this society was, by Malcolm's lights, to advocate their destruction as a race. He argued as heatedly as any unregenerate Southern seg that the real purpose of the integrationists was intermarriage. "They want your wife and your daughter and your sister and—and your *mother,*" he improvised during one debate. He was half-joking, but, one judged, only half. Malcolm often insisted that most of the prominent Negroes promoting integration were intermarried already, a list on which he included James Farmer, Harry Belafonte, Sammy Davis, Jr., Lena Horne and the playwright Lorraine Hansberry, among others. Miss Hansberry eventually cornered Malcolm at a party, eyes flashing, and told him she resented his harping on her mixed marriage. Malcolm, who by then had outgrown the idea anyway, was—possibly for the only time in his public career—speechless. A spectator remembers him laughing and stammering, "Well . . ." He and Miss Hansberry made up and became friends; Malcolm was among the mourners at her funeral, hardly a month before his own. But he remained an anti-integrationist long after he began losing faith in formal separatism as an alternative, and for some of the same reasons. "All that will happen," he told a friend involved in the school-integration struggles of the middle sixties, "is we'll get some more of these gray-eyed niggers. We've had nighttime integration for a long time now—that's why I look the way I do."

Malcolm presumed that integration wouldn't happen anyway on any significant scale—not without catastrophic violence and the imposition of a military dictatorship. "If all of the token integration which you see in the South, and it's only tokenism, has caused the bloodshed that it has," he said, "what do you think white people, both North and South, will do on the basis of *real* integration?" Malcolm thus saw "integration" as irrelevant to the lives of ordinary black people; it was rather a chimera to be pursued by middle-class Negroes fleeing their blackness and to be awarded by white people to those few they deemed acceptable, which was to say like whites in style, outlook and aspiration. These few token offerings were not to be confused with good will. "The man who tosses worms in the river," Malcolm said, "isn't necessarily a friend of the fish. All the fish who take him for a friend, who think the worm's got no hook on it, usually end up in the frying pan." The joke, moreover, was not only on them but on those whites who encouraged them. "After the black man who is seeking this integration which you promised him gets in and looks around and finds that all the whites have fled out to the suburbs and he still doesn't have what he wanted, he starts looking out to the suburb where you're now living, and he starts trying to get into the suburb. . . . And what he's doing, he's running you all over the country. He has you seeking someplace where you can lay your anti-integrationist head where the integration-intoxicated Negro can't make you run any farther."

If integration was a sham, the style then in vogue for seeking it —nonviolent protest—was a degradation; a beggarly style roughly equivalent, Malcolm said, to the sheep reminding the wolf that it was time for dinner. He contended that whites had never practiced "this little passive-resistance or wait-until-you-change-your-mind-and-then-let-me-up philosophy" themselves but had conjured it up to unman the blacks when they began getting restless. "When the Japanese attacked Pearl Harbor," Malcolm told me at our first meeting in 1962, "Uncle Sam didn't say, 'Forget Pearl Harbor.' No—he said, '*Remember* Pearl Harbor.' Uncle Sam said, 'Praise the Lord and pass the ammunition.' " I raised the Gandhi experience in India, from which King had consciously borrowed. "In India," Malcolm said, "their size was their strength. They were like an elephant sitting on a mouse. Here, the so-called Negroes are like a little tiny mouse trying to sit on an elephant."

Neither Malcolm nor the Muslims ever advocated armed, aggressive violence, but they were absolutely insistent on the right of self-defense. Their insistence seemed ominous to us at the time, as against King's doctrine of redemptive suffering; white people couldn't see where self-defense left off and the black revenge began, and Malcolm, who enjoyed their unease, did nothing to clarify the boundary lines. "If a man is struggling to keep a rope from being put around his neck," he said, "he's going to fight to preserve himself." I asked him once whether he meant us to take the rope literally or figuratively. "I'm speaking metaphorically," he replied. "It can be an economic rope. It can be a political rope. It can be a material rope. It can be a psychological rope or even a spiritual rope." He smiled; one did not know whether one had been listening to a discussion of human psychology or a declaration of war. The truth, as one discovered later, was that Malcolm was engaging in the only kind of combat his vows permitted him. Black Islam held him out of the active struggle—the Muslims in effect were waiting for the Mother Plane and the pilots who had never smiled—but he could at least stab at our consciousness with those shadowy words and those Aesopian figures. With luck, and art, he might even scare us into doing something.

He did not believe that the civil-rights movement ever would; he presumed, quite to the contrary, that white people had hired it to hypnotize the blacks and keep their rising restiveness in channels that would not unduly discomfit the rest of us. The greatest sin of the established Negro leaders, he thought, was their respectability: they were afraid to be demagogues, to be thought irresponsible, where Malcolm was not. "They controlled you," he told a black audience, "but they never have incited you or excited you. . . . They contained you. They have kept you on the plantation." He saw the new rebelliousness of the blacks as a forest fire and the official civil-rights struggle as an artificial "backfire" set by our Negroes to slow down the real conflagration. He believed that white people had taken over the civil-rights movement by joining and financing it, thereby diluting its blackness, and by flattering its leaders with media attention, rigged popularity polls and periodic invitations to tea and sympathy at the White House.

He could be particularly brutal about King. The press and public imagination had cast the two of them as adversaries in a great Manichaean contest, the forces of light against the forces of darkness, with the future course of black protest at stake. The deck in this game was stacked against him—the Age of Malcolm X began only after his death—but he played anyway, the harder precisely because King then held most of the cards. "Dr. King is an Uncle Tom," said Malcolm; a court magician who would never challenge our power or even seriously inconvenience us. "Martin Luther King's primary concern," he said, "is in defending the white man, and if he can elevate the black man's condition at the same time, then the black man will be elevated. But if it takes a condemnation of the white man in order to elevate the black man, you'll find that Martin Luther King will get out of the struggle. Martin Luther King isn't preaching love—he's preaching love the white man."

Malcolm, as John O. Killens put it, believed in love, too, but not in unrequited love; his capacity for fellow feeling during the Muslim years stopped roughly at 110th Street in uptown Manhattan, where Harlem ends and Central Park begins. He believed that the ruin of the blacks had begun with the destruction of their self-esteem and that their recovery had to start not with an access of brotherliness toward white people but with a decent regard for one another. "Once we accept ourselves," he said, "we're acceptable to everyone." This meant an end to the get-it-now hedonism of ghetto life. Malcolm well understood where that impulse came from—*now* becomes imperative to people when there may not be a later—but he knew from his own ravaged past where it led. Malcolm's get-right-with-God morality tends to be forgotten now as against his combativeness, which was more exciting to blacks and whites alike, but it was central to his leadership. "His moral force—that's what I dug him for," Dick Gregory, who was Malcolm's close friend, told me. "When you took a drink, you knew Malcolm wouldn't approve of it. I stole that part of him. I used to say, 'I sure want to be like you when I grow up.' "

It was a force he conveyed principally by example: his own life was a reproach not only to the white people who created Harlem but to those blacks who accepted its devastation. "Clean yourself up," he told a street crowd in Harlem. "Stand yourself up and look at yourself—with *your* eyes, not the white man's. Make yourself acceptable to God instead of the devil." He and the Muslims assigned women a subordinate role in the home and the mosque but insisted that they be honored by their men and protected from ours; in this respect, as Bayard Rustin put it, Malcolm "was the great male feminist, and all the women loved him for it." He urged with equal fervor the necessity of regular habits—Malcolm lived by his wristwatch and was intolerant of people who didn't live by theirs—and the rewards of deferred gratification. He really believed in the little mom-and-pop stores nursed to life by the Muslims out of the nickels and dimes they saved by living the clean life; he saw them for what Mr. Muhammad said they were—the beginnings of the Black Restoration. "The whites," Malcolm said, "came here uneducated and poverty-stricken, but still they were able to pool their resources. Many of them opened up little stores. They lived in the back of these stores, they sent their children to school, their children got an education, they came out and expanded their fathers' businesses. This is the principle that the American economy was founded on."

He believed that America was founded on white unity as well—Malcolm always suspected that factionalism was a special torment devised by the devil for the blacks—and he argued that black unity was the first requirement for survival. He preached this, particularly during the Muslim years, a good deal more effectively than he practiced it; unity in his view implied submission to the theocracy of Allah and Mr. Muhammad, and to hell, quite literally, with those who resisted. The contradiction seems not to have troubled him. He had rather a romantic view of the Bandung Conference, that first hopeful assembly of the Third World nations in Indonesia in 1955; he believed that its success lay in submerging political, economic and religious differences in the face of a common enemy—white people—and he saw no reason why the Bandung model shouldn't be equally applicable in Harlem or Watts. The language of his appeals to solidarity anticipated the Black Power movement by at least three years. "In this country," he said, "it seems to be all right for every group—Jewish, Italian, Irish and what have you—to come together on the basis of what they are and try and do something for their own kind. . . . But when black people begin to talk in terms of coming together base skin coloration—and that's about the only thing we have in (mon outside of oppression, exploitation and just pure catching ... —then people jump up and say that's racism or something of that sort."

Black unity in turn was only a prelude to Allah's final solution: the black exodus to "our home in the East"—the Muslims were always curiously resistant to coming right out and saying Africa— or, failing that, to some partitioned-off pro-rated share of the United States. This was the pie in the Nation's sky, as the dream of a Beloved Society was the pie in King's. Separation was of enormous psychic significance to the faithful, announcing as it did their final repudiation of everything white America stood for. But it was a slow seller outside the mosques; it began to sit uneasily not only with Malcolm's sense of reality but with his drumming instincts as well. Nevertheless, separation was what he preached as long as he lasted in the Nation. "Since we have this problem with America," he told me, "and one of the primary reasons is the inability of the government to force the whites to let the dissatisfied blacks into their white communities, Mr. Muhammad says let us go back to our own country. Ship us back to our home in the East. But the government has secret fears of any mass movement to go back to the East to be among our own kind. So, since they can't give us justice here and won't let us go home, and since we can't live in peace together, we say give us part of this country." The Muslims were always guarded about detailing the size of their claim, except that it ought to be equivalent to the black percentage of America's population, and about its location, though Malcolm used to joke that he hoped the Messenger would choose some place sunny, like Florida or California. The announced specifications were that the land be rainy, mineral-rich and fertile and that our government supply foreign aid for twenty or twenty-five years till the black Zion got going—a deal equivalent to the one the black authorities gave Yacub when he and his people left "the East" for Patmos six thousand years ago to create us.

Liberals, white and black, argued that he was urging flight from the struggle. "The sheep," he answered, "isn't running away when he leaves the wolf's den." We called his separatism segregation in reverse. "You never call Chinatown, an area where all Chinese live, a segregated community," he replied. "They control their own economy. All the stores in Chinatown are Chinese, the banks are Chinese, everything is Chinese. They control the economics of their own community, the politics of their own community, the educational system and the curriculum of their own community, so it's a *separate* community. It's respected because of their ability to provide job opportunities for their own kind, and because of this you never find Chinese on the welfare, Chinese in the breadline, Chinese in the unemployment line. But the stores in the Negro community are controlled by whites, the banks are controlled by whites, the politics are controlled by whites, the civic organizations are controlled by whites, and because the so-called Negro community is controlled or regulated by outsiders, it's a *segregated* community." We said separation was unrealistic—utopian from his standpoint and inadmissible from ours. Malcolm showed us Harlem and said: "We're separate already."

What whites often missed was that separation for Malcolm was less an issue of politics than an article of faith and that logic, in so devout a man, can be a long time overtaking belief. "Malcolm was so—*spiritual,*" Charles Kenyatta said. "He could quote the Bible by heart. The other ministers had to look it up." The Scriptures, as he read them, only confirmed his tragic view of the condition of the blacks in our midst. "Here in the 137th Psalm," he told one gathering of believers, "it says, 'By the rivers of Babylon, there we sat down, yea, we wept, when we remembered Zion.' When we remembered our homeland, we wept. 'We hanged our harps upon the willows in the midst thereof. For there they that carried us away captive required of us a song; and they that wasted us required of us mirth, saying, Sing us one of the songs of Zion.' And, beloved brothers and sisters, no one knows better than the black man here in America that our history here has fulfilled this prophecy 100 percent. We were *brought* here, and those who brought us here, they tell us daily, 'Sing. Sing for us. Dance for us.

Clown for us. Make us laugh. . . . Sing us one of the songs of Zion. Sing us one of those spirituals, or some of those blues.' And the answer came back, 'How shall we sing the Lord's song in a strange land?' How can *we* intelligently sing the Lord's song in this strange land?"

He found the future of the blacks affirmed in Scripture, too: in the flight of Moses from Egypt and of Lot from burning Sodom; in God's promises to Malachi that He would raise up a man named Elijah and that soon thereafter would come a day that would burn as an oven; in the prophecies of the Book of Daniel that the thrones would be cast down and that the Ancient of Days, the hair of his head like pure wool, would sit and rain fire till the beast was slain, and his body destroyed, and given to the burning flame. Malcolm, being spiritual, took solace in all of this and taught the faithful to await it. But Malcolm was an activist as well and did not expect to be merely a spectator at the judgment. He never stopped reading Scripture, but he was drawn more and more in his last years to the wild apocalyptic visions of the Book of Revelation, in which the righteous make war against the wicked and even Jesus takes up the sword.

13. We Are a World

One wonders when the doubts began; at what moment the snake first appeared in paradise.

The Nation of Islam is not a place that admits ambiguities. It offers its true believers a closed system of faith and behavior; it exacts in return a total commitment to that system—a body-and-soul submission to the will of God and His Last Apostle. "We are not an organization," Mr. Muhammad instructed the believers, "we are a world." So it was for Malcolm. He gave himself for a dozen years to the warm, dark embrace of Allah. His labors for the

Lost-Found Nation over that period brought it out of the back streets, enlarged its reach, its membership and its wealth, quickened its relevance to that other nation outside and attracted to it the notice of the world. His rewards were substantial, given that his aspirations to money and luxury died with Detroit Red in prison. Black Islam saved his life by retrieving his self-esteem; gave him a church, a pulpit, a program, a body of dogma, a living wage, a parsonage, a car, a bodyguard, a position of command and a following under iron, hierarchical discipline; provided him in sum with a life-support system so sustaining that, for months and possibly years, it sheltered his faith from what his wit and viscera had begun telling him.

The Kingdom of Allah is alien terrain for any white and most black Americans; a foreign country, close, protective, private and unsmiling to outsiders. My first glimpse of it was my own reflection in the one-way mirror set in the St. Louis temple door; the Nation looks out at the world, but the world cannot look in at the Nation. It is a society to which white people are never admitted and into which blacks are finally accepted only on evidence that they have passed through that profound inner dislocation called conversion. The new recruit typically is required to copy and recopy his letter to Allah again and again, sometimes a dozen times or more, before he is awarded his "X"; the rejections often seem to him to have been based on the most trivial whims of penmanship, but they are in fact the beginnings of his submission to Allah and his submersion in the body of Islam. The rebels, the jive-timers, the stubbornly autonomous fall out. The survivors are passed inside to a world that is at once constricting—"Islam," one of its adherents told me, "does narrow your life down some"—and profoundly liberating.

It is a world, for one thing, without white people and so without humiliation or fear. It offers its members respectability and security and the rare pleasures of seeing fear in the devil's eyes instead of in one's own. It admits the novitiate, a lesson a week, to a body of esoteric knowledge ranging from the identity of God and the Devil to the weights of the planets and the rituals of

Freemasonry—a secret wisdom that, as one former Muslim put it, "makes them believe they are getting something no one else got" and so invests them with a sense of personal and communal power. It provides a collective new identity that strikes outsiders as the death of individuality but which is experienced by the believers, quite to the contrary, as a rebirth. The streets outside are known in the language of the mosque as the grave and their inhabitants as the dead. The passage from the streets into the Nation is called resurrection.

Islam, if it is narrowing, still fills the days. There are services Sunday afternoon and meetings or socials at the mosque five nights a week; even at that, the faithful tend to spend their Saturday nights off visiting one another, since the Muslim code permits them so few other pleasures. The women of the Nation are expected to be good, chaste and dutiful housewives; they accordingly dress in floor-length gowns and head-scarves for modesty and are trained in various domestic arts, including Mr. Muhammad's own increasingly crotchety revelations about nutrition.* The worldly business of Allah is left to the men, who are similarly if less exotically uniformed (they wear close-cropped hair, narrow-cut business suits and white shirts with solid-colored ties) and are organized as the Fruit of Islam. The Fruit have got rather a melodramatic newspaper reputation over the years as an elite, karate-trained private army. Actually, their ranks include virtually all the able-bodied men in a given mosque. Their table of organization is in fact military, with captains, lieutenants and squads, and they do take karate lessons sporadically when instructors are available. But their duties are less those of an army than of a constabulary—

*In Malcolm's time, Muslims were limited to one meal a day (though fruit juice and coffee were permissible any time) and were required to fast three days a month; he kept to this regimen even after quitting and showed it in his 180 unfleshed pounds. In the years since, however, Mr. Muhammad has recommended taking only one meal in 48 hours, giving up meat entirely "except the little young pigeon (squab) that has never flown from its nest" and fasting periodically "for 3 days . . . 3x3 days . . . 9 days . . . 27 days." These teachings coincided with the development of a number of Muslim farms raising, among other things, beef cattle and chickens. Allah may not brook ambiguities in the Nation, but He has always seemed tolerant of contradictions.

policing the moral code, collecting tithes, bodyguarding the clergy and, it would appear, roughing up apostates who leave the Nation and set up potentially competitive temples of Islam. Some years before Malcolm's death made this last a public question, some defectors in St. Louis told me they had organized a breakaway storefront mosque and held a few "unity meetings" until some of the Fruit interrupted them one night and threw some chairs around; thereafter, one of the defectors said wanly, they kept the Muslim faith in their homes, "but we didn't have our unity meetings any more."

The more absorbing routine of the Fruit is selling *Muhammad Speaks,* which has grown up out of Malcolm's basement into a handsomely got-up tabloid weekly with its own printing plant in Chicago and a claimed circulation of 600,000. There is no way to certify this figure, but no reason to doubt it either. The brethren hawk their papers with enormous industry and zeal (Malcolm, in the era of bad feeling, started calling them "newsboys") and with encouragement in various forms from the FOI lieutenants if their enthusiasm flags. In Malcolm's day, before Chicago put sales on a commission basis, the incentives were economic as well as religious. Each man was required to buy $44 worth of newspapers every new edition at the face price and had to sell the lot just to break even—"sell them," one ex-Muslim told me, "or eat them." Malcolm could not ease this load—Chicago set the quotas and prices—but occasionally he would dip quietly into his own funds to help a brother going broke on unsold papers.

Some dropped out under this pressure, but the hardier souls seem to have accepted both the labor and the cost as simply one more religious obligation to be borne without question. With similar devotion, each of them, except in the most severe hardship cases, contributed a minimum $13.50 a week to Allah, plus $200 a year for the national "Savior's Day" convention every February on Mr. Farrad's birthday, plus various other ad hoc taxes and collections. The bulk of the receipts went to Chicago in regular cash-only pick-ups, some of it specifically for the comfort of Mr. Muhammad, his family and his court; the Messenger himself maintained an eighteen-room Victorian mansion in South Side Chicago and, after the Nation's fortunes improved and his chronic bronchial asthma got worse in the early 1960s, a second, $150,000 establishment in Phoenix. This allocation of resources was understood and approved by the believers, Malcolm included. "We have to take care of the royal family," the Fruit would say, laying on yet another levy; or, "Give so the Dear Holy Apostle can eat his soup." They gave, sometimes till it hurt. There was a double cost to the Nation in this—a steady attrition in the ranks and a progressive conservatization in the hierarchy. But Malcolm for years blinkered himself to both developments. He never exploited his own proximity to the Nation's wealth—he even paid his lecture fees and other outside earnings into the common treasury—and he did not allow the possibility that others might be less fastidious.

Even the rank and file were an oddly bourgeois lot, as against the white man's fantasies of them on one hand and their rejection of white America and all its values on the other. Some of them joined the Nation, Charles Kenyatta guessed, to wait for Armageddon, but others saw it as an upward-mobility route—a means to the economic betterment of the blacks, including their own. "They thought," Kenyatta said, "they could do like the Jews did." Some of the life-style is in fact Jewish burgher, from the family-owned corner groceries and dry cleaners—Allah's children are, or would like to be, a nation of shopkeepers—to the injunctions not to eat pork and to buy only kosher meat. (Malcolm himself used to announce that no civilized people ever ate pork, a test that anomalously conceded the status of civilization to the Jews but withheld it from the Chinese.) The Muslims believed in clean minds in clean bodies, which meant daily bathing, ritual ablutions before prayer and freshly laundered clothing. "We didn't have much," a former Muslim said, "but if you only had two pairs of underwear, you were taught to wear one and wash the other." They never used nicknames; Muslims were always William or Charles or James among themselves. The rigorous morality extended to language (Malcolm wouldn't even say "hell" unless powerfully moved) and to the arrangement of the believers in the mosque, the men on one side, the women on the other with a single row of the Fruit up front. "The Fruit was supposed to be there to protect them," a former Muslim said, "but it was also because the 'dead' women who would come to hear the teachings wore short skirts. By putting the Fruit up there, that kept anybody from looking up their legs."

The Muslims, moreover, shared the American faith in education, though on their own terms. Malcolm found the notion of school integration insulting to the blacks, apart from all its other vices; it presupposed, so he believed, that black children and black teachers were inferior to white children and white teachers and so could be made intelligent only by osmosis—by being put next to whites. The Muslims rejected this and opened their own parochial schools where they could, often against the stern resistance of the regular authorities. The New York mosque couldn't afford a school in Malcolm's day. But he developed his own adult-education program for the men, organizing a class that was called "public speaking" but which, as Benjamin Goodman recalled it, covered "a basic knowledge of things—etymology, archaeology, history, language, current events, decisive moments in world history, everything under the sun. We had to read the *Times* every day and *Newsweek*, *Time* and *U.S. News & World Report* every week, and we had to give reports." Malcolm himself ultimately got too busy to handle the class and turned it over to Goodman, who later became an assistant minister; but his own passionate interest continued. "He taught us to think things through," Goodman remembered. "Take something apart, look at it, put it back together. He called that 'cracking atoms.' "

What the Muslims offered was the possibility of respect, even to the most degraded down-and-outers in the ghetto. It found its earliest converts among the deracinated Southern blacks fighting for survival in the Northern slums. But in the period of its greatest growth, it began attracting and in fact actively seeking the hard-case cons, the junkies and muscat drunks, the spiritual desperadoes of the street—converts, that is, on the Malcolm rather than the Muhammad model. Malcolm, having been there himself, developed an authentic gift for reaching these men and women and resurrecting them from their particular graves. His work with addicts became the envy of Harlem's social-service community. "I've seen him do it," one black case worker said in those days. "He asks the guy, 'Are you an addict?' The guy says yeah. 'Where'd you get your stuff from?' He says from the guy upstairs. 'Where does he get *his* stuff from?' Well—from a guy downtown. Malcolm would trace this back until he showed the addict that narcotics is a multimillion-dollar business controlled by the white man. And then he asks the guy, 'Do you want to give money to the white man who's putting you down?' This shakes the guy up—it isn't hard to convince a Negro that the white man is his enemy. And then he shows him it's okay to be black." The case worker was impressed at the results—so impressed that he got his supervisor's permission to bring Malcolm around to Harlem Hospital and have him work with addicts there. It might have worked—might even have brought Malcolm and the Muslims a kind of public legitimacy that had eluded them before. But Malcolm, flattered, leaked the story to Handler of the *Times;* the hospital authorities got nervous about the publicity and called the whole thing off.

Silence was not Malcolm's gift; speech was. He was most engaging personally, I thought, after he left the Nation, not because he suddenly got brotherly toward white folks—he didn't—but because he accepted his own complexities as a man. But he reached the height of his powers as a public speaker in his later Muslim years, when he could still fit his own widening knowledge of the world to the certainties and the mythologies of Black Islam; doubt is unbecoming in evangelists and revolutionaries.

Malcolm was both in those years, a bishop of the church and an agitator among the dispossessed in the ghetto streets. He talked himself hoarse six or seven nights a week at mosques and meeting halls across the nation; he always kept a packed bag and an unread book ready in case he had to fly somewhere, and sometimes he wouldn't see his home or his home mosque more than once or twice in a month. He held street rallies on Lenox Avenue, speaking from midafternoon till dusk from fragmentary notes, printed on index cards if he had had time to prepare them or scribbled on scraps of newspaper or paper napkin if he hadn't. "He could speak for an hour from one word or ten," Benjamin Goodman recalled. Harlem, in his day, belonged to him. Once, Roy Wilkins, James Farmer, John Killens and a few other black leaders walked from an all-star rally of their own, to which they had drawn five thousand people, and found Malcolm haranguing fifteen thousand in Harlem Square; he had then been speaking for four hours. Harlem's politicians noticed his crowds; most of them thereupon stopped speaking ill of the Muslims, and a few sat on his platforms on ecumenical occasions. Civil-rights leaders mostly stayed away and trod gingerly on Malcolm's turf. CORE once called a series of street rallies there but thought better of it after the first, when some of Malcolm's people showed up looking baleful at the edges of the crowd. On the eve of a visit by Martin Luther King, Malcolm suggested in a speech that Harlem might want to show the reverend doctor what it thought of him; King appeared the next day and, whether or not at Malcolm's inspiration, was pelted with eggs.

Malcolm, as a prince of the church, was honored wherever it gathered. In *Muhammad Speaks,* which was not immune to the clichés of our journalism, he was invariably the "dynamic" or "hard-hitting young minister" spreading the word of God and confounding every adversary in debate. In the mosque, he would be introduced as "a man who has just returned from the Living Fountain"—that is, from one of his regular visits to Mr. Muhammad—and would open with personal greetings from the Messenger; the believers would be on their feet and the applause would come down like thunder. The Muslims made it a point of considerable pride that they didn't stomp, shout or get happy like sanctified-church Negroes, but Malcolm did punctuate his lectures asking rhetorically was he right or wrong and the faithful would shout back: *"Right! Thass right! Teach on!"* The lieutenants of the FOI would prowl the aisles looking for brothers who didn't respond and, when they spotted one, would whisper urgently: "Pass the word down—*bear witness! Bear witness!"* There weren't many such laggards when Malcolm spoke, though his temple lectures ran on for two hours or more and normally recapitulated the whole familiar body of Muslim revelation. (Ossie Davis, who later got to be fast friends with Malcolm, took in one of his Sunday sermons out of curiosity and thought him "very eloquent but a bit long-winded.") There were no laggards at all when Malcolm showed up dressed in blue with a white shirt and red tie. He called that his "burning suit," Goodman recalled, and when he wore it, the temple people knew he had something particularly "strong" to say.

Malcolm quite obviously relished his position in the Nation. Yet he seemed most powerfully moved by those occasions when he was not the star but a supporting player—the great rallies where the body of the church would assemble, thousands strong, to drink from the Living Fountain themselves. Malcolm had urged these occasions on the Messenger, not only as familial gatherings for the brothers and sisters but as spectacles of solidarity and competence and power for the outside world. The Nation would choose a city, hire the biggest hall available, promote the rally vigorously and bring in busloads of believers from around the country to guarantee a full and friendly house. The rallies were brilliantly laid-on affairs, with the Fruit wheeling in military formation, the sisters sitting in tiers of snowy-white robes and scarves, the balconies hung with banners demanding land and proclaiming the traditional *Shahada,* or profession of faith, required of all Muslims—"THERE IS NO GOD BUT ALLAH AND MUHAMMAD IS HIS MESSENGER." They commonly drew ten or even fifteen thousand people, and Malcolm, whose genius as impresario had helped assure their success, was honored in return with the privilege of introducing Mr. Muhammad. He did these devotions eagerly ("the wisest . . . the boldest . . .the most *powerful* black man in America") and sometimes was praised in return by the Messenger: "Minister Malcolm has been doing a very great work towards trying to help me get the truth to you." Increasingly, as his bronchial condition flared and left him gasping and wheezy, Mr. Muhammad would cancel out at the last moment, and Malcolm would have to go on. The faithful, having been deprived of the next best thing to seeing

God, were disappointed on these occasions. The unbelievers rarely were.

Islam was a world for Malcolm, and, for most of his years in Mr. Muhammad's service, he was secure and comfortable inside it. But the larger world outside discovered him, and he was drawn to it—to its complexity, its sophistication, its very worldliness. Percy Sutton, a lawyer and later a politician of great elegance, was an NAACP man by first allegiance, but he began accepting invitations to Malcolm's street meetings because he thought somebody respectable ought to, and they became not only attorney-and-client but friends. Ossie Davis and his wife, Ruby Dee, sought Malcolm out, attended some of his unity rallies and black business bazaars in Harlem and introduced him around their circle of artists and writers. John Killens met him on a picket line or two—Malcolm couldn't participate but would watch from the edges—and liked him immediately. Dick Gregory came around at Malcolm's invitation to speak at the mosque* and later reciprocated by asking Malcolm up to his dressing room at the Apollo. Malcolm got to know Kenneth Clark and Mike Handler and Jim Farmer and Irv Kupcinet and Sidney Poitier and Adam Clayton Powell.

Malcolm's world was widening, dangerously so for his faith. "He went around to colleges speaking," Kenyatta said. "He rode on *planes*. He met people. They influenced Malcolm to be more aware. Be a part of the community." They were, in effect though rarely directly, urging him further and further from the church. He never tried to convert these friends, not at least to Islam, or to exploit his relations with them; he could be an incorrigible name-dropper talking about the jazz musicians and blues singers he drank and smoked with in the old days, but he would not cheapen his new private connections by displaying them in public like so many dust-jacket testimonials or tooth-paste endorsements.

*"I started with a thang about how good pig-feet taste," Gregory recalled. "But then I did a serious thang about how freedom of religion is okay in this country until God becomes black. It's okay if he's white. Has blond hair. Blue eyes. I told them America always put a color to things she don't like. 'Black Muslims.' Everybody else call China 'China.' We call her *'Red* China.' "

His outside friends in turn did him the courtesy of not trying to convert him. Some, baffled by Malcolm's allegiance to Mr. Muhammad and his simplicities, probed to see if he really meant it; a very few pressed him to break away, but only in those last days when the tensions between him and Chicago began to show. Mostly, they respected the integrity and the privacy of his beliefs. "We felt his changes had to be made by him," Davis told me. "We felt we shouldn't attempt to advise him unless he asked for our advice. And we weren't going to smother him by adopting him or pushing him forward as *the* young leader. We felt we could best serve by standing a little bit distant, so that when he needed a disinterested point of view—someone to *talk* to—we would be there."

Yet one cannot let the world into the cloister without risking the possibility of being changed by it. Malcolm was too loyal to admit doubt and yet too alive to postpone questions forever; one can only guess at what inner tensions this caused him. The rigidities of the Muslim moral code, much as Malcolm believed in and observed them himself, were difficult to sell in the streets and to defend to one's friends; he began to see, one acquaintance guessed, "that you couldn't change people if they wouldn't come to you." People twitted him about Mr. Muhammad's dietary laws. "The biggest thing that keeps me from you," Livingston Wingate, the veteran Harlem community worker, teased Malcolm, "is that you want to come between me and the pig. I'm not prepared to separate from the pig." Malcolm would smile that stunning smile, but Wingate was kidding on the square, and he guessed that Malcolm was well aware of his problems.

Mr. Muhammad's solutions—the development of an independent black economy here and now and the ultimate separation of the Lost-Founds from the devil—became at least equally burdensome in Malcolm's private relations even while he was still preaching the line ardently in public. "I remember once at their restaurant on Lenox Avenue," Sutton told me, "when I said to him, 'Mr. Minister, here comes Mr. Pillsbury to deliver the flour so you can make your bean pies'—that's one of the Muslim specialties. I said,

'That must show you how independent you are.' And he said, 'Well, someday we're going to own all the wheat fields of Kansas.' But by then he knew it wasn't so."

It was a defense, nevertheless, that he was put to a thousand times in Harlem. James Hicks of the *Amsterdam News* used to needle him over the coffee cups at Chock Full O' Nuts: "How are you going to do all this?"

"Separate state."

"Okay, I'm whitey, I'm going to give you everything you ask for. What you want?"

"Well, all right—we'll ask for North Carolina as a separate state."

"North Caro*lina?* Hell, I don't want to live there. And you think the government's gonna give you *that?*"

Again the smile, warm but opaque, and Malcolm would say, "Brother Hicks, you been brainwashed. . . ."

Ordinarily, private conversations and public debates would end with Malcolm invoking the higher authority of the Honorable Elijah Muhammad; to press beyond this was like arguing the divine inspiration of the Bible with Billy Graham. " 'God said,' " James Farmer grinned in amused memory of their several confrontations. "How can you debate *that?*" For a long time, indeed, what God said spared Malcolm interior debate with himself: he forced problems of faith out of his consciousness. He had read about White Muslims, for example, long before his celebrated letters from Mecca announcing their existence in 1964; he had been in Arabia and Egypt, among other places, five years earlier as an advance man for Mr. Muhammad's own pilgrimage, and had actually seen some there. He simply rejected the evidence of his senses. He lectured light-skinned Arab Muslims on the blackness of God and on why it was necessary and proper that the world's least color-conscious religion maintain a black-only communion in the States; and he sent postcards home to friends announcing that he hadn't seen a single Muslim in his travels who wouldn't be Jim Crowed in the American South.

His first reaction to doubt thus was to repress it. "If the process was beginning," Eric Lincoln guessed, "he stoutly resisted it and carefully obscured it. One does not quickly cut away what is deeply embedded psychologically. As he traveled and became more sophisticated, he began looking at Elijah Muhammad and saying, 'My country, may she always be right, but right or wrong, my country,' and dismissing the matter there. When a man assumes a religious perspective, hell, it isn't easy for logic to dislodge it. I heard him say, 'When we tell you that Allah is a supreme black man, you laugh, because you can't conceive of God as black. But when the white preacher tells you that Jesus had blue eyes and stayed in the ground for three days and got up and went to heaven, you believe it. Now, which is more ridiculous?' He became more conscious of a world beyond the Muslims and beyond the ghetto, yeah; and one might argue that this itself might have become an erosive force. But it didn't reach the point where it would have set off within Malcolm himself an attitude of rebellion."

Doubt was impermissible in the Nation; rebellion was unimaginable. The Qur'an and the teachings of Mr. Muhammad are full of warnings of the soul-rending chastisement that will befall doubters, hypocrites and mutineers. These warnings had a palpable and terrifying reality for Malcolm; his own brother Reginald—the agent of his conversion in prison—had lapsed in the faith, blasphemed Allah and the Messenger and finally cracked up. The Nation is vigilant against every transgression, but most of all against heresy. "Muslims," Kenyatta told me, "never speak out against nothing. They called that 'seed planting.' They'd say, 'Look out for that bad seed planter.' "

A time came when that was said of Malcolm. But he struggled against it and lived with his two schismatic realities. It was a life-or-death struggle for him. The Nation of Islam is not an organization but a world, and nothing frightens a Muslim so much as the prospect of being cast out of it. The children of Allah call that going back to the grave.

14. Waiting for Allah

The trouble was that history overtook Malcolm and the airtight little Nation of Islam. The vision of the white man as the devil, revealed to the poor blacks of Paradise Valley during the Great Depression, endured thereafter as a powerful religious truth but a limiting one: it imputed a kind of divine intent to the fallen state of the Original People in white America and discouraged them from rebelling against it until Allah was ready. During the Nation's early years, this scarcely mattered, since rebellion—except in those relatively polite forms then practiced by the NAACP and the Urban League—was not a serious alternative for ordinary blacks. Even in the 1950s and 1960s, when the Negro revolt spilled out of the churches into the streets, the quietude of Black Islam kept its appeal for a fraction of Negro America put off by the tumult and the anxiety of the struggle or by its nonviolent submission to insult, injury and even death. But quietude could not have suited Malcolm forever. His own temper was activist, and he coaxed hundreds and possibly thousands of converts into the Lost-Found Nation on the supposition that it must be like him. It wasn't. The Nation was waiting for Allah, and the longer the wait dragged on, the more galling the necessity of waiting became for Malcolm X.

He could not, of course, have joined the civil-rights movement—not on its terms. Its announced goal was integration; Malcolm, like the younger movement radicals, came to appreciate the value of *desegregating* our society—forcing us, that is, to recognize the humanity of black people—but he could not have entered a struggle whose informing dream was to "free" the blacks by integrating them into the company of white people. Neither could he have submitted to nonviolence, even as a tactic appropriate to a minority in a society in which the majority had all the power and most of the guns. Malcolm's rhetoric was violent at times, in that carefully indirect way of his, but his soul and his stomach were not; he spoke violently and shrank from the fact of violence. Once, a group of one hundred white school integrationists announced plans for an all-night outdoor pray-in at 125th Street and Seventh Avenue. Civic Harlem was grateful for their concern but aghast at their innocence, until one community leader, in inspired desperation, paid two diplomatic visits. One was to a blood named Mississippi, a three-hundred-pound heavy who was well wired and not a little feared among the street people. The other was to Malcolm. "I told him the worst thing for the community would be if someone got clipped or mugged or had their pocketbook snatched," this civic leader recalled. "I told him, 'We can't let anything happen.' Malcolm saw it immediately. He spoke to the other nationalists, and between his people and Mississippi's, those white folks were safer than if they were home in bed." In a sense it was Malcolm's own variety of nonviolence that forbade him embracing King's, which was quite consciously designed to precipitate violence against the blacks. "If Malcolm had led black people somewhere and they'd got their heads broke," Ossie Davis guessed, "he'd have been absolutely done in."

Yet something drew him to the edges of the struggle and made him chafe under Mr. Muhammad's restraining hand. The Nation's policy was strict abstention, partly out of a fine ideological scorn for everything the civil-rights movement aspired to, partly out of its own deepening, don't-rock-the-boat conservatism at the top. "They clean people up, don't drink, don't smoke," Charles Kenyatta said, "but they don't *do* anything. Don't even *vote.*" Malcolm obeyed, increasingly unhappily. He saw that the locus of history was in the streets, however misguided the official struggle there seemed to him, and both his energy and his *amour-propre* impelled him to be where the action was. "The Messenger has seen God," he told Louis Lomax during his last days as a Muslim. "He was with Allah and was given divine patience with the devil. He is willing to wait for Allah to deal with this devil. Well, sir, the rest of us Black Muslims have not seen God, we don't have this gift of divine patience with the devil. The younger Black Muslims want to see some action."

Malcolm saw it, but only from the sidelines. Movement people got accustomed to that tall, priestly figure slouching in the back rows at their meetings or standing across the street from their picket lines, festooned with cameras, meters and accessory bags, watching and photographing them from a distance. "He would just go and look," Kenyatta told me. "He wanted to do it so bad." He sought out civil-rights people, though never hat in hand. He was persona non grata with the downtown Negro leadership during the Muslim years. A measure of the distance between them is the story, possibly apocryphal, of how Malcolm proposed a modest joint enterprise to Roy Wilkins of the NAACP and Wilkins told him to put it in letter form so he would have something to show his board of directors; Malcolm never did, and the proposal died of noncommunication.

Occasionally, in private, this or that civil-rights personage would praise him for the force of his indictment of the system; their compliments at first flattered Malcolm but came to irritate him in later years, when he wished some of them had the nerve to say something kind in public. They didn't; mostly, they used Malcolm as a bogeyman. Only the black trade-union ancient, A. Philip Randolph, among the elders of the movement made a conscious effort to break the quarantine and reach out to Malcolm; they would meet occasionally at Randolph's office, and Malcolm would sit for hours listening to the old man's reminiscences about DuBois and Garvey and the Harlem past. "The guy is so happy to communicate," Randolph told Kenneth Clark; he saw, earlier than most of his colleagues, the danger in isolating Malcolm and forcing him deeper into the rigidities of his positions. At one point, Randolph tried to organize a Harlem-wide leadership council to develop an economic program for the community and invited Malcolm to participate. "The thing finally fell apart," Bayard Rustin remembered, "for reasons that were built in—too many tendencies were represented. But Malcolm played a creative role—he kept the extremists pretty much in line and made that short year and a half of meetings possible."

The younger civil-rights activists, less troubled by questions of respectability since they lived at the margins of respect themselves, were accordingly more hospitable. Malcolm, on business trips to Atlanta, regularly dropped by the Southern Christian Leadership Conference office on Auburn Avenue, less to argue than to stay tuned in; he apparently never found King in on these occasions,* but he enjoyed standing around talking—one participant called it "nondirective chitchat"—with the field staff. ("A very winsome man off-camera," one of them, the Rev. Wyatt Tee Walker, recalled. "He showed us some Arabic letters, and we talked about their record, 'A White Man's Heaven Is a Black Man's Hell'—you might say we discussed the theology of that.") He was drawn even more to the Student Nonviolent Coordinating Committee for its forged-in-the-furnace radicalism; one of his young women followers went South to join SNCC, apparently with his blessings, and was known among movement people as Malcolm's "agent" in Mississippi for three years. He was locked out, but he crowded as close to the edges as he could. "He wanted to be involved with black people," said Ossie Davis, "whenever and wherever they were involved."

Privately, Malcolm developed a certain irony about his enforced lot as a noncombatant; he began telling people offstage that his contribution was precisely to be an "extremist"—to do his thing so it would be easier for the established leaders to do theirs. ("He was an instinctive social scientist," Kenneth Clark judged after one such conversation. "He understood roles.") Publicly, he ignored what was irresistible even to him in the movement—its

*Malcolm and King met only once, so far as I can determine, and then out of a prankish impulse of Malcolm's. In March 1964, just after Malcolm had quit the Nation, he visited the U.S. Senate to take in a day of the civil-rights filibuster and later slipped into the back row at a King news conference off the floor. King afterward left by one door; Malcolm popped out another into his path. "Well, Malcolm, good to see you," King said. "Good to see *you,*" Malcolm grinned. Reporters crowded around. Flash bulbs flared. "Now you're going to get investigated," Malcolm teased, and then they parted.

gallantries, its courage, its audacity in the face of white power and Jim Crow tradition—and kept up an acid running commentary on its mistakes and self-deceptions. The night after James Meredith enrolled in the University of Mississippi by force of Federal arms, one of those relentlessly earnest radio talk-show hosts tried to get Malcolm to say he was "impressed," to which Malcolm politely replied, "Uh—sir—one little black man going to a school in Mississippi in no way compensates for the fact that a million black people don't even get to the grade-school level in Mississippi." King and his people moved into a tacky Georgia backwater called Albany, vowing to turn the town nonviolently upside down unless it desegregated. It didn't; the campaign meandered on until the jails were full, the participants exhausted and the Northern media bored. "They didn't get anything but their heads whipped," Malcolm scoffed from the distance of New York. The judgment was literal-minded, and cruel to those black men and women who risked their lives in the challenge, but in a formal way—in terms of what was won and at what cost—he was right.

He publicly justified his own and the Nation's abstention by arguing the foolishness of the mainstream movement—it was spilling black blood unilaterally trying to go where Negroes weren't wanted anyway—and the contrasting don't-tread-on-me militance of the Muslims. "Up to now," he told one mixed crowd, "we haven't been involved in any violence because we don't force ourselves upon white people. . . . But by the same token, you might see these Negroes who believe in nonviolence and mistake us for one of them and put your hands on us thinking that we're going to turn the other cheek—and *we'll put you to death just like that.*" The Muslims, as Malcolm well knew, were not nearly that fierce. They are on the whole a conservative and a peace-loving lot; they expect that Allah will bring their enemies low for them and they take their here-and-now satisfaction from these prophecies and from the pro tempore evidences of divine wrath. "We believe," cried Malcolm, "that God is angry with America and that God will continue to whip America with rain and snow and hail and floods and drought like America has never known before. We believe that God will continue to whip America with sickness, disease and plagues like America has never known before." The movement was in the streets; Malcolm was reduced to standing on the corner applauding flu epidemics and blizzards.

In Harlem, where the cynicism of the fallen makes street reputations hard to win and easy to lose, Malcolm and the Muslims got by for years on the Hinton Johnson incident: maybe they weren't up front in the movement, but at least they took care of their people. Yet Malcolm's reputation even on his own turf was shaken in April 1962 by a distant event—a sort of *volte-face* version of the Johnson parable. The Los Angeles police, whose terror of the Muslims was eccentric even in those days, spotted a couple of them outside the local mosque passing some dry-cleaning out of a car and stopped them. One of the cops shoved one of the blacks against the auto and, so he testified later, "hit the gentleman on the head." A crowd gathered, mostly Muslims, and got surly; one of the policemen drew his gun and was quickly disarmed; more police arrived; there ensued what the Los Angeles *Times* next day described as a "blazing gunfight." The "fight" more nearly resembled a rout, or so the body count suggested: all but one of the gunshot wounds were suffered by Muslims, mostly in their backs. One of them died; another was paralyzed for life; five others were wounded and several beaten, some as they stood chanting, *"Allahu-Akbar"*—"God is the greatest." As testimony brought out later, the fatally wounded man, a Korean War veteran named Ronald X Stokes, had been walking toward the police unarmed, hands stretched out empty before him, when an officer opened fire. Why? "To stop him." Were the Muslims committing some crime? "Yes—they were fleeing." A coroner's inquest decided that Stokes's death was justifiable, and eleven Muslims ultimately were convicted of assault.

Malcolm wept. He had organized the mosque himself five years earlier and knew some of the casualties. "He wanted to do what most Muslims wanted to do—seek revenge," a former member told me. "You mean take heads?" I asked. He looked at me and nodded slowly. Malcolm had often roused the Fruit of Mosque No.

7 to fury—"Why, good gracious," Kenyatta recalled, "he'd get 'em to a point where if any white man had walked in they'd have ate him up alive"—and then had gently defused their anger. This time, flushed and raging, he pushed them further than he ever had. "What are you in here for?" he asked them. "What the *hell* you in here for?" He booked a jet seat to the Coast to preach Stokes's funeral and, so he hoped, to organize the revenge. He stopped by Professer Michaux's bookshop before he left. "Well," he said, "I got to go out there now and do what I've been preaching all this time."

He couldn't; the Messenger stopped him. "Mr. Muhammad said, 'All in good time,' " Benjamin Goodman told me, "and he was right. The police were ready. It would have been a trap. It was frustrating for the younger men, but he was the leader and he put them under restraint." Malcolm's rage spluttered out into a depression that some of us took to be mourning; what we didn't know then was that he was grieving not only a lost brother but his own helplessness. He did what he could to pick up the pieces. He took grisly photos of Stokes stitched back together after an autopsy, waved them about on TV and got Hicks to front-page one of them in the *Amsterdam News.* He haunted the coroner's inquest, commenting out of the back rows during recesses like some Greek chorus at the edge of tragedy. He involved the NAACP and a good deal of the local church and community leadership in joint protest actions, on the entirely reasonable ground that, as Malcolm himself put it at one popular-front rally, "It wasn't a Muslim who was shot down—it was a Negro." He made some promising ecumenical beginnings before Chicago inexplicably stopped his protest campaign, too; his only flat turndown came from the SCLC, which had organized a rally of its own at Wrigley Field and, smarting under Malcolm's continuing insults to King, suggested to him coolly that he go get his own ball park and his own crowd. Malcolm did preach Stokes's funeral, a traditionalist Black Muslim affair with no tears or flowers and with mints passed around at the end so that only sweet memories of the dead would linger; and he persuaded Chicago to put a 25-cent head tax on the faithful to buy a motorized wheelchair for the paralyzed brother and to help with his medical bills.

But his revenge, when he got it, was characteristically rhetorical, and even he came to regret it later. The inquest was still in progress when a charter jet went down in France, carrying much of the white cultural elite of Atlanta to their deaths—and Malcolm, having been denied any more satisfying retaliation, danced on their graves. "I would like to announce a very beautiful thing that has happened," he said at a Los Angeles meeting. "I got a wire from God today. Wait. All right, well, somebody came and told me that He really had answered our prayers in France. He dropped an airplane out of the sky with over 120 white people on it because the Muslims believe in an eye for an eye and a tooth for a tooth. We call on our God, and He gets rid of 120 of them at one whop." He spoke out of frustration; it came out raw, and Malcolm found himself forced to the defense for months thereafter. On one talk show, he got out his atrocity photos and held them up as evidence that God had intervened on behalf of black people "who are incapable of getting justice for themselves." The emcee called his joy nonetheless obscene. "Sir," Malcolm replied hotly, "just as America thanked God when she dropped the bomb on Hiroshima that wiped out 100,000 Japanese, I think that we are well within our rights to thank God when he steps in. . . . You did it in the name of God. Because we have no bombs and have no guns and have no weapons, when someone attacks us, we rely on God . . . and I think the white man has a whole lot of nerve, after all of the injustices that he has been committing against Negroes in this country, to be offended or surprised when someone says that God is after him."

Still, as he realized later, the remark had served nothing except the momentary satisfactions it brought him and those Muslims within earshot. It certainly didn't convince Harlem. The Los Angeles temple bust was seen there as a direct dare to the Muslims —and Malcolm's behavior as an ignominious retreat. The Muslim mystique wasn't quite the same uptown after that. "When he came back," Hicks told me, "people were saying, 'If you're saying you're Mr. Big—touch me and I'll knock you down—and then you don't, you're going back on your word.' They lost face out there —they hadn't fought back, and that aura of don't-touch-a-Muslim diminished a bit. Malcolm withstood it, but it got pretty rough. People were saying, 'Goddamn Muslims . . .' " Malcolm tried to retrieve some of the Nation's lost esteem by leading several hundred of the brothers into Times Square in February 1963, to protest some fresh affronts, including the arrest of two Muslims for selling their papers downtown and a police raid on the Rochester mosque. The march, unheard of for Muslims, frightened some of his own aides; Kenyatta remembered one of them at Malcolm's elbow, begging, "Please, Brother Minister, please, you don't understand—these brothers are frustrated, they'll do anything." Malcolm marched them anyway through the startled evening rush-hour crowds; he was, said Kenyatta, "so angry and depressed he didn't care *what* happened." Nothing did, and in any case the damage uptown was done.

The truth was that no gesture available to Malcolm as a Black Muslim could have placed him at the center stage of history; the stage then, so far as most of us could see, belonged to Martin Luther King and the Southern movement. King had in fact failed in Albany, but had learned from his failures and had chosen his next theater more carefully. One of his discoveries was that a morality play, if it was to engage the interest of the media and so the conscience of the nation, needed not only heroes but the possibility of violence and a single, identifiable villain. The search for an arena ended in Birmingham, an outgrown steel town so Klan-ridden that one black neighborhood was known as Dynamite Hill for the frequency of the bombings there; the role of foil went to T. Eugene (Bull) Connor, a gravelly, one-eyed, central-casting seg then serving as Public Safety Commissioner.

King's men and women moved in and spent four months organizing local blacks around an improbably grand bill of demands; then, with their normal strategic mix of well-laid plans and sudden insomniac improvisations, they filled the streets with marchers, including, at the psychologically neat moment, wave upon wave of schoolchildren. "They couldn't open up Birmingham to do business in the morning," Wyatt Walker remembered happily. "There were too many niggers downtown singing and sitting in." Connor responded first by jailing everybody and then calling out the police dogs and fire hoses; the vignettes of dogs nipping at children and jet-streams of water toppling women like tenpins filled our television screens and outraged our sensibilities. Birmingham's civic elite ultimately was forced to negotiate, though talks nearly broke down once because some of the whites couldn't bring themselves to call the blacks "mister" and again when, during a tense silence, one of the blacks absent-mindedly began humming "We Shall Overcome." In the end, the generals of the campaign settled for a modest few concessions, and even then the sense of victory was spoiled when King's motel and a brother's house on Dynamite Hill were bombed, injuring no one but touching off a furious one-night riot among the city's ghetto street people. Yet the real first objective of the Battle of Birmingham was won: President Kennedy, after two years of elegant temporizing, was forced to go on national television to plead that the battle be removed from the streets to the courts and to propose as the means for doing this the Civil Rights Bill of 1963.

Malcolm saw the flaws with chilly accuracy; saw, for example, that the blacks of Birmingham had been bloodied and jailed for the most marginal tangible gains; saw, too, that the government had approached the crisis not as the agent of morality and common decency but as a broker among conflicting interests. King, he said, was a "chump, not a champ" for committing black women and children to be hosed and clubbed and bitten; Kennedy was a fox who had talked prettily but had sent in troops only when white property was threatened, not when blacks were being brutalized in the streets, and had thereafter tried to buy peace with a bill permitting blacks to eat at white lunch counters. "Coffee with a cracker," Malcolm snorted. "That's *success?*"

It was, of course, in ways Malcolm could not then admit. Birmingham brought the civil-rights movement to its flood; it began a romantic period that even then carried the seeds of its own disappointment and exhaustion but which nevertheless endured through the great Selma crusade of 1965. Malcolm clearly sensed the revulsion black people felt at the images of their people—particularly their women—helpless before Connor's billy-swinging white cops. But he mistook, or rather refused to acknowledge, the extent to which Birmingham engaged black people as well—even up-North ghetto blacks who had no immediate stake in a struggle for the right to drink Cokes at Woolworth's or try on clothes at a department store. The real meaning of Birmingham for Malcolm lay not in the mass-marching or the dime-store counters or even the Civil Rights Bill but in that one-night riot of the street people—a native uprising he read as an omen of things to come. He was right in this, of course, but ordinary black people, for whom victories were rare enough, did not want to be told just yet that they had been cheated by Birmingham; they wanted to savor it for a while. Birmingham set an epidemic of street fever —"a contagion of heroism," one of King's people called it—spreading outward across the South and the nation. "Bull Connor did more for us than Martin Luther King or anyone else," Percy Sutton said. "He made black sacrifice a personal thing. He pushed black people to the point where it didn't make any difference any more. You developed out of Birmingham a number of crazy niggers; you learned that, if you defy the establishment, the establishment responds—it doesn't want to die."

Somewhere out of that contagion came the idea of a mass march on Washington. Malcolm liked to say that the march movement began spontaneously among street people who intended to shut down the government unless it delivered real justice to the blacks immediately—and not just some tricked-up civil-rights act either. It didn't happen quite that way; the idea germinated not in the streets but among the activist leaders of the recognized movement, King included, and the passage of the Civil Rights Bill was among its premier goals from birth. Still, the early, ad-lib planning did include acts of disruptive civil disobedience on Capitol Hill and elsewhere, and at length the movement elders—genuinely anxious that the whole thing not turn into a ruinous debacle—moved in and effectively took over. White churchmen and trade-unionists were added to the management, white marchers to the rank and file. The Kennedy Administration, which at first opposed a march, was persuaded to endorse it, though the President's language was cool and Robert Kennedy saw to such precautions as closing the capital's bars for the day. The events of the march were rigorously controlled by the official leadership, from what ground could be trod (the grassy expanse between the Washington Monument and the Lincoln Memorial) to what song could be sung ("We Shall Overcome") to what placards could be carried. Internal strains were smoothed over; Roy Wilkins and Whitney Young, for example, were miffed at King for skipping most of the planning meetings and for failing to contribute any money or marchers, but they agreed to let him do the inspirational windup speech anyway, knowing it would make him and not them the voice of the march. On the big day itself, John Lewis of SNCC arrived with a speech full of lines that sound mild enough today ("This nation is still a place of cheap political leaders who build their careers on immoral compromises. . . . I want to know, which side is the Federal government on?") but which seemed grossly impolitic at the time; the Roman Catholic Archbishop of Washington threatened to walk out unless they went, and Lewis finally yielded.

The march, tamed though it was, managed somehow to be enormously moving anyway—a communion of a quarter-million souls, probably two-thirds of them black, come peaceably to seek redress of their grievances. "We Shall Overcome" had never been so stirring; King, dreaming of a South suddenly struck color-blind, had never been so inspired. The wisest among the people who put it on understood the limitations of a march on Washington; understood that even if Congress had been moved to pass the Civil Rights Bill that afternoon, a major fraction of black America would still be ill-housed, ill-clothed, ill-fed and ill-used the next day. Bayard Rustin, who orchestrated the march, saw it even then as the last parade, not the first; Ossie Davis, who emceed it, stood looking out over that ocean of faces and told himself: *This is one of the most marvelous things that could possibly happen, but you can never do this again.* Still, for a day, that stretch of grass and that assembly of dreams *were* black America, and everything else was the margin. Malcolm, being sensitive to matters of color, understood this. He railed at the march before and after, called it a circus and a picnic, saw through its vanities and—in terms of direct material reward—its inconsequentiality. But he went.

He went to Washington, that is, and to the edges of the event; he haunted the headquarters hotel lobby and lectured marchers, newspapermen, passers-by and whoever would listen about how they had all been had. The grand marshals mostly treated him like Lazarus at the feast. Floyd McKissick, then national chairman of CORE and an old chum of Malcolm's, bumped into him coming out of a meeting at the Washington Hilton. "We hugged and kissed," McKissick told me, "but then some people from CORE grabbed me and said, 'Hey, Mac, there's something over here, you got to get over here right away.' But there wasn't nothing. They led me into a dark room and told me that was the worst thing ever happened to CORE. I said, 'We been knowin' each other for years.' They said, 'Man, that's bad. That ain't a thing for you to do.' "

The marchers by contrast accepted Malcolm and heard out his complaints; even those bourgeois blacks who had come to Washington, so he liked to say, as they might have gone to the Kentucky Derby or the Rose Bowl—for the status of being able to tell people, "I was there." Late the night before the march, Louis Lomax, all busy mystery, led me to a hotel room full of blacks, mostly middle-class and professional people from New York; and there in their midst was Malcolm, jackknifed into one of those low-slung, hotel-modern armchairs with his suit coat and tie still on—everybody else was in shirtsleeves—and a cup of coffee steaming on his knees. He was holding court, not trying to convert or to wound anybody but making gentle fun of the whole occasion. Scotch and bourbon splashed; Malcolm watched, smiled and reminded everybody that the first result of the march was not the delivery of the blacks but the closing of the saloons. "No firewater for the Indians tomorrow," he teased. Everybody looked awkward, as if they wished they could hide their drinks. Malcolm got onto Birmingham and the necessities of self-defense and challenged the room to name somebody really nonviolent. I bit, mentioning a black leader whom I admired but who was thought to be homosexual. Malcolm grinned and exchanged amused looks with a couple of the others. I flared, to my own surprise; I told him that that was the sort of reaction I would expect from Senator Eastland of Mississippi, say, but not from him. To my equal surprise, he backed off and said no, no, that wasn't what he had meant at all. The matter dropped there; Malcolm had deferred not to me but to the sensibilities of the black people in the room.

He deferred to them because, whatever he thought of the occasion, they were marching the next day. Malcolm might or might not have joined them, given his freedom; the point was he didn't have a choice and so once again he wound up a spectator. A year and a half before, when they had debated at Community Church, Bayard Rustin had given him a bad chivying about his enforced inaction; the Southern student movement, Rustin said, was committing its bodies to the militant struggle while Malcolm had to "wait for Allah to reveal to Elijah Muhammad, who will then reveal to him, who will then reveal to us, what their program is to be." Malcolm had sidestepped the challenge and had responded with an impassioned *cri de coeur* about the atrocities of slavery. But now he was an onlooker at Rustin's show—a pageant of which he disapproved but which he could not resist attending.

I asked some of his friends why they supposed he went to the march. The commonest and most satisfying answer was that he went because it was there—that, as John Killens put it, "Malcolm was gonna be wherever black people were gonna be." Black people, in the early 1960s, were in the street, and Malcolm found himself caught in an impossible two-way tug, between them on the one hand and his church on the other. The street, by 1963, was winning. Malcolm had for several years been lobbying Chicago, nearly to the point of heresy, to commit the Muslims to action of some sort—not nonviolent or integrationist action but action nevertheless. He very badly wanted recognition for Mr. Muhammad, and for himself, as legitimate claimants to a place in the Negro leadership, at least coequal with Wilkins and Young and King; he may even have imagined himself speaking from the steps of the Lincoln Memorial, pitting his religion and his gifts of oratory against King's, and trooping with the march leaders to the White House to confront John Kennedy. He saw no way to achieve any of this without making the Muslims relevant, which was to say involving them visibly in the struggle.

But Chicago kept saying no even to political action at the polls, let alone demonstrating—or defending demonstrators—in the streets. The Nation was stagnating in those days, after several years of steady expansion, and Malcolm, as growth-conscious as a General Motors executive, believed its policy of noninvolvement was to blame. Some of the New York Muslims wanted him to lead a party South to Birmingham, presumably to take on the cops and the dogs; Malcolm couldn't, but his own faith was eroding along with his patience. Other, more personal factors finally precipitated his break with Mr. Muhammad when it came, but his dozen unrewarded years of waiting for Allah conditioned him for it. "The Black Muslim movement," he said long after he had left it, "has nothing within its mechanism that's designed to deal with things on this earth right now. Most of the Black Muslim movement's objectives are similar to those of the church, the only difference being that the church says you're going to die and go to the Promised Land, and in the Black Muslims I was taught that we get to the Promised Land when God comes and takes us there. Nobody knows where this land is; no hint of it is ever given. Now, I believe in the Promised Land, and I believe in God. But I believe that we should be doing something toward trying to get to it right now. And if God wants to get into the act, good. But if He's not ready yet, we at least won't be sitting around here waiting."

15. Three Encounters at a Picnic

"The night before the march," Bayard Rustin said, "I came out of a strategy meeting of the Big Ten leaders at the Hilton and I saw Malcolm standing outside holding a press conference. He was denouncing the march. 'This is nothing but a circus, it's nothing but a picnic.' I said, 'Now, Malcolm, be careful—there are going to be a half-million people here tomorrow, and you don't want to tell *them* this is nothing but a picnic.' He looked at me, and there was a twinkle in his eye. He said, 'What I tell them is one thing. What I tell the press is something else.' Later on, I saw him talking to some of the marchers. I said, 'Why don't you tell them this is just a picnic?' He was being affable. He just smiled, and again there was a twinkle.

"But afterward I saw him again, and he said, 'You know, this dream of King's is going to be a nightmare before it's over.' There was no twinkle in his eye this time. I think he did feel a sense that there would be a hard period ahead. And I said, 'You're probably right.' "

16. Paradise Lost

What finally came between Malcolm and Mr. Muhammad was not the great debate over engagement vs. nonengagement but the tacky palace politics of an organization corroded by its own prosperity. The Nation of the Lost-Founds had come into a measure of visibility, wealth and power largely through Malcolm's agency;

the Messenger himself had recognized this, had blessed Malcolm's ever-increasing exposure in the world and had sealed this blessing finally by naming him national minister with a virtually open charter to travel and talk. The deadly irony in Malcolm's situation was that his very successes were his undoing. The Kingdom of Allah in the wilderness had passed into that condition identified by the sociologist Max Weber as the routinization of charisma—a time when the fires cool, when commitment becomes vested interest and the conservatism of the bureaucracy gradually supplants the passion of the street. The Nation in the 1960s had got clotted at the top with men who, as one well-informed outsider put it, had grown "fat and comfortable" in the service of Allah—"and when you become comfortable," he went on, "there's no point in making a big noise."

Malcolm thus became the object not only of jealousy, which is a normal condition of God's institutions as well as man's, but of fear as well. The combination cut him down. He might have stayed in the Nation indefinitely, for all his gathering doubts and differences over policy; he might even have succeeded to Allah's temporal throne. The choice, as it developed, wasn't his. "The decision was made for him," said Handler of the *Times.* "He didn't break with Elijah. Elijah broke with him."

Malcolm had seen signs of arteriosclerosis in the Nation well before the end. Mr. Muhammad had surrounded himself at the top with relatives and retainers—a circle, according to one black journalist who knew most of them, composed at least partly of "yes men and opportunists with a substantial investment in the movement." His middle management was crowded with ministers distinguished less for their brilliance than for their unquestioning loyalty to him. Malcolm was partly culpable in this; he had himself recruited some of the clergy and had held up the ordination of one particularly promising prospect on the basis of rumors that he was a Communist or a homosexual or both; not even he would breach some of our proprieties. Yet he eventually began to worry about the quality of the Muslim ministry. He was both proud and realistic enough to sense his own superiority to most of them; he thought them a "weak and incapable" lot on the whole, he said later, and was at once flattered and dismayed that their temple treasuries tended to red ink while his alone stayed consistently in the black. The ministry for its part began to resent Malcolm's pre-eminence and probably his gifts as well. Some of the ministers took to reminding outsiders pointedly that he wasn't the Messenger of Allah—he was only another minister, just like them.

Malcolm was further disturbed by what he saw as the creeping capitalism of the Nation—a taste for creature comfort that, so he and his circle believed, had seeped down from the theocrats in Chicago to the pettiest functionaries in the mosques. The Nation, even as it rejected the values of white middle-class America, imitated them; a noted black writer told with amusement how he had spent ten years arriving on Collier Drive, a prestige address for blacks in Atlanta, and had found the local Muslim minister already living there. Malcolm shared this get-ahead imperative, but only to a point; its abuse past that point was what he meant when, after he got out, he began telling people that the Nation had been the best black organization ever "until those niggers messed it up." He had himself worked for a modest wage, a car and a suburban house that was roomy enough when he took it but crowded by the time he and Sister Betty had their fourth daughter; he seems simply to have trusted his future to the Nation. He asked nothing more and believed that those who did so paid with a certain loss of limberness and soul. When he called his Times Square demonstration in 1963, he presumably had the Messenger's agreement, but a national officer who happened to be in New York begged him to call it off anyway. "Those guys," Malcolm complained to some of the brothers, "are on Easy Street." He fretted at the extent to which revenue collections and newspaper sales evolved from a simple matter of subsistence into major preoccupations; there were repeated tales of some brother being roughed up by the FOI "special squad" in this or that mosque for defaulting on dues or flagging at selling papers. Malcolm, who had previously accepted the necessity of keeping the hierarchy in comfort, began to have misgivings. "He thought some of them was exploiting it,"

Charles Kenyatta said. "He saw the oppressed was becoming the oppressor."

Some of the hierarchs in turn saw Malcolm as vain and publicity-happy at their expense and the Messenger's, and ill will stole into paradise. Malcolm got on well enough with most of the royal family, and particularly well with Mr. Muhammad's two ablest sons, Wallace, who was a fellow minister, and Akbar, then a student at Al-Azhar University in Cairo. But Malcolm suspected that John Ali, an old friend who had become national secretary, and Raymond Sharrieff, the Messenger's son-in-law and Supreme Captain of the Fruit of Islam, had turned against him. Friction arose, moreover, between him and Captain Joseph, who commanded the Fruit in Malcolm's mosque in Harlem. Joseph was nominally Malcolm's subordinate, but a 1961 administrative decree had made the temple captains answerable only to Chicago. The Harlem Fruit thus became an independent duchy within the mosque and Joseph a separate and nearly equal power. The two men coexisted amicably for years, even when Malcolm wearied of the officiousness of the FOI men as bodyguards (he thought all their glaring and shoving and body-searching gave the Nation a criminal look) and smiled at their bureaucratic airs: it was rumored among Malcolm's people that the dispatch cases the FOI officers carried everywhere had nothing in them. But the relationship soured badly in Malcolm's time of troubles; he tried unsuccessfully near the end to have Joseph removed as captain. Other animosities cropped up—wounded feelings among the peers he had overshadowed, jealousies among the ambitious men who saw him as a potential rival for the succession. Malcolm was accumulating enemies, and some of them began to hurt him with the Messenger. Malcolm was a contained man; he kept the tensions developing between him and Chicago to himself. But one day some of the brothers overheard him saying angrily to no one in particular: "I can't understand it—no matter *what* you're trying to do, you're wrong." He cut himself off there; they guessed what he meant.

His personal, filial bond with Mr. Muhammad might still have survived all this, except for the increasingly awkward fact of Malcolm's sheer size in the media and the public mind, and the Messenger's consequent eclipse. The epiphany of the stresses this caused between them was the publication in 1963 of Louis Lomax's Muslim book, *When the Word Is Given . . .*, with Malcolm's picture on the front jacket and Mr. Muhammad's on the back; Chicago was said to have been furious. *Muhammad Speaks,* after the break, insisted that the jealousy was all on Malcolm's side—that he had in fact tried to agitate the younger ministry to retire Mr. Muhammad and "elect" him Messenger; a man who had known and been commissioned by God, said the newspaper, could hardly experience anything so common as envy. Mr. Muhammad in fact did keep entrusting Malcolm with greater responsibilities in the Nation and so greater opportunities for public attention. He made Malcolm national spokesman; he put him in charge of the faltering Washington mosque in addition to Harlem for a time in 1963, till the double assignment got too burdensome and Malcolm asked out; there was even talk that he offered to send Malcolm and his family to Cairo to study orthodox Islam, although uncharitable spectators saw this less as a reward than as a way of getting him out of the country and the papers for a while.

The old man's public generosities disguised whatever private pangs he felt at the disparity between his reputation and Malcolm's. Yet one cannot easily imagine that, being human, he was immune to pain. It was Malcolm, not Mr. Muhammad, who was asked to sit for magazine spreads and television talk shows; Malcolm, not Mr. Muhammad, who was second only to Barry Goldwater among the most-sought-after campus speakers of the day; Malcolm, not Mr. Muhammad, who was approached by Doubleday with a $20,000 advance and a contract for an autobiography.* The Messenger assented to all of it; Malcolm in turn continued attributing everything he said to the Messenger, and he signed over his half-share of the book advance (and of the $20,000 the *Saturday*

*Doubleday later dropped the book, and Grove Press took it over, to its presumed delight: the *Autobiography,* published in 1965, sold 25,000 copies in hard covers and well over a million in paper within its first five years.

Evening Post offered for condensation rights) to the Nation. But, for all his deferences to Mr. Muhammad, the attention to Malcolm continued; and, whether for himself or the greater glory of the Nation, he loved it only too well. He complained in the *Autobiography* that his home phone number "somehow" got out to the press; it got out because he gave it out, along with alternate business numbers at the local *Muhammad Speaks* office and the Muslim restaurant in case he was out when we called. "A break was inevitable," one friend said. "An older man will never stand by and see a younger man get ahead of him. Muhammad thought Malcolm was running a game on him—every third word was 'The Honorable Elijah Muhammad' and pretty soon Elijah didn't believe it. He saw he wasn't the big man any more—Malcolm was." It is perhaps instructive that, while Malcolm was allowed to run free in the devil's media, he was frozen very nearly out of God's. *Muhammad Speaks,* once it moved to Chicago, gradually reduced him from a star to a spear-carrier; one issue typically dwelt at loving length on a Muhammad rally, then—in a "sidelights" column inside—noted in passing: "Out of town ministers included . . . Malcolm Shabazz, New York [Mosque] No. 7. . . ."

So there were already subsurface strains in their relationship when Malcolm began hearing—or, more accurately, listening to—scandalous rumors about the Messenger's private life. A number of secretaries to Mr. Muhammad had become pregnant and had been suspended from the company of Muslims under the codes against adultery and fornication. The faithful, Malcolm included, seem to have resisted drawing any invidious connections; they kept the story largely in the family until, after Malcolm's departure and with his encouragement, two of the women filed paternity suits against the old man in Los Angeles Superior Court. Both women claimed in their petitions to have had sexual intercourse with Mr. Muhammad over a period of years; one, Evelyn Williams, said he had fathered her four-year-old daughter; the other, Lucille Rosary Karriem, alleged that she had borne two daughters by him and was pregnant with a third child. Nothing came of the lawsuits except scandal and bad blood. Chicago issued a denial and suggested that Malcolm had himself had romances with both women before his marriage. The Messenger announced in *Muhammad Speaks* that he would not contend the charges of hypocrites before his enemies. The women never managed to get the papers served on him; they eventually dropped out of sight, and the litigation languished.

It was only later, under the pressure of the Nation's own cold war against him, that Malcolm tried to exploit the situation publicly. He actually had begun hearing talk in the middle 1950s, but had dismissed it out of hand; Mr. Muhammad had been his personal savior—had raised him up out of the degradation of prison —and Malcolm accepted the old man's moral perfection quite literally on faith. But the taletelling quickened at precisely a point when Malcolm's own ties with Mr. Muhammad were coming under stress. When he heard the new wave of rumors, he was still genuinely horrified—both at the possibility of imperfection in the Messenger of Allah and at the damage the stories might do the Nation if they got out—but was apparently somewhat less incredulous than before. He tried desperately to keep the lid on. The stories nevertheless leaked within the Chicago mosque, provoking some of the believers there to resign, and to a few outsiders. According to Kenyatta, one of Malcolm's show-business friends told him to his face, in street vernacular, that Mr. Muhammad had been less than completely abstemious; Malcolm, who might earlier have had the man's head for less, sat there numbly and took it.

Malcolm himself told in the *Autobiography* how, shaken and frayed, he sought out first the secretaries, then Wallace Muhammad and finally, in April 1963, the Messenger himself. They embraced and walked beside the old man's pool in Phoenix; Mr. Muhammad spoke of the Biblical tales of David's adultery and Noah's drunkenness; he said, so Malcolm remembered, that he had to fulfill all of those things. *Muhammad Speaks,* in months to come, would put rather a different cast on these Scriptural analogies; it contended that the Messenger, like those men of God in Biblical times, would be wrongfully charged by the wicked with misdeeds he hadn't done. "In the Bible," one of the newspaper's commentaries said, "a righteous prophet of God, Noah, stands accused of drunkenness; Lot, accused of having relations with his daughters; Moses was accused by his own sister; David was accused of Uriah's wife; Solomon was accused, and even Jesus. . . . Should we expect a change in the pattern of the wicked with God's last Messenger, Elijah Muhammad?"

But Malcolm apparently took their discussion as a confirmation, not a defense. He put together what he had heard and what he suspected, flew home and decided to tell it all to a select few Muslim leaders on the East Coast, where his influence was greatest, so they wouldn't be caught off guard if the story suddenly broke. This precaution proved to be a disastrous blunder. Among those he informed, Malcolm testified later when his own difficulties with the Nation got into the devil's courts, were Captain Joseph and the Boston minister, Louis X, a handsome ex-calypso singer who had recorded "A White Man's Heaven Is a Black Man's Hell" and who later was to succeed Malcolm at the Harlem mosque. "I told [Joseph] and the secretary and the minister in Boston that the Honorable Elijah Muhammad had taken on nine wives besides the one that he had," Malcolm said on the stand. ". . . I told [Joseph] that he had nine wives, that he had made nine sisters pregnant, or rather, I mean six of them pregnant." Louis, according to Malcolm's testimony, "confessed that he knew about it all the time"; he and Joseph nevertheless "sent in the report that I was spreading false rumors"—and the report, Malcolm believed, was his downfall.

Some of his circle inside the Nation and out were surprised that he made so much of the allegations about the secretaries in the first place. One outside friend suspected that his upset was really after the fact: "It's like being in love with a woman. As long as she's carrying on with *you,* you don't see what else she's doing. But when she locks you out, what she's doing becomes very important and very wrong." This friend argued that, quite apart from the question of whether the gossip about Mr. Muhammad was true or false, a certain patriarchal *droit de seigneur* is more or less assumed in most religions, black cults included. "The Cadillac is the open expression of it; you can guess at the rest. You don't even have to guess. Nobody gets upset when a cult leader is thought to have a harem. It's accepted. It's talked about. It's one of the fringe benefits." Some of the first temple people Malcolm confided in—even those who honored his confidence—reacted precisely that way and rather suspected the intensity of his concern. "I told him, 'Hell, don't talk to me about *babies,*' " one of them said. "That was just an issue he used. I imagine that when he told people, he was just trying to get the word out."

My own guess is that they mistook the depth of Malcolm's upset. It was true that in time he used the issue with a kind of chilly calculation; I think it equally true that what he had heard appalled him—that it turned some of the bedrock on which he had built his life over a dozen years to sand. "He wouldn't have wanted to believe a rumor like that," a close non-Muslim acquaintance said. "People would have been afraid even to tell him about it." Malcolm himself in the aftermath often identified the issue of the Messenger's morality as the beginning of the collapse of his faith. "I believed in him as a man 100 percent," he said in his last days. "I believed he was divine, divinely taught and divinely guided. And it was only when Elijah Muhammad—ah—something in his personal life—he found himself confronted with a moral question which he could not face up to as a man. And his failure to face up to that as a man made me begin to doubt him, not only as someone divine—divinely guided—but it made me doubt him as a man. And in the face of that, I began to analyze everything else he taught."

One immediate response to his doubts was the increasing secularization of his own ministry; his impulse to action and his increasing worldliness were tugging him that way anyway, and his suspicions about Mr. Muhammad only accelerated the pace. He spoke less and less about morality, more and more about politics and economics. He began referring to himself and the Muslims as black nationalists, to the dismay of some of them. He continued, as a nationalist, to preach the Muslim demand for land—but he began suggesting that the way oppressed peoples had got land historically was not by the intervention of God but by revolution.

He made the most influential single speech of his life in those days—a talk in Detroit in November 1963 that has survived him both in print (in the anthology *Malcolm X Speaks*) and, in the ghetto, as an underground best-selling record called "Message to the Grass Roots." The occasion was a rump "grass-roots" black leadership conference that had split off from a larger, more respectable assemblage over a variety of differences of opinion, among them the refusal of the mainstream group to let Malcolm and other black radicals speak. Gloria Richardson Dandridge, the leader of a radical civil-rights movement in Cambridge, Maryland, that Malcolm had admired from a distance, remembered spending two or three days in workshops at the official gathering; she grew more and more impatient as Martin Luther King's people, among others, kept deflecting the discussions away from the street issues she and the other militants considered important. "So every workshop we went to, there was this big fight," she said. "And I got tired of it. So finally I met some people in the hall and they said, 'You're in the wrong place—you should be over with the other people that split off.' So I went over there—it was at Rev. Albert Cleage's church—and Malcolm was speaking. That was the first time I had heard him, except over television, and I had the feeling that, *wow!*—you know, this could really be a great man if he could break himself from that sectarian thing. And in fact I began to wonder: how long?"

It was Malcolm speaking to a black audience and therefore at his best, slurred and inflected and cynical, and angry in a tempered way; it was a Black Muslim speech, full of the devil, but with Allah retired to the distance. He said the first fact of life for the blacks in America was that they weren't wanted. "You don't catch hell because you're a Methodist or a Baptist; you don't catch hell because you're a Democrat or a Republican; you don't catch hell because you're a Mason or an Elk, and you sure don't catch hell because you're an American, because if you were an American you wouldn't catch no hell. You catch hell because you are a black man." To recognize this was to identify the common enemy as the white man and thus to discover the single unifying fact that had brought the Bandung Conference together and made it important. "Once they excluded the white man, they found they could get together." Their condition was comparable to black America's; their enemy, too, had blue eyes and blond hair and pale skin. "Same man."

Malcolm talked about revolution, describing rather than advocating it. He laughed at the idea of calling the Negro struggle in America a revolution; not in its current phase, anyway. The American, the French, the Russian, the Chinese, the Mau Mau revolutions were all over land—"the basis of independence"—and all spilled blood. "Was no love lost, was no compromise, was no negotiation. I'm telling you, you don't know what a revolution is, because when you find out what it is, you'll get back in the alley. You'll get out of the way. . . . Only kind of revolution that is nonviolent is the Negro revolution. The only revolution based on loving your enemy is the Negro revolution. The only revolution in which the goal is a desegregated lunch counter, a desegregated theater, a desegregated park and a desegregated toilet. You can sit down next to white folks—on the toilet." No, revolution was bloody and destructive, not polite and nonviolent and psalm-singing. "These Negroes aren't asking for no nation—they trying to crawl back on the plantation." Malcolm did his house Negro/field Negro turn, and a long revisionist history of the March on Washington, in which he awarded Oscars to the white leaders for the best performances—"They acted like they really loved Negroes"—and to the blacks as the best supporting cast. What they called a movement, he said, was like a shot of Novocain at the dentist's: ". . . you sit there and 'cause you got all that Novocain in your jaw, you suffer—peacefully." He chuckled. "Blood runnin' all down your jaw and you don't know what's happening, 'cause someone has taught you to suffer—peacefully."

God hardly came into it at all; neither did Mr. Muhammad, except when Malcolm almost parenthetically rattled off the official bill of Muslim demands for "some land of our own" and some foreign aid to seed it with. "That was when I really wondered how long it would be before he would break with them," Mrs. Dandridge said, "because in my mind he was doing that part like—" she snapped her fingers in a flat, tired rhythm—"like his heart wasn't really in it, you know? Like he was just repeating something. A mechanical kind of thing."

The speech, in fact, was a good deal more heretical—had Mr. Muhammad heard it—than the one Malcolm gave a month later at Manhattan Center in New York and got in trouble for. The occasion then was a Muslim rally, at which Mr. Muhammad was the advertised speaker; the Messenger, as he often did, canceled out and asked Malcolm to go on for him. Malcolm wrote out his speech and, from the look of it, probably cleared it with Muhammad: it was partly political—a reprise of his critique of the March on Washington—but otherwise mostly standard Muslim stuff, heavy with obeisances to Mr. Muhammad and with predictions of "that great doomsday, the final hour" in which God's judgment would bring America to ruin. President Kennedy had been assassinated in Dallas only a week before, and, the morning of the rally, Mr. Muhammad called to remind Malcolm of a directive he had dispatched to all ministers: to "teach the spiritual side" and not say anything that could be interpreted as pleasure at Kennedy's death.

Malcolm agreed; his text did include some derogatory references to Kennedy's civil-rights record and his response to the Washington March but nothing at all about the assassination. In the question-and-answer period, however, somebody asked about it, and that impulsive tongue—not for the first time or the last—got the better of Malcolm. He called the President's death a case of "the chickens coming home to roost." Later he would offer the argument that he hadn't meant to crow at all—that he was really saying, as had a number of white eulogists, that the President's death was the inevitable consequence of a climate of hate and violence in America. "So this statement," he said, "was taken out of context and blown out of context to make it look as if I was having a—a *field* day over the assassination of the President." What he never mentioned in these defenses, or in the *Autobiogra-*

phy, was that the remark about the chickens had got a round of laughter and applause from the faithful and that he had thereupon felt impelled to top himself. "Being an old farm boy myself," he had said, "chickens coming home to roost never did make me sad; they've always made me glad."

The remark hit the *Times* next morning—the only whites in the audience were reporters—and Mr. Muhammad was shortly on the phone ordering Malcolm to Chicago. The Messenger, as Malcolm reconstructed their conversation later, hadn't objected to the content of the speech—"The Honorable Elijah Muhammad told me himself that he would have made the same statement I had made, that he had the same feelings that I expressed"—but had questioned its taste. "He told me that because of the climate of the country and the statement that had been made . . . it would be better for me to remain silent for 90 days." The terms of the sentence were that Malcolm could go on running the day-to-day affairs of his mosque, but was forbidden to speak or grant interviews from then until the end of February.

Malcolm and his circle seem to have acquiesced in this as an act of policy. It was true that he and every other Muslim minister worth the name had said far more outrageous things in public and that Mr. Muhammad himself had not hitherto been known for his patriotism toward America or his sympathies for its fallen leaders. "I thought that if the white man was the devil *before* Kennedy's death," Kenyatta said, "why should he be anything less after?" But it was equally true that the Nation had never before been confronted with the assassination of a President and with the emotional bath that followed it. Malcolm accepted that the suspension was best for the safety of the Nation and quite possibly for his own as well. The Messenger, he told one fellow minister, had probably saved his life; his chickens-coming-home line was a half-cocked statement and if the Nation hadn't disciplined him first, the public might well have killed him for it.

The trouble was that, as he suspected then and confirmed to his own satisfaction later, the remark about Kennedy had very little to do with why he was set down. His fall from paradise was full of painful ironies, not the least of them the fact that, with one facile wisecrack, he had handed his enemies the means to ruin him and had so compromised his own position that he couldn't resist or even complain. I remember calling him at *Muhammad Speaks* to ask about his suspension. "I'm in complete submission to any judgment Mr. Muhammad makes," he told me quickly. "I should have kept my big mouth shut." I jotted down what few notes I needed for a short *Newsweek* story and was about to say good-bye when he suddenly asked me what I thought about it. I was surprised; our periodic interviews had by then become almost conversations, but he had never asked my opinion before. It made him seem, for that fleeting moment, curiously vulnerable. I told him I was sorry he had been set down—that he had a lot to tell us and that white people needed his voice perhaps even more than blacks did. He seemed pleased, and we talked on for ten or fifteen minutes more. He never once grumbled about what had happened.

I had my quotes and my story, but what lingers in memory is that question; I had never heard Malcolm sound uncertain—had not even suspected the possibility of uncertainty in him. What I didn't know then was that everything he had been and had believed for twelve years was disintegrating for him. Most of us simply assumed that he would be back as a Muslim, that he was too valuable for the Nation to let go. Malcolm guessed otherwise. His chickens had come home to roost—the jealousies, the wounded vanities, the nasty business of the Messenger and the secretaries. He sensed that he would be cast back into the world, which was to say the grave; he saw that he had set himself up for it. He was exhausted. His nerves were shot. "He shed tears," Kenyatta told me. "He cried."

PART II

The Hour of the Knife

Brother, it is now or never the hour of the knife, the break with the past, the major operation.

—The Redeemer KWAME NKRUMAH, in a conversation with Malcolm X

17. At the Edge of the Grave

For a time, he thought he might be losing his mind.

He could feel everything coming apart—as if, he said in the *Autobiography,* something in nature had failed, like the sun or the stars. He had ordered his life for a dozen years around his absolute submission to Elijah Muhammad and his absolute faith in the ghetto theology Mr. Muhammad said he had got straight from God. His faith had flickered during his last months in the Nation of Islam, as his worldliness grew, but his reverence for the old man did not. "Malcolm loved Elijah better than his own sons loved him," Charles Kenyatta told me. "He never wanted to move away. If Elijah had come up to him five minutes before he got shot, Malcolm would have gone back." Even when he had collected what he took to be ample evidence, or gossip, as to the Messenger's human frailty, Malcolm found himself held back from rebellion not only by love but by a lingering awe of the old man's divine connections. He had seen how much the white man feared the Muslims; he believed quite simply that they all would have been wiped out, the Messenger included, if some higher power were not protecting the little Nation in the wilderness. He had always assumed Mr. Muhammad's reciprocal love for him. His devotion outlasted all the evidence to the contrary; some of his friends are persuaded to this day that, left to themselves, Malcolm and the Messenger might have composed their differences.

They might at least have postponed what was probably inevitable between them. Malcolm's lively and restless mind was in itself subversive in a theocracy as airless as Mr. Muhammad's; one suspects that the particular questions over which he was forced out of the Nation—his ad-lib about President Kennedy and even his taletelling on the old man—were no more than circumstantial. "Malcolm's intelligence and honesty had to come into conflict with Elijah Muhammad's concepts," Ossie Davis guessed. "Elijah Muhammad would have had to say, 'We have to change our doctrine and go out into the world,' or Malcolm would have had to go back to the religious doctrine. He couldn't. He had that nearly childlike quality—when he saw something, he embraced it. When I was a kid and I discovered some new truth, I assumed that everyone else would see it, too. That was Malcolm. He didn't consider the politics of it; it was *wow! a truth!* and he grabbed it. A man like that is dangerous. New truths disturb the old power relationships, and power defends itself."

Power in this case was vested in the elders of the Nation of Islam, and it defended itself by persuading the Messenger and later a working majority of the Original People that Malcolm's failures of discretion were really acts of dissidence against God. Malcolm moved numbly through those first weeks after his suspension. He assured the world that Mr. Muhammad would reinstate him in good time. "It's just as if you had cut off a radio," he said. "You can cut it back on when it pleases you." But he saw with a growing and shattering clarity that it wasn't so—that Mr. Muhammad had switched him off quite probably forever. "He knew it was all over," said Percy Sutton; and knowing this, he experienced that frightening dislocation any man feels on discovering that the ground he thought he knew has turned to sand.

The official word from Chicago was that Malcolm was being punished specifically for the chickens-coming-home remark and that the sentence consisted only of his suspension from public speaking, not from the day-to-day life of the Nation. "I have rebuked him because he has not followed the way of Islam," said the Messenger, and that, so far as the world was permitted to know at the time, was that. But Malcolm, who had understood his time in limbo to be a fixed ninety days, saw a first danger sign in an announcement from Chicago that it was indefinite and would be lifted "if" he submitted. Having told the Messenger at their first audience, "Sir, I submit," and having thereafter done suitable acts of contrition in public, Malcolm rather thought that he had bowed already. It wasn't enough. The real charge against him, as it developed, was not merely violating that be-kind-to-Kennedy directive but outright rebellion—and the particulars involved not what he had told the world about chickens roosting but what he had whispered to a few colleagues he had imagined he could trust about the Messenger and his secretaries.

The gravity of his situation became evident when, on January 6, 1964, he was summoned to the winter palace in Phoenix for a secret preliminary hearing and discovered that he would be heard not by the Messenger alone but by a panel also including John Ali and Raymond Sharrieff, both men whom he considered his enemies. As Malcolm told it in court months later, he was confronted at this session with what he had told Captain Joseph about the Messenger's private life. Mr. Muhammad, he said, was quite bitter about this and at one point told Malcolm sharply, "Go back and put out the fire you started."* Malcolm sensed trouble. He thought the secret hearing itself irregular—an attempt, so he guessed, to hush up the substance of his accusations against the Messenger. He demanded the chance to defend himself before the full body of the faithful in his own mosque, a well-established right of the accused in Muslim disciplinary proceedings. The Messenger, so he testified, promised him just such a hearing as soon as his original ninety-day sentence ran out at the end of February. But his punishment in the interim was made more rather than less severe. The word went out quietly among the believers back in Harlem

*The Muslim version of this exchange is sharply at odds with Malcolm's. According to one source within the Nation, Malcolm confessed that he had been undercutting the Messenger among the faithful over a period of two years and asked tearfully what he could do to make up for it. It was at this point, the source told me, that Mr. Muhammad told him to go put out the fire.

that Malcolm was not only suspended from public speaking but was to be "isolated" from the society of the Original People—a quarantine that meant Muslims he had brought to the faith and had loved as brothers and sisters for years were forbidden even to speak to him.

For a faithful Muslim, this order was tantamount to being forced to the edge of that grave the rest of us call the world. The evidence soon accumulated that somebody in the Nation had another, less metaphorical grave in mind. The great majority of Muslims are nonviolent in their daily lives; the men are instructed against carrying guns and normally will fight only if attacked. Still, with or without the knowledge of the larger Muslim community, heretics do get disciplined, and sometimes roughly. I once asked a black investigator well acquainted with the Muslims whether he thought them capable of having murdered Malcolm. "Oh, yes," he answered mildly. "They would be quite capable of killing him." He studied me for a moment, then smiled humorlessly and added: "Or me, or even you." The preferred mode of operation, a homicide detective told me later, was not the explicit "contract" to maim or kill but oblique suggestion—a dropped word upon which one or another of the faithful could be depended to act but which could not be interpreted by the devil's courts as a direct order.*

Malcolm shortly discovered, or guessed, that somebody had dropped the word about him. He and Kenyatta were walking along Amsterdam Avenue in Harlem one day when they noticed a young Muslim brother glowering at them, his feet thrown apart,

*During the investigation of Malcolm's murder, a sometime Muslim enforcer gave the police a case history that had very nearly turned into a tragedy of errors. Jackie Robinson, according to this story, had done an unflattering column about the Messenger in the *Amsterdam News.* Two mosque officials brought a copy of the paper around to the Muslim restaurant and, within earshot of the informant among others, speculated that it would probably be worth some cash and plane tickets to another mosque in another town if someone were to hurt Jackie. The brothers got the hint but bobbled the name: they thought the officials were talking about *Sugar Ray* Robinson. They waited for Sugar outside the *Amsterdam* for awhile, then—when he didn't appear—transferred their stakeout to his house. Fortunately he didn't show up there either; the hunters at length went home, tempers cooled and both Robinsons were spared the wrath of Allah.

his fists clenched at his sides, his face taut and knotted as if he were about to burst into tears. Kenyatta, a chunky, well-muscled ex-con who routinely packed a gun and who would willingly have died for Malcolm, marched up to the brother and asked him straight out what was on his mind. Well, said the brother, one of the officials had told some of the Original People, "If you knew what Malcolm said about the Dear Holy Apostle, you'd kill him yourself." Kenyatta exchanged glances with Malcolm, then growled something to the effect that the brother ought to go back to the mosque and ask the official why he didn't do his own killing. He and Malcolm walked away from that encounter, leaving the Muslim still staring after them. But Malcolm got the message, and it nearly pushed him past the breaking point.

He supposed later that Muhammad Ali saved his sanity. Ali was Cassius Clay then, a lippy manchild of twenty-two come out of Louisville and the Olympic Games to challenge the reigning monster, Charles (Sonny) Liston, for the heavyweight boxing championship of the world. Malcolm, contrary to the widespread supposition, did not begin Clay's conversion to Islam—Clay had already started attending Muslim meetings before they met in 1962—but he did complete it, and he became Clay's counselor in matters of faith, style and the psychology of combat against apparently superior power. Their widely publicized affiliation disturbed Chicago, which in the first place disapproved of Clay's profession and in the second assumed, like most of the rest of us, that he was going to lose to Liston. The friendship nevertheless endured, and, despite the official Muslim quarantine, Clay invited Malcolm and his family to come to Miami Beach and watch him train for the fight.

Malcolm, all raggedy-nerved in his enforced idleness, quickly accepted. He took rooms in a black motel in Miami, a knock-off replica of the devil's pleasure domes across Biscayne Bay, with a dark bar that he avoided and a clean luncheonette that reminded him of home. He was only a supporting player in the Clay camp, a marginal presence occasionally noted in the press as some black Svengali filling Cassius's ingenuous young head with Allah-knows-what, but he submerged himself gratefully in the role of second. The fight, for white people, was a taxing one, pitting as it did a stereotypical Bad Nigger, Liston, against a stereotypical Crazy Nigger, Clay. For Malcolm, with nowhere else to commit his energies, it became a jihad, with Clay as the bearer of Islam against the uncircumcised. This seemed to most reasonable people a hopeless cause; Clay's only known advantage over Liston was his speed, which Sonny, an unrecognized folk poet, had dismissed by wondering aloud whether Cassius could kiss a flying bullet or run through hell in a gasoline sportcoat. Malcolm undertook to convince Clay that he could, and in the end, with his marvelous gifts of persuasion, he succeeded.

Florida was a release for Malcolm. He spent time with his family, whom he felt he had woefully neglected. He warmed himself in the celebrity glow, the swirl of Jim Browns and Joe Louises and George Plimptons eddying around a heavyweight fight camp. He poked around the Beach like any tourist, taking the sun, snapping photos, buying picture postcards of dressed-up chimpanzees to send his friends back home. ("Negro *leaders,*" Gloria Dandridge's card said, "could learn something from these monkeys who have more freedom in America than Negroes do, and these monkeys haven't had to wait for civil-rights legislation. Maybe our leaders should let these monkeys lead us. Brother Malcolm X.") But his gathering war of nerves with Chicago went on, and even Clay became briefly a pawn between them. Clay had completed the requirements for membership in the Nation, but the hierarchy, out of the discretion of men of power, elected to hold up his registration and his Original name until they saw how the fight came out. Malcolm had by then persuaded not only Clay but himself that Liston could be conquered and had begun dreaming, for all his sentence to limbo, of what a gloriously marketable property the heavyweight championship would be for the Nation. Thus transported, he called Chicago and offered to deliver Clay, title and all, to the Savior's Day convention there the day after the big fight; his price was his own reinstatement. Chicago, still unconvinced of Clay's possibilities, turned the deal down. Clay, in the event, was not really Malcolm's to offer. The night he beat Liston, Chicago telephoned him at his victory party—an ice-cream social, more accurately, in Malcolm's motel suite—and awarded him his membership and his new name; the next morning, reborn Muhammad Ali, he confirmed his conversion to the world. Malcolm liked Ali too well to interfere in this or to involve him further in his private difficulties. When he broke with the Nation two weeks later, he counseled Ali to stay with Mr. Muhammad—and swallowed his hurt feelings when Ali took his advice.

Even that fleeting attempt to exploit his connection with Ali was unlike Malcolm. So was much of what he did in those strung-out days; one can explain his behavior toward Chicago only by understanding that he was a combative man engaged in a rough and dangerous fight and that he was a desperate man as well—the communicant first cut off from the church and then held up to the faithful as its enemy. Some of his tactics were chilly, like the offer of Ali's body; some were merely clumsy. During his suspension, the *Times* in New York and the *Sun-Times* columnist Irv Kupcinet in Chicago printed inside-dope stories of an impending split between Malcolm and Mr. Muhammad. The Nation assumed that Malcolm had planted these items, a not unreasonable guess given his acquaintance with Handler at the *Times* and his frequent appearances on Kupcinet's television talk show. Chicago accordingly was not impressed when Malcolm offered yet another trade—let him speak again and he could straighten out all those nasty rumors of a rift. The answer once again was no.

Hemmed in, his options very nearly exhausted, Malcolm tried a last, graceless effort to force his way back inside. His instrument —his bludgeon—was the gossip about the Messenger's secretaries. His demand for a full-dress hearing before his own congregation in Harlem was itself a ploy in this game; he was gambling that Chicago would rather reinstate him quietly, in spite of everything, than air the whole unlovely business before a jury of his people in his home parish. The Nation, as it developed, had no intention of doing either. Instead, so he believed, some of his antagonists used the period of his isolation to spread tales in the mosque that he had been mutineering against the Messenger of Allah; their purpose, as he saw it, was to poison the minds of the Original People so thoroughly against him that they would gladly see him sent to perdition without a hearing. Malcolm's gallantry was deep-grained but not limitless; it tended to quit him when the ante got high and the opposition nasty. At 3 A.M. one insomniac night during his suspension, he telephoned a black reporter friend on one of the downtown New York dailies and tried to get him to print the story of the secretaries for everybody, even the devil, to see. The papers couldn't touch it then—there were no court pleadings or public records of any sort to back up Malcolm's word—and Malcolm, so informed, was out of defenses.

The wonder was that all his desperate scrambling was directed at getting him back into a society to whose proprietors he was no longer welcome. He may have been moved by love, or loyalty, or anger, or ambition, or pain, or simply equity on his investment of time and soul in the Nation—or, as one guesses, by all of these strands tangled together. "He really thought they couldn't do without him," Kenyatta said; Malcolm continued acting on this premise long after his own good sense told him otherwise and after the contrary intentions of some of his ill-wishers in the Nation became quite murderously clear. In February, when he was theoretically near the end of his time in purgatory, some of the brothers from the Harlem mosque came to him and said they had been instructed by a Muslim officer to assassinate him. Whether the instrument of his death was to have been a shotgun or a bomb wired to the ignition of his Oldsmobile is not clear from Malcolm's various accounts of this episode. But its meaning seemed evident to him: his pursuers had escalated from politic hints to explicit orders to ice him. Malcolm, as it turned out, was more persuasive than they. He told the deputation from the doom squad his side of the story so convincingly that they went back to the mosque not only without his head but as his advocates among the Original People.

Even then Malcolm clung to the possibility that he could somehow recover his old place of honor in the Nation. Savior's Day came and went; Louis X took Malcolm's place introducing the Messenger to the annual Muslim convention; Malcolm wasn't invited or even mentioned aloud, although Mr. Muhammad was at pains to remind the faithful that he alone was the elect of God. "Allah has made me a Door," the old man said, short-winded and halting. "If you get out, you will come by me, and if you reject me, you won't go. I have been given the keys to Heaven. . . ." Afterward, Malcolm petitioned the Messenger one more time, by letter and then by telephone, for a hearing. The Messenger put him off and said he would answer by mail. Malcolm said later that the reply, when it came, was too ambiguous to puzzle out; the Muslims, to the contrary, said that Mr. Muhammad had advised Malcolm that he had not obeyed the order to be silent, "so now I will wait until you be quiet before I give you permission to speak in public." Malcolm, for all his professed mystification, seemed at last to accept that the judgment against him was final. "I could have remained quiet and walked the streets for six months or six years," he said in retrospect, "but I know it would have been six years. I knew they didn't intend to reinstate me as a Muslim. You don't put a shotgun at somebody who's suspended."

And so it really was over. Malcolm had been a Black Muslim from his twenty-eighth year, when he was a fire-baptised convert coming out of Charlestown Prison, until his thirty-ninth, when he was the Nation's best and best-known minister. He owed the little Messenger of Allah his life, his position, his ideology, his self-respect, even his name; he had in turn served the old man and his kingdom as nearly selflessly as a man so absorbed in public performance could. The anguish he felt putting all this behind him was enormous—the pain, one friend said, "felt by any man who loves his father and who is repudiated by him." But Malcolm had disciplined himself not to display emotion, and he hid his wounds from the people he knew he would need. "He had more plans than pain," Benjamin Goodman assured me, and in those last days Malcolm began to rush those plans together. He got a gun, a semiautomatic rifle, and advertised the fact openly as a deterrent to further visitations by enemies from the Nation or anywhere else. He totted up his assets and liabilities like a double-entry bookkeeper and determined that he measured up to his own exacting standards for leadership. He stayed in quiet contact with some of the more activist brothers in the mosque and some few well-wishers outside and began assembling a little cadre of people he could count on—people like Goodman, a bright, intuitive man with whom he could communicate with a nod or a glance; James 67X, a brainy inside operative educated in politics, languages (including Chinese) and karate; Kenyatta, then still Charles 37X, schooled in the street, but tough, loyal and comfortable. He got together the incorporation papers for his own church, which he called simply the Muslim Mosque, Inc.

Malcolm knew what filing those papers meant; the Holy Qur'an is quite severe about those who set up mosques in opposition to a messenger of Allah, and those few who had made the attempt before him had sometimes been roughly reminded of these Scriptures by the Fruit of Islam. But Malcolm was past the point of no return. On March 8, a week after his sentence was supposed to have run out, he issued a press release to the effect that he still revered Mr. Muhammad and had no intention of splitting the Nation but that he felt he could spread the word best "by staying out . . . and continuing to work on my own among America's 22 million non-Muslim Negroes." Three days later, he wired the Messenger directly, again pledging his fealty ("You are still my teacher and leader . . . I am still your brother and servant") and blaming their parting on a conspiracy of Chicago and New York officials against him. The Messenger is said to have wept then, and thereafter to have flown into a fury at the mere mention of Malcolm's name. Malcolm was sorry to hear this, but the deal was down. "It's hard," he said, "to make a rooster stop crowing once the sun has risen." The sun was up for Malcolm, flooding the darkness he had inhabited for more than a decade; and in its brilliant light, he could see his sanity, his only course of action and his death.

18. A Declaration of Independence

Malcolm set up his headquarters in Harlem, but when he was ready to go public, he put on a quiet pin-checked suit and a telegenic blue shirt, bundled up a stack of mimeographed press releases and came downtown to meet The Man. He booked a conventioneers' conference room on the mezzanine of the Park Sheraton, a faded commercial hotel in midtown Manhattan, and had his people invite the press to witness his declaration of independence. Malcolm rarely underestimated his own pulling power, but this time he hired too small a hall; it was already overflowing and noisy when he walked upstairs from the lobby, with James 67X at one elbow lugging the handouts and Professer Michaux at the other beaming out from under a rakish fez. He came bone-tired, after a harried, sleepless week dismantling his past and trying to create a future. But standing there under the hot TV lights, dabbing at the perspiration pebbling his forehead, he looked happy with his freedom and with the fact that so many of us were interested in it.

"Because 1964 threatens to be a very explosive year on the racial front," he began, reading from his prepared text, "and because I myself intend to be very active in every phase of the American Negro struggle for human rights, I have called this press conference this morning in order to clarify my own position in the struggle." He said he had been forced out of the Nation by "internal differences," not by his own choice; he still believed both in Mr. Muhammad's unshaded black-and-white analysis of The Problem and in his solution to it—"complete separation, with our people going back home, to our own African homeland." But separation was a long-term proposition, and the temporal needs of black people for better jobs, homes and schools couldn't wait till the boats began leaving. Malcolm planned to address himself to those problems, drawing on the Black Muslim model but using his new freedom to work with outsiders as well. "I do not pretend to be a divine man," he said. ". . . I am not educated, nor am I an expert in any particular field. But I am sincere, and my sincerity [is] my credentials." He hoped to call off his war with the recognized black leadership and join them in seeking some common approach to a solution. "As of this minute"—he smiled hugely—"I've forgotten everything bad that the other leaders have said about me, and I pray that they can also forget the many bad things I've said about them."

His new Muslim Mosque, Inc., he said, would give him a religious base from which to attack the debilitating vices of the black community. But its political, economic and social philosophy would be black nationalism, and there would be room for any blacks to participate in its secular programs whether or not they believed in Allah or in any god at all. Even whites could contribute money and ideas, though they could not join: "There can be no black-white unity until there is first some black unity. . . . We cannot think of uniting with others, until after we have first united among ourselves." The particulars of what the MMI actually would do were vague. Malcolm spoke only of organizing the blacks to recover control of the politics of their own communities —a hardy-perennial dream of the nationalists at 125th Street and Seventh Avenue—and of repudiating nonviolence once and for all as a strategy of revolt. He had advocated resistance all along; now, in careful language, he advocated armed resistance. "It is legal and lawful to own a shotgun or a rifle. We believe in obeying the law. In areas where our people are the constant victims of brutality and the government seems unable or unwilling to protect them, we should form rifle clubs that can be used to defend our lives and our property in times of emergency. . . . When our people are being bitten by dogs, they are within their rights to kill those dogs."

Malcolm was an intuitive public-relations genius; he complained later at how much of the attention fastened on the questions of politics and guns, but he clearly was not surprised by it. The conventional wisdom of the day held that he alone in Harlem could mount a credible challenge to Representative Adam Clayton Powell, and in this context his promise of a new black politics uptown sounded something like a threat.* Malcolm pushed it no further than that; he called Powell "a good friend of mine" and said only that the MMI would "encourage him to do better." His call for rifle clubs brought even more questions and got most of the headlines next day. Someone suggested that he was urging armed revolution. "I never would," Malcolm shot back. "I don't think I'm dumb enough to advocate armed revolt." Still, wouldn't rifle clubs raise the danger of civil war? "What would you prefer?" Malcolm answered. "Civil war or more Birminghams?"

Mostly, for Malcolm, it was an exuberant occasion. He ran his press conference with an easy professionalism, flattering some of the reporters by remembering their names and papers, handling the sharpest and silliest questions alike without missing a beat. Yes, he would keep his "X," he said, "as a reminder that I don't know who I am." Yes, he expected to muster a healthy following—"I'm not the most intelligent person in the world, but I'm too intelligent to take a stand as I do now if I thought I'd be alone." No, he wasn't becoming an integrationist, but there were projects they might work on together; he waffled briefly when pressed for examples, then hypothesized a joint effort with the NAACP and others to "stop the excessive number of bars" in the black communities. His new display of fellow feeling toward the established civil-rights leaders did not quite last out the morning, Malcolm being Malcolm. "I haven't met any that I thought were sincere," he said, "but I'll give them a break by saying that I haven't met many of them." Still, he was more than ordinarily careful to keep his differences with them to matters of policy. Assimilation, for example:

*This naturally occurred to Powell, too; so did the probability that Malcolm, as an ex-convict, was disqualified from voting or holding office. "I never checked that out," Powell told me comfortably. "I never got into that issue at all with him. I didn't want to pry into delicate affairs of his conviction." Neither had he worried, so he said, about Malcolm's good will. "Malcolm told me, 'You don't get any money from white people—it's all black money. That's it, Adam, that's why I love you.' He said, 'As long as you run, Adam, I'll support you.' He was a great man."

"During slavery, the house Negro coexisted peacefully with the master, but Negroes out there in the huts, they never coexisted. I still believe a completely separate black homeland is the only way to solve our problems; the servant can never coexist on the same level with the master. But that's in the future, and we want to get the best type of life out of our own community while we're still here." Malcolm had, in the space of an hour or so, come out for guns and vigilantism and separation—for the repeal, that is, of the American Dream—and had been positively ingratiating in the process. "He's so—*charming,*" a woman from one of the television stations exclaimed as we filed out. "So *intelligent.*"

The truth was that all of it—the politics, the rifle clubs, the offer of coalition with the civil-rights movement—was improvisation. There simply hadn't been time for him and his little circle to retreat and plan, and none was soon forthcoming; Malcolm, that morning and in the weeks immediately ahead, was making himself up as he went along. He carried on this act of creation not by meditation, which didn't suit him anyway, but by asking, listening and talking; he disclosed the results not in any single manifesto but in the accretion of words, spilled profligately in interviews and speeches and bull sessions that ran on till 2 and 3 and 4 o'clock practically every morning. A whole new set of operative terms came into his public vocabulary in those days, touchstone words like "flexible" and "radical" and "sincere," by which he defined himself and measured others. With his departure from the Nation, his friend Maya Angelou thought, he freed himself from being a totally "exclusive" person and, instead, became "inclusive"—aware of and open to differences in the people around him. To encounter him in those days was like meeting a man coming out of a lightless cellar and blinking at the day. "I'm reading five books a week trying to catch up," he told Dan Watts, the editor of the eclectic black-radical magazine, *Liberator.* Watts, a cooled-off man trained and disappointed as an architect, replied that it was late for that—the first book in the first grade was the one that counted. Malcolm didn't hear, or didn't care.

His transformation this time was as profound as his conversion to Islam in prison but not nearly so sudden or melodramatic; it happened as process, not revelation, and it ran out over weeks and months of trial and error, discovery and disappointment. Malcolm still thought of himself in the earliest days of his freedom as a Black Muslim in exile, and so did most of the forty or fifty Original People who had followed him out of the mosque. They had been the activists of the Nation—"I don't know whether you'd say the Left wing or the Right wing," said Malcolm, "but it was out on one of those wings"—and their single common assumption was that Malcolm would spread Mr. Muhammad's word farther and faster than the Messenger had been able to himself. They did not doubt that this word was accurate as to the identity of God and the devil; they had only grown impatient waiting for Mr. Muhammad to convert the black multitudes and for Allah to bring the enemy to judgment. They assumed that Malcolm could speed at least the former eventuality, and possibly the latter. It was, Benjamin Goodman said at the time, like the differences between one airplane sitting on the runway and another taking off. "Some who were very loyal went with Malcolm," Goodman told me years later; the plane flew off in directions none of them expected and for which some of them never forgave Malcolm.

The marriage they were proposing between the mosque and the world was probably impossible in the first place. The premonitory signs that it wasn't working out came as early as the second public rally of the Muslim Mosque, Inc., when Malcolm abruptly dropped the opening prayer to Allah—his God—on the ground that even this gesture was too sectarian and was keeping potential followers away. The unspoken objective of his new ministry, as it developed during those weeks, was not so much bringing the sinners to God as mobilizing them against the devil. Malcolm still wanted his religious base; he conducted services not unlike the Nation's at his new headquarters at the Theresa Hotel in Harlem and ordered a search for a more suitable mosque. But he came at the same time to understand that too much religion could be a bad thing, and most of the plans and projects he talked about were secular. He spoke of calling a black nationalist convention in the spring or summer, with delegates from every college and every back alley in America; of organizing a black nationalist party, or a black nationalist army if necessary; of supplying MMI legmen to the established organizations to go from door to door and register every black vote in New York; of setting up a Muslim-style drug-addict program in Harlem; of doing a monthly column in Watts's *Liberator;* of getting out his own newspaper, a sort of *Malcolm Speaks,* with a Muslim editorial line but without the Messenger's meandering prose.

That none of this ever happened was neither surprising nor critically important. Malcolm didn't have the resources to make it happen and in any event was no more to be held literally to his campaign promises than any charismatic political leader. His real contribution to the struggle, as he himself seemed to realize, was catalytic, not corporate. He began to think of himself as potentially a black Billy Graham—an evangelist seeking decisions for blackness as Graham sought decisions for Christ. "Graham," said Malcolm, "has an evangelical gospel of Christianity, which in my opinion is white nationalism. He has put or tried to put the Christness back into a lot of white people. He has been successful by not trying to start an organization himself and arousing jealousy among other ministers. His strategy has always been to tell people to go out and join any church that preaches the gospel of Christ. My gospel will be black nationalism. I won't tell Negroes to come and follow me—I'll tell them to join any organization where black nationalism is practiced."

He imagined at the beginning that he could bring this off as a free-lance disciple of Mr. Muhammad, and he tried, at least in his public behavior, to avoid provoking the old man. Some friends saw a double motive in his continuing public pledges of allegiance to Black Islam—an investment in life insurance as well as an expression of love. "It couldn't have worked, of course," one told me. "I don't mean the analogy literally, but suppose you were leaving the Mafia—the first thing you'd do is say that the Mafia is a fine organization. That's what I'd do. Now, I happen to believe that Malcolm believed it. But here you are running around with the Mafia secrets. Your public relations about how nice they are isn't enough to guarantee that you're going to stay around. And the Black Muslims weren't having any of it. Their attitude is you're either with us or you ain't." Malcolm, being a realist in matters of survival, surely recognized this; nevertheless, he made the effort and probably meant it. Friends thought they heard a catch in his voice every time he mentioned Mr. Muhammad at the Park Sheraton press conference. I saw him afterward, in the back room at Michaux's bookstore; he seemed less guarded than usual about the Nation's business, possibly out of relief or exhaustion or both, but even then he carefully blamed his troubles on the courtiers, not the king. It was they who had poisoned the Messenger against him, he told me. "If you put the wrong information into a computer, it can only come back the way you put it in."

The Nation did not meet his peace-keeping efforts halfway. The Messenger denounced Malcolm as a hypocrite—the worst name one Muslim can call another—and rejected his offers of continuing solidarity. "He broke with me, I didn't break with him," the old man said bitterly. "He don't want me." *Muhammad Speaks* began a flow of nearly weekly commentaries, the first a tirade by Minister James of the Chicago mosque, accusing Malcolm of being a self-seeker ("He loves worldly praises") and a fraud. "I am sure that Malcolm has not believed the Honorable Elijah Muhammad to be the Messenger of Allah," James wrote. "If he did, he would be afraid for his future." The Nation even produced Malcolm's own brother Philbert X, Mr. Muhammad's minister for Lansing and several nearby Michigan cities, to read a prepared statement likening Malcolm to Judas, Brutus and Benedict Arnold and suggesting that he was crazy in the bargain—a thought that, for some in the Nation, became father to the wish. "I am aware of the great mental illness which beset unfortunately many Americans," said Philbert, "and which besetted my mother whom I love and one of my other brothers and which may now have taken another victim, my brother Malcolm."

There was, in much of this, a visible undercurrent of nervousness that Malcolm was about to spill the story of Mr. Muhammad's secretaries; Minister James's piece warned prospectively against imputing sin to a Messenger of God, and Philbert's statement charged Malcolm with trying to use certain unnamed "weak" women to "accuse and smear" certain unnamed Muslim leaders. Malcolm in fact was in touch with several former secretaries, and at a point then or later, he started collecting affidavits from them for use as necessary. But after his first effort under quarantine to plant the story, he apparently suspended trying to exploit it in public and bit his tongue as best he could under the abuse of his old comrades—an effort that was largely but not completely successful.

Philbert's statement particularly rankled Malcolm. It caught him on a day when his office was crowded with reporters waiting to see him, each wanting a response to his big brother. Malcolm had a fierce headache, which he was dosing with aspirins and paper containers of coffee; he handled the question gracefully enough the first time or two, but as the day dragged on and his headache wouldn't go away, he started matching Philbert *ad hominem* for *ad hominem.* His brother was, he said, the minister of the only mosque in the Nation with no members; he had been flown in from Lansing to Chicago and handed a prepackaged script to read; he had never been in the papers before and likely never would be again. Malcolm refused even to concede that there was anything tragic in having brother set against brother. When Helen Dudar of the *Post* proposed this to him during an interview, he hid whatever upset it caused him behind the mask of the leader who is, or must seem to be, impervious to human feeling. "When you're involved in a revolution," he told her brusquely, "nothing is painful." Later, she quoted him the newest warning of divine retribution emanating from Chicago and said it sounded to her like a prelude to a bullet in the back. "This is true," Malcolm answered. "It's more than likely." The mask was still in place; he said this, she thought, with no more emotion than he might have expended agreeing that the grass is green.

The civil-rights leaders to whom Malcolm had offered the possibility of coalition were barely more congenial than the Black Mus lims he had left behind. A minor undercurrent of black nationalism was then stirring to life in the action wing of the movement, notably in CORE—a few of its Harlem members quit to join Malcolm—and SNCC. But those days were, as Floyd McKissick put it, the Great Age of Martin Luther King; to question his strategy or his goals, if one was black, was to be thought a Tom on the one hand or a Muslim on the other. It was too much to expect, really, that the war between Malcolm and the integrationists could be waved away with a single declaration of good faith and good will at a press conference. Their mutual history of no faith and ill will stood between them; so did their irreconcilable ideologies and strategies for change; so did Malcolm's wretched media reputation as an antiwhite, anti-Semitic demagogue and now as an advocate of taking up guns as well. And so did the sheer force of his personality. James Farmer of CORE, who belonged tenuously to the black leadership establishment of the day but had grown rather fond of Malcolm in their several debates, sensed a little edge of anxiety as well as mistrust among some of his colleagues when Malcolm's name came up. "He had charisma, a great deal of it, and a great deal of the best qualities of leadership," Farmer said. "So I think there would have been too much fear of his competition. Rivalry. The civil-rights movement would not have taken him."

Some of Malcolm's new friends in the movement warned him that the distance was too great to be bridged. "Forget it," Gloria Richardson Dandridge told him, " 'cause it's too set in. You may have some younger guys coming up that you can deal with *outside* of these organizations, but you're not going to be able to deal with Whitney or Wilkins." It didn't seem to register then; she figured that Malcolm would learn but that it might take a year's disappointments for him to get the message—and a year, as it developed, was slightly more than Malcolm had left. Some of the Old Muslims who had quit the mosque with Malcolm were similarly dubious, for reasons that were parochial and predictable and yet more realistic than he was then prepared to be. "How you going to work with these people?" Benjamin Goodman asked him. "Why, you called them Uncle Toms yourself." Malcolm shrugged.

"If you're in a car with someone going to Chicago," he told Goodman, "and you know they're going the wrong way, and you ride along and pretty soon you pass a sign that says 'Boston,' sooner or later they'll stop the car and say, 'Take the wheel.' "

The first returns were not promising; the movement was not prepared even to let Malcolm get into the car. Mrs. Dandridge made the mistake of telling reporters that she thought Malcolm's position on guns for self-defense altogether reasonable; some of the outside financial support for her Cambridge, Maryland, movement promptly dried up, and not many other black leaders were so incautious. Martin Luther King, who had privately been predicting a break between Malcolm and Mr. Muhammad, said a bit loftily when it happened that he would have to talk to Malcolm about his position on rifles. (He never did.) Farmer called Malcolm a talented demagogue and predicted that, out of his essential intelligence and honesty, he would become an integrationist within a couple of years.* Even SNCC, at the radical Left edge of the movement, held back from Malcolm's embrace; its kids were hardly less scornful of King—they called him "De Lawd" behind his back—but were not quite ready to give up the dream of reconstructing America nonviolently, beginning in the boondocks of Mississippi. Stokely Carmichael, who two years later contributed "Black Power" to the vocabulary of race in America, boasted that summer of having told Malcolm: "You keep your talk, and you can say what you want, I don't even think you put me in better bargaining position, you know, because you don't say anything." James Forman, SNCC's executive secretary, was no more receptive when Joseph B. Cumming, Jr. of *Newsweek* asked him whether any joint enterprise was possible. "Come on, man," Forman said, "I don't know anything about Malcolm X. Come on, man. Look." Would SNCC work with him? "Look, man, come on." Or feel challenged by him? "I don't feel threatened. We're pretty

*Malcolm responded in a radio interview that he didn't know what a talented demagogue was and that Farmer, out of *his* essential intelligence and honesty, would become a black nationalist within a couple of years. "In a sense," said Farmer, "both of us were right."

secure psychologically." Or coalesce with him? "Look, man, nobody's worried about Malcolm X."

Malcolm's first points of contact were not with the insiders but with the outcasts of the respectable movement, and even they were leery of letting him too close at first. The black revolt, in its spread northward, had indeed begun producing a rebellious new generation in the cities—a breed of radical local leaders who sometimes shared the goals of the mainstream movement but whose style of pursuing those goals was thought dangerously harum-scarum. Their ranks included Mrs. Dandridge, then Gloria Richardson, whose mass marches had brought Cambridge under something like martial law; Jesse Gray, a street-wise rent-strike organizer in Harlem; the Rev. Milton Galamison in Brooklyn and Lawrence Landry in Chicago, both of whom had led successful black boycotts of the schools; Stanley Branche, a renegade NAACP leader in Chester, Pennsylvania; Julius Hobson, a CORE radical in Washington; Dick Gregory, even then half-timing between nightclub comedy and the movement; and kindred spirits in increasing numbers around the nation. They shared a common disillusion with the operating style of the national civil-rights organizations, which seemed to require okays from their front offices and boards of directors for anything but the tamest protest actions. The outsiders were further discouraged by the heavy concentration of the energy and money of the movement on the South; they did not question the value of doing away with formal Jim Crow, but the problems that immediately concerned them and their people had to do with rats biting babies and children going hungry and trade-unions barring Negroes and men dying of nothing to do. Common interests and the common disapproval of the respectable movement brought the outsiders together; a group of them met in Dayton, formed a loose confederation called ACT (the name was a declaration of purpose, not an acronym) and scheduled a second session in Chester in March 1964 to begin pooling war stories and technical expertise.

Somebody at the Dayton meeting proposed inviting Malcolm, then still a Black Muslim, to join them at Chester. Hardly anyone there actually knew Malcolm or anything much about him except his press reputation; the notion may in fact have come up out of a certain sense of obligation to do something outrageous. Several of the conferees were quite nervous about it, and one—a man of established radical credentials—argued strenuously that they should have nothing whatever to do with Malcolm. They finally did agree to ask him and, a bit gingerly, chose Mrs. Dandridge to bell the cat, since she had met Malcolm, had been mentioned flatteringly by him in a speech or two and didn't seem to be afraid of anybody. She phoned him. Malcolm rather liked the company—"He was just coming out of that whole, enclosed, sectarian thing," Mrs. Dandridge recalled, "but there were people across the United States that he had been noticing and that he respected"—and he put Chester in his datebook. The meeting chanced to fall on the weekend just following his declaration of independence; his talk to the ACT people, as Mrs. Dandridge remembered it, was well done but "essentially his thing—you know, the Muslim thing, the fact that he wasn't for integration," and they exchanged no commitments about working with one another. Still, Malcolm did establish his availability for certain kinds of activities, so long as he wasn't expected to be nonviolent or integrationist, and he promised to work some of their pet projects into his speeches. They in turn got to see him and were not quite so nervous about him the next time.

His situation nevertheless remained painfully awkward. "He desperately wanted to belong," Ossie Davis told me. Davis, among others, tried to put Malcolm in touch with the right people in off-the-record settings, where they could get to know one another without the necessity of doing battle. Yet he was still unwelcome to much of the movement, and even where he was accepted, he had to calculate whether he would help or hurt a cause with his controversial presence. He looked in on one of Rev. Galamison's school boycotts and was shown upstairs to the study at Galamison's church in Brooklyn. He was shortly joined there by Adam Clayton Powell and Jesse Gray, who likewise were mixed blessings PR-wise, but not by Galamison—not for a long while. The guest stars spent an hour or so waiting amid a litter of empty coffee containers for their host and being interviewed about the occasion and one another. Malcolm said that he had come because he was against segregation, not because he was for integration, and that he and Galamison "don't discuss that which we don't agree upon." Galamison told me he meant nothing by his absence: he had been downstairs on the telephone collecting school-absentee estimates so that his figures on the success or failure of the boycott would get to the papers before the Board of Education's. "When you're in the kind of trouble I was," said Galamison, "you want all the friends you can get." His trouble at the moment was the terrible hiding he was taking in the press for trying to bring about the integration of the schools by calling black children out of them. Malcolm was hardly the antidote for this, and they both knew it. He paid his respects and posed for pictures, his smile brilliant and Galamison's rather restrained. But when the Reverend headed out to march his followers to the school board, Malcolm said goodbye and went home. "There's no reason for you to take on my enemies, too," he told Galamison.

"I was involved," Malcolm liked to say thereafter. He was involved at the margin; Malcolm remained, no longer by choice but by force of circumstance, a spectator at the battle—a warrior confined unhappily to the sidewalks and to commenting on the events in the streets. Some days he was quite cynical about his purposes in wanting to join the movement—"The only way to uncover what's inside the pot," he said, "is to put some heat under it"—yet even this was denied him: Malcolm had to apply his heat from the outside looking in. I was downtown one day in that period covering a civil-rights demonstration against the Plumbers Union when I noticed James 67X watching from a nearby doorway. I asked him conversationally what he was doing there. "Looking," he said. He wasn't being curt—just matter-of-fact. Looking, in those days, was pretty nearly all Malcolm and his people could do.

Looking and talking. Malcolm wanted badly to be recognized not as a street agitator with religious pretensions but as a clergyman with political interests, on a footing with Martin Luther King, say, or Adam Clayton Powell. "The same as they are Christian ministers," he said, "I am a Muslim minister." But their ministries were activist, King's in the street and Powell's in the precincts, while Malcolm's was a ministry of words. His objective was to heighten the consciousness of the ghetto and to cost white people sleep in the process; his technique for political education was not to call people into the streets or to solicit their votes but to make that marvelous voice and that acid vision limitlessly available to them. He talked as long as anybody would listen. One day a reporter protested that he was rattling along too fast to keep up with. Malcolm apologized, thumped his chest with two fingers and said, "I speak from the heart."

His new rectory was Suite 128 at the Theresa, a single long room on the mezzanine crowded with folding chairs and stacked cartons of handouts and partitioned off at one end to make a more or less private office for Malcolm. The suite itself bore witness to Harlem's failed dreams; it had been abandoned by a cosmetics company (the name EVE NELSON COSMETICS on the door never got painted over) and by the branch office of a Wall Street stock brokerage, which unwittingly bequeathed its ruled green blackboard to the revolution. ("We must obtain a mosque," said one of the first notices to go up in Malcolm's tenancy. "We can accomplish said above with a little study.") The big room served as headquarters and temple, but most hours on most days it was full of people wanting Malcolm's time and attention—reporters, photographers, followers, competitors, visitors from Africa and the United Nations, street people with problems they hoped he could solve or visions they thought he could use. Speaking requests, mostly from colleges, stacked up "that high," he would say, flattening out one hand three feet above his desk. The radio talk shows asked him on regularly and prodded him to say something shocking about white people or guns. Malcolm rarely told any of them no. He asked his wife to take a bow at one of his early Harlem rallies and discovered she had already left for home; he stood there looking sheepish for a moment, then found himself apologizing to his public for "the worst crime I ever committed"—having neglected his family in the press of the black man's business. "This man's flesh were *so* valuable," Kenyatta said; he looked unhappy in retrospect that he and the brothers had let Malcolm parcel it out so freely.

Malcolm decided early in his new ministry on a separation of church and state. The Muslims among his followers rendered unto God that which was God's at weeknight religious services, but his Sundays were for public rallies and for settling accounts with Caesar. He booked the Carver Ballroom in Harlem for the first of these open meetings, but somebody influential applied some heat—Malcolm suspected the powerful black City Councilman J. Raymond Jones—and Carver canceled his rental. The meeting had to be switched at the last minute and with only minimal public notice to another Harlem dance palace, the Dawn Casino, where Malcolm sat smoldering with his platform guests under an arbor of fake flowers, counting a disappointing house of about six hundred. He tried not to let the snafu spoil the occasion; it was, as he told his audience, "the first time I've had a chance to open my mouth to a group of so-called Negroes in 105 days—since December 1, when them chickens came home to roost." He was halfway through his talk—a reprise of his formal declaration of independence with some impromptu marginal comments—when an aide walked onstage and passed him a note to the effect that the Dawn Casino no longer wanted his business either. Malcolm laughed. "They say they can't rent the place to us any more because people in the neighborhood were scared by all the commotion," he said. "Can you imagine that—people worried about people in *Harlem* being scared?" The crowd laughed, too; Malcolm finished his speech and thereafter hired other dancehalls—first the Rockland Palace and later the Audubon Ballroom. His crowds swelled, to two or three thousand some weeks. They rarely went away disappointed. Malcolm had only a provisional public philosophy in those days—not so much a single, coherent system of thought as a loosely strung set of positions that were changing even as he announced them—but he had never been in better oratorical form.

He called his new gospel black nationalism, but it was no longer the classic nationalism of territory—of repatriating to Africa or partitioning off a separate black state within America. Malcolm's nationalism, instead, was a prototype model of the doctrine we got to know two years later as Black Power, which held that the separation of the races had already happened and that, since black people weren't going to be allowed out of the ghettos, they ought to run them. Malcolm remained nominally a back-to-Africa man, but he retired the idea quickly to the middle distance and began presenting it less as a real possibility than as a strictly "philosophical" concept. "We have to be realistic and flexible," he said at one March rally at the Audubon. "Africa is a long way off and there's a lot of water in between." One of his reservations, as Malcolm himself candidly admitted, was that the return to Mother Africa was then rather a drug on the market in Harlem, at least as a literal proposition. "Millions of so-called Negroes in this country," he said, "have a distorted image of our homeland. They think Africans eat each other and live in mud huts. They've been brainwashed by the white man—why, I'll show you muddier huts in Harlem than they've got over in Africa." It would thus take considerable doing, or rather undoing, to get black people on the boats home. Malcolm spoke of educating them around to the idea by involving them in exchanges of aid and sympathy with independent black Africa—"One hand," he said hopefully, "will wash the other"—and by reminding them constantly of their lost African past. He undertook both of these efforts with a will, but he soon quit talking about the return to Africa at all.

The blacks, he said, had to live here and now; the best way for them to improve their lot in America, and to prepare for their destiny in Africa, was to achieve dominion over their own communities and their own lives. Malcolm was far less concerned with the details of how this was to be done than with persuading black people that they could do it—with showing them, that is, that they were men and women of intelligence and worth and so entirely competent to order their own affairs. His nationalism began with self-respect: "That's what black nationalism *is*—personal pride."

The outlines for action thereafter were general and beguilingly simple. "The political philosophy of black nationalism," he said, "only means that . . . the black man should control the politics of his own community. The economic philosophy only means that we should control, own and operate the businesses of our community, and thereby be in a position to create job opportunities for our own people so that they won't have to boycott and picket and beg others to give them a job. And the social philosophy of black nationalism only means that we should do what is necessary to eliminate the vices of alcoholism, drug addiction, bastard children and things of that sort that are destroying the moral fiber of our community and elevate the social standards of the community to the point where we would be more happy in our own social circles and won't be trying to force ourselves into the social circles where we're not wanted."

It was a gospel of retreat, or, as Malcolm would have preferred, retrenchment; he was arguing that black people ought to come together, throw off their dependence on and their subservience to whites and create a *de facto* black nation not unlike ours except in soul and human feeling. His radicalism directed itself only gradually and fragmentarily at the basic institutions of American democracy and American capitalism; Malcolm attacked those institutions savagely for their hypocrisies and cruelties, but he accepted them then as given and proposed that they might even be used. It took him a considerable while to get over the folk capitalism of the Nation of Islam—the notion that the pennies of the black poor could be pooled over a generation or so into an independent industrial economy. "Woolworth didn't start out big like they are today," Malcolm said. "They started out with *a* dime store." The blacks, by contrast, had allowed white people to get control of the ghetto economy and were squandering their spending money with "a man who doesn't even look like us . . . a man who, when the sun goes down, takes that basketful of money in another part of town." The only point of superiority Malcolm conceded white people was their wealth; he thought then, or argued, that the blacks could reproduce it by exploiting their $20 billion annual buying power—Malcolm never deducted the share of this Black National Product that went merely to buy survival—and by practicing the middle-class virtues of thrift, industry and continence. Black capitalism, he said, was the beginning of black independence. "It will eliminate the need for you and me to act ignorantly and disgracefully, picketing, boycotting some cracker . . . trying to beg him for a job. Any time you have to rely on your enemy for a job, you're in bad shape."

Malcolm contended as well that the white man's political system might be bent to the black man's purposes. Starting at one rally at the Rockland Palace in late March, Malcolm worked up a more or less set speech he called "The Ballot or the Bullet"; its purport was that it was almost but not quite too late for the ballot.

There was nothing whatever romantic in Malcolm's view of our politics as it existed then. He had last experienced patriotism in a civics class in Mason, Michigan, and had seen nothing in our public life since to reawaken it. He dismissed even the best efforts of American liberalism as palpable frauds. The then pending Kennedy-Johnson Civil Rights Bill, he said, was a counterfeit that would create havoc whether it passed or didn't; the whole long run of court decisions desegregating the schools was equivalent to giving the black man a paycheck he couldn't cash anywhere. "He'll *never* collect," Malcolm said. He hadn't stopped believing that for black people to demand integrated schools was to concede the inferiority of their own children; Malcolm was advocating black-run schools for black children long before "community control" came into fashion as a battle cry. His single comfort was his secure belief that integration wasn't going to happen. How was the government going to desegregate the schools of Mississippi and Alabama, he demanded, if Galamison & Co. were catching such hell just for trying in New York?

Neither did Malcolm accept the then standard apology for the failures of American liberalism—the argument that a Southern minority in Congress had slipped into the key centers of legislative power by right of seniority and so could work its racist will on everybody else. Malcolm, having been a hustler, thought he knew a hustle when he saw one; he argued that the Dixiecrats had got all that power with the secret connivance of the liberals, who needed the South to keep the Democratic Party afloat. The Southerners, he said, had come out of a system of politics in which white men voted and black men died trying; they had thrived in a Congress which, under the Constitution, ought to have expelled them but instead had rewarded them with positions of prestige and influence. This cozy arrangement, Malcolm believed, was the product of a conspiracy between the Southern white segregationist and the Northern white liberal—that man who came around Harlem once every four years "smiling and wagging his tail and telling us how much he can do for us if we vote for him" and who then betrayed Harlem the first chance he got. "You today are in the hands of a government of segregationists," he told one black audience. "Racists. White supremacists." His evidence for this was that one Southern white man occupied the Presidency—"They'll lynch you in Texas," said Malcolm, "as quick as they'll lynch you in Mississippi"—and that others held the chairmanships of ten of sixteen standing committees in the Senate and twelve of twenty in the House. "And at the same time," he scoffed, "they're going to tell you and me that the South lost the Civil War."

Malcolm's answer to this white politics of conspiracy was a black politics of independence—and still, at that stage, a politics of ballots rather than bullets. He scolded his black audiences mercilessly for having indentured themselves to the Democratic Party too long for too little. "You put them first," he said, "and they put you last. 'Cause you're a chump—a political chump." Malcolm was caught up then in the enduring dream of a third-force black politics—a cohesive bloc vote that would operate outside the two major parties and would be the balance of power in any close election. The dream had taken flesh in 1960, when John Kennedy in fact might not have won without a massive black vote, and Malcolm saw no reason why this situation couldn't be repeated—and exploited far more profitably—in elections at every level. The keys to exploiting it were the re-enfranchisement of the blacks in the South—the ballot was one issue on which Malcolm made common cause with the civil-rights movement—and the registration of a large nonaligned black electorate in the North. He was adamantly against registering black people as Democrats or Republicans, a commitment that struck him as a sellout in advance. There was a vein of political naïveté in this, since most of the real political decisions in Harlem are taken by signed-up Democrats in Democratic clubhouses and Democratic primaries; to register blacks as independents would, whatever its spiritual satisfactions, cut them out of the real electoral process. Malcolm blinked this fact of life on the platform but was less fastidious in practice. The first candidate he favored with his active support was not an independent or a third-party man but his lawyer, Percy Sutton, then a rising and more-or-less-regular Democrat; Malcolm quietly fielded nearly ninety of the brothers to slog up tenement stairs and punch doorbells in Sutton's maiden state-legislative campaign in Harlem that summer and autumn. Still, nonalignment had a kind of moral force to it—it announced to the power brokers that the blacks were no longer to be bought, sold, traded or taken for granted—and Malcolm kept on prescribing it for everything from precinct to Presidential politics. "Any minority group that is in a position to control a bloc of votes," he said, "can determine whether Lyndon Johnson will sit in the White House or whether he'll go back to the cotton patches of Texas."

Some of Malcolm's admirers cannot quite bring themselves to believe that he really meant all of this literally; their retrospective guess is that even then he despaired of finding salvation for the blacks in the electoral process and was only trying to lead them the long, hard way around to the same conclusion. "That was the whole ballots-and-bullets thing," Mrs. Dandridge told me. "I'm quite positive that Malcolm knew better at that point than to think the ballot was a way to help people. But in terms of trying to politicize people, there are certain steps that you have to take them through. And sometimes, hopefully, they may work out, even if you don't think they will. But most of the time"—she smiled thinly—"it seems like it was our bad luck for them not to work out, just like we thought to begin with." One is tempted by this theory, out of respect for Malcolm's sophistication and his deep-grained skepticism about the system. But it is equally so that he had not been to the end of the electoral road himself and had spent the past several years of his life itching to give it a try. Now that he was permitted to do something, he spoke of great wonders that might be worked with the ballot—perhaps even the first bloodless revolution in human history. The glow was no doubt partly style: Malcolm, like most public moralists, tended to paint everything in heightened colors. Yet one suspects that it was partly sheer enthusiasm as well—that old *wow! a truth!* excitement with which he embraced any fresh insight and propounded any new strategy.

Still, there was an apocalyptic undertone in his speeches and sermons of those days: Malcolm conceded only the possibility of the bloodless revolution, not its likelihood. He was rather more cautious with his language than his reputation as a fire-eater suggested; he had an almost lawyerly sense of where consciousness-heightening ended and where sedition began. "Malcolm," said Sutton, "had a marvelous ability for brinksmanship. He knew how far to escalate his rhetoric. If you start out telling people in New York to take up guns, when you get to Washington you have to *get* a gun. By the time you're in Richmond, you have to put bullets in it. And when you get to New Orleans, you have to shoot. The press will push you into that. Malcolm knew this, and he knew how far to go." Accordingly, he stopped short of advocating armed revolution.

But he described revolution, always in dire terms ("They haven't never had a bloodless revolution or a nonviolent revolution—that don't happen even in Hollywood") and often in affectionate ones. He would not be deterred from this by the odds weighing against a black revolution in a society that was nine-to-one white. "What do we care about odds?" Malcolm asked rhetorically. "Wasn't nothing nonviolent about old Pat"—Patrick Henry—"or George Washington. Liberty or death was what brought about the freedom of whites in this country from the English. *They* didn't care about the odds, and here you got 22 million Afro-Americans, black people today, catching more hell than Patrick Henry ever saw." Neither ought the blacks be unduly frightened of revolution simply because whitey had The Bomb. "It's useless," Malcolm said, as the Third World discovered in its wars of independence. "They put some guerrilla action on him, and a white man can't fight a guerrilla warfare. Guerrilla action takes heart, takes nerve, and he doesn't have that. . . . You take that little man from Africa and Asia, turn him loose in the woods with a blade—that's all he needs. All he needs is a blade and when the sun goes down and it's dark, it's even Stephen."

Malcolm's revolution was distant and abstract, more pep talk than battle plan; but it blurred at the edges into his call for rifles and rifle clubs right now, and the reaction in the press and the civil-rights movement was instant and furious. Malcolm on guns was even more cautious than Malcolm on revolution—surprisingly so for a man who seemed beyond caution on a public platform. He sought out legal guidance before he ever got onto the subject at all. The advice of counsel was that he neither carry a gun himself nor urge any specific person to get one, and Malcolm never did; instead, when people raised the question outside his own circle, he would dip into his wallet, pull out a dog-eared card and read from Article II of the Bill of Rights: ". . . the right of the people to keep and bear arms, shall not be infringed." Occasionally, confronted with some fresh atrocity out of the South and with the professed helplessness of the government to do anything, he spoke of a bloody revenge and may in fact have yearned to be a part of it. "The Negroes should not wait for white investigators," he told one interviewer. "They should find the guilty ones themselves and execute them on the spot." But more often he found himself explaining half-defensively what he *hadn't* said. "I wasn't advocating that Negroes go out and buy rifles and become involved in some kind of militia designed to initiate acts of aggression," he announced on one radio panel. " . . . I've never said go out and initiate acts of violence or acts of aggression—only to defend. And I also pointed out that this was necessary only in instances and in areas where the government itself has failed to protect the Negro.

Actually, the burden is on the government. If the government doesn't want Negroes buying rifles, then let the government do its job."

Even so, the mere fact that Malcolm had raised the subject at his breakaway press conference gave guns a kind of priority in his politics that he may or may not have fully intended but that he was stuck with for the rest of his life. The irony was that Malcolm, having once lived by the gun, was uncomfortable having guns around; one senses that he understood too well that they exist to go off. He was in a cab in Chicago once with James 67X and Kenyatta, riding from Irv Kupcinet's TV studio to the airport and talking happily about the show he had just done. It had been a particularly successful one, a discussion with U.S. Senator Paul Douglas, and afterward they had heard Douglas telling someone that Malcolm had one of the most brilliant minds he had ever encountered. All of them had felt flattered. They hardly noticed at first when their driver swung off down an unfamiliar back way. But they popped awake as the streets got darker and the route twistier. "You going right?" Malcolm asked. The cabbie, a black man, grunted and drove on. The three of them exchanged glances. Kenyatta closed his hand around a pistol in his pocket. The route turned out to be a shortcut; the cab deposited them safely at the airport and they caught their plane home. Later, when they were alone, Kenyatta fished out his gun and showed it to Malcolm. "Believing in Allah is one thing," he said, "but I believe in this. I had my finger on the trigger all the way." Malcolm's eyes widened for a moment; then he forced a laugh.

Even later, with his life in real and constant danger, he had to be talked into getting a rifle. Once he posed for pictures, peering out the front blinds of his home, with the gun on his hip. The photos were like stills out of *The Battle of Algiers*; Malcolm posed for them, one guesses, precisely for melodramatic effect, as a deterrent to his enemies. His new public reputation as the prophet armed had a similar value at first; it was only later that it began to frighten away potential friends as well, and at that point his original purpose was lost. Malcolm had advocated storing up guns because black people were being clubbed, bitten, hosed and killed in the South for asserting the most trivial rights; because the recognized Negro leadership of the day was encouraging them to suffer this without reprisal or even defense; because the government had too many correct and heartless reasons why it could not intervene; and most of all because he considered America quite beyond the reach of appeals to conscience or humanity and so susceptible only to threat. "Whites," he told me that March afternoon in the back room at Michaux's, "will never correct the problem on moral, legal or ethical reasons. But they're realists enough to know that they don't want Negroes running around with rifles."

He thought we might bend at the threat of embarrassment as well, and he sensed a perfect theater for our humiliation no farther away than the United Nations. Malcolm by then had made a considerable circle of friends among the Arab and African delegations, notably the militants from Tanzania, Zambia and Kenya. He had become a regular visitor, teetotaling at the delegate parties* and gossiping in the delegate lounge. He had been a distant but interested spectator when a group of American blacks put on a clamorous demonstration there in 1961 over the slaying of Patrice Lumumba; Malcolm, who was commonly blamed for the outburst, actually turned down an invitation to join the demonstrators—he was still under Mr. Muhammad's restraining hand—but he sent his respects and his sympathy. He was positively entranced by the arithmetic of the General Assembly, where, since Bandung, the dark majority of the world had become a voting majority of the world's nations. The cynicism of the street seemed to desert Malcolm in UN Plaza; he took that majority to be a locus of real power, or at least great psychological leverage, and he wanted desperately to identify the American black nation with it.

This meant rewriting the entire vocabulary of race relations in

*Malcolm was pained by the sight of the Africans sipping martinis at these occasions, though he was of course too much a gentleman to say so outside the company of Muslim brothers who shared his own abstemious ways. Malcolm wanted the Africans to fit his idealized image of them; to the extent that they imitated our bad habits, they disappointed him.

America. It meant creating a new national allegiance based on one's color, not on the accident of one's birthplace. "We're not Americans," Malcolm said at a Harlem rally that spring, "we're Africans who happen to be in America. We were kidnaped and brought here against our will from Africa. We didn't land on Plymouth Rock—that rock landed on us." It meant forgetting about *civil* rights, which were America's to grant or withhold, and recasting the movement as a struggle for *human* rights, which belonged inalienably to everybody everywhere. Malcolm, as a man of words, believed that one could alter reality by changing the terms with which one described realities. "When you are begging for civil rights," he said, "you're putting it in Uncle Sam's lap. You're taking it to Uncle Sam's courts. You're taking the criminal to the criminal—asking the criminal to solve the crime. Whereas, when you're attacking this thing at the level of human rights, you can take it to the United Nations. You can take Uncle Sam, the one who's really guilty, to the UN and accuse him or charge him with violating the UN Charter on Human Rights."

To bring the plight of the blacks before the nations of the world —to rattle their chains where all mankind could hear—became the informing dream of Malcolm's life over the next several months. Some of his friends tried to persuade him that he was wasting his time—that the very best he could hope for was a propaganda victory and that even this was unlikely given the power of the Yankee dollar in the politics of the United Nations. But Malcolm pressed on. He asked Dan Watts, who knew his way around the UN, how one went about getting a genocide case before the Commission on Human Rights. Watts asked around, with largely discouraging results; he discovered, among other things, that the Commission was less a functioning investigative body than a letterhead for documents and statements and that his African connections were sympathetic only to a point anyway. "They'd say, 'Oh, good brother, you can count on us,' but they weren't about to do anything," Watts told me. "I passed this on to Malcolm, but it didn't seem to bother him." Watts went away exasperated; Malcolm got somebody else to work on the project.

He argued, out of that furious logic, that the blacks in America were as entitled to the notice of the UN as the blacks in South Africa and Angola and that once they got their case on the docket, "some kind of meaningful results" would follow. He was unclear as to what these meaningful results would be but not as to the justice of the indictment. "Here he is standing up . . . Uncle Sam . . . with the blood dripping down his jaws like a bloody-jawed wolf and still got the nerve to point his fingers at other countries," cried Malcolm. Sam was the criminal, his crimes compounded by his hypocrisies; America, founded on the proposition that all men were created equal, was still debating two hundred years later whether that proposition really included the blacks as men.

Malcolm understood that the attention of the UN one afternoon did not mean that the massed armies of the Third World would land in New York and Los Angeles the next morning to deliver the blacks. He believed for a time that he really could bring off his UN venture, but he knew even then he was dealing in symbolic action. His objective was to expose whites to themselves and to black people as a minority in the world—a minority temporarily in power but irrevocably in decline. For blacks to see the white man in this new light was to recognize that he was vulnerable after all and that, much as the present might be his property, the future belonged to them. A black man so informed, said Malcolm, "doesn't beg. He doesn't thank you for what you give him, because you are only giving him what he should have had a hundred years ago. He doesn't think you are doing him any favors." And for whites to see blacks who didn't beg or say thank you, Malcolm believed, was to recognize them at last as men and potentially enemies. He thought that this discovery might even shock white America into action.

He was optimistic about the UN enterprise, as he was about anything new he undertook. But he was full of brooding, cataclysmic gloom about our future together. The black struggle as most of us saw it in those days was that continuing otherworldly war against Jim Crow in the South—a war between a dying white order and a few score black preachers and black students who read Camus and praised God and said you could get your freedom if you had the courage to stand in the bright sun and cast a sharp shadow. Martin Luther King had taken his crusade on to St. Augustine, Florida; SNCC and CORE were heavily involved organizing something they called Freedom Summer—a campaign they hoped would turn Mississippi into Spain for a whole new generation of white college kids. The poetry of it was not for Malcolm; he once confessed that he had never really liked freedom songs. He saw only the portents of disaster—that one-night uprising of the unwashed in Birmingham, a bunch of black kids winging rocks at the police in Cleveland, a premonitory few Molotov cocktails setting the night afire in Jacksonville. Each was in itself a trivial episode, lost in the headlines that mostly followed King, but Malcolm knew what they portended. The discontents of the blacks who had already arrived in the promised land—the big-city ghettos far distant from King and his dreams—had been accumulating unseen and unabated and had now reached the flashpoint. "They're fed up," Malcolm said. "They've become disenchanted. They've become disillusioned. They've become dissatisfied." The casbah was restless, he told us, and was about to blow up— "and when a racial powder keg goes off, it doesn't care *who* it knocks out the way."

19. A Declaration of War

On March 10, 1964, two days after Malcolm first announced his break with the Nation of Islam and two days before his formal declaration of independence, the Nation quietly sent him a certified letter announcing that it would like its house in East Elmhurst back and requesting that he and his family move out forthwith. A month later, with only the scantiest attention in the press, Maceo X, as secretary of Muhammad's Mosque of Islam No. 7 in

Harlem, filed suit in civil court in Queens to have Malcolm evicted. The elders of the Nation, being men of affairs, saw these actions as matters of simple equity. Malcolm, who had served and enriched the Nation over a dozen years and who owned nothing, read them as a declaration of war.

20. A Pilgrim's Progress

Malcolm came out of the Nation of the Lost-Founds still preaching the blackness of God and the whiteness of the devil—and seeing with a deepening clarity how little this had to do with true Islam. Allah, whatever He may have told Mr. Muhammad about the colors of good and evil, had not shared this particular wisdom with His half-billion followers in the East; they include every shade under the sun and are absolutely insistent on the irrelevance of race in the sight of God. Malcolm had known this for some time, though he sometimes professed not to, and so had the brothers who did their homework in his catchall "public-speaking" classes: he in his travels and they in their reading had discovered that there were in fact White Muslims somewhere out there.

They lived with this knowledge for years by ignoring it—by telling outsiders, and themselves, that Allah had made a special case of the so-called American Negroes and had sent them a Messenger and a message of their own. "There is no racism in Islam," Benjamin Goodman agreed, "but you can't take Islam as it is practiced in the Middle East and transplant it to America. When you're speaking to people who are mentally dead, you've got to have something strong." Malcolm accordingly preached the gospel according to Elijah Muhammad; when the followers of the original Prophet Muhammad complained of his heresies, Malcolm replied tartly that *his* Muhammad had brought "hundreds of thousands" of American blacks to Allah while all the orthodox Muslims put together had managed fewer than a thousand Stateside conversions.

He did not vary the Muhammad message significantly in his first weeks on his own—not where anybody could hear him. One guesses that by then the devilishness of white people had become less an article of faith than a principle of politics for him, but, in the pulpit, he continued teaching it as the gospel truth. The only concession forthcoming out of his new flexibility was the wispy possibility of cooperation between blacks and well-meaning whites, but not yet—the blacks had first to coalesce around their blackness and their common oppression—and not in one another's company. The best thing whites could do, said Malcolm, was to stay out of the black man's sight—"Make him help himself"—and attack the system from within, among their own kind. He didn't expect many to volunteer. He doubted that most whites were capable of feeling guilt about the condition of black people; he believed that those few who could were most often driven by it to get next to Negroes—to join their organizations, dilute their blackness and subvert their independence. He was merciless about the presence of white people on the boards of all the major civil-rights organizations; the blacks in those organizations valued the whites as points of access to sympathy, money and power, but Malcolm saw them as enemy agents.

There remained the alternative possibility of alliance with whites like John Brown, though Malcolm expected even fewer volunteers of his sort; it meant you had to be ready to kill or die for black people. Merely to die was not enough. That spring, a young white minister, Bruce Klunder, was crushed under a bulldozer during a CORE lie-in on a muddy construction site in Cleveland. Malcolm, who was in Cleveland at the time, may have been touched by Klunder's death but was angered by the headlines: the white press, it seemed to him, never broke out type that big for black martyrs. He went back to New York still simmering and, next night, kept a speaking date before the Militant Labor Forum, a regular affair put on by the Trotskyist Socialist Workers Party.* During the question-and-answer period, a liberal in the audience confronted him with Klunder's sacrifice. "We're not going to stand up and applaud any contribution made by some individual white person," Malcolm retorted hotly, "when 22 million black people are dying every day. What he did—good, good, great. What he did—good. Hooray, hooray, hooray. Now Lumumba was murdered, Medgar Evers was murdered, Mack Parker was murdered, Emmett Till was murdered, my own father was murdered. You tell that stuff to someone else. It's time some white people started dying in this thing."

Still, when he departed the Nation, Malcolm left some of his certainties behind; the White Question was no longer quite so simple for him as it had been in the days when Yacub's History answered all one's questions about the origin of species. Even then, Malcolm knew from his almost daily encounters with whites that they were not nearly so terrifying an enemy as Satan. He had, moreover, to deal with the awkward and heretical discovery that there were a few devils he respected and a very few he even liked. Mike Handler of the *Times* was one of these—a blunt, worldly man who seemed to Malcolm to have survived being white with none of the usual prejudices or sentimentalities about black people. Charles Silberman of *Fortune* was another; Malcolm admired his book *Crisis in Black and White*, and, when one black scholar gave it a sour notice in the *Times*, he called Silberman to see if there wasn't something he could do. He was incurably admiring of radio talk-show hosts: they gave him air time, microphones and leading questions—a level of generosity one hardly expected from the devil—and he repaid them by crediting them with intelligence.

Most of all, Malcolm was drawn to the white young—the student generation he met in his travels as one of the two or three pre-

*The Socialist Workers, trendiest of America's Old Left parties, saw Malcolm's potential as a mass leader while he was still in the Nation and were eager for a liaison with him after the break. Malcolm accepted their hospitality. Whatever he thought of their color (mostly white) or their politics (revolutionary socialist) at that point in his career, he was grateful for a platform downtown.

eminent free-lance university lecturers of his day. He liked their openness, their questions, even their arguments; he saw in them, as he once put it, "a sense of collective guilt and rebelliousness against their parents" for the sorry state of American race relations. One day, Kenneth Clark and his wife took a little group of high-school students, most of them white, to see Malcolm in Harlem. They found a clutch of reporters already there, and Mrs. Clark, feeling their business with Malcolm suddenly trivial, told him: "We'll wait." But Malcolm said no—"The important thing is these kids"—and showed them to the head of the line. "He said the reporters could wait," Clark remembered. "He didn't see a difference between white kids and *kids.*"

To have reached a point where one lost sight of color was, for a Black Muslim, to have sunk in error. Malcolm understood this and resisted the consequences as long as he could; he clung to the letter of his faith, in the classic way of priests in doubt, and dealt with his heretical tendencies by repressing them. But his last years in the Nation had eroded his belief, and his exile freed him from the necessity of believing. He was drifting free, open and light-sensitive and susceptible. He remained a religious man, a true believer cut loose from one system of faith and looking for another that would more nearly suit his experience of the world and would offer him religious legitimacy as well. He sought it in true Islam. Some orthodox Muslims in America remembered their quarrels and were suspicious of Malcolm even after he renounced the Nation. But others welcomed him out of the fold, and some of them suggested that he go see Dr. Mahmoud Youssef Shawarbi.

Shawarbi, then forty-two, was an Egyptian learned in Islam—a professor of soil science, normally, at the University of Cairo but at the time on leave to direct the Islamic Center of New York. Malcolm had been hearing his name around for a while and had once been introduced to him by a reporter. But he put off paying a call until after he was out of the Nation and could meet him as pupil to teacher rather than as heretic to priest. Malcolm finally did visit him in March, appearing one day at Shawarbi's third-floor office in a graystone building at the foot of Riverside Drive. He told Shawarbi he was a Muslim and believed in Allah. He said: "I want to learn about the real Islam."

It was, given Malcolm's disciplined calm, an extraordinarily emotional encounter. Shawarbi liked him immediately—"He was," the professor said, "a thorough gentleman, full of glamour and humor"—but was dismayed by his cultish visions of God and the devil. The first thing to know about Islam, he told Malcolm, was that it is a religion of peace and love. He got down his Qur'an, flipped it open and read Malcolm a verse, which Shawarbi translated: "Muslims are all brothers regardless of their color and race." It was elementary stuff, and Malcolm surely knew it by then. But, as Shawarbi recalled the scene, Malcolm jumped to his feet and asked him to repeat the reading. He did, and suddenly, standing there, Malcolm was shivering and weeping.

The tutorials continued over several weeks, Malcolm railing nightly against the devil and slipping downtown days when he could squeeze an hour out of his schedule to meet with Shawarbi. One day early on he brought along a tape recorder and asked the professor to read some verses from the Qur'an into it. Shawarbi did, choosing, among other readings, some verses about the enormous regard of Islam for education. One of these said that a scientist was of greater benefit to the world than a martyr's blood; Malcolm, who believed in learning and expected martyrdom, seemed powerfully moved. Shawarbi read him other scriptures about the democracy of Islam—"You are all," says the Qur'an, "the rulers and the ruled"—and lectured him at length about its colorblindness. He told Malcolm that sometimes Arab Muslims consider themselves first among equals, since the Prophet Muhammad was an Arab, but that Allah recognized no such distinction—that He would judge men solely by their deeds. Once again Malcolm seemed affected.

Some orthodox Muslims remained suspicious of Malcolm's motives and were unhappy with the time and authenticity Shawarbi was granting him. Shawarbi in effect held the keys to Mecca—the Saudi Arabian government required a letter from him certifying any American Muslim attempting to make the obligatory hajj, or pilgrimage, to the Holy City—and skeptics in the Islamic community felt that Malcolm might be faking conversion in a play for recognition as *the* legitimate Muslim minister to black America. The principal difference was that Shawarbi had seen Malcolm's progress in Islam at first hand and they hadn't. The professor had been touched by Malcolm's tearful receipt of the faith and was in fact eager that he make the hajj and experience the classlessness of Islam for himself at its most sacred shrines. He urged the journey on Malcolm; so did some non-Muslim friends.

Malcolm responded eagerly. He was back to living on the proceeds of his collections and his lecture fees and was as usual nearly broke. But his half-sister Ella lent him the money—she had been saving up for her own hajj—and he booked a single seat via Frankfurt to Cairo and Jedda. Shawarbi gave him the required letter and put in a discreet call to the Saudi Arabian Embassy to smooth the way. Malcolm packed his suitcase and his cameras, told a few of the brothers he would be gone no more than three weeks—the trip as it developed, ran nearly to six—and, on April 13, took off to discover the faith he had followed for a dozen years.

He spent a couple of days in Cairo being a tourist—the things that impressed him enough to write home about were not the monuments but the schools, the highways and the automobile factories—and a few more days in Jedda feeling gawky and tongue-tied among the pilgrims while the hajj authorities mulled over his unconventional history in the faith. He was billeted briefly in an airport dormitory and became a point of interest among the faithful; some of them, he learned later, had heard that he was an American Muslim and guessed that he must be Muhammad Ali. The whole adventure was beginning to look chancy when Malcolm finally made connections with a powerful Saudi family—a White Muslim family at that. They retrieved him from the airport, put him up in their suite at the Jedda Palace and left him happily holding court in the hotel lobby while they helped get him on the way to Mecca.

Malcolm was well conditioned by his reading, his travels and his conversations with Dr. Shawarbi for what he found there. But it struck him still with something like the force of revelation—one of those sudden, impulsive, flare-in-the-night recognitions that he trusted and by which he had ordered and reordered his life. "I think that the pilgrimage to Mecca broadened my scope probably more in twelve days than my previous experience during my thirty-nine years on this earth," he said when he got home. "I am a man who has tried to train myself to face certain facts whether they are pleasant or unpleasant. And many of the things that I experienced, that I witnessed, and many of the people that I conversed with, I don't know whether or not they *changed* my mind, but I must say they did *broaden* my mind. They broadened my scope. They broadened my outlook."

What had happened was that, just as Shawarbi anticipated, he had seen and immersed himself in the leveling democracy of the hajj. The pilgrims had all dressed alike, Malcolm loping tall among them with his long, copper-brown legs poking out of a snowy loincloth; had all followed the course the Prophet walked thirteen centuries before and had cried after him, *I come, O Lord;* had all made the ritual circuit of the holy places of Mecca, Muzdalifa and Mina; had all prostrated themselves, equal in their humility before God; had all cast the traditional seven stones at a devil who had no color. The beauty of it struck Malcolm standing outside his hotel in Mina one day, chatting with a Turkish MP who had befriended him. "This would be an anthropologist's paradise," the Turk said, gesturing at the swarm of pilgrims. "Every specimen of humanity is brought together at Mecca during this pilgrimage. It's probably the only incident and the only time and the only place on earth where you can find every specimen of humanity—all cultures, all races, all shades, all of everything." Malcolm was stirred by the sight, and the thought. "Where our people in this country are concerned," he said, "almost anything we look at, without realizing it, the yardstick that we use subconsciously always has something to do with color. Most Afro-Americans are this way. And it's natural for us to be this way because our entire life is governed by color—the racial ingredient is there." Malcolm felt suddenly free of this necessity in Mina; he discovered that he did not miss it.

That same afternoon, the pilgrims moved on to Mount Arafat and assembled in a huge tent there; Malcolm naturally used the time between devotions to educate any of the pilgrims who understood English and would listen on the agonies of race in America, but even as he spoke he was seeing things he had never seen before. "Right present in that group," he said, "was every shade, every complexion, every type of color. There were Chinese, Indonesians, people from Afghanistan, Persia; there was one Russian and his wife, who were very white; there were some Nigerians and some Ghanaians. And all of these were under the same tent. And in this religious pilgrimage you eat with your hands—everyone eats from the same plate—so this involved me in a situation where I was eating from the same plate with people who in this country would be considered white. I found myself drinking from the same glass, and sleeping on the same cot, and praying on the same rug with people who in this country would definitely be classified as white people."

Malcolm could hardly credit his senses; he had trouble sorting out whether he was more surprised by the brotherly assembly of peoples or by his own unself-conscious participation in it. "To me," he recounted later, "a white man had always been a *white man*—this was my blanket classification. But I had to finally reach the conclusion that the thing that made them different there was the fact that they had accepted the oneness of God, and in accepting the oneness of God, their intelligence demanded that they also accept the oneness of humanity. They didn't judge people according to color. Their attitude toward the differences in complexion was the same attitude that one might have toward the differences in the size of the fingers on his hand. The different sizes were needed to make up the whole hand. And these different complexions were needed to make the human family complete—to give it variety and give it beauty. When one of them would say he was white, he had a different connotation and a different meaning. It was my experience that here in America, when a white man says he's white, usually the weight of his voice or the weight of his words, the impression that the nonwhite person gets is that *he means more than color.*"

Malcolm was full of his discovery and his wakening faith in the Islam of the East. He made his daily obeisances to Allah and sat up nights excitedly writing home about the oneness of men before Him. As always the drummer for God, he was typically unhappy that the elders of the faith had not adequately advertised the pageantry and democracy of the hajj to the world; he thought, just as he had in his earliest days in Mr. Muhammad's service, that conversions could be doubled or tripled with the application of modern sales techniques. He bought up picture postcards of the Great Mosque and the pilgrims on Arafat and sent them to friends, followers, even casual acquaintances—practically everyone black he knew. His style, confronted with a postcard, turned half American tourist and half Muslim novitiate, all exclamations and underlinings and wish-you-were-here enthusiasm. "I have just visited the Holy City of Mecca," he wrote James Farmer, "and witnessed pilgrims *of all colors,* from every part of this earth, displaying a spirit of unity and brotherhood like I've never witnessed during my entire life in America. It is truly a wonderful sight to behold."

The cards suggested only elliptically the changes Malcolm was going through; friends were puzzled by them and put them away for elucidation when he came home. But he sent a few longer, more intimate letters to his family, his inner circle of associates and finally to Handler for publication to the world. He wrote how, in the hajj, he had been thrown together with "some of the earth's most powerful kings, cabinet members, potentates and other forms of political and religious rulers—but also with fellow-Muslims whose skin was the whitest of white, whose eyes were the bluest of blue, and whose hair was the blondest of blond." For the first time in his life, he said, he did not see them as white men at all, because he had looked into their faces and had seen that they didn't regard themselves as white.

Seeing this, he said, "has forced me to 'rearrange' much of my own thought-pattern, and to toss aside some of my previous conclusions." This rearrangement did not apply to white America—not, in any event, to white Judeo-Christian America. The colorblindness Malcolm witnessed among whites on the hajj seemed to him specifically and exclusively a property of Islam; color, he wrote, "ceases to be a determining factor of a man's worth or value once he becomes a Muslim." White Americans, by contrast, practiced "conscious racism" and had created a reflexive antiwhite animus among the blacks—an animus which he had shared and would not now apologize for. The single hope he saw was that what had just happened to him might someday happen to whites. "If white Americans would accept the religion of Islam," he said, "if they would accept the Oneness of God (Allah), then they could also sincerely accept the Oneness of Man. . . . As America's insane obsession with racism leads her up the suicidal path, nearer and nearer to the precipice that leads to the bottomless pits below, I do believe that their own young, less hampered intellectually, will see the 'handwriting on the wall' and turn for spiritual salvation to the religion of Islam and force the older generation of American whites to turn with them."

What Malcolm thus offered white Americans was not absolution or even pity but fantasy—the convert's starry dream of an entire nation now lost in sin being led to Allah by its own children. His letter home was the occasion of some quiet rejoicing among liberal whites, who found in it the possibility of their personal exoneration from Malcolm's frightening judgment. The celebration was premature; the prodigal had come home but not to white people. All Malcolm saw in Mecca, and all his various messages conceded, was the humanity of white people, nothing more. A white person, if he was capable of brotherhood with blacks, could not after all be the devil. But, in Malcolm's sight, white people in America remained guilty of a collective and historic devilishness toward the blacks, and they would stand so judged collectively until that millennial hour when they received Islam.

Even this modest breach of faith with his past was the source of great anxiety among Malcolm's constituents back home; the white man's celebration, for some of them, was the black man's wake. "There's a segment among my brothers and sisters who would rather feed on hate than have a three-inch steak," Dan Watts observed. Those who had followed Malcolm in and out of the Mosque assumed that he shared this appetite. The message from Mecca particularly disturbed the Old Muslims who had left the Nation with him, sometimes with considerable pain, and who made up the cadre he depended on to keep things going back home. Benjamin Goodman thought that Malcolm in Mecca had been like a married man looking at pretty girls in mini-skirts in the street; you felt loyal sexually to your wife, but if you responded to those flashing thighs, something important was lost. "Malcolm compromised," he said, and compromise put a strain on their relationship from which it never quite recovered. Kenyatta, too, was disconcerted, although, out of his dogged personal loyalty, he was willing to follow Malcolm anywhere. "That letter he sent back, when he was up on the mountain and he ate with whites out of the same bowl—why, the average black in this country *lives* on hatred," he said. "Good gracious, they had been told for twelve years that the white man was the devil, and then you turn around and say some of them was *different?*"

Some black spectators who were not so personally involved guess that Malcolm's transformation in Mecca was as much political as religious—that he had known when he left home that he needed to broaden his base and had seen the opportunity in the hajj to begin remaking his image accordingly. Kenneth Clark for one believed that Malcolm had always been a compassionate man and that now—"not necessarily with guile"—he was trying to work the appearance of compassion into his public persona. "He had to have a bridge back from the extreme positions and the rigidities of his days with Muhammad," Clark thought, and Mecca gave him an opportunity to display to the world a vein of humanity that had always been there.

His image no doubt did figure in the reconstruction of Malcolm X; he wanted legitimacy and respect, not just as a matter of pride but as a means of reaching a wider black audience than the Black

Eve Arnold—Magnum

The old glory: Malcolm X at a Black Muslim rally, 1961

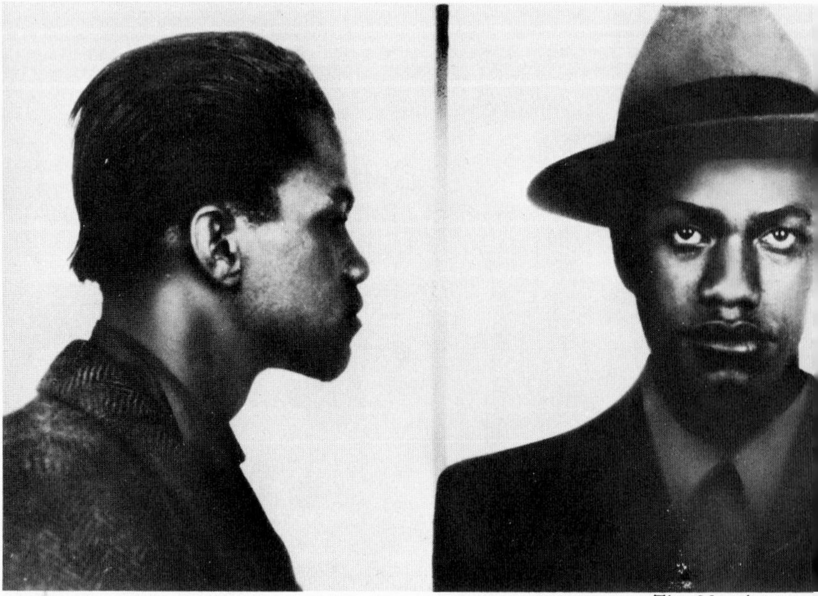

Time Magazine

The hustler: A police mug shot, 1944

Richard Saunders from Pictorial

The word: Teaching etymology in the Harlem mosque (above) and the sisters at a Muslim rally

Eve Arnold—Magnum

Eve Arnold—Magnum

The man who knew God: Elijah Muhammad and his star pupil

Eve Arnold—Magnum

Wide World

Don Hogan Charles, *Ebony*

After the split: A prankish meeting with Dr. King, an informal lecture to the faithful, a curbside audience (Charles Kenyatta, second from right)

Don Hogan Charles, *Ebony*

Don Hogan Charles, *Ebony*

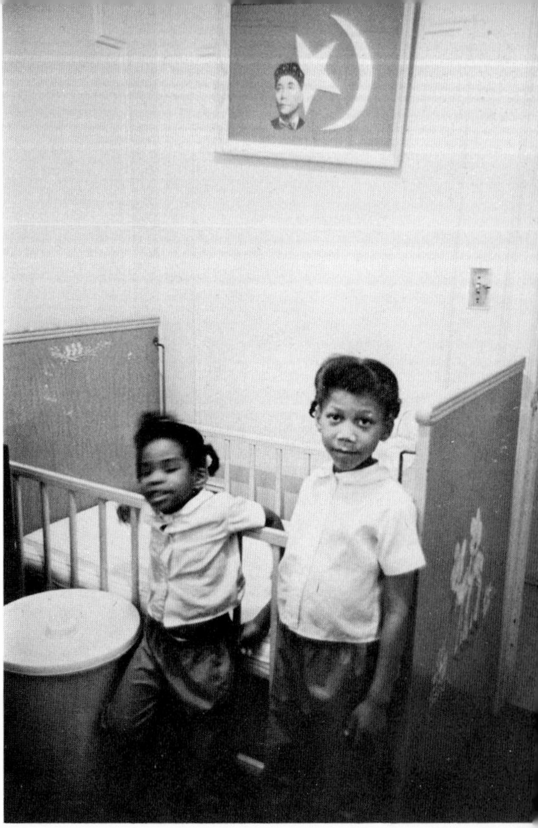

The family: Two of Malcolm's daughters, and Sister Betty after the birth of the fourth, July 1964

Don Hogan Charles, *Ebony*

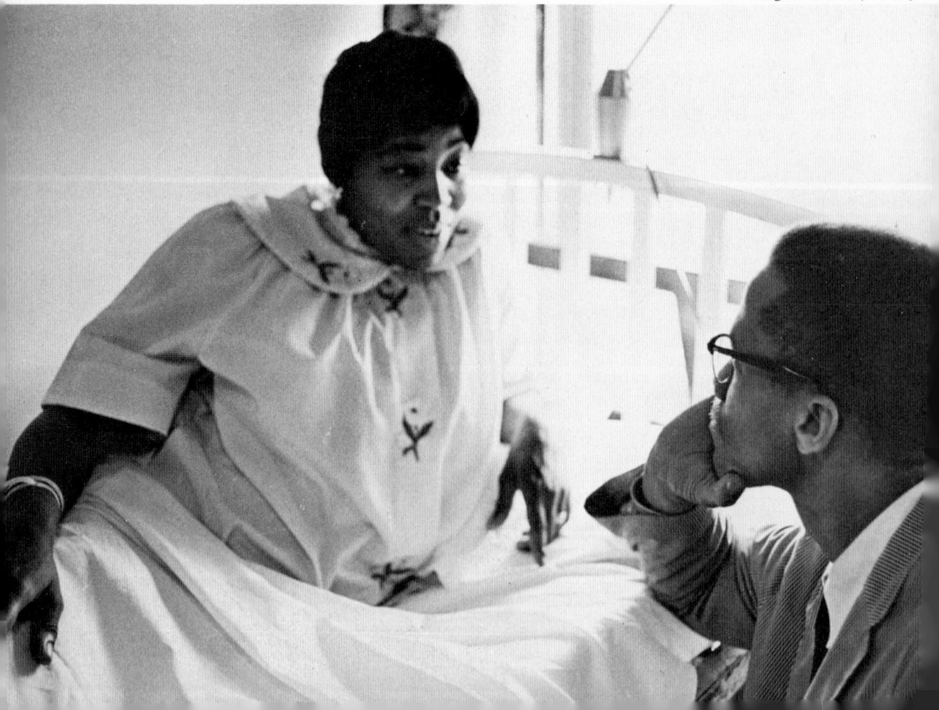

Don Hogan Charles, *Ebony*

The house: A moment's relaxation, and a tense vigil with a gun Malcolm didn't really want

Don Hogan Charles, *Ebony*

John Launois from Black Star

The pilgrim: Kneeling in prayer in Cairo, 1964

Muslims with their exoticism and their bad notices ever had. As a salesman, Malcolm knew you couldn't make a sale unless you first got the customers under the tent. Yet to fix on what might have been calculated in his pilgrimage was to miss what was surely spontaneous. The discovery that whites were the devil had been a sudden revelation; the realization that they were not was more gradual—a wave of recognition that had been welling to a crest for months before Mecca—but still had the force of spontaneity and surprise. The change, moreover, was an incomplete one: he had, just as he said, broadened his scope and opened his mind but had not abandoned his war. He may in fact have hoped that his letter home would improve his press and his chances for coalition with the respectable black movement—or even, at some point still blurry in the distance, with certain committed whites. While Malcolm was still abroad, he had James 67X write a conciliatory letter to various integrationist leaders mentioning his "new position" after the hajj and praying that it would be "attractive to you"—attractive enough to bring them together with him in a united front. But Malcolm still needed his past and the people in it, and he could not bring himself to a total break with it—not on the moving but fragmentary evidence of Mecca alone. "A man who has a religious commitment to an ideology just doesn't tomorrow flip like a damn pancake," Eric Lincoln insisted. "Malcolm after a time may have come to a new ideological position concerning white people, but it could not happen *in toto* overnight. What he felt was too deep, and none of the motivations for his feelings had been removed."

He was Malcom X, the Black Muslim, when he set out on the hajj, a pilgrim with barely acceptable credentials for the pilgrimage. When he left, he was El-Hajj Malik El-Shabazz, an accredited Sunni Muslim, a novice in the largest single sect in Islam. He had done far more than shuffle names and religious affiliations. He had achieved the security of belief without the costs of belief exacted by Mr. Muhammad; he had identified himself more closely than ever with the Muslim seventh and the nonwhite majority of the world; he had even squared with his conscience the uncomforte fact that there were possibly a half-dozen or so white journal- and a generation of white college kids that he actually rather liked. But Mecca did not alter his politics or his conviction that most white Americans and all white American institutions were hopelessly racist. The chief difference after the hajj was that white people were evil *de facto* rather than *de jure.* Malcolm in a sense buried the devil in Mecca. Thereafter, whites were merely his enemy.

21. The Child Has Come Home

"For Malcolm," said Maya Angelou, who saw him in Ghana that spring, "Africa was a promise." He went on from Mecca to the mother continent with clear political purposes in mind: he wanted to establish diplomatic ties between the black nations of Africa and the black nation back home, and he hoped specifically to line up sponsors to take the case of the American Negro before the United Nations. The dream, as one friend paraphrased it, was so to involve the Africans that, if the white man stepped on a black foot in Harlem, they would say, "Ouch! That's *our* foot!" Malcolm did his homework, consulting his UN contacts for advice before he left; he even took tutorials in a midtown hotel from an American relation of Kwame Nkrumah's, who helped him put together an itinerary and briefed him on each country down to the finest details of what would be ingratiating for a visiting black American to say.

But none of this prepared him for the emotional bath of the homecoming. He moved with a dazzling ease among men of power and affairs, as though he had been doing it all his life; Africa's rulers impressed Malcolm, but it was Africa itself that enthralled him. He hopped from capital to capital across the north and west, alone and, to the dismay of friends and admirers he saw along the way, unguarded. His itinerary stretched and unraveled as he went. He would materialize at an airport, tall, sun-reddened and beginning a goatee, lugging his own bags and cameras; if no one was there to meet him, he would fish out his address book and call somebody. Once he made connections, Miss Angelou remembered, "he wanted to look at everything. He never wanted to be driven anywhere fast—and we were always rushing so." He took pictures and home movies as obsessively as any tourist, explaining half-apologetically that he could use the films and slide-shows back home to raise some money and pay for his trip. "He had a lot of cameras that I wound up carrying from place to place," the writer Julian Mayfield, another of Malcolm's hosts in Ghana, recalled with wry amusement. "He took pictures everywhere. He was a lousy photographer." He wanted to drink it all in—the sights, the sounds, the politics, the gossip, the *blackness* of it—and freeze it all on film and then sit up talking about it into the small hours every morning. "I got the feeling that he always knew intellectually that Africa existed," Miss Angelou said, "but on that visit he got to know it emotionally. The smell of the earth in Africa is heady to a black person." Malcolm couldn't get enough of it, nor Africa enough of him. In Nigeria, a student association gave him yet another new name, Alhadji Omowale Malcolm X. Omowale, in Yoruba, means "the child has come home."

Malcolm's reception in political Africa was uniformly fascinated and friendly in tone but uneven in consequence: the old anticolonial revolutionaries loved him, but some of those who had already got hold of governments received him with the caution of men for whom a simple politics of race had become a luxury as against the requirements of survival in a world still dominated by whites. The out-of-power radicals and the liberation underground adored Malcolm; so, most of all, did the students. Their affection was foreshadowed in Beirut, at the beginning of the grand tour, where he worked a largely Sudanese Muslim student audience into a passion that looked riotous to white spectators but which Malcolm recognized as love. "Was no riot there," he smiled afterward. There nearly was at his next stop, Nigeria, where he spoke at the University of Ibadan. The press there, in contrast to his other stopping places, virtually ignored him, and the U.S. Information Agency had got the word around that he was regarded back home as a hatemonger. A standing-room-only student crowd turned out anyway and very nearly tore Trenchard Hall down. Malcolm denounced the U.S. government, laughed at its claims of progress and denied that he taught hate or needed to. "Any American Negro who still does not hate the white man after all the white man has done to him in America could never be taught to hate the white man, and I wouldn't waste my time trying." Afterward, during the question period, a black faculty member took the microphone and called Malcolm's furious stress on the past and the crime of slavery "fundamentally dishonest." A muttering welled up in the audience, then shouts. A dozen students rushed the stage, grabbed the mike and milled around until the dissenter stood down. Afterward, some of them flocked to the USIA headquarters and ringed it, but the police had got there first and nothing happened.

Ghana was the best. Ghana was to Malcolm's developing politics what Mecca was to his faith: it was the home of the Redeemer, Kwame Nkrumah, and the fountainhead of Pan-Africanism—the dream of a united and powerful mother continent and a world community of the children of Africa wherever they happened to be. W. E. B. DuBois had lived there and had taken Ghanaian citizenship; he died the year before Malcolm arrived, but his widow survived in a kind of resident sainthood and a small but talented colony of American black expatriates had grown up in his train. The leader of this colony was Mayfield, a large, dark and many-gifted man who was then in his second exile from home—he spent the first in Puerto Rico during the McCarthy era—and was working as a press official in the Nkrumah government. He had met Malcolm some years before at Ossie Davis's and had liked him, but was put off by his religion. When he read that Malcolm had split with the Nation, he wrote a letter proposing that they organize some sort of association for black Americans in Ghana. Malcolm, pleased, wrote back that it was the first letter he had got from outside the States and that he was interested. When he announced that he was actually coming to Ghana, the Mayfields and Maya Angelou, among others, got up an instant Malcolm X Committee and programmed a busy week for him.

The single difficulty in their planning was that Malcolm neglected to tell them exactly what day he would get there. He called the Mayfields' house from the airport; Mayfield was out taking a French lesson, but his wife, Ana Livia, fetched Malcolm, dropped him at Miss Angelou's place and dashed off after Julian. "She rapped on the window and said, 'Malcolm is here,' " Mayfield remembered. "That was the last time I studied French." Miss Angelou had also met Malcolm in the States—she had been one of the organizers of the UN demonstration over Lumumba's death—but didn't recognize him at first standing outside her house in the Ghanaian sun with his grown-out hair and his feathery beginner beard. "How are you?" she said tentatively. "Hello, Maya," he said; the voice was unforgettable and the face was suddenly familiar.

They all adjourned to the Mayfields', rounded up the committee and from then on filled Malcolm's days with visits to nearly everybody important in Ghana. "Some of us knew journalists, some knew diplomats, some knew government ministers," Miss Angelou said; they forgot about their jobs, organized a breathless relay and saw to it that Malcolm got to all of them. He met most of the African ambassadors and several of Nkrumah's key ministers. He visited the Cuban mission and got on famously; they had not only current affairs to talk about but memories to share—a celebrated meeting between Malcolm and Fidel Castro at the Theresa in 1960 when the Maximum Leader was in New York for a UN session. The Chinese invited him to dinner, reminded him that Chairman Mao had sent comradely felicitations to the March on Washington and showed him some of their documentary films. (Malcolm was excited by the movies and was too gallant to remind his hosts that he had opposed the March.) The Nigerian High Commissioner laid on a luncheon and gave him a robe and turban; afterward, some of the Malcolm X Committee posed the two of them for pictures, Malcolm dressed up in his new costume and at six-feet-three towering ludicrously over the Commissioner at four-feet-eleven, and everybody had a good laugh. The Ghanaian Defense Minister threw a party for him and was so impressed that an invitation to address Parliament followed—an unheard-of gesture to anyone less than a visiting head of state.

Malcolm's speech there was a diplomatically short and pointed appeal for unity between Africa and Afro-America. His major speaking date was at the University of Ghana, with the Marxist Forum as his host; some of the committee were nervous that the auspices might embarrass Malcolm back home, but he said the Forum was all right with him, Marxist or not, and went on. "I'm from America, but I'm not an American," he said straightaway to heavy applause. "I didn't go there of my own free choice. . . . I don't feel that I am a visitor in Ghana or in any part of Africa. I feel that I am at home. I've been away for 400 years but not of my own volition, not of my own will." He was self-assured and acid and brilliant, lavishing praise on the Redeemer, warning the Redeemed to beware of those white Americans who had brutalized African-Americans back home and now were "over here in Africa smiling in your face trying to integrate with you. . . . Actually, what it is, they want to integrate with the wealth that they know is here." Still feeling his way with African audiences, he ran into awkward silences at moments but talked through them until he got the crowd with him again. The single sour note came when, in the question period, someone asked what about the Jews in Nazi Germany, and Malcolm, as he was accustomed to doing in the States, answered sharply that everyone was always talking about the Jews—what about *us?* "It sounded callous," said Preston King, a black American professor who had introduced Malcolm that evening, "and various of us said as much. And he said to Julian Mayfield, 'Why didn't you tell me that was the sort of effect I was likely to have? I didn't mean to communicate that.' " The speech otherwise was an unmixed triumph. A dissenter was run out of the hall, and the students rose in a storm of cheering and chanting—a phenomenon one officer of the Forum called "the Ghanaian violent elation." Malcolm stood there, shining with perspiration, his eyes rimming with tears.

What ought to have been his best moment in Ghana—a private audience with Kwame Nkrumah at Christianborg Castle—was by contrast a bit of a disappointment. Malcolm did come away lit by the mere presence of a man he so admired and quoting those bits of wisdom he remembered—Nkrumah's famous homily on politics and the blacks ("Seek ye first the political kingdom") and his conviction that 1964 would be a year of revolutionary change: *the hour of the knife.* Malcolm the pilgrim thus was rewarded; Malcolm the diplomat was not, apart from the genuine coup of having won an audience at all as a kind of minister without portfolio from black America. "They were two different kinds of men," said Mayfield, who delivered Malcolm to the President's door and picked him up afterward. "They weren't on the same wavelength. One was dealing with a government and with power; the other wasn't. Nkrumah could more likely be compared to Martin Luther King with power and a nation of people behind him than to Malcolm X." I wondered whether Malcolm had made any headway with his UN proposition; Mayfield guessed not. "Ghana was in serious economic difficulty at the time," he said. "Nkrumah would have been sympathetic, but his actions would have depended on other things he had to consider. He wasn't free to act just out of his sympathies. A lot of things would have made him hesitant to take on the United States government. The United States and the Soviet Union were too important to offend. You're a poor country—that's the difference." Whatever tenders of aid and comfort may have been exchanged remained private between the two men; the impression among the Americans, according to Preston King, was that the Redeemer had been curious and encouraging but in the end distant and that Malcolm had left feeling his idol a degree or so cooler than he had expected.

But Malcolm had neither the time nor the energy to spend on disappointment; the days were too crowded with event and mission, the nights too bubbling with talk. "He was expansive," Miss Angelou remembered. "He was open. He was learning. He was no longer in love with a position—he was in love with truth. When he shuffled off that Black Muslim coil, he shuffled the whole thing off. You'd tell him something, and he'd say, 'That's a very good point. I see. I was wrong about that.' And he was absolutely as strong in his new position as in his old one. He had no loyalty to old misconceptions." One morning they all bumped into Muhammad Ali, who was then on a countertour of the continent. It was an awkward moment for Ali, being thus confronted with an old friend turned chief hypocrite of all Black Islam, and ought to have been for Malcolm as well; but he smiled (*sweetly,* Miss Angelou thought), called Ali "brother," introduced him around, then moved on and left him standing there, tongue-tied and embarrassed. They were buoyant, bouncy times. Days, Malcolm and Mayfield and Miss Angelou, all of them giants, would fold themselves into her car—"All those legs in my little Fiat 600"—and bounce around between appointments, Malcolm constantly after them to go slower so he wouldn't miss anything. Nights, they would all crowd into his room at the Ambassador, order up drinks—mostly Scotch for the Americans, tea for Malcolm—and sit around talking, laughing, gossiping and feeling black and beautiful.

Malcolm normally liked parties but despised partying—that compulsive desperate gaiety that seemed to him the invention of whites and the narcotic of the black middle-class. One brilliantly moonlit night, the Press Club threw a dance for him. "It was outside, as most things are in Ghana," Miss Angelou said. "They had a big dance floor and two bands and everybody was dancing. At 11 o'clock, Malcolm was asked to speak. He got up and stood there under that big moon and said, 'I'm very grateful for this party. But I must tell you, I'm not dancing because I'm thinking of my people being oppressed at this very moment in America. I'm not *laughing* because I'm thinking of my people being oppressed at this very moment in America. I'm not asking you not to dance and not to laugh, but I'm thinking of my people in South Africa and Southwest Africa and Mozambique. . . .' Well, our troupe had danced its last for *that* night." But those late evenings at the Ambassador, he relaxed—they had all earned their respite—and sometimes they even forgot The Problem. "He could talk for hours about the race situation," Miss Angelou said, "but it wasn't always politics. He could talk for hours about Betty, about his children, about love, about food, about religion. Even fashion —Malcolm was not a man without eyes."

His days in Ghana were a time of learning for him—of experience flooding in and crowding some of his assumptions about Africa and Negritude. "When he came," Preston King said, "he seemed to be pretty sure of where he was. I think he sort of supposed that what he was going to confront in Ghana was a situation in which, quite simply, black people were in power and control. When he got there, he found that to an extraordinary degree it was a very mixed kind of picture—a sort of strange combination of white socialists, Communists, liberals and blacks all mixed up together in this peculiar governmental show—and he wasn't quite sure how to handle this." He had supper one night with, among others, King, his white wife, Richard Wright's daughter Julia and her French husband. Malcolm was then still ardently against intermarriage, but under the circumstances, as King recalled it, "he was not in a position to object. . . . You could see him being rather cautious and you could see him sort of getting used to the idea, and it was interesting to watch this as a piece of social dynamics on the ground." Nkrumah himself had a powerful sense of blackness but had become a determined nonracialist in power. This may have been one source of his wariness with Malcolm; the Redeemer couldn't be sure then how much the hajj had changed him. One measure of the distance between them was Malcolm's wide-eyed surprise at passing the last desk before Nkrumah's office and seeing a white woman working there. It was one of the travel stories he told the brothers privately back home. "If the people found out about *that,*" he would say, "they'd hang him." Then he would laugh, but it seemed clear to them that he hadn't quite got over it.

Still, as the hajj had transformed the theology of race for Malcolm, the visit to Ghana began subtly to alter the politics of race. He had one memorable conversation with the then Algerian Ambassador to Accra, Taher Kaid, an African and a revolutionary but, at least in skin color, a white man. As Malcolm told the story to friends in the States, Kaid had asked him, "Brother Malcolm, what are your plans? What are you going to do?" Malcolm responded with a long disquisition on the political, economic and social philosophy of black nationalism and on his dreams of linking the destinies of Afro-America and Africa around the single fact of color.

"Brother Malcolm," Kaid said, smiling gently, "that sort of leaves me out, doesn't it?"

"What do you mean?" Malcolm asked.

"Well," said Kaid, "I'm a Muslim brother and a revolutionary, but I'm not black—I'm Caucasian."

Malcolm, for a rare moment, wasn't sure what to say. The hajj had made it possible for him to forget Kaid's color but not his own. He began to wonder after that whether the politics of blackness might be cutting him off from important sources of support, not so much on the white American liberal-to-radical Left—Malcolm hadn't changed that much just yet—as among the White Muslims of North Africa and the Middle East and the nonblack nations of the Third World. Malcolm remained conscious of his own color and his enemy's. But the Accra experience, and his talk with Kaid, lent new shadings to this consciousness. Black nationalism thereafter no longer seemed to him quite so adequate a name for what had to be done; he used the term somewhat less often and worried whether it had got him into another semantic box.

Malcolm rethought his organizational apparatus in Ghana, too. His initial decision to incorporate himself and his fellow refugees from the Nation as a spin-off Muslim mosque had seemed natural at the time but had turned out in practice to be prohibitively narrow—a cage for Malcolm and a deterrent for nonbelievers who might otherwise have been tempted to follow him. He had been worrying this problem during his tour and had come to Ghana still thinking about that letter of Mayfield's proposing some sort of black American organization there.

Mayfield guessed in retrospect that Malcolm may have overestimated the size and importance of their expatriate colony. "We had a large number of younger people who'd come because they couldn't get into the Martin Luther King thing," he said. "They were mostly pretty well-trained and educated people, and they were functioning as heads of departments and near-heads of departments. But you're talking about possibly 120 Afro-Americans in all of Ghana, and around Accra, the young artists, writers, scholars, technologists, electronics people, maybe thirty. And they had no influence on the President's policies whatever." Malcolm was undeterred by any of this, and out of those late-night talks at the Ambassador was born the charter chapter of a new, nonsectarian group, the Organization of Afro-American Unity. It took its name and purpose from the Organization of African Unity, the fledgling all-African confederation whose promise had greatly stirred Malcolm. The goals of his little circle in Ghana were perforce more modest, once he was persuaded how little say they had with the Nkrumah government. They got an information center going, to counter the USIA's cosmetic version of the racial struggle back home and to orient black American visitors to what was really happening in Africa; they thought it might also be useful for bringing pressure if Malcolm were ever detained by the authorities in America. Mayfield had the additional idea of setting up some kind of refuge from the Stateside struggle—a quiet place where a Malcolm, a Martin Luther King or even a Roy Wilkins could retreat, rest and think in peace.

The day Malcolm left Ghana, five ambassadors followed his party to the airport in an impromptu motorcade to shake hands good-bye—the kind of send-off normally reserved to the ministers of states more widely recognized than the black American nation. Malcolm went off on day trips to Liberia, Senegal and Morocco and a short visit to Algeria, where he walked through the casbah of Algiers and was reminded of the casbah in New York called Harlem. When he booked passage home in May, the outposts of the U.S. government in Africa were relieved; they had not precisely been alarmed by his tour or the excitement it stirred but had been interested enough to monitor it—to keep up, for example, on his flight numbers, his hotel reservations and presumably his appointments. This interest would shortly increase. Africa remained a promise for Malcolm X; the day he left, he knew he was going to be back.

22. The Return

Malcolm came home on May 21 with his wispy beard and an astrakhan hat, both of which immediately became fashions in Harlem, and a slightly moderated view of white people, which did not. He was met at John F. Kennedy Airport by Betty, the children, a sizable force of the brothers, an equally sizable force of airport policemen and an enormous swarm of reporters, who cornered him in the terminal for one pell-mell press conference and followed him in to the Theresa for another. The brothers had booked the Skyline Room on the eleventh floor for the homecoming and had draped the front of the building with a great streamer that said: WELCOME BACK BROTHER MALCOLM. The only thing was they weren't really sure he had come back to *them.* The letters from Mecca had unsettled some of them, and so had the turnout of white reporters; it was almost as if we were trying to woo Malcolm away from them with our attentions. Harlem, cynical and worn by too many betrayals, had brooded on this during the weeks of his travels and waited charily to see how he would act now. "A lot of people thought, 'Well, he's getting his,' " John Killens told me. "When he came back, I heard a brother say, 'They must of given him some money.' " The suspicions, as Killens quickly added, were nonsense—nobody ever bought Malcolm—but suddenly, on his home ground, he was required once again to prove it.

He felt obliged, first off, to assure us that the outpouring of reporters had not in fact turned his head. "No matter how much respect, no matter how much recognition, whites show towards me," he said, "as far as I'm concerned, as long as it is not shown to every one of our people in this country, it doesn't exist for me." Yes, he said, his racial philosophy had changed in Mecca, but only to the extent that his brother Muslims of every color had treated him like a human being; he saw little possibility of anything like that happening in America, short of a mass conversion to Islam, and in the meantime the chance that there might be a few "good" whites wasn't going to alter his judgment that, collectively, the lot of them were bad. He said he had come back with pledges of support for the case against white America in the UN and would prepare it for submission later in the year. He confirmed that he wanted to enter a united front with various civil-rights leaders and would treat with them, secretly if necessary, toward this end; in the next breath, out of habit or irritation at some obstinately silly question, he called them all Uncle Toms. He was pressed repeatedly to say what he knew about the "Blood Brothers," a probably fictitious Harlem "hate gang" that had been discovered by the *Times* and was said to have been trained or inspired by Black Muslim defectors to kill white ghetto storekeepers. The fact was that Malcolm didn't know anything much about them—he had first heard of the Blood Brothers in Nigeria—but he wouldn't disown them entirely, not to us. "If it does exist," he said a little wearily, "I am surprised that white people are surprised that Negroes are reacting like that." Did he then condone them? "I don't think I should even be asked whether or not I condone the reaction of any people who are exploited and whose reaction is to criminal exploitation."

What he said suited the necessities of the homecoming—the tenor of his press notices and the provisional judgment of his followers was that he was the same old Malcolm after all—but at the same time sharply illuminated his problems after the hajj. He was anxious to come into what he described as "a new regard by the public, especially Negroes," as neither an outlaw nor a fanatic but a legitimate third-force leader—a radical alternative for blacks who were too angry to surrender and too proud to beg. Yet he was caught between his future and his past. "His personality—his power to excite—attracted the institutions of society," Ossie Davis said. "Whites found him exciting, particularly when he moved into an area where color was no longer decisive. There was a tremendous desire to get him—to discover him. This creates a tremendous pull away from your own community. The danger of being swept over into another world is a real one, and Malcolm realized it. And he did not want to move faster than the brother could move. There were those who were still blinded by the need to keep pummeling the white man and who would say, 'Shit, this motherfucker sold out.' He couldn't move too fast, and that restricted his progress."

To this degree, he was a prisoner of his past. Malcolm had made his name and his constituency burning whites, all of them, uniformly and mercilessly. He had won a following not merely because he was charming or magnetic or manly or had sex appeal but because of his rage; a good many ordinary black people saw in him the vicarious agent of their own secret furies. To the extent that his fires now burned cooler, he was breaking faith with that following—and since he had not yet established a new audience, he could not yet afford to lose the old one. He tried, at different times and in different places, to address them both; neither was wholly satisfied. The downtown press, upon whose mercies he depended for that new regard he sought, was pleased enough with his access of humankindness after the hajj but was quickly bored by it as copy and began ignoring him except when he said something outrageous. His older followers, for their part, remained suspicious—sometimes violently so. Quarrels broke out among them. "In a room one night," Kenyatta told me, "I had to hold some brothers off Malcolm."

Malcolm was imprisoned by his language and his combative style as well. He had a clear tactical sense of words; he understood, that is, that even benign institutions move slowly and that a powerless minority addressing corrupt institutions, as he believed America's to be, had to get rhetorically rough even to be heard. "You have to walk in with a hand grenade and tell the man, 'Listen, you give us what we've got coming or nobody is going to get anything,' " he said at one of his Audubon rallies. "Then he might listen to you. But if you go in there polite and acting responsible and sane, why, you're wasting your time, you have to be insane." As it happened, hand grenades—the verbal kind—suited his temper anyway. Malcolm was instinctively a fighter, and, like any great fighter, most dangerous backed into a corner with the taste of blood in his mouth and the crowd roaring. In the quiet of a friendly interview, he would patiently and carefully define his new position on the White Question: he had indeed discovered the humanity of white people in Mecca, he would say, and while he would not now embrace them in brotherhood, neither would he damn every last one of them out of hand any longer. He was not, he insisted in these situations, a racist; he had been "used" by Elijah Muhammad in the past, but he would no longer "sentence anyone who has not first been proven guilty." In combat conditions, he behaved as though the proof and the judgment were already in. No hajj, no religion, no revelation on Mount Arafat would alter his certainty that white people collectively were the enemies of black people collectively. "I'm not saying all of them are bad," he told one black audience. "There might be some good ones. But we don't have time to look for them. Not nowadays."

At the same time, the pulse of violence in Malcolm's rhetoric quickened. He was a *Fanoniste* without having read Fanon: he lived, in spirit if not literal fact, in the native quarter and understood its vocation for destruction. He did not advocate the rioting that surprised us so that summer, but he predicted it regularly and was furious when we taxed him with contributing to the atmosphere that produced it. What he did insist on was that the blacks ought to answer white violence tit for tat. He began after his return from Africa to talk about dispatching trained guerrilla teams South to revenge atrocities by whites, and the revenge might or might not be selective, depending on whom Malcolm happened to be addressing at the time. Robert Penn Warren, the poet and novelist, visited him at the Theresa that spring and interviewed him for his book *Who Speaks for the Negro?* Malcolm, judging by the published results, was in a dueling mood—that almost sportive fighting humor he got into sometimes when the morning's news had been bad for black people or when a white liberal irritated him with a line of what he considered to be "subjective" questions. He chilled Warren with a smile, drew him into a pointless metaphysical debate about the relative guilt or innocence of, say, a three-year-old white child and positively toyed with him on the issue of selective vs. nonselective reprisals. "If I go home and my child has blood running down her leg and someone tells me a snake bit her," Malcolm said, "I'm going out and kill snakes, and when I find a snake I'm not going to look and see if he has blood on his jaws." Warren asked him if he was then urging indiscriminate revenge. "I'm just telling you about snakes," said Malcolm.

His unrelenting stress on self-defense spoke to a very real undercurrent of feeling in Harlem—a helpless fury at the almost daily brutalities visited by whites in and out of uniform on the Southern civil-rights movement. The cost for him was that, in the public eye, he sometimes seemed to stand for nothing else; he had no other way except our media to reach the great mass of black Americans, and so he paid the price of admission, which in most cases meant saying something scary. His situation as a public ogre pained him at times, but Malcolm hid his feelings and in fact developed a kind of good-humored irony about it. Between planes one day at Washington National Airport, he bumped into Martin Luther King's man Wyatt Walker. The two of them weren't exactly pals—they had nearly come to blows once during a station break in a TV talk show when Walker called Malcolm a liar—but the relationship had since mellowed a bit, and Malcolm let Walker tease him about the matter of getting guns. "Look, baby," Walker said, "a good gun costs $80 or $90 or $130, and black people are poor. They're gonna say, 'If I can get my hands on $80 or $90 or $130, I'm gonna get some bread and potatoes.' " Malcolm chuckled. "I have to say that," he told Walker, "to make it easier for you and Martin."

He had to say it, really, because nobody else would. Most of the civil-rights leadership—those who believed in physical resistance to violence and those who didn't—wished he wouldn't harp on the matter so; they saw no purpose in making a public issue of something that seemed to make white people that nervous. In Malcolm's view, that was precisely the point. He *wanted* whites to be frightened and blacks to be brave, and to these ends he spoke to both in a visceral language he assumed we could both understand. He did this at the risk of seeming violent himself and so forfeiting that new regard he wanted. It hardly mattered that he was trying, more or less carefully, to differentiate between aggressive and defensive action; his insistent hammering on the subject itself gave his nonnonviolence a canted importance in his politics. Even the membership card in his fledgling Organization of Afro-American Unity locked it in high on his agenda. The single declaration of purpose on the card was not "We want justice" or "We are brothers with Africa"; it said, "We assert and affirm the right of self-defense, which is one of the most basic human rights known to mankind."

The price of defenselessness, as Malcolm saw it, was everywhere visible in the South that spring and early summer. King's people were being regularly roughed up in St. Augustine; the SNCC-CORE "Freedom Summer" in Mississippi had opened to a wave of beatings, church-burnings and police harassment, and three young volunteers—two white college boys and a local black youth—had vanished the very first night. Some of the brothers were itching to retaliate; they wanted Malcolm to take a party of them South, to Mississippi, say, and while he did the speechmaking, they would organize the local Negroes into armed units trained and equipped to defend their communities and to take a head for a head if necessary. This, like so many of the projects they discussed in those days, never actually got organized. But it did get advertised, which was Malcolm's gift and was probably just as important; one need not actually take heads if one can persuade the enemy that there are people angry enough to take them. Malcolm wired King and James Forman of SNCC that spring, offering to send some of his people South to "give the Ku Klux Klan a taste of their own medicine." He knew they couldn't accept; he knew also that the papers would pick up the story, and he hoped we would read it correctly. "Any time you lay a few Klansmen out dead, the government will step in," he told one OAAU rally in Harlem. His gamble was that talking about laying out Klansmen might well accomplish the same thing.

Even the talk deepened Malcolm's estrangement from the respectable leadership. A certain despair had begun to tinge the edges of the movement—a cumulative weariness with broken heads and nights in jail and the apparent impotence of the Federal government—but not to a point where Malcolm was persona grata. He did his best to stay out of fights with the civil-rights people and urged his followers to do likewise; he even looked in on the NAACP national convention, and, so he reported, "learned a lot." He may actually have expected his sudden mannerliness to melt hearts among the respectables. "Just because I'm going a hundred miles and they're going only fifty doesn't mean we can't walk together," he told the brothers. The fact was that they were going in opposite directions; they could not have walked together without him surrendering to them or them to him on all the questions that then seemed central—nonviolence, integration, even the meaning of blackness. Malcolm argued that those were really questions of means and that they all wanted the same end, justice for black people. But means and ends were in fact inextricably intertwined for the civil-rights people, and for Malcolm as well, and the movement held to its fifty-mile road without him. "They've been pretending for five years that I don't exist," he complained in the midst of his moratorium on public squabbling. "In Kenya, the respectable blacks kept saying the Mau Mau didn't exist, but the Mau Mau won the country."

Malcolm in fact was trying as best he could to be flexible. He shucked off more and more of his Black Muslim past, not just the old inflexibilities about color and activism but the last wisps of the back-to-Africa dream as well; he took to saying that the return was strictly a psychological matter—a sense of identity with Africa—and that the real fight was right here. Having only just come out of one closed system of thought, he was uncomfortable with ideology. He did come home impressed by his glimpses of socialism and his introduction to its vocabulary. He worked some of it tentatively into a few speeches and interviews, arguing that racism wasn't the only problem—that it was the handmaiden of colonialism and capitalism. When people asked him whether he would accept Communist support, he would smile and quote an old African proverb: "The enemy of my enemy is my friend."

One guesses that Malcolm's interest in African socialism at that point was more that it was African than that it was socialist; it was in any case a minor motif in his speeches. But it was noted with great interest by the Left, which had always dreamed of finding a black leader with genuine grass-roots appeal, and particularly by the Socialist Workers, who now dared hope that the dream might be coming true. Others were less impressed at that point by the depth of Malcolm's apparent drift leftward. Charles Silberman did a five-hour radio panel with him and was surprised by his first awkward detours into dialectic. "I got the feeling that he really didn't know what he meant by the words and that he didn't have any real conviction about them," Silberman said. "He was trying out any idea that would come to him and asking himself, 'Is this the way I go?' I remember thinking he was really floundering." Or improvising. Socialism remained a downtown idea and a downtown theme for Malcolm; uptown, at the founding rally of the OAAU, he predicted that the true ideology for liberation would one day "come out of the bosom of this black man" spontaneously, like riffs at a jam session, and that it would be something nobody ever heard of before.

He put together the OAAU precisely that way, in a jam session of philosophizing and programming that ran over four weeks. The Muslim Mosque, Inc. seemed more clearly than ever not to have worked out as he had planned: it was a hybrid, too worldly for some of the Old Muslims and too religious to bring in either the first-class leaders or the mass following that Malcolm wanted. He didn't scrap the MMI—he still wanted a pulpit—but he decided he needed a political platform as well. So he assembled a brain trust of writers, academics, politicians, students, celebrities, professional people, Old Muslims and budding revolutionaries and put them to work devising an organization and a program. They met secretly in a motel on the north fringe of Harlem, well away from the Theresa and its traffic, and at length produced a six-page mimeographed "statement of basic aims and objectives" for the new organization. Its tenor was rather well suggested by its cover, an outline map of North and South America enclosed in—and dwarfed by—an outline map of Africa. This reflected Malcolm's own perspective on the worth if not the actual power of the nations of man—a perspective he had begun to call "global black thinking."

The document, like the OAAU itself, was constructed to suit Malcolm; he was named chairman before there were any members. The prospectus of the OAAU reads today like a Black Power manifesto two years ahead of its time—a declaration of the controlling importance of color and of black control of every aspect of the black community. The OAAU announced itself to the world as "non-religious and non-sectarian" (though Malcolm couldn't quite bring himself to say "non-religious" at the founding rally) and as being concerned principally with human, not civil, rights. Its economic policies, far from being socialist, turned out rather like the old shopkeeper capitalism of the Black Muslims. Its agenda was to include voter registration, school boycotts, rent strikes, housing rehabilitation, programs for addicts, unwed mothers and kids otherwise in trouble, a war on organized crime, a black cultural revolution "to unbrainwash an entire people"—more activities, that is, than an organization with eight or nine hundred or less active members at its peak could possibly have undertaken. Whites once again were forbidden to join (though we could, if we wanted, set up a White Friends of the OAAU in our part of town) and, this time, even to give money; Malcolm wanted absolute freedom to attack "the structure" with no strings attached. He announced an initiation fee of $2 and dues of $1 a week; he hoped that this, plus the collection buckets, would bring in enough to keep him and the OAAU going outside the reach of white charity and white control.

"It's rough," Malcolm acknowledged, reading the prospectus to that first OAAU rally; he and the brothers meant to smooth it out as they went along, but they never quite did. The OAAU's greatest single asset was its star; its fatal flaw was that it was constructed specifically as a star vehicle for a man who didn't have the time to invest in making it go. Malcolm's attention had always been fragmented by the multiple demands on it and by his inability to deny them. In that moment of his career, his time and energy were further taxed by two overriding concerns. One was pursuing the case against Uncle Sam in the United Nations. The other was staying alive.

23. The Far Side of the Rubicon

It was the house that brought them to the verge of war. It wasn't much of a house, really—just an overgrown brick bungalow, assessed at $16,200, with five tiny rooms downstairs and a nook up under the gabled roof where Malcolm used to go when he wanted quiet to think or nap in. But it was all he had, his home and, more important to a man living so close to the edge, the only estate he had to leave Betty and the children should anything happen to him. The Nation of Islam knew this and acknowledged in *Muhammad Speaks* that its real interest in seeking to evict Malcolm was precisely to show him up as "a foolish rebel" incapable of providing for his own family—a devastating accusation in the middle-class world of the Lost-Founds. The lawsuit by this measure was right on target. It hit Malcolm literally where he lived; he fought back furiously, even viciously, to a point where not only his home but his life was at hazard. The house meant that much to him. "It was *mine*," he said in his wintry last days, when its price had become clear to him. "From the start. Absolutely. Elijah Muhammad knows that—this is another thing that made me see him as he really is."

He meant that he saw Mr. Muhammad as his enemy, and he

thereupon quit even pretending that they could continue as prophet-and-disciple or father-and-son as though nothing had happened. The Nation had never taken this possibility very seriously in the first place, and Malcolm's proclamation from Mecca that the white man was not the devil was the heretical last straw. *Muhammad Speaks,* in some issues that spring and summer, was an index of Malcolm's crimes against the faith, as told and retold by one after another of his sometime brother ministers. The newspaper hooted at his transformations on the hajj; the Messenger himself announced ex cathedra that the pilgrimage had been nothing but a "shrewd hypocritical move" and that even the beard Malcolm came back with was a gimmick to make him look religious when he wasn't. The Scripture lessons were full of veiled warnings about the coming wrath of Allah and the certainty of hell for hypocrites—a retribution from which not even the Messenger's own family would be spared. In one issue, Eugene Majied, the paper's brilliantly cruel cartoonist, drew Malcolm's severed head bounding down a roadway toward a pile of skulls, growing horns and a satanic leer en route and crying, "I split because no man wants to be number two man in nothing . . . bla-bla-bla-bla. . . ." In another, one of Mr. Muhammad's loyal ministers proclaimed Malcolm "the number one hypocrite of all time. . . . If it were not for the Messenger, you would still be just another unheard-of penny-ante Harlem hustler. Now that you have defected, you are a FAMOUS penny-ante Harlem hustler. The Bible accurately describes you as 'a dog returning to his own vomit.' You've even gotten shaggy like a dog. . . ."

Malcolm, a materialist in matters of human motivation, thought he saw reason enough for this in the competition his new mosque posed for the Nation. He had brought no more than a few dozen of the Original People out of the Harlem mosque with him and had in fact encouraged some to stay behind and "be helpful" to his cause behind Mr. Muhammad's lines. But some two hundred turned out for his first public rally in Harlem after the schism and others followed in the months thereafter, some to join him, some dropping out of the movement entirely. The Messenger's own son

Wallace, who was the only minister in the royal family and for a time was considered the heir apparent to the throne, left or was put out and granted several interviews charging members of his father's court with high crimes ranging from smoking to fornication to misusing the Nation's wealth. Malcolm took the regular biweekly attacks in *Muhammad Speaks* to be the inevitable consequence of this exodus and for a time suffered them in silence, even when they were delivered by men whom he had made and who he thought by rights ought to be outside with him. "He never expressed hurt," Percy Sutton remembered. "He never discussed people I would have considered traitors. One of his people would come in and say, 'So-and-so did such-and-such.' And he'd say, 'Peace, brother, you have to understand—when a man's mind is not his own, you can't blame him.' "

His tolerance faded, however, as the mid-June docket date for the eviction case drew closer, and so did his unaccustomed pacifism. The attacks on him quickened and got more personal. The prospect of being turned out into the street with his family and belongings grew daily more real. He and Louis Lomax, debating in Chicago just two days after Malcolm's return from Africa, noticed John Ali and a contingent of the Fruit of Islam glowering at them out of the audience; simple curiosity may well have brought them out, but Malcolm thereafter began seeing Muslims practically everywhere public he went. The Nation, deliberately or not, had crowded him into a corner and so had brought him to his most dangerous condition—that reckless, free-swinging, gut-punching fury in which he would use whatever weapon came to hand.

What came to hand most readily, to the dismay of practically everybody who cared about Malcolm, was the issue of Mr. Muhammad's private life. Malcolm had sent first one, then another, of his most trusted people to Chicago to see some of the Messenger's ex-secretaries and had written, telephoned and visited some of them himself. Some turned him away, but he and his people eventually collected affidavits from three of them, and two were willing to take their cases to court. With this material in hand, Malcolm started hinting in public that something in the Messenger's private conduct was involved in their split and that people would be shocked to know what it was. Some of Malcolm's counselors, particularly the Old Muslims, were against raising the subject at all, on the grounds that men shouldn't use women to split an organization and that what Mr. Muhammad did in his non-Messengerial hours was in any case nobody's business but his and Allah's. Malcolm may in fact have been counting once again on the cocked fist to accomplish what he wanted without the necessity of throwing a punch. If so, the strategy didn't work. Mr. Muhammad, weary of the innuendo-dropping, finally called him on it: he wrote Malcolm that he could get on a housetop or a mountaintop for that matter and shout whatever he wanted to the whole world. Malcolm's choices at that point were to back down, which was not in his nature, or to talk. He talked.

He told the tale first during a radio interview in Boston on June 12. It got almost no mileage; the media still didn't want to touch the story with no public record to back it up. But there was quick and compelling evidence that Malcolm was on dangerous ground. He had been scheduled to stay on in Boston for a day or two more but, instead, had Benjamin Goodman take over a speaking date for him and left for home, early and unannounced. Goodman made the speech; afterward, seven of Malcolm's people were riding out to Logan Airport in two cars when they noticed two more carloads of black men following them. They shook off one of the tail cars in a dash into Callahan Tunnel. But the other cut them off in the tunnel, and three men they identified later as Black Muslims got out flashing knives and shouted, "We're going to kill the so-and-so —you're not going to get out of here alive." The so-and-so they were looking for was Malcolm; he wasn't there, and, when one of the brothers poked a loaded shotgun out of the car window, the Muslims backed off.

Malcolm didn't. The eviction suit was docketed for Queens Civil Court the very next day, and, whatever the outcome, he saw the courtroom as a perfect setting for his disclosures—a theater in which the relationship of provocation to response would be clear and where anything he said was privileged against litigation for libel or slander.

The trial even without this digression was a tindery affair—the first public confrontation between Malcolm and the Nation since his apostasy. The newspapers started getting anonymous telephone tips that Malcolm was going to be shot in open court. "Oh, shucks, I don't worry," Malcolm said, but he did. Eight of his own people brought him to court and thirty-two uniformed and plainclothes policemen took over there, surrounding him so impermeably that he could barely be seen from the gallery. Even on the short walk down the hall to the men's room, he was escorted by five officers. The court authorities judiciously chose one of the smallest courtrooms in the building and kept the shades drawn through the two-day trial so nobody could draw a bead on Malcolm from outside. Malcolm nevertheless sat fidgeting at the defense table, glancing anxiously around the room at unexpected noises; during the breaks, he tried to persuade the reporters there that he wasn't jiving about the danger he was in—that the Muslims were in fact capable of murder and that he knew this "because I taught them." The tension in the room was almost palpable. Malcolm's people and the Nation's sat on opposite sides of the gallery, glaring at one another across the aisle. The court stenographer was struck by their almost eerie silence. "Usually, in a case that touchy, you'll be sitting there taking down testimony and you'll hear gasps, or somebody muttering, 'How can he lie like that?' " he said. "This time, there wasn't a sound. Not one word."

The defense that Percy Sutton had prepared for Malcolm was valiant and skillfully presented but in the end obtrusively thin. They had to argue (1) that the house really was Malcolm's, no matter what the deed said, and (2) that even if it did belong to the mosque, he had never been properly fired as minister and so was entitled to stay on anyway. The Nation spent the first day presenting the testimony of various officials of the Harlem temple, Captain Joseph included, that they had bought the place specifically as a parsonage in 1959 and were still paying off the mortgage. Sutton managed to establish that, while the mosque was nominally a religious corporation with officers and a board of trustees, it was in fact run pretty much by the minister in consultation with Mr. Muhammad. This meant the other officers couldn't testify as to what Malcolm's arrangements with the Messenger really were—whether, for example, the house was meant to be his or the Nation's. Captain Joseph remembered only that, some years before, Malcolm had come home from Chicago and had told the brethren that he was supposed to get $150 a week plus "the necessary living quarters, etc. . . . and we took him at his word." The temple people couldn't even swear of their own knowledge that Malcolm wasn't their minister any more. "He put into the paper that he no longer was a member of Muhammad's Temple No. 7," Joseph said; so far as the rules of evidence were concerned, the Muslims—like the rest of us—knew only what they had read in the *Times.*

Malcolm himself spent two hours on the stand the second day and, as on any stage he ever graced, was the commanding presence. His case was somewhat less prepossessing. It required, first, that he testify that he hadn't quit at all—that the papers had misquoted him as saying he had and that he still considered himself a Black Muslim minister "under suspension," waiting for his hearing.

"Did you ever have a hearing?" Sutton asked him.

"No."

"Were you ever removed?"

"No, I was suspended."

"Have you ever resigned?"

"No, I asked for a hearing. They wouldn't give me one. . . . Never gave me a hearing."

His real moral claim on the property was that Mr. Muhammad had given it to him outright as a reward for his service to Islam; his legal problem was that there was nothing but his own word to offer as evidence. "The Honorable Elijah Muhammad told me it was my house, that the house was purchased for me. . . . I had gotten married and had my wife and child, and we were living in cramped quarters, and the Muslims had been trying to get me to move into larger quarters for a long time, which I kept refusing until finally the Honorable Elijah Muhammad insisted . . . and when the house was purchased, he told me over and over that it should be in my name, that it was for me because of the work I was doing and had been doing." The Muslims' lawyer, Joseph Williams, confronted him on cross-examination with the facts that the deed was in the temple's name and that the formal report of the brothers who bought the house referred to it as a "ministry home." Malcolm replied that these were simply devices to make the place tax-exempt and that that had been Mr. Muhammad's idea, too. "I never sought to gain anything personally from the Nation of Islam," he said. "That is why I lived in a room and then lived in three rooms. . . . [The members felt] that it was not good for me to live where I had been living, and since I was working so hard, they insisted that a house be purchased for me."

All the while, Malcolm kept skittering closer and closer to the point of telling on the Messenger and then drawing back, almost as though he were still debating the wisdom of his decision with himself. Early on, he said that his remark about President Kennedy's death hadn't been the reason for his suspension—that the real issue was something concerning Mr. Muhammad and that his only purpose in seeking a hearing had been to keep the whole business in the family. "I tried to keep it private," he said. ". . . I asked them for a hearing in private so that it would never come out to the public and because there were facts that I thought would be destructive to the Muslim movement. . . ."

"You're making it public now?" Williams asked him sharply.

"Yes," said Malcolm, "only because they have driven me to the point where I have to tell it in order to protect myself, but I have been trying to keep it quiet."

Even then, having marched himself to the brink, he drew back, and the questioning wandered off onto something else. Both lawyers, his and the Nation's, seemed almost equally reluctant to get into whatever it was he was trying to say. At one point, he repeated that "something private" had forced his suspension. Williams interrupted and tried to change the subject. "*Very* private," Malcolm got in. "Just a moment," his own lawyer, Sutton, protested, and once again the line of inquiry meandered away from The Subject.

One might have expected cross-examination to have forced the issue, given Malcolm's instinct for counterpunching. Instead, it surfaced on a matter-of-fact question of Sutton's about whether he had or had not had a hearing; Malcolm suddenly took the plunge, saying no, he hadn't, but that he had been promised one and that the question it was to have taken up was his having told Captain Joseph among others that the Messenger had taken on nine wives. "I'm not asking that," Sutton interjected. "*This* is the reason for my suspension," Malcolm blurted. ". . . My mouth was closed so that I couldn't talk. Then they poisoned the Muslim body to keep them from demanding that I get a hearing. That's all. That's what I fought against. I said I would have kept the whole thing secret and private if they would give me a hearing. They would rather take the public court than keep it private among the Muslims simply because I told Joseph that the Honorable Elijah Muhammad had taken on nine wives." Moments later, on cross, Williams asked him if he had proof of his charges. Malcolm invited him sardonically to ask Mr. Muhammad "and see if he denies it. . . . See if *he* can give you a yes or no answer."

And so it was out. The hearing wound anticlimactically down; Malcolm left the stand, sat nervously through the last routine testimony, then rode home to Harlem in a caravan with Sutton and twenty of the brothers. He wasn't even in the country when Judge Maurice E. Wahl ruled routinely three months later that the house was indeed the parsonage of Muhammad's Mosque No. 7 and that Malcolm would have to get out. Malcolm still cared, of course, and fought on, but for him the act of real consequence had been taken on June 16, in a badly lit little courtroom in Queens, when he bore witness before the devil against the Last Messenger of Allah. The papers duly noted his charges, though not quite so splashily as Malcolm had expected; his testimony to the Messenger's supposed seraglio was buried in the trial stories and accompanied by word from Chicago that he was a liar and that Mr. Muhammad would not dignify him with a reply. Still, the deed was done. That day in court, one of his closest advisers told me, "Malcolm crossed the Rubicon."

That night, he discovered when he got home that his telephone had gone dead. The phone company, when he finally got through, told him that a "Mrs. Small" had called and asked that it be disconnected because he was going away on vacation. Small sounded like a play on his slave name, Little, and Little was what the Nation had taken to calling him after the break; Malcolm put two and two together and guessed, fairly or not, that "Mrs. Small" had been a Black Muslim sister. His people agreed. One of them had tried to call Malcolm's house and had been alarmed by the recorded "disconnect" message. He rounded up a half-dozen or so of the brothers, appropriately equipped, and dashed out to Malcolm's place to be sure he was all right. Afterward, so they told police later, they drove back to Harlem and stopped innocently to buy a paper; the newstand they picked only happened to be at 116th and Lenox, a door or so away from the Muslim restaurant. A crowd had collected there, idly watching a white john arguing loudly with a black prostitute. Suddenly, in the swirl, an undersized Muslim threw a punch at one of Malcolm's people, a full head taller, and caught him flush on the jaw. Malcolm's man retreated to the car and came back with his friends—six men, a Muslim said later, "with these *wild*-looking beards and red eyes." One of them flashed a knife, another a .30-caliber rifle. A crowd of Muslim men spilled out of the restaurant to meet them, some of them carrying sticks, bottles and broom handles. The man with the gun shouted, "Get in the restaurant." One of the Muslims, a lieutenant in the Fruit, was trying to wave them inside when a squad car arrived and everybody scattered. The police locked up six of Malcolm's people, confiscated three guns and effectively stopped the confrontation.

The bad blood only got worse. The Muslims had been inflamed by the trial, Malcolm's people by the news that the Messenger himself planned to come to Harlem for a rally on June 28. The rally actually was to be only one in a series in several major American cities and had been booked in May, while Malcolm was still abroad and might have been planning to stay forever so far as anyone knew. But the coming of the Messenger looked to Malcolm like a direct challenge on his own home ground, and on the very day he planned to announce the founding of the OAAU at that. The visit became the focal point for all the deepening bitterness between the two factions. Rumors flew that each side was plotting to kill the other's leader—that Mr. Muhammad was to be murdered at the airport the morning of the rally, that Malcolm had been ordered slain no later than the following day. In the midst of this, Malcolm dispatched an open letter to the Messenger proposing that they work with one another and with other black leaders in the interests of black people "instead of wasting all this energy fighting each other." He expected nothing to come of this; an open letter under the circumstances was not a gesture of peace but a gambit in the developing state of war.

Malcolm no longer doubted that war was what was happening. In Queens one night, one of his younger followers—a seventeen-year-old kid—got into an argument with a Muslim official. The Muslim shoved him. The youth disappeared and came back with an older comrade—a charter OAAU member who was the brother of one of Malcolm's best celebrity friends. The OAAU man pointed a .30-caliber carbine at the Muslim. The Muslim took it away from him, bashed him on the head with it and knocked out a window of his station wagon. Both men were arrested. Malcolm, furious, got Kenyatta and went to the stationhouse to arrange to get their man out. "It was the first time I ever saw Malcolm lose his cool," Kenyatta recalled. "He said it had come to the point that he were in deep trouble with the Muslims and he felt he had to fight them violently. He told the *police* that, right there outside the stationhouse, and a black detective who was his friend cautioned him about it. On the way back, Malcolm said, 'What did I *say?*' I told him, 'You blowed your cool.' "

They were tense days for Malcolm. Publicly, when his big brother, Philbert X, had read him out of the family, Malcolm had denied feeling any pain. But privately he was hurt at having had to break with Philbert and another brother, Wilfred X, the Muslim minister in Detroit, and when they came to town for Mr. Muhammad's rally, Kenyatta told me, Malcolm secretly arranged a meeting with them. So strained were the times that they could think of no place in the city secluded enough for a rendezvous and so picked a spot in the woods just up the Hudson Valley. The three of them met there the night before the rally and walked and talked among the trees. Malcolm came back looking wounded. He had not penetrated that frozen Muslim loyalty—had not been able to talk to them, really. He told Kenyatta, "They don't understand."

Kenyatta wanted to go to the rally at the 369th Regiment Armory the next afternoon; he thought they ought to provoke a confrontation. Malcolm said no. "I know you got the guts," he told Kenyatta, "but don't go there." Kenyatta went, but only to watch the events from a nearby tenement rooftop. Everybody was nervous; the police were out nearly in riot force and even at that were outnumbered by the Fruit of Islam, shaven-headed and icy-eyed, patrolling the sidewalks with plastic armbands that said, WE ARE WITH MUHAMMAD. At one point, while the queues of spectators were still backed up into the street waiting to be searched and let inside, a young black man suddenly came tumbling out the armory door into the smoky-hot afternoon. *"He's one of Malcolm's men!"* somebody yelled. Nobody stopped to check his credentials. The Fruit swarmed over him; some of them locked arms in a double line to hold the police back while others pummeled him to the ground. A crowd closed around them, shouting: "Kill him, kill him!" The Fruit beat him nearly senseless, then carried him across the street and dumped him against a fence. A short distance away, a man named Jesus Emmanuel, who called himself the Blood Son of Mother and Father Divine, handed out some homemade leaflets calling the Messenger a "mix bred phony." Two men attacked him, smashed his nose and knocked loose two of his teeth.

The rally itself was uneventful. The crowd was responsibly estimated between 6,500 and 8,000, considerably less than the hundreds of thousands the Muslims had predicted or the 15,000 they claimed afterward in *Muhammad Speaks,* but a splendid showing nevertheless in a community normally thought to be Malcolm's property. The day was sweltering, the acoustics wretched, the Messenger's bronchia particularly troublesome. He came in hidden in a phalanx of the Fruit; they walked him to the stage, then parted to reveal him, tiny and eggshell-fragile, looking faintly surprised through a strenuous three-minute ovation. He coughed and gasped through his speech, with Muhammad Ali close by leading the applause and yelling, "Teach us! Teach us!" He spoke mostly about the evils of integration and only obliquely about Malcolm. "There is some person who wants to be what I am," he said, "but that person is not able to be what I am. . . . I know what you do not know, I have heard what you have not heard, I have seen what you have not seen." Mr. Muhammad survived the heat, the sound system and his own wheeziness for an hour or so, the words coming out halting, almost as if there were periods between them; then, abruptly, he sat down without finishing. Ali followed with a report on *his* trip to Africa; if he had seen any White Muslims there, he did not mention them.

That evening, while Malcolm was waiting to go on at the Audubon Ballroom, Jesus Emmanuel materialized like some apparition out of the night, his face a blood-streaked ruin. The sight sickened Malcolm; he turned away, to one of his people, and said, "Get him out of here." In his speech, he said that any black group that really wanted to crack heads ought to go South and crack some cracker heads, not black people's; and at the end, he extended this invitation directly to the Muslims. "They've got all the machinery, don't think they haven't," he said, "and the experience where they know how to ease out in broad daylight or in dark and do whatever is necessary by any means necessary. They know how to do that. . . . That's my closing message to Elijah Muhammad: if he is the leader of the Muslims and the leader of our people, then lead us against our enemies, don't lead us against each other."

It was a pretty sentiment, but events by then had driven Malcolm and the Messenger past the point where reconciliation or even détente was possible. They fought as they had loved, as father and son, in sudden storms of emotion and long brooding passages of hurt feelings. Each had friends in the other's circle; word got back to Malcolm that the Messenger's people hardly dared even mention his name in the old man's presence. Malcolm equally felt betrayed. He was sitting around talking with a few of the brothers one Sunday, half-listening to the radio, when Mr. Muhammad's regular weekly sermon came on. Malcolm snapped it off. "Don't listen to that thing," he said, suddenly hot. "I know what they're doing—they're brainwashing people." A reporter in those days confronted him with the rumors of a plot among his people to assassinate Mr. Muhammad, and he scoffed at the thought; he said that the old man's own deeds would bring him to his grave without outside help. Actually, the idea had been presented to Malcolm; one of the brothers had come to him and said, "I'd even kill *God* before I'd let Him kill me."

"You're losing your religion," Malcolm answered angrily.

"They're getting ready to kill you," the brother said.

"No," said Malcolm. "If someone killed him, it would make a martyr out of him."

The Nation, for its part, announced that death was too charitable a punishment for Malcolm. In *Muhammad Speaks,* the Messenger, who had previously let his ministers do the denunciations of Malcolm for him, wrote a little page-one homily on "the hypocrites who go out from me today" claiming to believe in Allah but rejecting him as Allah's Messenger. There was mention of a "chief hypocrite," but not Malcolm or anybody else by name—only the blanket warning that a prophet of God was bound by Scripture to "be unyielding" with hypocrites and disbelievers and that the fire of hell would surely be their abode. "They are not to be killed," the Messenger wrote, "for Allah desires to make them examples for others, by chastising them like a parent does a child. He chastises one with the strap to warn the other not to disobey."

For Malcolm, on the far side of the Rubicon, this declaration was small comfort. On July 2, he complained to a wire-service reporter that he had been made to look ridiculous in the dispute—that he had been unable to make his case adequately because it involved a moral matter that "can't be brought into public before it is brought into court." That same day, in the State Superior Court for the County of Los Angeles, the prominent attorney Gladys Towles Root filed complaints to establish paternity against Mr.

Muhammad on behalf of Evelyn Williams, Lucille Rosary Karriem and their four minor children. On July 5, getting into his car outside the house in East Elmhurst, Malcolm saw four black men coming at him with knives; he hit the gas hard, roared off, then circled back and got his rifle, but the men had gone. That evening in Harlem, during the question period at the end of the second public rally of the OAAU, he apologized for not taking appointments too far in advance. "Right now," he said, "things are pretty hot for me, you know. Oh, yes. I'm trying to stay alive, you understand. I may sound like I'm cracking, but I'm facting." On July 9, he left John F. Kennedy Airport for London and then Africa. He planned to be gone six weeks. It was nearly twenty before he came home to the wars.

24. On Standing on the Tops of Trucks During Riots

It was said in Harlem that Malcolm X was the only man who could order a riot to happen. This may well have been so; the truth was that he would not have tried. Malcolm did not doubt that white America deserved to be rioted against; it was just that he was a percentage player and that he saw none for the colonials in tearing up the colony. Malcolm was a force *against* rioting in Harlem, because he loved Harlem too well. "In his street rallies," Percy Sutton remembered, "he would say, 'This devil has been awful, we've got to get him off our backs. But let's don't let him trap us into burning down our houses. Oh, yeah, they own 'em, but we got to live in them. We're going to take this over, but we don't want to take over a shambles when we get it.' And there would be applause, but you could see what he was doing. Or he would say, 'None of these blue-eyed devils in blue uniforms are going t touch us. But there are some Uncle Toms who might agitate the police to hit us on our heads. Well, we're not going to help those Toms—we're going to go in peace. . . .' "

When Harlem's riot happened, Malcolm was a world away, trying to persuade the assembled chiefs of state of the Organization of African Unity that Harlem was really an African city and that its problems were of as much concern to them as Accra's or Nairobi's or Stanleyville's. The trigger incident was a flash fight outside a school downtown in Yorkville, in which a white police lieutenant named Gilligan shot and killed a fifteen-year-old black kid named Powell. Two nights later, an angry crowd marched on the 123rd Street police station, the same one from which Malcolm had peaceably liberated Hinton Johnson seven years before, and demanded Gilligan's arrest for murder. The police started making arrests; the crowd fragmented and spread howling through Harlem, battling cops, smashing show windows, firing buildings, liberating clothes and TV sets and cases of Scotch and all those gaudy appurtenances of the American Dream that white people had hidden behind steel gratings and prohibitive price tags for all those years. The Long Hot Summer had not yet become a cliché of our journalism or a recurring reality of our calendar; some of us saw the events in Harlem as an insurrection, others as a storm of criminality loosed on us by Communists or civil-rights agitators or maybe even Malcolm, by telepathy from Cairo. What we missed was the sheer joy of it—the exhilaration of making something happen in a place where nothing ever did. One night a sweaty cop faced a crowd of rioters and told them through a bullhorn to go home. "We *are* home, baby!" a voice taunted back. Tomorrow was soon enough for arguing over pennies with the welfare lady or shoving a handtruck through the garment center; tonight was windows dissolving and whitey's riches spilling out and cops looking scared and black kids running in the streets, faces shining orange in the fires, shouting: "Malcolm! We want Malcolm! Wait till Malcolm comes!"

It was said in Harlem, too, that Malcolm X was the only man who could order a riot to stop. He probably would not have tried that ither. There was, for one thing, the pragmatic risk to his legend: ne does not command the waters to part unless one is quite sure that they are going to. More important, no matter how much he disapproved of anything so suicidal as rioting, Malcolm could not have stood at so great a distance from the street people—his people—as to criticize them for it or to ask them to quit. He wasn't in the streets with them, but he read about the rioting in the papers and, on about the third day, put in a call to Sutton. The connection was terrible and conversation difficult, but Malcolm got his message through.

"There were suggestions," Sutton told him, "that you might have got onto the top of a truck and tried to get people to cool it."

"If I were you, counselor," Malcolm replied, "I'd stay off the top of trucks. Black people didn't start the riot and they don't have any obligation to stop it. It's bad destroying our own community because someday we should own it. But I don't advise you go get on the tops of any trucks. I wouldn't if I were there. If I were there, I'd be doing the same thing."

25. The Second Time Around

For our men in Cairo, it was—*extraordinary.* There they were, two U.S. Foreign Service officers assigned to cover the Second OAU Summit Conference for the State Department, and they couldn't get past the lobby at Shepheard's or into the Nile Hilton at all—couldn't even talk to their African *friends* without a couple of Egyptian security men maneuvering close and their friends suddenly going gray and saying, "I've got to go now." And there, smiling on the other side of the cordon, they could see Malcolm X, sometimes sitting by himself waiting for an appointment, some times moving among the delegates with that elegant ease and whispering in their ears—what?—that Africa and Afro-Americ were one. The U.S. team—a senior Africanist and a young OAU specialist on loan from the American Embassy in Addis Ababa—had a hard time going anywhere; Malcolm seemed free to go everywhere. The OAU had given him observer's credentials, a floor pass and a berth on the yacht *Isis* with the leaders of the major African national liberation movements. He wasn't permitted to address the conference—Malcolm blamed American wire-pulling for that—but he was allowed to circulate a memorandum making his case among the thirty-three assembled heads of state.

For our men in Cairo, on the outside looking in, it was all most awkward. They had no special instructions from home about watching Malcolm or dealing with his presence at the summit; still, there he was, a small embarrassment among all their other problems in Cairo, but an embarrassment nevertheless. One of them inadvertently got maneuvered face to face with Malcolm; they both smiled unhappily and shook hands, each clearly wishing he didn't have to. The other saw Malcolm at a cocktail party laid on by the British. He felt *fascinated* by the man but stayed discreetly on the far side of the room. "He was not a person we could associate with," he said. "I never did talk to him. I felt I couldn't."

Malcolm might have been, so far as Washington's people were concerned, the minister of another country—an envoy hostile to America and welcome in the presence of African premiers, presidents and kings whose friendship America wanted. Just being there was in this sense Malcolm's victory: when the nations assembled in the great soaring conference chamber at Arab League headquarters, his was the favored American diplomatic presence. He understood African politics well enough to know that further victories would be enormously more difficult. But he lobbied industriously around the hotels, struck up friendships especially among the younger, more radical members of delegations and invested all the passion he had in his eight-page memorandum begging the support of the Africans in haling America before the United Nations. He had come, so he wrote, to speak for 22 million Africans trapped in the U.S. "by a cruel accident in our history," and deprived daily by the government, or with the government's assent, of the most basic human rights. "Our problems are your problems," he said. ". . . You will never be recognized as free human beings until and unless we are also recognized and treated as human beings." He understood their tenuous hold on nationhood and their consequent dependence on U.S. foreign aid; he told them in effect that there were more important things than their own survival if its price was doing America's bidding. "We pray that our African brothers have not freed themselves of European colonialism only to be overcome and held in check now by American dollarism," Malcolm wrote. "Don't let American racism be 'legalized' by American dollarism."

They had little choice. Malcolm was moving in a dreamscape, an Africa whose power in the world he romanticized and which did after all place national survival ahead of questions of color, conscience and even meaningful independence. "They weren't in Cairo to fry his fish," one American diplomat said comfortably and accurately. The Congo that summer was in turmoil; the Angolese liberation movement was stagnating; apartheid was hardening in South Africa, with the rest of the continent impotent to stop it; the spirit of unity that had brought the OAU into being the year before was coming undone in a tangle of private jealousies and political quarrels over, among other issues, how and how quickly unity was to be achieved. Malcolm under the circumstances was like a guest at a gourmet feast talking about starvation in Bangladesh: everyone suspected he was right and wished he wouldn't keep reminding them of it. The Africans didn't want to pick a fight with the Americans, not just then. The tip-off came the very first day when Gamal Nasser of Egypt, who actually rather admired Malcolm, praised America in his opening speech for having put the Civil Rights Act of 1964 on the statute books two weeks before. Since Malcolm was trying to persuade the Africans that the law was a fake passed specifically to fool them, and that the real issue was *human* rights anyway, his cause was undermined before he had seriously begun to fight.

That he came away from Cairo with anything at all was a tribute less to his charm, though he did captivate the Africans, than to his stubbornness; Malcolm was never afraid to be rude in a good cause. He nagged and lectured and cajoled, and when there was nobody at hand to talk to, he haunted the hotel lobbies making himself and his quest unremittingly visible. His persistence in the end was rewarded with a resolution—a cautiously balanced affair praising the U.S. on one hand for the Civil Rights Act, worrying on the other about the continuing evidence of racial oppression in the States and concluding with the wish that the government intensify its efforts against color discrimination. This was disappointingly tame stuff for Malcolm, since it credited Washington with trying to deal with the problem, and it was substantially identical in thought and tone to a resolution passed without his lobbying at the first OAU summit in Addis Ababa the year before. Still, it was something—a first gingerly gesture in what he hoped would become a continuing diplomatic connection between Africa and Afro-America—and it was unmistakably Malcolm's doing. "He is the only real American leader of the people to tell us what is the problem in the U.S.," said A.M. Babu, a radical Tanzanian government minister, in a reciprocal visit to one of Malcolm's Harlem rallies that winter. ". . . He did not go to Geneva —he went to *Cairo.*"

He lingered in Cairo for two months. His purposes were partially political, pushing the UN venture and hunting moral and material support for his activities back home. Some of the brothers had been pressing him to do this last—to come back from this trip with something for them besides Islamic religious tracts. Malcolm wrote excitedly from Cairo that he had been meeting with everybody from Nasser on down with the most heartening results—"so hold your head up high."

But his purposes were religious as well. He had come to Cairo surprisingly sophisticated in politics and naïve as a child in Islam; some of the more worldly Egyptians he met were privately amused by his bubbling convert's innocence in the faith. Malcolm wanted to move beyond that—wanted to grow in his religion and to be legitimated as a religious leader. He spent a good part of his time in Cairo (and in shorter trips to Jedda and Mecca later) studying Islam at its fountainheads and preparing himself for an authentic Muslim ministry. He did have more religious tracts shipped home, and he recruited a spiritual adviser for the MMI as well, an ancient Sudanese imam named Sheik Ahmed Hassoun, whom he found in Mecca. He got the credentials he wanted: the rector of Al-Azhar, the great Islamic university in Cairo, certified his ministry ("Mr. Malkulm X . . . with his true and correct faith is one of the Muslim community . . . and it is his duty to propagate Islam") and the World Muslim League in Mecca made him its man in America.

There were purely pragmatic reasons for acquiring these papers: they certified Malcolm's religion to the ghetto, where he and Mr. Muhammad were coming into open competition for souls, and to that larger American audience whose regard he had lately begun to value. But in a deeper sense his new credentials testified to the tumbling rush of discovery and renewal and change he was going through during his last year. Early that autumn, he sent Handler and the *Times* a second letter from Mecca as remarkable in its way as the first. "For twelve long years," he wrote, "I lived within the narrow-minded confines of the 'straitjacket world' created by my strong belief that Elijah Muhammad was a messenger direct from God Himself and my faith in what I now see to be a pseudo-religious philosophy that he preaches. . . . I shall never rest until I have undone the harm I did to so many well-meaning, innocent Negroes who through my own evangelistic zeal now believe in him even more fanatically and more blindly than I did." He suggested that Mr. Muhammad was a "religious faker" and swore he would wear a straitjacket no longer—the Messenger's or anybody else's. "I am a Muslim in the most orthodox sense," he wrote. "My religion is Islam as it is believed in and practiced by the Muslims here in the Holy City of Mecca. This religion recognizes all men as brothers. It accepts all human beings as equals before God, and as equal members in the Human Family of Mankind. I totally reject Elijah Muhammad's racist philosophy, which he has labeled 'Islam' only to fool and misuse gullible people, as he fooled and misused me. But I blame only myself and no one else for the fool that I was, and the harm that my evangelic foolishness has done to others."

For Malcolm to confess error in the white man's presence was rare enough. What followed was rarer still—Malcolm the black Jacobin suddenly addressing whites in language that would hardly have raised an eyebrow at a luncheon of the National Conference of Christians and Jews. He wasn't anti- or un-American, he wrote —just an open-minded man trying to follow his intelligence wherever it led him. Some of his best friends were Christians, Jews, agnostics, atheists, capitalists, Communists, socialists, moderates, conservatives, extremists—"some are even Uncle Toms." He included everybody on this list except, specifically, white people; he still believed that those who were well-meaning ought to quit talking about it so much and do more about the racism of their own kind. The difference was that he was now conceding that some white people might in fact *be* well-meaning. "We must forget politics and propaganda," he said, "and approach this as a Human Problem which all of us as human beings are obligated to correct."

Given his normal recklessness of what official America thought of him, Malcolm was curiously anxious to get across in this letter that he was really neither seditious nor subversive. He may have imagined that, with these disclaimers, he was investing cheaply enough in life insurance for his continuing travels through the Middle East and Africa. While the OAU summit was still on, he became violently ill one night after dinner at the Nile Hilton and was briefly hospitalized. He suspected that he had been poisoned and guessed that American agents had done it.

There was no tangible evidence for this; Washington in fact was slow responding to his trip even as a policy problem, much less as grounds for assassination, and did not get seriously interested until after its people in Cairo pouched home a copy of his memo to the African heads of state. Its attention thereafter increased visibly, however, and as it did, so did Malcolm's anxiety. The Justice Department began quietly inquiring into where he got the money for his trip. The best information available in the States was that he was traveling on borrowed cash, publisher's advances and the hospitality of the host countries, but the fact that such an inquiry was undertaken at all suggests that Justice was looking for something more sinister.* Handler got wind of the government's concern and did a *Times* piece reporting that not only Justice but State had got worried after seeing Malcolm's memo. What troubled Washington, Handler wrote, was that if Malcolm could persuade a single African government to carry the ball in the UN, the United States would be confronted with "a touchy problem" indeed—a challenge to its claim to primacy among nations in the defense of human rights.

Someone sent Malcolm a clipping of this story; he read it, folded it up, put it in his wallet and worriedly showed it to friends he met on his travels. He had come in Africa, as he had earlier in the States, to that point in the life of a revolutionary where paranoia and reality intersect. People began following him—U.S. agents, he presumed—and when he couldn't pick out his particular shadow, he was suspicious of any stranger. "He was very frightened," said Melvin McCaw, a young black American who then directed the Nairobi office of the Institute of International Education. "Every person he saw, he'd want to know: *Who's that? What are his connections?* We took him to a nightclub, the Equator Club, and sat at a table where he had his back exposed. He was very uncomfortable. He kept looking over his shoulder, kept noticing people he thought he'd seen before. . . ."

His travels this time took him from Egypt and Arabia down the east coast of Africa as far as Tanzania, then west and north roughly along the route he had followed on his first trip. He visited four-

*One measure of the discretion with which the matter was handled was the fact that Burke Marshall, then the Assistant Attorney General in charge of civil rights, did some of the inquiring himself and that when he wanted to see Alex Haley, Malcolm's collaborator on the *Autobiography*, he arranged that they meet informally in New York, at the offices of a foundation friendly to civil-rights causes. Marshall, when I inquired, had forgotten this meeting and remembered generally having been "more curious than concerned" about Malcolm's activities. "We were awfully ignorant about the Muslims and about Malcolm X." But not alarmed by what he was doing? "Not me. Now if you ask Mr. [J. Edgar] Hoover or somebody like that—"

teen nations and had audiences with seven heads of state; he spent several days with Prime Minister Jomo Kenyatta of Kenya, took a plane ride from Dar-es-Salaam to Nairobi with Prime Minister Milton Obote of Uganda, visited Conakry for three days as the house guest of President Sékou Touré of Guinea. His sponsors from country to country were usually the old revolutionaries or the young radicals, but he seemed to be welcome everywhere. "Even the conservatives were impressed by him," Melvin McCaw remembered. "He had a great gift for explaining the situation—for bringing the issue to the Africans. He even talked the way they do, with those animal metaphors—the whole language of the Kikuyu is made up of them."

Where his first trip had been impromptu and private, his second was formal and public—a VIP tour down the corridors of power of a third of the then independent nations of Africa. He didn't get stuck waiting at airports this time; this time he was expected, and received, like a visitor of state. He stayed at the grand hotels, like the Nile Hilton or the richly gardened Federal Palace in Lagos or the New Stanley in Nairobi, where the doormen used to chase passing Africans across the street in the old colonial times. On his diplomatic rounds, said Julian Mayfield, who saw Malcolm this trip in Cairo as well as in Ghana, "it was open sesame everywhere he went. And he took it all in stride. He was completely at ease with men who dealt in world affairs. He understood power and they understood power. I used to wonder what he would be like if he had been born in a country where we were in a majority and if he had been the head of state. He understood right off something that it took me a long time to find out—that the United States government doesn't run much differently than a little old chickenshit government like Ghana." Malcolm invested himself with the authority to speak for 22 million black Americans, and a good part of Africa believed him. Other American black leaders traveling the continent in his wake—a group from SNCC and, later, James Farmer—discovered that they had to relate themselves to Malcolm to be heard, not only in Left and student circles but among some government ministers as well. "Almost everywhere he'd been," Farmer said, "I was asked, 'What do you think about Malcolm X?' His reception had been splendid. Fantastic."

By the time he got to Nairobi, barely a third of the way into his journey, the State Department had indeed got interested in his travels—particularly in the success or failure of the UN effort. This interest, so far as I could determine, was rather low-key at the top—aides to the then Assistant Secretary for African Affairs, G. Mennen Williams, did not, for example, trouble him with the Malcolm Problem—but it grew more intense further down the line. "We got cables from State that he was a suspicious character and we should keep an eye on him," said William Attwood, the magazine and newspaper executive who was then U.S. Ambassador to Kenya. "They wanted to know what he was saying, who he was seeing, whether he was undermining American interests, whether he was spreading false rumors. . . . State was saying watch him."

Attwood didn't catch up with the watch personally until Malcolm had been in town a few days, visiting government people and doing press and television interviews. "I saw him out at the race track one Saturday afternoon sitting in the Presidential box with Kenyatta and the cabinet," Attwood remembered. "I thought he was white; American Negroes don't look so black in Africa and in fact some of the Africans were a little put off by the color of his skin—they called him an albino at first. I said to Mungai"—Dr. Njoroge Mungai, a government minister friendly to the U.S.—" 'Who's the new face?' He said, 'That's Malcolm X. He's the leader of 22 million American blacks.' I said something like he didn't look very black to me, and besides, from the polls I was familiar with, I thought Dr. King would have a better claim to that. Mungai said, 'Well, that's who he says he is.' The fact was that they didn't know who in the hell he was."

Neither did Attwood, really, not at that point, and he found himself in a bit of a scramble putting out fires. He wasn't worried about Malcolm turning Jomo Kenyatta's head—"Kenyatta," he said, "didn't quite figure him out"—but the visit made problems for him nevertheless. Malcolm predicted on television that Barry Goldwater was going to win the Presidency in a landslide—that he was the candidate of the whites and that whites outnumbered blacks ten to one. Some of the Africans were nervous about this and descended unhappily on Attwood. "He'd made it sound pretty convincing," Attwood recalled. "I told them, 'I'll give you ten-to-one odds that Johnson wins with forty-five states.' I lost twenty pounds. If I'd said forty-four states, I would have won." The trip was making waves in the American black colony, too—some of Attwood's own embassy people among them. Mel McCaw, who had met Malcolm once as an undergraduate at Atlanta University seven or eight years earlier, threw one party to introduce him to the black Americans and planned a second for some of the same crowd and some Kenyans as well. The embassy tried to persuade its people not to go, and, McCaw told me, Attwood himself called him over for a dressing-down. "He said, 'What are you trying to do, set up some kind of cleavage in the U.S. community here?' I said no. He said, 'Well, what is the point of raising these issues by having special black parties?' " McCaw said Attwood threatened obliquely to have his job (his institute was getting government scholarship money) and assured him that no staff people would go to his second party. In the event, some did, and some who didn't show sent around liquor along with their regrets.

McCaw got back to his office and found Malcolm waiting on the phone. "They're very upset about you over at the embassy," McCaw said. "Why don't you go over and talk to them?" Malcolm had heard good things about Attwood in his travels—he was by common consensus America's best hand in Africa at the time—and phoned for an appointment. Attwood was not overjoyed at the prospect but said yes—"he was an American citizen." As the tale got out later, he made a date for that afternoon, hung up and instantly began jabbing buttons to get his political people together for consultations.

But when Malcolm finally loped up the embassy stairs and dropped into a chair opposite Attwood, they got on like civilized men. Their conversation, once past their first mutual wariness, ran on for hours; Malcolm counted it afterward as another of those moments of sudden, flaring insight that, strung together, made up his continuing re-education. "He was discovering Africa," Attwood said. It took Attwood a few moments of sparring to discover Malcolm. "I expected a lot of raving and ranting," he remembered. "I started right out saying, 'Look, I want to warn you, I've got no use for racists, black or white, and as far as I'm concerned, you're a racist.' And he said, 'No, I'm not anymore, and I'd like to explain why.' " Malcolm talked about his travels and about having seen black and white people for the first time outside the context of America and its ruined racial climate. "He started coming to life," said Attwood, "when I started telling him on my own what he was going to tell me about color-consciousness in America. I told him that in Africa I had become all but color-blind but that back home I was far more aware of color.

"He really warmed up. He thought we were *talking,* not just making conversation. This was a theory he had, and here I was, a member of the establishment saying something that he felt. It pleased him enormously. He said that in America all of us are under strong pressure—some electricity in the air—that forces us to be race-conscious. People could act more *relaxed* outside America. So the white man was not the devil, he wasn't evil in himself—it was the atmosphere." Malcolm, for all his growing interest in African socialism, didn't seem to Attwood to be identifying American racism with American capitalism; the problem he was describing was more neurotic than economic. "He was saying that in America we're reminded of color by the scenery and the furniture of our past. Abroad, we're just Americans." Malcolm argued that this racism was decisive in America, if not quite universal. Attwood dissented at this; Malcolm smiled and told him, "I think you'll notice it when you get back." Retelling the story years later, Attwood still seemed faintly surprised by the whole experience. He had expected a fire-eating racist; he had received an oddly gentle man, three-buttoned and bespectacled, who called you "sir" not as black to white or servant to master but out of the common courtesy of equals. When Malcolm left Nairobi soon thereafter, Attwood cabled ahead alerting the next diplomatic post, as State had instructed him to do, but was himself considerably less troubled. "Travel," he said, "*is* broadening."

Travel in Africa that summer could be diminishing to one's dreams. Malcolm seemed subdued in the later stages of his journey, perhaps out of jet fatigue, or anxiety over being so constantly watched, or perhaps out of discouragement about getting help for his UN adventure. There was, as Malcolm eventually was forced to recognize, a disparity between the warmth with which Africa welcomed him and the yes-but caution with which it received his call to arms against America. In the end, he discovered that he was bucking not only the vast distance between Harlem and Africa—a distance he blamed perhaps too easily on white American propaganda—but the great reach of U.S. foreign aid. Africa liked Malcolm X but couldn't afford him. "They were all polite to him," said Attwood, a man whose realism was respected as much by the Africans as by his employers. "The Africans have a way of being pleasant to people. He would get some vague promises from some of them—'If So-and-so does, *we* might.' But in the crunch what they cared about was staying in power. Except for a few intellectuals, they didn't really care that much about what happens to the American Negro—they considered him *American.* If there ever was an isolationist continent, it was Africa, and with good reason." The American estimate at the time was that Malcolm might have picked up some support in Tanzania, which was home to many of the liberation movements, and in the north, in Egypt and Algeria; that he missed some stops that might have been profitable for him, notably Congo (Brazzaville) and Zambia; that he was wasting his time elsewhere, pragmatically speaking, even with men like Nkrumah of Ghana and Touré of Guinea—the radicals he most admired.

Malcolm's innate optimism seemed to fade accordingly. In Nigeria, two-thirds into his tour, an African friend asked him how the UN project was going. Malcolm, normally bullish about anything he undertook, seemed suddenly vague; he answered only that no doors had been closed to him on the trip and that he wished the radicals and moderate heads of government could find some way to work together. In conversations and in letters home, he began to talk in more general terms about internationalizing the struggle and less about the particulars of bringing America formally to book before the UN. He did not give up the project, but he invested less hope and less energy in it. "He got all those great official receptions," said Handler, who witnessed Malcolm's disappointment when he got home. "But the one thing he wanted of them he couldn't get. He got very rough with them. He told them there were all kinds and forms of colonialism and that as long as you take money from America, you'll have only the external appearance of sovereignty. But every one of them was on the handout line. He discovered that they weren't going to help except in a verbal way—they weren't going to jeopardize those handouts."

Washington's concern began proportionately to diminish. Malcolm was still followed, but his trip was seen increasingly as a problem in propaganda, to be dealt with by normal counterpropaganda techniques. The USIA saw to it that Africa was plentifully informed of the progress of the government and the regular civil-rights movement against Southern segregation and of Malcolm's outlaw role in this struggle. After Malcolm's return, the American Negro Leadership Conference on Africa, whose letterhead included most of the name civil-rights groups, from the Urban League left through SNCC, sent Farmer on his tour over much of the same ground. It was reported years later that the CIA had been putting some money covertly into ANLC and may in fact have promoted Farmer's trip. If so, neither Farmer nor his colleagues in the movement knew about it; Farmer, in fact, was painfully embarrassed and not a little peeved to hear that he was supposed to be going to undo what Malcolm had done in Africa. The person who brought him this news was Malcolm himself, in a phone call just before Farmer's departure.

"Brother James," he said, "I hear you're going to Africa."

"Right," said Farmer. "How'd you hear that?"

"Well, they've been announcing it on the radio, every hour on the hour. They say you're going to counteract *me*. Tell me—what about me are you going to counteract?"

"There's no truth in that at all," Farmer said, horrified. Malcolm asked if he could come over and talk about his experiences; he did, lounging on a couch at the Farmers' apartment on the Lower East Side with their dachshund curled up on his lap, spinning travel stories and suggesting African government people whom Farmer might want to see. Farmer, when he took his trip, went as nobody's servant; some American authorities at the time considered him, too, rather irresponsibly militant. Still, after Malcolm, America's men in Africa were pleased enough to have him come. "His trip was helpful," Attwood said. "He wasn't any CIA puppet—he was thought to be quite radical at the time, and some of the more radical African elements picked him up. What he did do was show the diversity of the American movement."

Malcolm thus wasn't going home from Africa empty-handed—not if the most powerful government on earth felt he needed answering. Quite apart from the particulars of his mission, he had gone really to renew a bond of brotherhood that had been broken by the slave trade centuries before. He may or may not have succeeded in this; he at least got the proposition of unity between Africa and Afro-America on the table, and he left behind a network of new OAAU chapters across the continent (and in Paris and London en route home) to keep that proposition alive. These would have been extraordinary achievements for any man. For Malcolm X, who read world history in prison and whose first notions of Africa came out of the revelations of W. D. Farrad, they were incredible.

Still, something was wrong when he came back to Ghana near the end of his journey. He looked up the old crowd and went back to the old places where they had been so happy together the first time; he even enlisted a few recruits for the OAAU back home, among them Maya Angelou, who had good African connections plus solid administrative experience in the Stateside movement raising money for Martin Luther King. But it was all *different* this time, because Malcolm was different. "There was a sense of—not desperation, you know, but it was like the hand of fate was on him," Miss Angelou said. All of them saw it. He was worried about those people tracking him; he got out the Handler clipping, showed it to Julian Mayfield and told him that if anything happened to him in the States they shouldn't necessarily think it was solely the doing of the Black Muslims.

Yet the shadows in Africa still were not nearly so ominous to him as his enemies back home; Malcolm, for the first time in his life, was afraid of going back to Harlem. "He looked very much like a fighter who had had a bit of the wind taken out of him, who'd had a blow to the solar plexus," Preston King remembered. He intimated to some of the Americans that he had actually been stretching out his trip to delay going home. He said there were brothers in the street in Harlem who would kill you for a dime; he said there were Muslims there who wouldn't even cost that much—who would do it for Allah if somebody further up the hierarchy told them to. The little circle of Americans—his circle—was frightened for him. "All of us begged him to stay," Miss Angelou said. "We were afraid for his life, and we thought he was being cavalier about it, traveling around a-damned-lone like that. One mark of a friendship is if you can say that's dumb—that's *duh-umb*—and the foundations of your friendship don't tremble just because you're shouting. We shouted. We said, 'Just spend six months here, let that jazz cool off.' We told him to bring Betty and the children. We told him he could give lectures anywhere. We told him any government would have taken him in."

But finally they had to put him on a plane, still a-damned-lone, no gay send-off this time but a little group of people watching him walk away across the tarmac with his overstuffed briefcase and his cameras and wishing he weren't going back. Julian Mayfield watched him and thought: *He's got nowhere to go* but *back.*

26. By Any Means Necessary

It was, said Percy Sutton, looking pained, like the ancient fable of the blind men and the elephant—"One feels the ear, one feels the trunk, one feels the tail and so on, and each of them thinks he can describe the whole animal." We had met years after Malcolm's death at Sutton's Democratic Club, in a drafty brownstone crowded with black petitioners in their overcoats; the room was full of Harlem's unmet daily hunger, and, seeing that, one saw Sutton's point—saw the irrelevance of trying to crowd Malcolm and his furies into some square-cornered ideological box and announcing that *this* was the real Malcolm X. Yet it remained a game that anybody could play and everybody did. Integrationists assured me that Malcolm was becoming an integrationist. Nationalists told me that he never left home. Marxists were sure he would have been a socialist had he lived. White liberals wanted him to be a black liberal. His special affection has been claimed by Trotskyists, Maoists, Nkrumists, Garveyites, orthodox and unorthodox Muslims, civil-rights organizations from the Urban League to CORE and SNCC, and Adam Clayton Powell. And out of that mystery of becoming that was Malcolm's last year—out of the extravagant spill of words in speeches and interviews and chance conversations—all of them could produce evidence to prove it.

The truth, as Malcolm himself kept telling us, was that he didn't know where he was going or what he wanted to be, except *flexible.* He thought of himself as a teacher, a minister, a Muslim, an African, an internationalist and in the most general terms a revolutionary; and, before any of these things, as black. The details were vague and fluid and improvisational, subject to change from speech to speech or even answer to answer in an interview or radio panel. He was searching (some said groping) for his bearings; in the meantime, he said straight out, he would ride with the wind, changing his mind and his course as circumstance changed around him. Where was he headed? "I have no idea," he told one black writer that last December. "I have no idea. I can capsulize how I feel—I'm for the freedom of the 22 million Afro-Americans by any means necessary. *By any means necessary.* I'm for a society in which our people are recognized and respected as human beings, and I believe that we have the right to resort to *any means necessary* to bring that about. So when you ask me where I'm headed, what can I say? I'm headed in any direction that will bring us some immediate results." He paused for a long moment and toyed with the cup of coffee in front of him. Then he added slowly, "Isn't anything wrong with that."

By any means necessary: the words, for Malcolm, were slogan enough, program enough, ideology enough. They carried a little edge of menace, which troubled him not at all; they gave him enormous political maneuvering room, which pleased him greatly. He had trusted in fixed answers for most of his adult life and now saw that they had betrayed him. He said, "I'm not dogmatic about anything any more."

He had come home from Africa in late November tired and shivering a little in the chill; he hadn't packed for winter, since he had planned to get back in August, and was grateful when Charles Kenyatta pushed through the homecoming crowd and handed him a topcoat. There wasn't time to rest. He arrived to find both his organizations in disarray, their projects languishing and their cash so desperately short that some weeks they had to borrow money to pay for a meeting hall. Malcolm was forced to book a heavy schedule of speaking dates, those he wanted and those he didn't, just to bring in some cash. He lived in a condition of flight, his enemies behind him, his future somewhere dimly ahead. His days were full of audiences of one or two or five or ten or a hundred or a thousand waiting to hear him; his nights disappeared in people's living rooms in conversations that didn't end but died, like a fire going cold. Malcolm made a rule for himself that he would try to get at least four hours sleep a night; sometimes, he kept it. Whole weeks slipped by when the only moments he could steal for unwinding and thinking were on a jet plane going somewhere. "I've got no time to do *anything!*" he exploded one day.

His ideology and his program, to the extent that he had any at all, took form out of the slow agglomeration of all those words. His priority project was still internationalizing the struggle and his primary theater for this, the UN. His international politics ebbed and flowed between Pan-Africanism—the unity of black people everywhere around their color and common origin in Africa—and a wider identification with the entire Third World from Cuba to Vietnam against the colonialist (and capitalist) white West. Which label more nearly applied was not nearly so important as Malcolm's underlying purpose—making black and white Americans alike see themselves on a larger stage where the old majority-minority arithmetic was reversed and the future, if not the present, belonged to dark mankind. "Till Malcolm," said John Killens, "most people believed it was a family affair between black people and this government. What Malcolm was saying was that's like the woman whose husband beats her and she doesn't scream because she doesn't want the neighbors to know." Malcolm wanted not only to let the neighbors know but to persuade them to bring the law down on America—an international law whose authority he may have overrated but whose psychological value he understood. SNCC brought a bunch of teen-agers from McComb, Mississippi, to see him that fall—black children to whom even Jackson was a great and distant place—and Malcolm spent an afternoon telling them that there were men of power who looked like them and cared about them in Dar and Accra and Conakry. "It is important," he told them, "for you to know that when you're in Mississippi, you're not alone."

Malcolm spent more than half his last year traveling abroad in quest of his dream *entente noire* and devoted increasing time at home to lobbying around UN Plaza. The day-to-day domestic politics of survival in America got proportionately less of his attention, to the distress of some of his followers, and his home-front program was accordingly more difficult to define. He talked about revolution, without defining either its means (except that it probably wouldn't be nonviolent) or its ends (beyond "respect and recognition" for black people). He no longer insisted, as nationalists classically had, that land was the single objective of revolutions; the blacks already occupied land of a sort—the ghettos—and Malcolm had begun dreaming in the vaguest terms of change in the larger American system. He remained fascinated though not deceived by the possibilities of elective politics for achieving change, provided black people organized, registered as independents and ran their own militant candidates. "Even I prefer ballots to bullets," he said, as though even he were surprised by this declaration. The difference between him and the respectable movement was that he didn't rule out bullets as an alternative; he was otherwise equally concerned to register black voters and "make our people become involved in the mainstream of the political structure of this country."

He talked about brotherhood, too, a new word for Malcolm; in his haunted last days particularly, in speeches to mixed crowds and interviews with the white media, he kept repeating it with a kind of desperate persistence. His downtown politics by then had become a cry for help. Uptown, he spoke differently. "I say one thing in Harlem and another downtown," he acknowledged once, "because you're dealing with two different people." He did not mean by this that he was running some hypocritical game, truckling to whitey south of 110th Street and baiting him to the north. He meant simply that one addressed one's audiences in a tongue they would understand and that whitey, in the vocabulary of his audiences in Harlem, remained the enemy. He seemed mellowed the night he dropped by Farmer's place that late autumn, lounging there on the couch talking about Mecca and White Muslims and the experience of having prayed alongside men he had thought irredeemably wicked. "Brother James," he said at length, "I've come to the conclusion that anyone who will fight not *for* us but *with* us is my brother. And that goes for your three guys, too."

By Farmer's three guys, he meant Michael Schwerner, Andrew

Goodman and James Chaney—the three CORE volunteers, two white and one black, who had been lynched the first night of the Mississippi Freedom Summer and buried in an earthen dam. Farmer's eyes widened. "Why didn't you say that last Saturday noon in Harlem Square?" he asked Malcolm.

"Brother James," Malcolm answered, smiling, "you're enough of a politician to know that if a leader makes a right-angle turn, he turns alone."

All Malcolm was saying was that to die for black people was after all enough to certify one's good intentions toward them; that this should seem to him a right-angle turn was a measure of the continuing weight of his past upon him. His brotherliness of the last days was the composite of small concessions painfully and haltingly yielded. He would consider alliances with whites, so long as they knew their place. He accepted the willingness to die as a credential, though he still thought whites should be willing to kill as well. He even relented on the question of intermarriage, a step as difficult for him as for any Southern segregationist. That night at Farmer's, he asked for cream in his coffee. "Why, Malcolm," boomed Farmer, turning a favorite joke back on him, "I'm disappointed in you. I take *my* coffee like my women—black. Strong and black." Malcolm, who had so often attacked Farmer for having married a white woman, looked up and saw Mrs. Farmer standing there. "He started to laugh," Farmer said. "He roared. I thought he was going to fall off the couch." A month later, he announced publicly that intermarriage was "just one human being marrying another human being," nothing more. What would have been a platitude for anybody else so civilized was a confession for Malcolm; he made it, by chance or design, where few of his friends could hear it—on a television show in Canada.

Even these modest changes were extraordinary, given Malcolm's past; the danger lies in making too much of them—in sentimentalizing Malcolm into a black white liberal. He had seen White Muslims in Mecca and white revolutionaries in Africa; had met a few American whites he actually liked; had even discovered and enjoyed a capacity for relaxing with that minority of whites who seemed able to relax with him.* In his last days, he was codifying his experience into his politics; he thawed just enough to satisfy the evidence of his sensibility and the requirements of his new notions of leadership, which included the possibility of arm's-length alliances with the right kind of whites. What he never retreated from was the first premise that white American *society* was deeply and perhaps irretrievably racist—that our past and present together had so poisoned all of us, black and white, that we could not even look at one another independently of color and all that color meant between us. Mecca remained one thing for him, America another. "When I got back into this American society," he said, "I'm not in a society that practices brotherhood. I'm in a society that might preach it on Sunday, but they don't practice it on *no* day."

He had a problem selling even this much lovingkindness in Harlem, which was the audience that finally counted with him. The vague brotherhood he spoke of among liberal and radical whites took on a we-know-better edge of cynicism there. At one of his last rallies, a turned-off follower got up during the question period and said bitterly, "We heard you changed, Malcolm. Why don't you tell us where you're at with them white folks?" It wasn't the sort of challenge Malcolm was used to on his home ground, but he improvised through it. "I haven't changed," he said. "I just see things on a broader scale. We nationalists used to think we were militant. We were just dogmatic. It didn't bring us anything. Now I know it's smarter to say you're going to shoot a man for what he is doing to you than because he is a white. If you attack him because he is white, you give him no out. He can't stop being white. We've got to give the man a chance. He probably won't take it, the snake. But we've got to give him a chance."

*When Percy Sutton was inaugurated for his first state assembly term that January, Malcolm rode up to Albany to watch on a chartered bus. His seat-mate was a white preacher, a friend of Sutton's, who knew Malcolm only by his press reputation. Afterward, Sutton asked the minister teasingly if he had learned all about Malcolm's legendary hatred for white people. "You should have heard him," the minister said. "We talked about the weather, the scenery, the cows we passed on the way—everything else but. *I* had to introduce the subject with *him*."

Uptown, where it counted, white people were still The Man, the snake, the enemy. Uptown, Malcolm made his disclaimers about racism almost apologetically. "I'm not blanketly condemning all whites," he said at one Audubon rally. "All of them don't oppress. All of them aren't in a position to. But most of them are, and most of them do." These asides were obligatory for him simply as ghetto politics; he had created himself as a leader attacking whites and he could not quit just like that. But they accurately reflected his private feelings as well. The day Martin Luther King came to Harlem with his new Nobel Prize, he spoke as he often did about conquering hate with love. Malcolm, who was there, remained unmoved. "No," he said a few days later. "Negroes been loving the white man for four hundred years, and he hates us as much now as he did when we started. We see nothing in his behavior toward us but hate." Nothing in Islam demanded unrequited love. "I can get along with white people who can get along with me," the New Malcolm X said, "but you don't see me trying to get along with any white man who doesn't want to get along with me. I don't believe in that. You got to get some kind of another religion."

Neither did Malcolm retreat from the politics of violence as a legitimate option for black people—a means that might become necessary and in any case should never be renounced in advance. Violence for Malcolm remained a matter of rhetoric rather than physical fact. He was quite consciously engaging in brinksmanship; he knew who had the guns—knew, as Killens put it, that you don't go up against the establishment with a Molotov cocktail—but he also knew how frightened white America was of the black revenge. "We must make them see that we are the enemy," he told one interviewer. "That the black man is a greater threat to this country than Vietnam or Berlin. So let them turn the money for defense in our direction and either destroy us or cure the conditions that brought our people to this point." He saw no way to make white power move except violence— "or," as he added, "a real threat of it." One cocked one's fist and gambled that cocking it would be enough. "Nobody who's looking for a good image will ever be free," Malcolm argued. ". . . You've got to take something in your hand and say, 'Look, it's you or me.' And I guarantee you he'll give you freedom then."

The New Malcolm accordingly spoke even more violently than the old. He held up the Mau Mau terror as a proper model for American blacks and was angry afterward when the papers wondered editorially what had become of his new religion of brotherhood. "The Mau Mau believed in brotherhood," he said, "and I believe in brotherhood. But I also believe that our people need organizations that will fight against those who fight against us." He identified himself with the Harlem rioters and said he probably would have died fighting among them if he had been home. He said there was no point demonstrating unless a demonstration carried the implied possibility of bloodshed—"and it should be reciprocal. *Reciprocal.* The flow of blood should be two ways." He came out again for armed self-defense units in the South to meet white violence with black violence. ("If a man speaks French," he said, "you can't speak to him in German if you want to communicate.") He sent a blustery open telegram to George Lincoln Rockwell, the then American Nazi fuehrer, who had been agitating against Martin Luther King's latest campaign in Alabama; he was, he wrote, "no longer held in check" by Mr. Muhammad and would answer Rockwell with "maximum physical retaliation" if King or anybody else black was hurt. "And," said Malcolm in a radio interview, "I haven't seen anything else of Rockwell in Alabama since."

King, of course, remained uninterested in that sort of help, and to the extent that King and his ideology dominated the public face of the movement, Malcolm remained as distant as ever from the connection he sought. He rather liked some of the recognized leaders as private men—Farmer for one ("He seems *sincere*") and Whitney Young for another, though Malcolm thought he didn't spend enough time around Negroes. He and Young met one Saturday afternoon at an off-the-record discussion group assembled by some of Malcolm's artist-and-writer friends; they still had hopes of involving him in a broad united-front coalition and had invited a number of civil-rights people to the meeting, though only Young among the name national leaders showed up. Malcolm thought

Young "more down to earth" than most of the other movement celebrities—blacker, that is, than his board-room manner in public suggested. "I can't say the things you can," Young told him. Malcolm by then had got a bit tired of hearing this from respectable black leaders, but he smiled anyway and kidded about how his hell-raising was frightening the more timid Negroes in droves into the Urban League and the NAACP. "You ought to pay me $5 a head for recruiting," Malcolm said; they both laughed. The group talked through the afternoon about the possibilities of joint action, down to what issues they could come together on and what tactical role Malcolm might best play. "Malcolm wasn't politicking, but he was eager," Ossie Davis remembered; Davis for one believed that they parted having made at least a beginning toward some kind of functional unity.

But nothing came of it; there wasn't enough time, and even if there had been, one suspects that the price of unity between Malcolm and most of the mainstream leadership was still too high for either party to pay. Malcolm by then had given up on formal separation of the races as a goal but had not adopted integration in its place. He believed simply that separation had already happened in America, that integration wasn't about to and that neither was something that you could sensibly organize a movement around. He and the established leaders thus remained a vast distance apart on first principles. Malcolm was color-conscious where they aspired to be color-blind, nonnonviolent where they submitted willingly to pain, a child of Harlem where they were preoccupied with Louisiana and Alabama and Mississippi. "Malcolm really thought he could convert them," Benjamin Goodman told me, "or at least convert enough of their followers so they would have to go along." He couldn't. The movement took him at face value, which was to say on his incendiary image in the downtown media, and Malcolm for his part never could live up to his own resolution not to attack them. He thought he had; he would flatter himself in an interview with having left them alone for a solid year and in the next breath attack them all as Toms and traitors. King especially was his *bête blanche;* Malcolm's charity began and ended with the patronizing concession that King was trying—"probably a good man, means well and all that"—but didn't know any better. "White people in the South," he said in the midst of the armistice, "are praying in the secrecy of their closets that King never dies. King is the best thing that ever happened to white folks. *For* white folks. As long as anybody can keep Negroes nonviolent, it helps white folks."

King was Malcolm's nominal beneficiary when he finally did make connections with the Southern movement, but his real patrons were the cooled-off children of SNCC. They had been as much put off as anyone else in the movement by Malcolm's public reputation. But they had had a trying summer in Mississippi—a summer of beatings, bombings, arrests, harassments and constant low-grade tension between them and the white college kids they had brought South to help. It had ended at the Democratic Convention in Atlantic City, where their friends and enemies met without them and compromised away their dream of seating a biracial slate of "Freedom Democrats" as *the* Mississippi delegation. They went away feeling betrayed and were never quite the same again. They had always lived at the radical fringe of the movement, which kiddingly called them the Nonstudent Violent Noncoordinating Committee; now, in the ashes of Freedom Summer and the convention compromise, the vein of alienation widened and deepened. "They used to tell me, don't have anything to do with Malcolm X," said Gloria Dandridge, who had worked with SNCC in Cambridge. "After they'd gotten their heads whipped hard enough and long enough, and got an awareness of things, they had to begin looking in that direction."

They did, and when a couple of them learned that Malcolm was coming to Alabama that February to speak at Tuskegee Institute they invited him over to Selma for a voting-rights rally. SNCC, which had begun the Selma campaign two years earlier, had been shunted aside that winter when King moved into town with his usual retinue of reporters and cameras and his crisis scenario of mass marches and mass arrests. The SNCC kids felt left out, their identity as individuals and as a group lost somewhere in the catchall newspaper label "civil-rights workers," and their invitation to Malcolm had an edge of provocation to it. "They came in ready to fight for his right to speak," said King's deputy, the Rev. Andrew Young. The SCLC people were hardly happy with the prospect, but rather than go to war defending the premise that free speech didn't apply to civil-rights rallies, they agreed uneasily to let Malcolm go on.

King was in jail at the time, along with several hundred local youngsters who had been doing most of the marching; the crowd waiting to go in Brown's Chapel A.M.E. Church was made up mostly of kids from tiny outlying hamlets and crossroads, where, SCLC's people figured hopefully, nobody had ever heard of Malcolm X. Still, they thought certain precautions were in order. "Our concern was that he not in any way try to inflame the situation," Young remembered. They felt uncomfortable telling anybody what to say, but they took Malcolm aside in the parsonage before the rally and leveled with him—told him, look, we're trying to stay on the single issue of voting, nothing else; we're not even raising police brutality, though God knows we're catching enough hell; it's *voting* we're looking to get across to the nation, through the press, and we can't afford any—*incidents.* Malcolm sat there smiling at them; he seemed cooperative enough, though some of them shivered a little when he said on the way to church that nobody ever put words in his mouth. The SCLC people sandwiched him between two of their own best speakers, Fred Shuttlesworth and James Bevel, both hell-raisers but both committed to King, SCLC and nonviolence. "We felt," said Young, "that we were in control."

They weren't so sure when Malcolm's turn came to speak from King's own adopted pulpit. "I'm 100 percent for the effort being put forth by the black folks here," he said. "I believe they have an absolute right to use whatever means are necessary to gain the vote. But I don't believe in nonviolence—no. I don't think anyone expects a sheep to go into the den of the wolf and love the wolf, because the sheep would end up in the *stomach* of the wolf." He did his house Negro/field Negro monologue; he said that whites should thank God for King & Co., "because they're giving white people time to get things in shape"; he went on for an hour or so, then sat down saying he hoped he hadn't put anybody on the spot or stirred anybody up. He had done both. The kids applauded furiously; the SCLC people thought better of sending them out on a march at all that day and hastily got King's wife, Coretta, to say a few inspirational words to help quiet them down. She and Malcolm had a brief whispered conversation; he asked her to tell King that he hadn't really come to make his work harder—that he hoped in fact to make it easier by showing white people "what the alternative is." She thanked him. He told some of the SNCC people to call him any time. Then he got in a car and left.

Selma was as close as Malcolm ever got to taking the plunge. His contribution was that single speech; he had to rush off to keep some commitments in England and France and didn't believe in marching in any case. He never got South again. He wanted to; some people from the Mississippi Freedom Democratic Party, a SNCC spin-off, booked him for some speeches two weeks after the Selma trip, but Malcolm had to postpone going at the last minute and did not live long enough to keep the new date. For much of the movement, he remained as unwanted as ever, and even where he was welcome, he was uncertain of what his role ought to be. His chat with Mrs. King was revealing; he had wanted to join and had bumped up against the ego-bruising proposition that his real place in the struggle of the blacks might be to play the bogeyman after all—to make Martin Luther King's life easier by showing white people that there were other, scarier kinds of black people around. "He always had that feeling," Ossie Davis told me. "He'd say, 'I don't see why they hate me—I raise hell in the back yard and they run out front and The Man puts money in their hands.' He knew that if there's a situation out there that frightens people a little, it helps." Malcolm was willing enough to play the role but cannot have felt entirely comfortable in it. He was a proud and gifted man, trying to create a new politics of his own, and all the movement seemed to want of him was that he glower a lot and say something fierce and stand aside when it was time to do business with The Man.

That new politics remained a composite rather than a system—a loosely strung series of positions held together more by Malcolm's militant bearing than by any single coherent philosophy. The American Left, and especially the Trotskyists, have tried since his death to wish him into a revolutionary socialist and have produced appropriate passages from his late speeches to suggest that that was what he was becoming. Malcolm had in fact come home from his second trip powerfully stirred by his talks with African revolutionaries and pleased with what he had seen of African socialism. The African leaders he had liked best were all socialists of one sort or another—Nasser, Nkrumah, Touré, Ben Bella of Algeria and Nyerere of Tanzania—and, to the extent that he identified with them, he identified with their politics as well.*

After his return to Harlem, the attentions of the Socialist Workers increased. They invited Malcolm back to the Militant Labor Forum, covered him heavily in their newspaper, *The Militant,* and offered to arrange a campus lecture tour for him. Malcolm, who needed both platforms and honoraria, was grateful for all this; he repaid the SWP's favors with some kind words and occasional reciprocal gestures, as when he opened some doors around Harlem for the party's Presidential candidate, Clifton DeBerry, a blond and extremely fair-skinned Negro. The dalliance was an exciting one for the SWP. "They really jumped on Malcolm's bandwagon," one radical black journalist told me. "They'd never made any real inroads with the brothers before." They saw Malcolm as a revolutionary becoming a socialist—and, they dared

*There have been persistent rumors, around Harlem and occasionally in print, that one or more of these leaders agreed clandestinely to finance Malcolm in return for his services agitating in the United States on behalf of causes they favored, including their own survival. Those most commonly named are Nkrumah and Ben Bella (the fact that Malcolm was killed and both of them toppled from power in the space of a year is thought to be significant) and/or Gamal Nasser. Some of these men may in fact have helped with Malcolm's travel expenses—may, for example, have picked up some of his hotel bills—and may even have spoken of sending him foreign aid back in the States. But if Malcolm ever got any actual cash from them, his bank balance didn't show it. "Where was the *money?*" one associate asked rhetorically. The answer was that there wasn't any; Malcolm was down to his last $150 the day he died.

hope, a Socialist Worker. Once, sitting in the folding chairs in the back of the SWP meeting hall, I asked DeBerry if he thought Malcolm might someday have taken out a card. "I can tell you this," DeBerry answered. "If he had asked the Socialist Workers Party for a card, the Socialist Workers Party would not have turned him down."

A strand of Left rhetoric did appear in some of Malcolm's later speeches and interviews, particularly but not exclusively downtown. He continued to see color as central but not necessarily the single motive force in his world: Malcolm began arguing that the nonwhite peoples of the world had not only their nonwhiteness in common but their exploitation by the West. Occasionally, he identified capitalism straight out as an enemy— "You show me a capitalist, I'll show you a bloodsucker"—and socialism as the almost universal system among the new Third World nations coming into independence. "Instead of you running downtown picketing city hall," he told one Harlem audience, "you should stop and find out what they do over there to solve their problems. This is why the man doesn't want you and me to look beyond Harlem or beyond the shores of America. . . . I mean, what they use to solve their problem is not capitalism."

But his Left language and Left themes were hardly more than asides for Malcolm—and in his very last speeches and interviews they abruptly vanished. This may have meant nothing more than that he was too preoccupied with staying alive in those days to talk coherent politics; or it may confirm what some of his friends suggest—that he had begun to feel crowded by his new vocabulary and his new comrades and that he was trying at the end to disengage from them. "He never really thought in Marxist terms," Handler told me. "He had no use for Marxism. He considered Marxism another political ideology invented by white men for white men, to shift the seat of power from one group of white men to another group of white men. He thought it had no relevance to the black man." His romance with socialism, while it lasted, was with African socialism. Leslie Alexander Lacy, a black writer and teacher, wrote of a moment during Malcolm's first trip to Ghana when, riding in a car from Winneba to Accra, somebody asked him what he thought of socialism. "Is it good for black people?" Malcolm asked. The questioner said it seemed to be. "Then I'm for it," said Malcolm. His interest in socialism may have quickened for a time thereafter, but his priorities never changed. To the day he died Malcolm was black first; his concern was what was good for black people, and everything else was a question of tactics.

At the very end, he seemed to be moving away from Marx and back to Allah—to the mosque as his real base of operations. One can again interpret this as the retreat of a dying man who saw not only Black Muslims but police agents in the shadows; or, again, one can read it as a withdrawal from a system of thought and a society of men that had grown claustrophobic for him—a strait jacket as constricting as the one he had only just shucked off. "He had been moving with a number of people who thought they could use him," one close associate said. "They didn't think Malcolm was as bright as he was. At the end, he was looking at where he would be the leader and where he would be the victim. It became clear to him that some of his newfound friends had their own course to follow and that he would be walking in their path, whereas if he went back to a religious base, *he* made the decisions. He wanted to detach from the Left and reassert himself as a Muslim. He wanted to really compete with Elijah Muhammad. He wanted to be his own man." Old friends who had always regretted his new comradeships encouraged this trend—told him that he could use the pulpit as an instrument for social change, just as King had, and that he would be free to create whatever political theology he wanted. These friends are convinced that they were winning; *their* evidence is that Malcolm had begun laying in supplies of orthodox Islamic literature, had installed Sheik Hassoun as his spiritual adviser, had begun classes in Arabic at the Theresa and had in his last days begun shopping actively again for a mosque. He saw a place he liked, a church on 116th Street that was up for sale, and though it would have meant mortgaging his future, he had Percy Sutton open negotiations to buy it. (Their offer was turned down just before Malcolm's death.) A Malcolm ministry would surely have been political, as King's was, and might have incorporated elements of wing-it socialism into its design. Its real value was that it would have permitted him to say whatever he wanted and so would have suited his real genius. Malcolm was never so much a politician as a moral commentator on politics, and a Sunni Muslim mosque would have meant having a pulpit of his own for the first time.

There was something sad in the competition for Malcolm—that hunger to possess him that began probably the day he came out of the Nation of Islam and has continued since his death. "He never got the chance to be *Malcolm,*" Charles Kenyatta told me wanly. One might have carved those words on his tomb.

The chance to be Malcolm would have meant the chance to be recognized as an authentic man of God *and* as a legitimate political leader; to create a black theology and a black politics as a thousand Charlie Parkers and Billie Holidays and John Coltranes had created a black music, extempore, out of one's heart and anger and pain; to exist today with or without reference to yesterday, as one wished and the exigencies of politics required; most of all, to be free. The answer to the mystery is that Malcolm would most probably have gone on as he was, neither integrationist nor separatist, neither nonviolent nor actively violent, neither socialist nor capitalist nor even *Fanoniste,* but Malcolm, black, bad, gallant in private, remorseless in a fight and committed to nothing except freedom by any means necessary. *I am the man you think you are,* he announced to white America. He meant that he would behave as rudely and as dangerously as anyone would—as whites would—in reply to the systematic ruin of one's people and one's pride.

One day during those last months, he and Claude Lewis, the black reporter, sat talking over coffee at 22 West, Malcolm all nerves and sadness among his bodyguards; he knew Lewis well enough by then but had insisted, out of a suspicion that no longer discriminated between acquaintances and strangers, that they meet in a public place. The tape of their conversation, while it followed the form of an interview, had in long passages the quality of a man composing his own obituary. Malcolm's voice was heavy; his answers were shorter and his silences longer than one remembered; his anger had curdled into something nearer bitterness, or despair. He spoke of his religion and his new feelings of brotherhood and how neither of them altered the single, central fact of his life—"that I'm a black American living in a racist society that does not practice brotherhood." He spoke of his life in the imagery of war, a psychic landscape in which one saw the other side—the white side—not as the opposition but as the enemy and so prepared oneself to deal with them as one properly deals with enemies. He spoke of the world around him as one subsisting on lies. "This is an era of hypocrisy. When white folks pretend that they want Negroes to be free, and Negroes pretend to white folks that they really *believe* that white folks want 'em to be free, it's an era of hypocrisy, brother." He chuckled, a short, leaden laugh. "You fool me and I fool you. You pretend that you're my brother and I pretend that I really believe you believe you're my brother."

And he spoke about himself. One listened, if one had known him, waiting to hear the old interplay of rage and wit, fire and laughter; instead, one heard another Malcolm, tired, harried, diminished. He might have stayed in Africa, he said; he had been offered jobs there—"*good* positions, that would solve my problems as an individual forever. But it would not solve the problems of our people. And I feel much—pretty much responsible for much of the action and energy that's been stirred up among our people for rights, and for freedom. And I think I'd be wrong to stir it up and then run away from it myself." King had just got the Nobel Peace Prize, on the premise that it was *he* who had stirred up the action and the energy; Malcolm had watched his celebration in Harlem from the back benches and had clearly not joined the rejoicing. Lewis asked him if he had ever got an award. "Naw," Malcolm started, then switched tacks. "Yeah, I've received an award—whenever I walk the streets and I see people getting ready to get with it, that's my reward." That those people did not always make themselves visible to anyone else did not concern him. "All I need is to walk through the street or anyplace else and really find out where people are at. In a silent sort of way. I know where they are, in a *silent* sort of way."

Near the end of their talk, Malcolm spoke of death. "I'll never get old," he said. Lewis asked him what he meant. "Well," Malcolm said, "I'll tell you what it means. If you read, you'll find that very few people who think like I think live long enough to get old. When I say by any means necessary, I mean it with all my heart, my mind and my soul. A black man should give his life to be free, and he should also be willing to take the life of those who want to take his. When you really think like that, you don't live long." There was a long silence. "So I never think about being an old man. That never has come across my mind. I can't even see myself old." Again, the leaden little chuckle; again, a space of dead silence. Lewis asked him how then he would like to be remembered. Malcolm answered quickly, as though he had been thinking about the question. *"Sincere,"* he said. "In whatever I did or do. Even if I make mistakes, they were made in sincerity. If I'm wrong, I'm wrong in sincerity. I think that the best thing that a person can be is sincere."

Sincere, and true to his blackness, which in the end was Malcolm's politics, his theology and his life. At the very outset of their talk, Lewis had asked him the obligatory question one was sent by one's city desk to put to Malcolm in those days—whether or not there really was a New Malcolm X. And Malcolm had laughed that sharp, suddenly unmusical laugh and said, "The white man asks the question is there a New Malcolm X. 'Cause what he has been demanding is, politically, a new me while there's not yet been a new him. Which means I'm supposed to change before white people change. As long as there's an old problem, the same old problem, I don't see how there can be a New Malcolm X." The laugh again; a silence filled with background whispers and clattering lunch-counter china; then that toneless voice: "Or a new any other kind of a black man."

27. Coming Apart

He had always assumed he was going to die young. He accepted this simply as given, as the patrimony one came into as the son of Earl Little and the dues one paid as a revolutionary, and was utterly matter-of-fact about it. *Mathematical,* one friend thought; as logical and as businesslike as a CPA contemplating an adding-machine tape. Once, after a particularly discouraging day in the court proceedings over his house, he and Percy Sutton rode off homeward in a convoy of the brothers, shotguns poking out of their car windows. "With all these guns, don't you get scared?" Sutton asked him. "Don't you think you're inviting trouble?" Malcolm answered him with a little parable he had found somewhere, a Persian tale, as Sutton remembered it, about a man named Omar. "I've seen the face of Death," Omar had said one day and had asked for the fastest horse in the kingdom. He knew that Death would not take him after nightfall; he raced Death headlong all day for three days. Each evening before sundown, he came to a fork in the road and chose one branch or the other thinking to throw Death off his trail. On the third day, he chose the left fork, rode on for a distance—and met Death. "And Death said to him, 'Omar, Omar, where have you been? I've been here for three days. Why have I had to wait so long?' " Malcolm and Sutton drove on in silence for a moment, Malcolm sitting there surrounded by guns and knowing that they were worthless except for the comfort they gave the brothers guarding him. "So, counselor," he said finally, "you can run and run and run. But when the time comes, you're going to die."

His sangfroid sustained him through much of his last year, even when his world was turning into a paranoid fantasy come to life. But at the end, when Malcolm was broke, raggedy-edged and shadowed everywhere by Black Muslims and Allah-knew-who-else; when he couldn't make the papers except by attacking Elijah Muhammad or advocating an American Mau Mau; when his dream of indicting the U.S. formally before the United Nations was dying of Yankee dollarism; when his two organizations were teetering near collapse and some of his oldest brothers in the struggle were drifting away disillusioned; when Harlem was getting impatient waiting out his changes and confusions and still he couldn't flog a program together; when everything else was coming apart, Malcolm's marvelous calm in the face of death began to come apart, too. He never did run from death, even when flight still seemed possible and friends urged it on him. He kept up his furious schedule, crowding his little red pocket diary with speaking dates and interviews and holding himself together on energy, will and faith. He found a passage in Islamic scripture that comforted him and quoted it from memory to some of the brothers: *Do you think that Allah will not try you when He has tried other men before you?* There were days and circumstances when he managed a kind of fatalistic cool—when friends who were frightened for him came away thinking he had been the only unfrightened man around. There were other days and other circumstances when he bridled at shadows and snapped at his own people, when his fine tall walk turned into a tense half-crouch, when he told some of the brothers that his mind felt completely *paralyzed.*

He had wanted the UN project as his monument—wanted it said of him that he had renewed the link between black America and the mother continent and so had been able to bring the plight of his people before a tribunal of the nations of the world. He kept his part of his implied bargain with the Africans, lacing his speeches heavily with passages attacking American neo-colonialism generally and America's half-veiled involvement in that autumn's Congo crisis in particular. U.S. pilots had flown in Belgian paratroopers on what was officially a rescue mission to liberate several hundred hostages, mostly white, from the Congolese insurgents, but had also delivered Stanleyville over to the control of the conservative Tshombé government. During the UN debate on this enterprise, several African delegations with whom Malcolm had established liaison—notably the Ghanaians, the Guineans and the Kenyans—connected the oppression of blacks in the States with America's behavior in the Congo. Ghana's Foreign Minister, Kojo Botsio, argued typically that the United States had no more business there than Ghana would have intervening in the American South "to protect the lives of Afro-Americans . . . tortured and murdered for asserting their legitimate rights."

The attack ran over several days and clearly surprised and embarrassed Washington. Adlai Stevenson, then the U.S. Ambassador, replied passionately that America had no apologies to make as a force for social justice and that while whites had indeed sinned against nonwhites through history, "the antidote for white racism is not black racism." The defense was well received in UN Plaza, by some of the Africans and Asians as well as the white West. Malcolm nevertheless regarded the whole episode, the attack and the fact that America had been forced onto the defensive, as a victory—not the victory he had hoped for, but a victory still. "That wasn't an accident," he told interviewers; he meant that his travels and his lobbying had had everything to do with it.

It was the only victory he lived to enjoy. He never quite abandoned the dream of a formal human-rights case against the United States. But the people he had working on the petition never finished it—only a rough outline ever got on paper—and Malcolm had begun to despair of bringing it before the UN anyway. The project required African and Arab support, not just one nation to raise the issue but others to see that it wasn't filed and forgotten after a single speech. Publicly, Malcolm professed optimism, though perceptibly less than before his second swing abroad. Privately, among the brothers, he admitted his discouragement—conceded that the support wasn't there and wasn't likely to be as long as the Africans depended on American aid and American investments. "A lot of promises was made to him," Charles Kenyatta said, "but none was ever kept. Some of those ambassadors over here, it was like he owned them, but they couldn't deliver. They constantly shove you toward the cliff and say, 'We're with you,' but they're not." Neither could Malcolm interest anyone influential in the civil-rights movement, which might have helped; they were men of affairs where he was a public moralist, and they considered the UN project a waste of time and resources. The Congo debate in the end was Malcolm's consolation prize. His monument never got built.

He felt equally defeated trying to persuade the press that he had really changed or "broadened his scope" at all. Malcolm's brotherhood period made good human-interest copy for a day or so but palled thereafter; the media covered his speeches irregularly, missed the point of his new politics, headlined the most incendiary-sounding passages and set him down editorially as The Same Old Malcolm X. "As long as people could see him screaming," said John Killens, "he was okay. But when he came back, he couldn't buy television time because he was talking sense." Malcolm understood the trap and fell into it anyway. He wanted a wider public; he couldn't reach it without the media; he couldn't crash the media without saying something excessive; all too often, he obliged. The result was a wide incongruity between the warmongering Malcolm one read about and the rather more winning man one encountered at first hand. His outlaw reputation had certain values to him, particularly in the streets uptown, but only to a point. "They won't let me turn the corner!" he complained once to Alex Haley. He told those audiences he could reach that they shouldn't be buffaloed by his image—that you could pull a drowning baby out of the water and *still* be called extremist once the papers had you typed that way. He ultimately came to see his own complicity: he was the prisoner of his clippings, and he had helped write them. By then, even his extremisms had begun to bore the city editors and talent coordinators downtown. In the end, when everybody else knew it, Malcolm couldn't even make the media believe that he was going to die.

Malcolm's image troubles compounded his difficulties in trying to put together a broad-based membership organization. He didn't exactly need one—a political leader is often more effective when his following cannot be counted precisely—but he wanted one anyway. He couldn't bring it off. His two fledgling organizations, the Muslim Mosque, Inc. and the Organization of Afro-American Unity, had languished badly in his long absences; one visitor found the brothers sitting around quoting Malcolm's letters like Scripture and waiting for him to come home to tell them what to do next. They fell to quarreling among themselves, the Old Muslims polarizing around Benjamin Goodman and the more political people around James 67X. The MMI was itself split between those who resented Malcolm's drift away from Mr. Muhammad's brand-X Islam and those who wanted to accelerate it. The OAAU was an ill-mixed mélange of cultural nationalists, artists and writers, Maoists, Trotskyists and nonsectarian black revolutionaries, including some of the men later charged by the police with "conspiracies" to blow up the Statue of Liberty and to assassinate some name civil-rights leaders. The political people quarreled not only with the MMI crowd, who finally moved out of the Theresa to be away from them, but among themselves; one caucus even began issuing its own membership cards. "The OAAU was the worst mistake we ever made," one brother told me. At the very end, Malcolm himself came to agree and ordered its thorough overhaul.

He had got word of some of the problems while he was still in Africa that summer and fall. Charles Kenyatta wrote him worriedly that the MMI and OAAU were polarizing, that some of the older brothers were beginning to feel left out and that both unregenerate Black Muslims and hard-line leftists were joining the two organizations. "Some of them aren't *right,*" he said; he suspected that some might in fact be trying to set Malcolm up for murder. "You can't see the birds for the trees," Malcolm wrote back. But the bad tidings kept coming—reports of bickering and jealousy and defections and challenges to his leadership. At length, Malcolm wrote the brothers impatiently that he was doing important and dangerous work abroad, that he would be away another month and that if somebody else felt better qualified to lead than he, fine—this was the time to show it. For the meantime, he nominated Goodman as "the best teacher I left behind" and begged them all to rally around and forget their differences. "You can make the Muslim Mosque and the OAAU a success, or you can destroy both organizations," he wrote. "It's up to you. You have one more month."

But he was away nearly three, and by the time he got back, his organizational base was a shambles. Goodman, unhappy with the new directions Malcolm had taken, had not tried to assert his leadership—"I didn't have the spirit for it"—and all the tensions continued unresolved. Nothing ever seemed to get done. In the Nation, with its rigid chain of command, Malcolm had only to give an order to get action. Outside, with no such lines of authority and with Malcolm himself available only part-time, discipline collapsed. "It was like having a lot of people and giving them each a brick and telling them, 'All right, when I shoot this gun, go over there and build a wall,' " Goodman said. "You wind up with a pile of bricks and people." The older brothers were used to taking orders, but the newer OAAU people free-enterprised, each according to his tendency. Artists and writers accepted assignments, then laid them aside when book contracts or movie jobs came up. Malcolm put a group to work on an OAAU program and promised it successively for December, then January, then February. When it didn't materialize, he pressed for it privately and argued publicly that the first duty of leadership was to "analyze, analyze, analyze" until people knew they had a problem and only then to organize them around specific goals. "No organization meets any time schedule," he said. "Time schedule was yesterday. *No* time schedule will put us on time. We were already behind time when we got started." A draft "Basic Unity Program" finally did get written in time for what was to be Malcolm's last rally. But it was really more manifesto than program, a mostly black-nationalist declaration of faith in unity, Mother Africa and self-defense; Malcolm, for whatever reason, didn't think it ready for public presentation.

He never got the time to take hold—his booked-up calendar and his fragmented attention kept him from it—and he had no single, strong administrative officer to put things together for him. He may have had some such role in mind for Maya Angelou, who was due in from Ghana in February to go to work for the OAAU and who had both the experience and the presence to take charge. But even the proper place of women was then a source of angry argument among the brothers, with Malcolm already beginning to phase them into leadership roles and some of the Old Muslims strenuously objecting. ("You don't let something that's *weak* lead men," Goodman said.) In the absence of authority, pressing business went untended. Theological and political arguments rattled endlessly on. Old faces vanished out of disillusion; new ones appeared, strangers of uncertain intentions, and after a while neither Malcolm nor anybody else knew who was who any more. "He would speak to an audience," Kenyatta said, "and some of them was wishing him well and some of them was sitting there stalking him and some wanted him to make a mistake so they could jump for joy. People that was truly not his friends was demanding that he would deliver a product they could use. And everybody completely silent. No one was saying, 'Right! Right! Malcolm, you're right!' any more."

The pull of the world, which had helped bring Malcolm out of the Nation, was drawing him away from the Old Muslims. One after another slipped away. No more than two dozen were left when he got back from Africa; the drain continued thereafter until hardly any remained but Goodman out of the old crowd that had come out of the Nation expecting Malcolm to spread Mr. Muhammad's word about God, man and the devil. And finally Goodman, too, was estranged, hanging on out of habit and personal loyalty long after he had left in spirit. "I guess you could say I was one of the last to stay with him," Goodman told me one day years later, walking me to my subway stop in Harlem. "I stayed and I didn't stay." He felt that Malcolm had left the brothers, really—had turned unfairly on Mr. Muhammad, compromised his teaching and gone wandering off in pursuit of a religion of brotherhood and a politics of internationalism that had no real meaning for Harlem. "I loved him," Goodman said. "I thought he was the wisest man I ever knew. I used to tape his speeches and write down all the hip things he'd say in the mosque. I was his assistant and I was a *good* assistant. I know I was good—he used to send me all those places to speak for him. But it's no secret I was discouraged." He never spoke, and Malcolm did not ask him what was bothering him. "He didn't need to ask—he knew what was bugging me. We didn't need to talk. He knew me. It was that kind of relationship —like a love affair." We stood there in front of the IRT entrance, Goodman blinking into the August sun. "The man who died," he said, "was a stranger to me."

Even Kenyatta, his old retainer, came near the point of quitting; he had stood resentfully behind, watching Malcolm move off among his new friends, men and women—*intellectuals*—who Kenyatta thought meant him no good. "You *knew* it was a conspiracy going on," he said. "I began to question Malcolm's judgment." He stopped going to the Audubon rallies for a few weeks and sat one whole day alone and brooding in a movie house, thinking about Malcolm and not seeing the movies. They didn't get back together until near the end; then Malcolm told Kenyatta, "I'm a dead man."

Some days, the man who died seemed a stranger to most of the people who knew him—tense, frustrated, irritable, exhausted, unsure of himself, freezing at street noises, jumpy around strangers. One night, after a speech at the Palm Gardens in midtown, some friends walked him to his Oldsmobile. "As he was crossing in front of the car to the driver's side," Dan Watts remembered, "another car came down the street, and there was suddenly a loud backfire —*bang!* Malcolm froze. A look of real horror came over his face. We all saw it. We didn't ask him about it and he didn't say anything. But we knew then he was worried for his life." He was followed regularly. He believed that the Old Ones—the name some of the brothers called the white establishment—regarded him as an enemy of the state for his hell-raising at home and in Africa and might very well want him dead. But he believed even more powerfully, and with substantially more visible evidence, that elements in the Nation were after him, too. The night he visited Farmer's place in December, a bodyguard showed up with him. Farmer, surprised, asked him teasingly, "Why did you bring this fellow with you? You think I'm going to kill you or something?" Malcolm smiled faintly. "No, Brother James," he said, "*you're* not going to kill me, but there are other people after me, and they're going to get me." Farmer asked him who. Malcolm hesitated a moment, just long enough so that Farmer surmised he had some doubts; but when he answered, it was the Black Muslims he named. "I honestly think they're the only black people in this country who are capable of assassination," he said. "I taught them what they know, so I know what they can do."

For the Nation, Malcolm was both competitor and blasphemer—a heretic who had slandered God by questioning the morality and authority of His Last Messenger. A second of Mr. Muhammad's own sons, Akbar, who had been studying in Cairo, had deviated in the faith and in December was publicly read out of the Nation as a "hypocrite." He did not join Malcolm. But since Malcolm had lately been in Cairo, and since Akbar had said a kind word or two for him in a newspaper interview confirming the split, Malcolm was blamed for his defection as for Wallace Muhammad's before him. This became another white mark against Malcolm's name, along with the question of the secretaries—the Nation was sure he had instigated the paternity suits—and his continuing oratorical war against Mr. Muhammad as a "religious faker." This latter charge had particularly infuriated Chicago; when the *Egyptian Gazette* played it up, the Messenger himself warned "the entire world" that it might be "playing with fire, and a very hot fire at that."

Muhammad Speaks that fall was more vituperative than ever. Louis X, then the Boston minister and once Malcolm's close associate, filled almost five full pages in one issue denouncing his old comrade as "an international hobo," indexing his sins and daring him to come home from Africa "and face the music. . . . You are now the target of both your own followers (which are very few) and the followers of Muhammad." The piece read in passages like a death warrant, though Louis drew back at the end and left vengeance to the Lord. "Only those who wish to be led to hell, or to their doom, will follow Malcolm," he wrote. "The die is set, and Malcolm shall not escape, especially after such evil, foolish talk about his benefactor. . . . Such a man as Malcolm is worthy of death, and would have met with death if it had not been for Muhammad's confidence in Allah for victory over his enemies." Malcolm, who read the piece on his return, was stung by it ("Here's an organization spent its whole newspaper telling lies about me") and was not reassured by its disclaimers of any deadly intent. A month later, the Messenger himself did a page-one attack on him as "the chief hypocrite of them all. . . . I will never forget this hypocrite's disgraceful acts against me. If he is the last of the 22 million, I shall remind him of his evil and wicked acts done to me in return for the good I did for him." Allah's punishments for hypocrisy, Mr. Muhammad wrote, were "grief, regret, shame and disgrace"—a chastisement of the soul so fierce that, receiving it, one cannot pray or even blink one's eyes. "It begins with their feeling of fear and excitement—fear that someone is going to do harm to them (as they plan to harm those they oppose). . . . They even wish for someone to kill them. . . . But Allah, the Holy Qur'an says, will not permit anyone to kill them, because death would take them out of their chastisement and grief."

This threat alone still held a powerful reality for Malcolm, distant though he was from the sway of the Nation; he had seen one brother broken, so he believed, by Allah's chastisement, and he could feel his own nerves fraying in the round of haunted days and sleepless nights his life had become. "They knew about his mother and his brother," Kenyatta said. "They was relying on him to break." The Black Muslims seemed uncannily well tuned in to where he was going and what he was doing. Deputations of the Fruit of Islam started materializing mysteriously around his hotel lobbies and meeting halls. Some of them showed up at a Philadelphia ballroom where he was speaking; the police had to get him out. Associated Community Teams, a group working with Harlem youth, invited Malcolm to speak at a seminar of Domestic Peace Corps volunteers in December. Two dozen FOI members showed up, in dark suits and I AM WITH MUHAMMAD buttons. Frightened, some of the ACT staff called the police and hid Malcolm in an office until they arrived. He finally went on and spoke for an hour, the Fruit sitting there staring at him out of expressionless eyes. A half-dozen police stood watch, and nothing happened.

There were tales of violence against other apostate Muslims—reports of beatings and stompings in Boston, Detroit, Chicago, Los Angeles. Kenyatta happened by the Muslim restaurant one day; one of the Original People told him, "You fell in love with that red nigger, but we're going to kill him." Leon 4X Ameer, a tiny Muslim karate expert who had been assigned most recently to the Muhammad Ali entourage, defected to Malcolm that fall and brought along another chilling tale: four Muslims out of Chicago, he said, had come to him, announced that they were going to assassinate Malcolm and asked if he could get them a pistol silencer for the job. Ameer said he stalled them off by saying he couldn't find one and finally was able to talk them out of their mission. Whatever Malcolm made of the story, he liked what it told him about Ameer's loyalties and, over the dissent of some of the brothers, took him in as New England organizer. On Christmas Day, Ameer, who was staying at the Sherry Biltmore Hotel in Boston, got a call to come downstairs to the lobby—a French journalist wanted to see him. As he stepped off the elevator, somebody clubbed him on the back of the head, dropping him to his knees. A policeman who chanced to be in a shop off the lobby dashed out, rescued Ameer and arrested four men, all of them Muslims, one the local temple captain. (They were eventually convicted and fined.) Later that night, a second squad of black men bulled into Ameer's room, pummeled and stomped him, popped both his eardrums, fractured one rib, bloodied his face and dumped him senseless into his bathtub; he lay in a coma for three days with a bloodclot on his brain. Ameer couldn't identify the men but thought he recognized their style: they used some tricks he had taught as a Muslim instructor in karate.

Two weeks later, another defector—a New York prison guard named Benjamin Brown—was attacked outside a little independent mosque called "Universal Peace" that he had opened in the

Bronx. Brown was not affiliated with Malcolm; he considered himself loyal to Mr. Muhammad and had hung out a picture of the Messenger in his storefront window. On the evening of January 6, three Muslims came by, complained briefly about the picture, then left. Two hours afterward, Brown locked up and was walking to his car with three followers when a single shot from a .22-caliber rifle hit him in the back and collapsed his right lung. Based on what Brown and his followers told them, the police quickly arrested three men, once again all Muslims. One of these was Thomas 15X Johnson, husky and soft-spoken, an out-of-work house painter and a nominee for FOI lieutenant who had lately turned thirty. The police found a .22-caliber Winchester repeating rifle in his home; it had jammed, they reported, after one shot. Another of the suspects was Norman 3X Butler, then twenty-six, a tall, flat-muscled young man full of the dogma and the certainty of the faith. He was an FOI lieutenant and was trained in karate. The party dispatched to arrest him, knowing his reputation, went in with nylon-covered steel-alloy face masks. A detective named John Kilroy was the first man through the door. Butler staggered him with a backhand karate chop; when Kilroy got the mask off later, according to departmental legend, there was a deep crease in it.

Toward the end, the net drew closer. In late January, Malcolm stepped out of his house one day, saw three Muslims standing there and guessed—"thanks to Allah for good intuition"—that they planned to jump him. He scuffled with them—beat them up, he said later—and chased them away. Six days after this encounter, he flew out to Los Angeles to get the OAAU chapter there going and to meet with the two secretaries in the paternity case and their lawyer, Gladys Towles Root. The local Muslims apparently hadn't known he was coming, but a half-dozen of them bumped into him by chance in a hotel lobby, and he was shadowed everywhere thereafter. He wouldn't go to the secretaries' place himself, fearing it was staked out; he sent a friend ahead instead and had him fetch the women to a covert rendezvous point a few blocks away, then went on to Mrs. Root's office. "He was afraid," Mrs. Root remembered. "Frightened. He told me he had been threatened. I called the Wilshire police and asked for protection for him while he was in Los Angeles and in my office." He got back to the Statler Hilton late that night, found the place aswarm with Muslims and sprinted past them into the hotel and upstairs to his room. They were still there next morning; Malcolm holed up until plane time, calling likely local Muslims on his room phone and coaxing some of them to defect. En route to the airport, he and a local friend saw two carloads of Muslims tailing them. They shook one, but the other pulled alongside them on a freeway, the two cars doing seventy side by side. Malcolm, unarmed, snatched up a cane, poked it out the window and sighted along it as if it were a rifle. The Muslim car fell back and disappeared. They spotted two more Muslims at the airport; a flying squad of policemen smuggled Malcolm out through an office and an underground tunnel to his plane.

He flew on to Chicago, where, among other errands, he was to be questioned by the state attorney general's office in an inquiry into the Nation's mysteriously unchallenged tax exemptions. The Los Angeles police intelligence unit had sent word ahead that he was plainly being stalked and might be killed publicly. A heavy force of Chicago cops met him, took the suite next to his at the Bristol Hotel and kept him under guard for three days. He did the Irv Kupcinet television show one evening, showing up with three bodyguards of his own. "The police, that was standard, but the bodyguards weren't," Kupcinet said. "I asked about them. He said *they* were trying to kill him. I asked him who, but he would only say, 'You know who.' " When the police took him back to the Bristol, a dozen or so black men were hanging around outside. Malcolm recognized some of them as Muslims—at least two of them from New York—and told one of the detectives assigned to him that they were out to kill him, probably in some public place. "It's only going to be a matter of time," he said.

The brothers organized elaborate security measures for him, a pursuit that by the end became a preoccupation to the exclusion of practically everything else. They slept with their guns, dashed around on midnight missions, bodyguarded Malcolm everywhere, wouldn't let him go outside until two men had slipped out first to scout the street and peep around the nearest corners. Malcolm for a time maintained a kind of detachment about this, as though he were watching some distant melodrama that brought some feeling of purpose to the players but could not guarantee his life if somebody meant to take it. The trouble with bodyguards, a radical black leader once told me, is that they can't protect you or do anything else much, really, except make you paranoid. Malcolm saw this. He cut out body searches at his meetings; he thought they gave the organization rather a criminal look and so would frighten away potential followers. Whether or not the brothers should carry guns was a matter of continuing debate and shifting policy. Some did, whatever happened to be the rule of the moment; Malcolm did not disapprove but laughed at them and called them "spooky." One day, he had coffee at 22 West with an old Harlem racketeer named Bumpy; Malcolm talked about the threats against his life, and Bumpy argued that he ought to go to war against his enemies. "Malcolm," he said, "they ain't ready to die no more than anyone else. You pinch them, they'll holler, too." Malcolm seemed mostly amused. He valued life but understood the vanity of trying to outrun or outgun death. The day the Muslims gate-crashed the ACT meeting in Harlem, it was the ACT people who were frightened, Malcolm who was cool. "There's *always* a danger," he told ACT's director, Livingston Wingate. "If somebody is really intent on killing me, there's nothing anybody could do."

As danger became a daily fact of life, that calm weakened and at moments seemed about to break. Malcolm never did carry a gun and never sanctioned a shooting war with the Muslims. But he did lay in a pistol along with his rifle at home, and he bought himself that most futile of weapons, a tear-gas fountain pen; his defense against assassination was a single pellet of gas in the ready position and a second in a little leather jacket in his pants pocket. He responded to the Muslims' attacks on him with his own answering charges against them, a line of accusation that got less restrained and more personal in direct proportion to his own deepening desperation. He charged the hierarchy with chicanery, immorality and high living on the dimes and quarters of the faithful. He said they had run a clandestine romance with George Lincoln Rockwell of the American Nazis. He said that once, on orders, he had himself negotiated a mutual nonaggression treaty with the Ku Klux Klan, which granted the Muslims immunity so long as they preached separation of the races.

His only certification for these charges was the continuing threat to his life. "I know too much," he kept saying. His retaliatory war dismayed his friends, angered the Old Muslims, was largely ignored by the media and in the end served no purpose except to inflame the Nation further against him. It was as if he were crying out for help from behind soundproof glass. One night in the last days he visited John Killens's place in Brooklyn. When he got ready to leave, the bodyguards went out first, as usual, then signaled for him. Malcolm waited, looking tense; he had become part of the game. He left with Clarence Jones, a young black lawyer who had done some work for King but had got friendly with Malcolm, too. "You know," Malcolm said heavily, "you're taking your life in your own hands walking me to my car." Jones had no doubt that he meant it.

In February, Malcolm went abroad again, a short trip this time to England and, so he thought, to France. He spent three days at a meeting of the Council of African Organizations in London, then flew the Channel to Paris for a scheduled speech at one of the city's biggest halls, the Salle de la Mutualité. He never got past the transit lounge at Orly Airport. Nine policemen and immigration officers met him with an order from the Ministry of the Interior —"Your presence is undesirable in France"—and whisked him away to an office, where three of the gendarmes stood watch over him. For all his alienation, Malcolm's first impulse was that of any American traveler in trouble abroad—to call the U.S. Embassy—but he wasn't allowed near a telephone. He sat there fuming for a while, finally dug into his pocket, fished up an English penny and shoved it toward a French security man. "Give that to De Gaulle," he said, "because the French government is worth less than a penny." The security man wouldn't take it. Malcolm flung it to the floor. Moments later, he was bundled into a car, sped across the apron to a London-bound Air France Caravelle and officially deported as a threat to the peace of Paris. The rally at the Mutualité went on without him, the speakers denouncing not only the involvement of white mercenaries in the Congo and the U.S. intervention in Vietnam, which had been the main agenda items for the evening, but the detention and forced departure of their guest star.

The French had their reasons, though not the ones they announced publicly—or the more sinister ones Malcolm and his followers suspected. The official government explanation was that Malcolm's speech could have "provoked demonstrations that would trouble the public order." This access of caution was not very convincing, given that Malcolm had spoken in the same hall without incident a scant three months before, and the lack of official candor gave rise to the widespread and enduring suspicion that the United States government was involved—perhaps criminally so. Malcolm himself blamed the State Department, though it surely occurred to him that State would have intervened to keep him out of England as well if silencing him abroad were American policy. Since his death, a considerable folklore has grown up around a far uglier rumor—that French intelligence had learned that the CIA planned his murder and that France didn't want his blood spilled on its soil. There is even a published quotation to this effect from an unnamed North African diplomat, declaring—"in elegantly modulated French"—that his country had been quietly alerted by Paris in case Malcolm flew in from there.* A more credible version was that the French acted on the representation of two of their lately liberated colonies, Senegal and the Ivory

*The quotation appeared in a piece on the assassination by Eric Norden in the February 1967 issue of *The Realist*, an early underground journal that styled itself "the magazine of wrongeous indignation." The quotation is impossible to evaluate; the piece as a whole is crowded with error, supposition, hearsay and casual reporting and is informed by a double-o-seven view of the role and power of intelligence agencies in the real world.

Coast, that Malcolm—aided and abetted by Nasser and Nkrumah —might try to incite African students to overthrow moderate, pro-Western governments like their own. They naturally preferred that he not be allowed in Paris, where there was a large African student colony and a small but active OAAU chapter of two dozen or so Afro-American and Latin-American blacks. Malcolm had been scissored once again in the power politics of Africa and its continuing liaison with the white West, the medium of exchange being francs this time instead of dollars. The tact that forbade anyone's saying so at the time has nourished the conspiracy theory of Malcolm's assassination ever since, and conspiracies, in the popular culture of the Left, are the monopoly property of America and the CIA.

Malcolm went back to England, for a speech at the London School of Economics and a controversial side trip to Smethwick, a working-class satellite of Birmingham then much troubled by a swelling nonwhite immigrant population. A camera crew from the BBC *Tonight* show had got him there, hoping for an on-scene debate with Smethwick's Tory MP, Peter Griffiths. When Griffiths didn't show up, the BBC people were uncertain what to do with Malcolm except walk him around town, pose him in front of a "for sale" sign and interview him on the town hall steps, where he likened the treatment of black people locally to that of the Jews in Nazi Germany. "I would not wait," he said, "for the fascist element in Smethwick to erect gas ovens." The visit created a great furor, the mayor calling it "deplorable," the papers viewing it with alarm, Griffiths proposing that Malcolm be barred from England forever and the BBC nervously shelving its film unshown.

It was the kind of controversy Malcolm loved; seeing the pictures of him walking down Marshall Street in Smethwick in his topcoat, astrakhan and a yard-wide grin, one guesses that he enjoyed himself—quite possibly for the last time in his life. He ran out his stay abroad for a week and liked it all; liked being a statesman and a celebrity and an object of high debate in the press and in Commons; liked feeling safe, as it was no longer possible for him to feel at home. While he was away, he wrote a painful letter to

Julian Mayfield in Ghana. If I'm killed, it said, would you do what you can to see that some African government takes in Betty and the children? On February 13, he flew back to New York. He had eight days to live, and it was already as though he could hear Death saying, "Malcolm, Malcolm, why have I had to wait so long?"

28. The Malcolm File

The funny thing was that they liked him—liked him personally, that is, even when they abhorred his politics. They thought him dangerous, a demagogue and a threat to the peace and good order of New York, but not even policemen were immune to Malcolm's extraordinary private magnetism. "He's a gentleman, though you'd never know it from his sheet," one top-level police official remarked off the record in Malcolm's day; that a man might have a sheet—a felony record—and still turn out a gentleman is accepted among policemen as an irony. Another high-ranking officer, an intelligence man whose daily duties included the Malcolm watch, made several opportunities to meet him and thought: *He's brilliant.* Still another, a senior hand at headquarters, called him vicious but conceded in the next breath that this was a purely professional—and purely white—judgment. "Don't get me wrong," he told a reporter who was forbidden even to take notes, let alone quote him. "If I were a Negro, I'd follow Malcolm. I wouldn't take that crap. But I'm not a Negro. I'm not going to follow him, I'm going to fight him."

It was just that sort of schizoid fight to the end. Federal and local police agencies subjected Malcolm daily to microscopic surveillance. They tapped his telephones; they bugged his office, his meetings, even the tiny dressing cubicle just offstage at the Audubon; they shadowed him; they taped and transcribed his speeches;

they bought fact and gossip from informers; they infiltrated at least one undercover agent into his inner circle; they questioned friends and neighbors of his followers, a practice whose intent was the collection of intelligence but whose collateral result was to frighten believers away. Once, while Malcolm was still under suspension from the Lost-Found Nation, two FBI agents even came calling on him at the house in East Elmhurst and tried by heavy indirection to buy secrets about the Nation, mainly names; Malcolm was not *that* far gone in controversy with the Messenger and politely sent them packing. The watch was constant, intrusive and totally nonselective, a seine that swept up everything from Malcolm's political beliefs and associations to the intimate details of his private life. To the extent that raw unevaluated data constitute knowledge, the police knew Malcolm better than anybody else and so understood that they were dealing with a man of quality. They seem to have accepted this as another of the ironies of police life and did not let it interfere with duty. "Sure, we're watching him," the headquarters cop said in the days immediately following Malcolm's split with the Nation. "Not as much as he thinks he's being watched but more than most people would imagine."

That this ought to be done was not seriously questioned. Intelligence-gathering is not the license-to-kill occupation fantasied in the Bond movies—a lot of it consists of reading dusty dialectics and running credit checks—but it does tend to operate according to its own imperatives. Intelligence has a voracious appetite, a consuming interest in names and data that passes quickly from the professional to the bureaucratic; it tends in the process to lose sight of the difference between dangers that are clear and present and those that are speculative and remote. It is intensely literal-minded as well: its mission is preventive, to alert the authorities to troublesome situations that may happen, and it does not therefore draw overly fine distinctions between what is really criminal or revolutionary and what is just talk. The boundaries have got particularly blurry in the Federal intelligence bureaucracies, the FBI and Army intelligence particularly, which were caught out in the 1970s monitoring everything from bomb factories to Earth

Day rallies. The New York police were more fastidious in Malcolm's day: their intelligence operations were under the management of literate, sophisticated men who understood the dangers of unbridled political surveillance and so insisted on the working premise that what wasn't criminal wasn't subversive. But what was criminal included various political acts, among them conspiracy and anarchy. The judgment accordingly was that both Malcolm and the Nation bore watching, not so much for what they did—police intelligence conceded that they were law-abiding—as for what their teachings might incite. They sounded dangerous; therefore, they were.

The watch employed the usual techniques of surveillance with all the usual hazards, plus several new ones peculiar to the Muslim beat: some paid informers got converted, and even some regular black detectives brought back word that the Muslims weren't so bad after all—that they were problack, not antiwhite, and really rather conservative in the bargain. Various units participated at various times, sometimes without one another's knowledge—and sometimes presumably turning in reports on one another's people. At one point when Malcolm and the Original People were only just coming into the public consciousness, the department even created a special M (for Muslim) Squad to keep tabs on them. Normal detective operations were hampered, however, by the fact that Harlem is at heart a small town and that its black professionals, including black detectives, tend to get quickly and widely known. The inside assignment accordingly fell to a secret intelligence unit whose operatives were unknown even to the rest of the department. Malcolm had become a job for the men from BOSS.

BOSS was the Bureau of Special Services, a lineal descendant of the old Radical Bureau of pre-World War I days*; it had languished

*The agency has gone through a succession of name changes, sometimes reflecting its major concerns (it became the Neutrality Squad in 1915, the Bureau of Criminal Alien Investigation in the 1930s) and sometimes disguising them (it was briefly the Public Relations Squad in 1945–46). When some of its operatives surfaced during a Panther trial in 1970–71, the defense, in cross-examination, kept calling BOSS "the SS Division." Its name, probably coincidentally, has since been changed to the Security and Investigation Section.

in the 1950s, when the FBI pre-empted most of the subversive-chasing field, but it came back to life in the boil of Left-wing, Right-wing, student and Negro militancy of the sixties. It became by conscious design an elite corps—a high-wage, high-morale, computer-screened outfit whose hiring desiderata included a 120 IQ, a college diploma, a foreign language, a knack for writing, some skill with bugs, taps or cameras, a solid personnel folder, a sound body and a clean, *nuancé* mind. "The work," as one alumnus, Anthony V. Bouza, wrote mildly in an unpublished master's thesis on BOSS, "is interesting, stimulating, challenging and varied." For the sixty or so men and women assigned to overt operations, it can also be prosaic: the Malcolm File, assuming that it fattened according to formula, included not only reports on his politics but the sweepings available from his birth certificate, his grade-school transcript, his rap sheet, his prison folder, his marriage license, his credit history, his utility bills, his driver's-license application, his MMI and OAAU incorporation documents—that whole trail of more or less public paper that everybody, tame or rebel, leaves behind in the punch-card society. The routine even included a garbage check: BOSS had discovered that you could tell a lot about a man by filching and sorting through the things he throws away.

But BOSS's heart was in its clandestine-operations section. Like any intelligence agency, BOSS used paid informants but understood their limitations, among them the possibility that they might make up information to keep their wages coming in. It vastly preferred its own undercover operatives—men who were commonly recruited out of town, secretly inducted into the force, equipped with a cover address, job and identity and set afloat to establish themselves in the community. There was nothing to identify them as policemen even to other policemen; their folders and ID photos were held secretly at BOSS headquarters, and they never set foot in police stations unless they were arrested in the line of duty. There was thus no reason to be suspicious of Gene Roberts, clothing salesman, of the Bronx, New York, when he appeared among the brothers in 1963 or 1964. The charter of the

BOSS agent was to work his way inside the target group, make himself constantly available, volunteer for the nastiest jobs and get as close to the center as he could; the extent to which this required participating in and even promoting precisely those activities the department was worried about was left to his discretion and his daily covert contacts with his Control. Roberts succeeded admirably in his mission; the brothers got to calling him "Brother Gene" and admitted him to the circle of two dozen or so true believers who served Malcolm as staff, advance men and bodyguards.

The Malcolm File was opened as a dossier on his politics and political connections, but by the end its major concern, like Malcolm's own, was his life expectancy. BOSS's analysts had no serious doubts as to the real source of the danger to him. They had Roberts in Malcolm's own court, at least one other agent similarly well placed in Mosque No. 7, plus a rich assortment of other sources ranging from newspaper clippings to informers and telephone taps. The intelligence picture they assembled out of all these mosaic bits was schematic and simplified as to motive but not unlike Malcolm's. The police tend to take a radical-materialist view of the world around them: they perceive conflict as originating not in the abstractions of politics and theology but in the baser appetites for money, power and license. They believed that the first source of conflict between Malcolm and the Nation was simple jealousy—Malcolm as competition for the crown and the treasury—and that their quarrel had been inflamed beyond recovery by his personal insults to the Messenger. Malcolm understood very well what he was doing when he breached this last taboo, a BOSS alumnus told me, and he saw the beating of Leon Ameer and the shooting of Benjamin Brown as direct warnings to him. "He knew it was all over," the BOSS man assured me, with the authority of a man for whom Malcolm had had no important secrets. "Don't forget—we knew what he was telling his associates."

In late January and early February, the danger signs began quickening—the continuing name-calling, the rising tensions, the then unpublicized scares in Los Angeles and Chicago, the increasingly worried reports from the undercover operatives in both camps. Two weeks before the end, at around the time Malcolm was getting off for England and France on his last trip, BOSS's analysts sat down with everything available and reached a chilling judgment—that the crisis between Malcolm and his former brethren was coming to a head and that they would shortly make an attempt on his life.

An intelligence estimate always comes down to an educated guess; this one was passed on to the police command as a strong and imminent possibility, not a certainty, and, as one BOSS officer told me, "We'd been wrong about things plenty of times." Still, with all the caveats, it was taken seriously by the department and was the subject of considerable command debate as to what to do about protecting Malcolm. The traditionalist line apparently was that they ought to continue only with routine coverage of his public activities, nothing more. ("The guy had a bad sheet," a headquarters officer who had not participated in the discussions told me years later. "You don't offer somebody like that protection.") But in this case the decision was to make Malcolm a formal offer of a twenty-four-hour police guard. This proposal was advanced by a man from BOSS; he accompanied it with the second educated guess that Malcolm would have to say no.

He was right, of course. Malcolm had always given the police a certain minimal and distant cooperation; he would have somebody telephone them, for example, when he was planning a speech or a rally. But as BOSS well knew, the visible presence of police protectors was impossible for a man whose politics included regularly excoriating the police. Malcolm had turned down several proposals—seventeen, by one police count—that uniformed men be posted inside the Audubon at his rallies; his usual reply was that his own men were protection enough. The uniformed details as a result were limited to the sidewalk outside and were assigned there in erratic numbers, a handful one week, several dozen the next. I asked my BOSS source whether or not protection might have been forced on Malcolm whether he wanted it or not. "You can't do it," he said. "There's no guarantee you can do it even with the full and complete cooperation of the person involved. We did have our guy near him, Roberts, and I'm sure he was armed—an automatic or a Derringer, maybe, not a police weapon. But if someone's out to get you, there's very little you can do about it—certainly not until the fellow acts. That always shocks people, but it's true. You can't take out an injunction against an assassination."

Accordingly, following the BOSS scenario, representatives of the New York police department made three approaches during the final two weeks to Malcolm or to men presumed to speak for him and offered to put him under round-the-clock guard. These offers were made formally and before witnesses. In each case, also following the BOSS scenario, Malcolm or his people refused. The refusals were duly noted in the Malcolm File, "and as far as I was concerned," the man from BOSS told me, "that took us off the hook."

29. The Hour of the Gun

He had come in from London on Saturday the thirteenth frayed and jet-weary and had gone to bed with a sleeping pill to be sure for once that he would get some rest; but in some dim fraction of consciousness he heard glass breaking and a sudden *whoom!* as the first Molotov cocktail hit the living room and he was up and moving before he was really awake. The clock said 2:45 and the house was boiling with smoke and sudden licks of fire, and there was a second *whoooom!* and he and Betty, big with twins, were running in the dark scooping up children, the three older girls from the single bedroom next to their own, the baby Gamilah out of a tiny made-over utility room just about big enough for her crib. They heard a third Molotov clunk against the back door and bounce away into the grass, where it died, and somehow he got them all, Betty numb and the children crying, into the back yard and the twenty-degree cold, and then he went back in, still in his pajamas, and got out what clothes and belongings he could; in a minute or so he stumbled back outside bundled in a charred topcoat and coughing, and watched the firemen save what was left of the house. The word spread quickly among the brothers; Kenyatta, all injury, wouldn't come—"Malcolm have picked new friends," he told the lady who called him—but the others did, crowding around with their good intentions and their useless guns. The man from the *News* asked Malcolm who he thought had done it. Malcolm stood there in the dark, the glow of the red domelights playing over him, and started to laugh.

The Muslims said he did it himself; they called a press conference, invited the devil media and said that after all Malcolm did love publicity and, besides, his last appeal on the eviction case was coming up before Judge Wahl on Monday morning with no credible hope that he could beat it. "We *own* this place, man," Captain Joseph told the representative of the *Herald Tribune,* a newspaper of enlightened but still property-conscious Republicanism. "We have *money* tied up here." The authorities did not precisely agree with the Malcolm-did-it theory but quietly encouraged it with the matter-of-fact mention that, oh, by the way, they had found a whiskey bottle containing a clear liquid standing upright on a dresser in the girls' room and that the liquid had turned out upon analysis to be gasoline. The implication of this and the Muslim charges was that Malcolm would have risked the death by fire of his own wife and children for a day's cheap publicity. The notion sent him into a fury. He said it had been Betty who pointed the bottle out to the firemen in the first place; he was convinced it was a plant—what would he have been doing with a whiskey bottle anyway?—and the publication of the find led him to suspect that the police, the fire department and the press were somehow in league with the Muslims to get him, or at least to permit him to be gotten. "Only I won't burn to death," he told the fire inspectors assigned to the case. "I'll probably be shot to death in the street one day. Or maybe while I'm speaking . . ."

Malcolm wept, not because he was going to die but because his family had been made part of the stakes and because he couldn't get anybody to believe him. He found a place for Betty and the kids—a friend and OAAU comrade in Queens put them up—and flew out to Detroit Sunday afternoon in his scorched topcoat for a speaking date he had agreed to and couldn't be persuaded to cancel. He was by then close to breaking; a doctor gave him a shot of something calming, and he napped backstage until it was time to go on. He came out in a rumpled suit and an open-necked sweater and apologized for them; one of the few good things you learned in the Muslims, he said, was to be conscious of your personal appearance. It was an odd and sad performance for Malcolm, stammery and meandering and only spottily applauded, a slow-motion tour of his entire politics. He talked about his efforts in Africa and how they were causing the white man great concern; about the necessities of self-defense and the preciousness of blackness; about John F. Kennedy and American neo-colonialism; about the Black Muslims and how in the good days they had made the whole civil-rights movement more militant but then had strayed in ways at "which, when they come to light, you will be shocked." He said the Muslims now were trying to silence him because of what he knew. "I'm not a racist," he said at the end. "I don't believe in any form of segregation or anything like that. I'm for the brotherhood of everybody, but I don't believe in forcing brotherhood upon people who don't want it. Long as we practice brotherhood among ourselves, and then if others want to practice brotherhood with us, we're for practicing it with them also. But I don't think that we should run around trying to love somebody who doesn't love us."

He came back to New York on Monday the fifteenth in the midst of the rising furor over the house. Almost the first news he got was that, having been bombed out of the place, he no longer had any lawful claim on the ruins; Judge Wahl had indeed refused to vacate his ruling, and, a couple of nights later, Malcolm wound up stealing out to the place at 1 A.M. with a pick-up, a couple of station wagons and a crew of the brothers and moving his last belongings out a jump ahead of the city marshal. The eviction order compounded his anger. He had called an OAAU rally for that Monday night, supposedly to announce his long-delayed program, but, instead, he spent the evening raging that the Muslims had fired the house and endangered his family and then had made him out to be the criminal. "I have no compassion or mercy or forgiveness for anyone who attacks sleeping babies," he said. His retaliation was faint and desperate—the charge, by now thrice-told, that the Nation was in league with the Nazis and the Klan and that the lot of them "want me out of the way" because he was on to them. "I'm waking up America," he said, "to the great Muslim menace." During his speech, there was a small commotion in the audience, a quarrel between a couple of spectators that drew some of the brothers standing guard away from their posts and distracted the crowd for a moment until Malcolm prevailed on everybody to cool it. It was a transient flurry, barely noticed at the time, and Malcolm's continuing rattling on about dying made a couple or three paragraphs inside the next day's papers.

The week thereafter was like a dream in which one ran without moving, cried out without being heard. Malcolm took a scheduled day trip to Rochester and kept a speaking date at Columbia University but otherwise started clearing his calendar of virtually everything not directly connected with his and his family's survival. He postponed his trip to Mississippi, called off a weekend he had planned with Haley in upstate New York to rest and think about the *Autobiography*. He made a date with Sutton for Friday the following week to talk about drawing a will. He called a press conference at the Theresa, a frantic affair at which everything seemed to run together—the fire-bombing, the expulsion from France, the naked ill will of the Muslims, the indifference of the police and the press—in a single conspiratorial tangle. He demanded an investigation by the FBI and an explanation from the State Department, the latter in a long telegram to Dean Rusk that he had written out in Magic Marker. "He was hysterical," said one old acquaintance who was there. "He kept looking over his shoulder. It was spooky—the only person in the room more frightened than Malcolm was me." He finally gave in to the pressure from the brothers to carry a gun, or at least to take out a permit to carry one. He stopped by the 28th Precinct stationhouse in Harlem to pick up the application papers; whether for want of time or out of some last secret reserve, he never filled them out.

Everybody worried for him. The Ossie Davises sent him a little money, hoping it would entice him to go back abroad until things cooled down.* Maya Angelou arrived from Ghana and called him from the airport. "They almost caught me," he told her. She could hear the desperation of it; she urged him to get away somewhere —to go on out to her mother's house in California if nowhere else and just sit around for a while—but he shrugged off the idea. One day a friend called him to make a date for the following Tuesday. "I'll be *dead* by Tuesday," he said. He repeated it several times; he sounded terrible. His friend asked what about calling the police. Malcolm laughed. "The police know I'm going to be dead by Tuesday," he said.

He sat for several print and broadcast interviews, seeming now desperate, now superbly cool. "I live like a man who's already dead," he told Theodore Jones of the *Times.* "I'm a marked man . . . This thing with me will be resolved by death and violence." Jones asked why. "Because I'm me," Malcolm answered. He said he felt like a sleepwalker come awake and suddenly out in the world on his own. "I won't deny I don't know where I'm at," he said. "But by the same token how many of us can put the finger down on one point and say, 'I'm here'?" The next day, with Gordon Parks of *Life,* he spoke again of his Black Muslim past; it was as if it had been another life, somebody else's, with only the most distant connection to his own. "I was a zombie then," he said, "like all Muslims—I was hypnotized, pointed in a certain direction and told to march. Well, I guess a man's entitled to make a fool of

*There is an enduring story that Malcolm had in fact decided on another trip to Africa, that air tickets had been bought for him for Monday the twenty-second or Tuesday the twenty-third and that his execution had to be hurried accordingly. I found no evidence to support this—only the contradicting facts that Malcolm had made appointments to see Percy Sutton and Kenneth Clark, had tentatively accepted a campus speaking date in New England and had agreed to keep his deferred date in Mississippi, all between Tuesday the twenty-third and Sunday the twenty-eighth.

UPI

The beginning of the end: Malcolm outside his fire-bombed house, February 1965

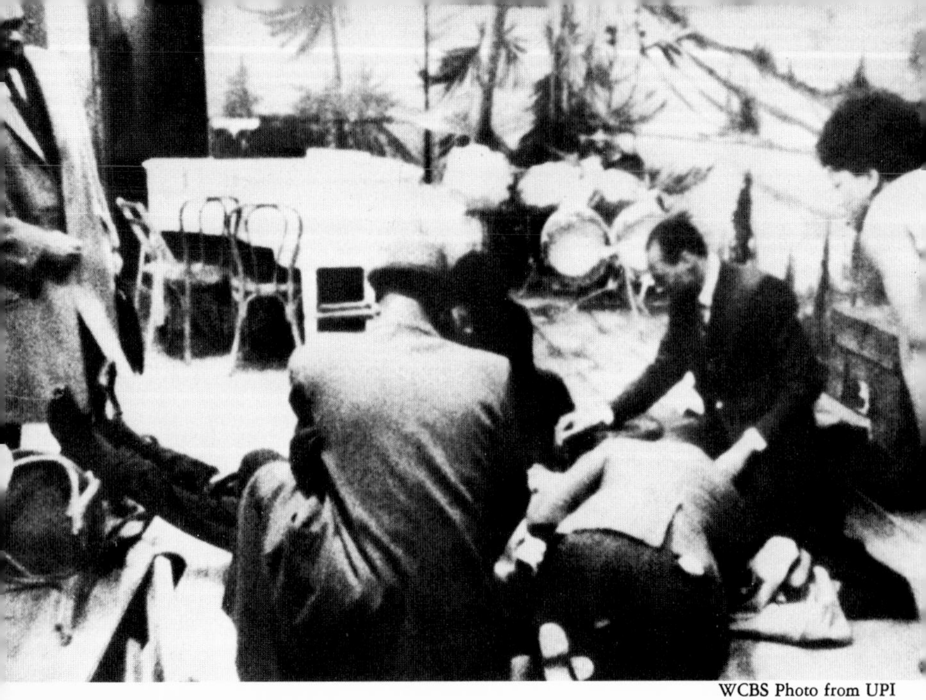

WCBS Photo from UPI

The death of Malcolm X: On stage at the Audubon (with police agent Gene Roberts, kneeling in light jacket, attempting resuscitation) and en route to the hospital

UPI

Wide World Photos

ire and ice: The burning of Muhammad's Mosque in Harlem the night
ter Malcolm died

A.F.P. from Pictorial

Wide World

The suspects: Talmadge Hayer in the hands of the crowd and the police; Norman 3X Butler . . .

Wide World

UPI

. . . and Thomas 15X Johnson, waiting to be booked for homicide

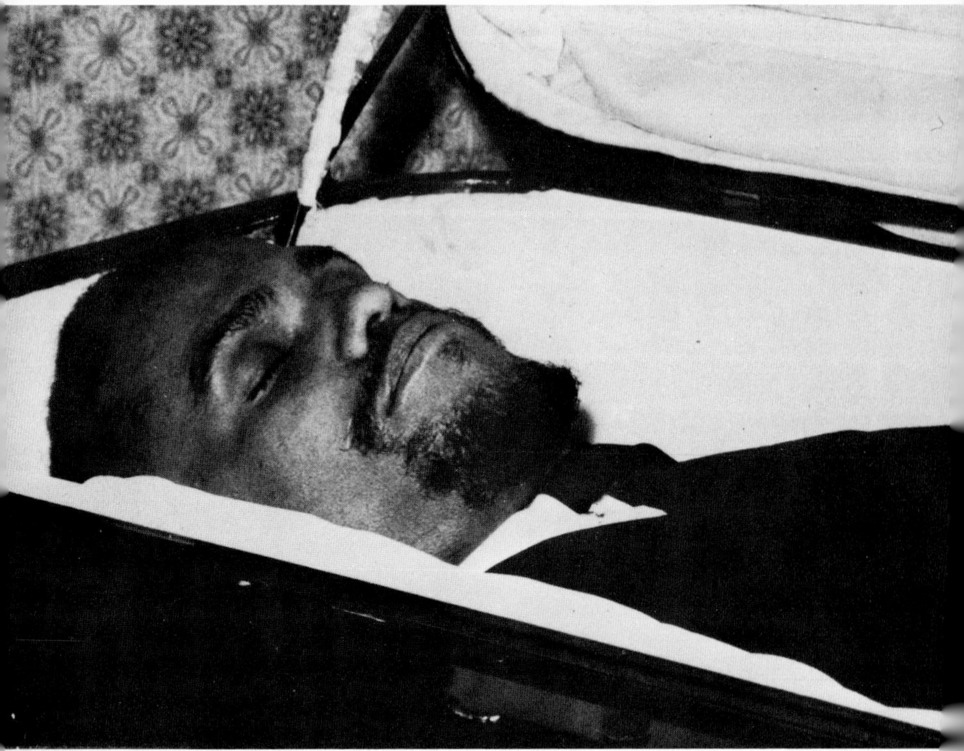

Wide World

The last rites: The body on view . . .

Wide World

. . . Sister Betty at graveside, mourners in Harlem

UPI

Ebony Magazine

"Every goodbye ain't gone"

himself if he's ready to pay the cost. It cost me twelve years." He sensed now that the cost would be higher still. "That was a bad scene, brother. The sickness and madness of those days—I'm glad to be free of them. It's a time for martyrs now. And if I'm to be one, it will be in the cause of brotherhood."

In all these talks, he identified the Muslims as his antagonists—"those folks down at 116th Street," he told Jones, "and that man in Chicago." One day, sitting at the Theresa with Betty bottle-feeding Gamilah nearby, he attacked the Nation bitterly as shot through with "gangs of criminals and fiends" who pretended to militancy but never attacked white people—only their fellow blacks. Some days toward the end he believed that they were acting with the complicity or at least the acquiescence of the white establishment, which he considered equally interested in silencing him. The day before he died, he told Haley that he had changed his mind about blaming the Nation; he had by then been brooding about his expulsion from France, and the contours of the conspiracy had widened suddenly and dizzyingly to include the government itself. But he never doubted that the Muslims were the principal instruments of this conspiracy. One day that last week, he wrote down the names of five men he believed had been assigned to kill him. One man who saw this list would not repeat the names to me and did not himself believe that the Muslims had assassinated Malcolm; his own suspicion was that the CIA did it, using borrowed or hired Muslim gunmen. But he confirmed by implication that the men on the list were Muslims and that Malcolm never amended it. "Certainly he thought it was the Muslims," this source said. "My guess would be that at the moment they started shooting he assumed it was the Muslims."

Malcolm made time in the last days to be with Betty and to go hunting for a new house. They saw a place they liked in a white neighborhood; they needed $3,000 for a down payment and $1,000 to move, and Malcolm got on the phone trying to scratch it together in supplemental advances on the book. He left the family Saturday with the friends who had taken them in. He went to a last business meeting with the brothers, a worried affair whose principal topic was the reorganization of the OAAU; Malcolm was distressed by its inability to get anything done and had come to mistrust some of the ideologues and adventurers who had been joining. On Saturday night, he took an $18 single on the twelfth floor at the New York Hilton; Malcolm rejected most of white America's material values, but he had never been able to resist the laminated push-button luxury of the big hotels downtown. He slipped downstairs during the evening to the Hilton's Old Bourbon Steak House, a pleasantly half-lit room done in New Orleans *fin de siècle* with lots of red velvet and red flocked wallpaper, and had dinner by himself—a small, well-done steak, most likely, and several cups of integrated coffee. He never left his room otherwise. While he was upstairs, several black men materialized in the lobby and asked around for his room number. Somebody notified the hotel security man, a former cop who had read the papers and was immediately suspicious. He asked them to leave, and they did.

Malcolm came awake rattled on Sunday the twenty-first, the telephone ringing at his bedside. He picked it up. "Wake up, brother," a voice said, then clicked off. It was 8 o'clock. The day outside was spring-mild, but Malcolm dressed warmly for it, tugging on a pair of long johns and buttoning up a black cardigan under his dark-brown Alexander's suit. He called Betty; he hadn't wanted her to come to his rally at the Audubon that afternoon, but something had changed his mind and he asked her to bundle up the children and bring them. At around 1 o'clock, he checked out of his room, ordered up his two-year-old Olds from the hotel garage and drove uptown to 146th Street and Broadway, twenty blocks south of the Audubon. He parked there, outside an RKO movie house and stood at the corner for a few moments waiting for a bus; the police guessed later that he suspected somebody might be waiting for him around the Audubon and that he didn' want to arrive there in his own instantly identifiable car. Anothe auto with New Jersey plates pulled up in the bus stop, and th driver, a youngish black man named Fred Williams, waved Ma colm over. Malcolm peered at Williams anxiously, not recognizin him or Mrs. Williams beside him. Then he glanced into the bac seat and saw one of the brothers, Charles X Blackwell, from Jersey City, grinning out at him. Malcolm grinned back and got in.

There was just a single cop outside the front entrance, a kid patrolman from the Three-Four Precinct named Thomas Hoy, when Malcolm got there. Usually there were at least four or five officers on the sidewalk and sometimes a couple of dozen. But one of Malcolm's senior people had asked the duty captain in the precinct to take the main force off the door and put them somewhere less conspicuous. He said this was Malcolm's wish. The duty captain may or may not have been advised by then of the BOSS deduction that Malcolm's life was in imminent danger; in any case, he obliged. Hoy was stationed at the door. Two uniformed patrolmen, Gilbert Henry and John Carroll, were posted discreetly in the Rose Ballroom adjoining the main hall with a walkie-talkie and orders to yell if anything happened. The rest of the twenty-man security detail was hidden in the Columbia Presbyterian Medical Center across the street. Malcolm and his people still did not want a police presence inside the hall, and the department made no effort to persuade them.

This left the inner-perimeter defense to the brothers, and it was in some respects oddly slack that day. Several dozen spectators, familiar and unfamiliar, had arrived and taken seats before anybody responsible for security showed up to get the watch organized. Even then, nobody was searched coming in; that was orders from Malcolm. Nobody was supposed to be carrying a gun; that was orders, too, though the policy caused furious debate among the brothers and several of them brought their pieces anyway. Screening at the door was cursory. Malcolm, angry at the press, had directed that reporters be barred that day. Two black newsmen showed up; they were asked to remove their press badges and then were passed inside. One white man was stopped and asked if he was a reporter. "Yeah," he lied, unaware of the ruling. "No reporters allowed," a guard told him. He stood there a moment, then walked on in past the man who had stopped him. A second white man carried in a tape recorder; nobody checked it, or him. A Muslim from New Jersey with a Fruit of Islam pin gleaming in his lapel somehow slipped through unnoticed and took a seat down front. Somebody in the guard detail finally spotted him and asked him to step to the rear, where a couple of the brothers questioned him. He told them he had been getting disillusioned with the Nation and its teachings; they asked him to put his FOI pin in his pocket, then let him return to his seat without a search or even special instructions to any of the brothers to keep an eye on him.

It was going on 2 o'clock and the hall was filling when Malcolm clumped up the stairs with Blackwell and Mrs. Williams and walked heavily down the 180-foot length of the main ballroom to his little offstage dressing room. People watched him go by and thought he looked tired. Haggard. *Old.* His presence alone had always lit the place, but this time he was only a spent and anxious man and the hall wasn't a theater or a temple after all but an aging second-story barn with folding chairs and a plywood lectern and a backdrop painted with bilious blue-green trees and a cigarette-scarred piano that looked like it had been around since the great glory days of the Audubon when Georgie Raft used to dance there for pay. The floor was set up for four hundred and was filling; the stage was set up for eight or ten guests and was empty. Malcolm had asked Milton Galamison to speak, but Galamison had a secretary call to say that he had already conducted two services, some baptisms and a wedding that day and was too tired for anything else. Professor Michaux was to be there with the back-to-Africa crowd but he had an errand downtown and got stuck in traffic. Another man was supposed to do a fund-raising speech, sparing Malcolm the necessity of begging, but he never showed up. The Ossie Davises had wanted to come but were committed to a Negro-history banquet that night. Malcolm had invited Clarence Jones—he had always loved the idea of Martin Luther King's lawyer being at his meetings—but Jones, too, was otherwise booked.

So Malcolm waited in the little room, slumping in a folding chair, jumping up, pacing the floor, staring out at the empty guest chairs, slumping in his seat again. "He was more tense than I'd ever seen him," Benjamin Goodman remembered, "and I'd seen him for seven years. He just lost control of himself completely. I never saw him do that before." He had promised his program, but it wasn't ready; this made the bill of guest stars doubly important to him, and he got sharper and testier with his people as each new no-show report came in. Kenyatta, by then suspicious of everybody but Malcolm and himself, reported the seemingly loose security at the door. "I'm with my people here," Malcolm told him peevishly. "I have nothing to worry about." Another of the brothers looked in and said he had passed Galamison's message that he wasn't coming to one of the sisters. "You gave that message to a *woman?*" Malcolm flared. "You should know better than that." He had in fact planned to let one of the sisters do the customary "opening-up" speech introducing him, but with no program ready and no one to share the platform, he asked Goodman to do it one more time, as he had at hundreds of rallies and services in the past. Goodman nodded across the widening distance between them. Malcolm slouched back into his seat, his head bent, staring at the floor. Sheik Hassoun, the old Sudanese Muslim who had followed him home from Mecca, stepped over to him and touched his shoulder, trying to comfort him. Malcolm's head came snapping up. "Get out of here!" he growled. The sheik left, and Goodman followed him out.

Goodman was an experienced and skillful supporting player; he knew how to work a crowd—how to bring it to the right pitch for Malcolm's best days, how to make veiled excuses in advance when something wasn't right. That Sunday was a day for excuses. Goodman improvised through a half-hour; he remembered doing one extended metaphor about a captain on stormy seas and another, "from the Book," about that wall so high you couldn't get over it, and all of it was to let the people know that Malcolm once again would be talking about something other than his program. Malcolm sat offstage half-hearing the speech. He told the little group in the room that something felt *wrong* out there. He told them he was nearly at his wit's end. He told them he was sorry he had snapped at them. Then he stood to go on. Goodman saw him in the doorway and hurried into his wind-up: ". . . I present . . . one

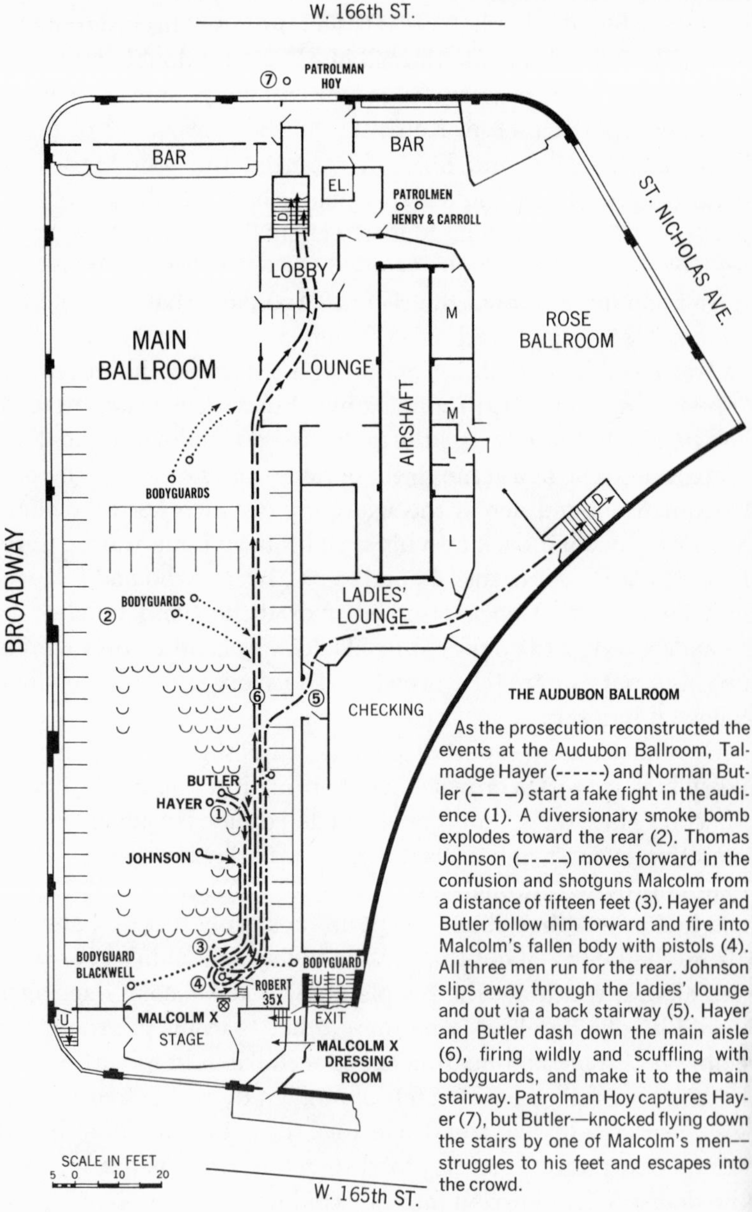

THE AUDUBON BALLROOM

As the prosecution reconstructed the events at the Audubon Ballroom, Talmadge Hayer (------) and Norman Butler (— — —) start a fake fight in the audience (1). A diversionary smoke bomb explodes toward the rear (2). Thomas Johnson (–·–·–) moves forward in the confusion and shotguns Malcolm from a distance of fifteen feet (3). Hayer and Butler follow him forward and fire into Malcolm's fallen body with pistols (4). All three men run for the rear. Johnson slips away through the ladies' lounge and out via a back stairway (5). Hayer and Butler dash down the main aisle (6), firing wildly and scuffling with bodyguards, and make it to the main stairway. Patrolman Hoy captures Hayer (7), but Butler—knocked flying down the stairs by one of Malcolm's men—struggles to his feet and escapes into the crowd.

who is willing to put himself on the line for you . . . a man who would give his life for you. . . ." He hadn't meant anything special by this, had had no premonition or anything—it was just something you said. He finished and started offstage, back to the little cubicle in the wings, and passed Malcolm coming on.

It all happened so terribly fast. Malcolm was standing there alone in the wintry sunlight filtering in over the booths off to his left, and everybody was applauding, on and on for a minute or more, and he was smiling that slowly widening smile as if after all those years he hadn't expected people to carry on so. He let them quiet down and said, *"As-salaam alaikum,"* and they said back, *"Wa-alaikum salaam,"* and suddenly, deep in the crowd, two men were on their feet, bumping backward against their wooden chairs, one hollering at the other, "What you doing in my pockets, man? Get your hand out of my pocket." The two jostled one another. The rostrum guards, Blackwell at stage left and Robert 35X at stage right, left their posts and started back toward the fight. Cary 2X Thomas popped toward them out of a booth. George 28X Whitney and Gene Roberts, the undercover cop, started forward from the back of the hall. And there was Malcolm all alone, saying hold it, hold it, brothers, let's be cool, and maybe he glimpsed the black man coming at him half-hunched over a sawed-off double-barrel 12-gauge J. C. Higgins and maybe he didn't, but if he did it was too late to do anything, even move.

A shotgun makes a fearful roar when it goes off and does even more fearful damage; men who live around guns will tell you they would rather go up against almost any other kind you can name. The one that killed Malcolm X was perfectly aimed from the point-blank range of fifteen feet. A dozen double-0 buckshot pellets, each the diameter of a .32-caliber bullet, ripped through the plywood lectern as if it were paper and made a perfectly patterned seven-inch circle of holes dead center on Malcolm's chest. Malcolm's hands flew halfway up. His eyes rolled back. There was blood on his face and his shirt front. He rocked on his heels and toppled over backward, crashing into two of the empty guest chairs. His head thudded hard on the floor. The man with the shotgun fired his second load, and almost simultaneously two more black men in overcoats came out of nowhere, one with a Luger and the other with a .45 automatic, squeezing off shot after shot into Malcolm's body, and by then it didn't even mean anything any more—Malcolm was lying there gray and dying, maybe dead already, and the bullets that hit at all were burrowing into his calves and thighs for no purpose except to make clear his final humiliation.

Everybody was running, screaming, bumping, falling, shouting, diving for cover, crashing into folding chairs. A man was crawling somewhere with a baby under his arm. A woman was on the stage flinging herself over a prostrate figure thinking that it was Malcolm and she could shield him, but it was somebody else. Betty, in a booth near the stage, heard the shots and one of the children wailing were they going to kill everybody, and she got them all under the seat somehow and covered them with her body. Near the back, somebody yelled, 'There's a *bomb* in here!" A homemade flare made out of a man's sock wrapped around some matches and some film lay there spluttering and smoking; people eddied around, some trying to get away from it, some trying to fight close to douse it and stomp it out. The guard detail dissolved, some ducking, some pinned in the tangle of people and folding chairs, some too stunned even to move. Most of those who brought their pieces never got them out. One or two tried to shoot through the crowd at the assassins, the bullets ricocheting in the vast room, and the wonder was that only two bystanders got hit, one with a stray shotgun pellet in the foot, another with a .32 slug in the gut. Patrolman Henry, one of the cops in the Rose Ballroom, said something into his walkie-talkie and couldn't get an answer. "Shots fired, Audubon Ballroom," he hollered helplessly, then flung the radio down, ripped his .38 out of its holster and, with Patrolman Carroll, ran into the madness too late.

The man with the shotgun by then had tossed it away where he stood and faded into the tangle of colliding bodies; somebody thought they saw him duck into the ladies' lounge, which had one door opening on the ballroom and another leading to a back stairway down to the street. The two men with pistols pounded down the aisle toward the main exit stairway, hurdling chairs, ducking bullets, firing backward toward the crowd. "Get out the Goddamn way!" one of them yelled, waving the .45. Brothers grabbed at him and ducked away as the gun came round. One of them threw a rolling body block at the second man—the one with the Luger—and sent him crashing down the steps toward the main door. The man with the .45 came straight at Gene Roberts. Roberts picked up a chair. The man squeezed off a shot. It caught Roberts moving and went through the bottom of his suit coat. Roberts flung the chair at the man, knocking him down. The man got up limping and stumbled toward the steps. Another of the brothers—the police identified him later as Reuben Francis—got a bead on him from eight feet and fired three times. The second shot caught the man in the left thigh. He lurched and said "Oh!" but kept going and made the stairway and started down, half-hopping, half-sliding down the banister, vaulting over the gunman who had been knocked downstairs. The brothers clawed at his arms and clothes. He dropped the .45. A brother snatched it up, pointed it at him and squeezed the trigger. It wouldn't work. George Whitney got the man's collar and slowed him. Others poured down after him, and they all came spilling out the door just as Patrolman Hoy came dashing in.

"People were coming out yelling, 'They shot Malcolm! They shot Malcolm!' " Hoy remembered. "The first guy down, the crowd was beating him with chairs, yelling, chasing him. I reached out and grabbed him. I had a piece and the crowd had a piece." The second man—the one who had the Luger—melted away through the pack. The brothers closed around the first man, pulling, pounding, kicking, stomping, wrestling Hoy for him. *They'll kill him right here,* Hoy thought. He drew his gun and knew instantly it was useless—knew they could disarm him if he tried to use it. So he hung on to the suspect, the man's body stretched between him and the crowd like the rope in a tug-o'-war, till suddenly two more cops, Sergeant Alvin Aronoff and Patrolman Louis Angelos, came bulling in out of a squad car and into the crowd, people punching and shouldering them every step of the way. They joined the struggle, but Aronoff saw the crowd was winning, so he drew his revolver and ordered them back and fired once into the air. The crowd froze for a split second; Aronoff, Angelos and Hoy wrestled the man away and got him in the back of the squad car.* The crowd regrouped and closed around. Angelos raced the engine. Someone leaned in and punched him in the face. The car stalled. The crowd started rocking it. More cops came running out of the Medical Center and got them loose, and they headed uptown to the Three-Four Precinct station on Wadsworth Avenue.

They saw that their captive was a kid, and that he was hurt. He was saying, "My leg, my leg, I'm shot—my leg, my leg." Aronoff patted him down, felt something in his pants pocket and pulled it out. It was a cartridge case for a .45, with four live cartridges in it. "What's this doing in your pocket?" Aronoff asked. The kid moaned. "What's your name?" He moaned some more—"My leg, I'm shot"—and didn't answer. Look, said Aronoff, if it hadn't been for me and this other police officer here, those people would have killed you back there, so the least you could do is cooperate—what's your name? "Tommy," the kid said. And your second name? "Hayer," he said, but he slurred it, and Aronoff got it down as Hagan. "Is that Tommy or Thomas?" he asked. Hayer may have answered "Talmadge," which was his given name, or "Tommy," his family nickname, but it came out slurred again, and he went down forever on the records of the State of New York as Thomas Hagan, with his rightful name, Talmadge Hayer, appended later as an alias.

Malcolm lay on the stage where he had fallen. Somebody had

*Hoy and Aronoff were debriefed separately at the time, Hoy at the scene and Aronoff at the stationhouse, and the early editions of the next day's papers reported that there had been two arrests. The two policemen, as it developed, were talking about the same man, but the confusion lasted long enough to create a whole folklore around the "arrest" of a mysterious Second Suspect—a mythology that endures to this day.

ripped open his shirt and tie and torn away his T-shirt, soggy with blood. A nurse got to him first, then Gene Roberts; each in turn tried giving him mouth-to-mouth resuscitation. Betty fought through to the stage screaming—"They're killing my husband"—and dropped to her knees beside him. He had gone ashy, his face stretched into a terrible smile, his eyes slitted and lifeless. A half-dozen of the brothers dashed over to the Medical Center, found an intern and a wheeled stretcher and said, "Come on, baby, you're coming with us." The intern, terrified, told them, "No—*you* take the stretcher." They did. The full police contingent got in late out of the roiling crowd in the street, and one of them moved slowly up the main aisle—*sauntering,* the brothers said resentfully afterward—and said, "Okay, what's the name of the guy who got shot?" The brothers stood there staring at Malcolm and wandering aimlessly around the stage, crosshatching it with paths of bloody footprints. "I'm going home," George Whitney said numbly. "There's snakes, snakes, snakes, snakes in the community," Cary Thomas answered, bruised and bitter; maybe they should have searched everybody coming in—just paid Brother Malcolm no mind and searched everybody. He waited till the stretcher appeared at last. The brothers hefted Malcolm onto it and ran him down the aisle and out into the street, yelling, "Get out the way or we'll kill you!"

It was too late. They got Malcolm across to the Medical Center, the brothers jostling the cops all the way to be nearest to him. They were still in the entranceway to the Vanderbilt Clinic when the residents and interns met them, took one look at Malcolm and did a fast stab tracheotomy, opening his throat to let him breathe around the thickening blood. They got him upstairs to a third-floor emergency room and did what they could—"the usual heroics," said one staff doctor out of that detachment one requires if one is to watch people die. They laid open his chest to massage his heart, knowing without looking that it was over already. Seven of the twelve slugs from the first shotgun blast had destroyed Malcolm's heart; others had shredded his aorta, punctured both lungs and burrowed into his spine. The doctors worked fifteen minutes anyway; then they quit and closed him up and pulled a sheet up over his head.

He had been born Malcolm Little, a kid baptised into blackness when they killed his daddy for it; had come up Detroit Red, fleeing blackness in a street world where you never thought about yesterday and never knew if there was going to be tomorrow; had become Malcolm X, a minister of Allah preaching blackness with a fury as intense as the shame of blackness had always been; and at the end was still becoming El-Hajj Malik El-Shabazz, Muslim and revolutionary, prophet and demagogue, a decent and supremely gifted man who was martyred by his past and never got to see his future as an authentic black American hero. His life had been a series of contingent lives—a procession of changes that was broken, not completed, by his death in his fortieth year. It was at once shabby and appropriate that they checked him into the hospital as "John Doe" because there wasn't time to search him for identity papers. They knew who he was, of course; we all did; but lives are one thing and records another, and one had to wait in an airless little office clogged with family and brothers and reporters until the man came downstairs and told us all, "The gentleman you know as Malcolm X is dead."

PART III

A Detective Story

Any time you catch a homicide case, there's a lot of confusion. But most of them are committed by your wife, your husband, your boy friend—someone who *cares* for you—and most of them clear themselves up in the first ten minutes of investigation. This one took a little longer.

—A detective assigned to the Malcolm X murder case

30. The First Day

Rocky Cavallaro was suffering in the squadroom, feeling lousy after a late Saturday night out and thinking gratefully that nothing ever happens in the Three-Four Precinct on Sunday afternoons. John Keeley and Bill Confrey were winding up a tour at their back-to-back desks at Manhattan North Homicide, talking cases and every so often noticing the minute hand wandering past 3:15 and toward 4 o'clock, when they were due off. Herbert Stern, the DA's man, had left his number at the office and put on something sporty and was on a date at Ondine's in midtown when somebody who knew him came over and said, "Hey—you hear Malcolm X was shot?"

"Where?" asked Stern, hoping: *Let it be Brooklyn or Queens.*

"Manhattan. The Audubon Ballroom."

"Was he killed?" Stern asked, thinking: *If he's just wounded, I'm all right.*

"Yeah, he was killed, and they seem to have caught somebody," the guy said, and almost before the words were out Stern was moving, breaking his ass to get to a phone, because if it was a homicide and they had caught somebody, they would be looking for an Assistant District Attorney so they could book him. Stern called in, dialing fast, and whoever picked up the phone on the other end said, "Where you *been?*"

They were the main men on the case, along with Cavallaro's

partner, Tom Cusmano, and the two black detectives, Jimmy Rushin and Warren Taylor, and maybe fifty other guys the first few days, and probably all of them wished in that very first instant that somebody else had caught it. All of them possibly excepting John Keeley: he was a tough, grainy, wiry Irishman who loved being a homicide detective—who had talked his way into the assignment, with no rabbi, no hook, no nothing, by promising to be the best homicide cop in the whole city and who figured he was keeping the promise. Keeley always loved a good case, the kind you could get the *feel* of and get some results, and even his first reaction when the console phone rang on the back-to-back desks at Manhattan North and they got the news was that he could say good-bye to the wife and kids and everything they had planned for a while. The others all liked a good case, too, sure, but some days you had a date or the blahs or just forty minutes to go till quitting time and. Well. "Your first reaction is 'oh shit,' " one man in the investigation told me. "You're human. You go up there and look at the body and your stomach turns over, not because of all the blood but because you see right then and there it's going to be a bitch of a case."

The first one in it, willy-nilly, was Rocky Cavallaro—Ferdinand Cavallaro, actually—a lean, dark mod cop who was then thirty-fiveish and into writing, photography, acting (mostly TV commercials, but *who knows?*) on the side. The day detectives on the 34th Squad had divided their tour into three three-hour shifts and Cavallaro mercifully had drawn the third, which meant he was catching from 2 to 5 that afternoon and was sitting in the second-floor squadroom when Aronoff and Angelos came in from the Audubon half-dragging, half-carrying Talmadge Hayer and plunked him down on the big table in the muster room like a trophy of war. Then they saw the blood on his left pants leg. Somebody called for an ambulance and somebody started giving him first aid. Cavallaro and Cusmano heard the commotion and came pounding downstairs. "Malcolm X was shot at the Audubon," Aronoff told Cavallaro. "This is one of the perpetrators." The kid was groaning on the table. Cavallaro automatically threw a few questions at him—was he in the Audubon, did he have a gun, did he shoot Malcolm X?—but all he got was the name, which he heard as "Tommy Hagan," too, and some more moaning. He quit after a minute or so. The ambulance came and took Hayer/Hagan first to Jewish Memorial Hospital, the closest available, where they discovered that, along with the gunshot wound, his left thighbone had been broken in the brawling outside the ballroom; the doctors there spent an hour working over him, and then the cops took him to the prison ward at Bellevue, where the leg was put in traction. Cavallaro meanwhile had raced down to the Audubon. He noticed leaving that it was 3:15 P.M.

It was 3:20 when Manhattan North Homicide got the call, a time Keeley and Confrey remembered clearly because if it had been 4 o'clock "we wouldn't of caught it." Keeley caught it, actually, because the two of them alternated taking on cases as they came in and Keeley happened to be up at the time, but the distinction existed mainly on paper in the days and weeks ahead—days and weeks in which everybody worked their butt off. Keeley and Confrey, an amiable, thick-chested Irishman with wavy gray hair and a shamrock tie clasp, got in Keeley's car and headed for the hospital first. Cavallaro by then had looked in at the Audubon long enough to give the uniformed cops there a couple of instructions about corralling witnesses and preserving evidence and then had gone over to Columbia Presbyterian himself, riding up to the third floor in an elevator choking with brothers, cops, hospital people and a grieving black woman who turned out to be Betty Shabazz. The detectives converged on the operating room. "I pulled open the curtains," Keeley remembered. "His whole chest cavity was open. They had massaged his heart. I saw him there on the table and I knew we had a homicide."

They scrambled back to the Audubon and immediately discovered the price they would pay for the low-visibility police deployment that Malcolm's people had requested that afternoon and that the precinct command had so readily granted. Putting the full contingent of twenty men out on the sidewalk instead of hiding most of them indoors would not have saved Malcolm's life; a team of assassins brazen enough to shoot him before two to four hundred eyewitnesses was clearly quite beyond being put off by the normal deterrents. Neither would the police necessarily have caught any more of the killers at the scene, since there was no way for them to tell who was who in the crowd boiling out of the building. What they might have done, as one man from the DA's office conceded long afterward, was contain some of the people and so hold their witnesses together until orderly questioning could begin. As it developed, Patrolman Hoy at the door had had his hands full just keeping Hayer from getting killed, and the two cops who had been posted in the adjoining ballroom had been swallowed up in the chaos inside. It was telling that Aronoff and Angelos, the next officers to get to the scene, had strayed in from another precinct; the detail from the 34th didn't get out of Columbia Presbyterian and into the street until afterward, and by then most of the brothers and a good many of the spectators at one of the best-witnessed murders in history had scattered and disappeared.

There were maybe twenty to forty people left around the Audubon; the detectives had some of the uniformed men start taking names and delivering anybody who had seen anything back uptown to the Three-Four stationhouse on Wadsworth Avenue. Cops prowled the ballroom, scooping up slugs and cartridges, making little chalk circles around bullet-holes. The specialty units started showing up, from ballistics and the crime lab. Keeley found the diversionary smoke bomb, still sopping wet, and picked it up with a piece of newspaper. Cavallaro looked in the offstage dressing room and discovered the shotgun, wrapped up in a man's coat. He hefted it; it was a 12-gauge, a common Sears Roebuck model, with the double barrel sawed down from thirty inches to eight and a half so you could hide it easily, under a coat, say. It developed later that Freddie Williams, the man who had driven Malcolm to the Audubon, had found the shotgun and the Luger and shown them to his friend Charles X Blackwell; Blackwell, as he would testify at the trial, wrapped them up in coats and gave them to Reuben Francis. The Luger had vanished by the time the detectives got there.* So had the .45 automatic; the brother who had picked it up and tried to fire it at Hayer had stuck it in his pocket, taken it home, dismantled and reassembled it and only then, apparently mistrusting the city police, telephoned the FBI to come get it.

The detectives went back to the Three-Four that night with only the roughest idea of what had happened beyond the basic facts that Malcolm X had been shot full of holes in front of a roomful of people and that several guns had been involved. Most of them hardly knew who Malcolm was except for his reputation in the papers and the muster rooms as a guy who was stirring up the colored and was probably getting rich off it. They came into the squadroom at the Three-Four and found it in tumult, moiling with cops and witnesses and worried-looking police brass, whose presence (though none of the detectives on the case would put it quite that way) meant there was going to be big pressure downtown for some collars. If the case had been a routine one, its day-to-day management would have been left principally to the detectives officially carrying it, Cavallaro from the precinct squad and Keeley from Homicide, plus Herb Stern as the Assistant DA. But the Malcolm X case was enormously more than routine: they didn't know then if Harlem was going to blow up or what, and besides there was the embarrassment of having accurately guessed that somebody was going to try to kill Malcolm and not having moved vigorously to keep it from happening. The brass

*The Luger never was surfaced, and its disappearance remains one of the tantalizing mysteries of the case. One intriguing possibility is suggested by Blackwell's testimony before the grand jury, where he said he had given the shotgun to Francis and the Luger to "Brother Gene"—Gene Roberts, the man from BOSS. If Roberts in fact had come into possession of the gun, the police would have been confronted with a real dilemma: getting it into evidence would have required his testimony, and they were anxious to preserve his cover. In the event, Roberts's cover was preserved; he went on successfully to infiltrate the Black Panther Party when it succeeded Malcolm's two groups as the pre-eminently frightening black organization in New York. At the Malcolm X murder trial, eleven months after his grand-jury appearance, Blackwell testified that he had been mistaken the first time—that he had given both weapons, the Luger as well as the shotgun, to Francis. Since the state never called Francis, the question of how the Luger thereupon dematerialized never got answered or even asked.

poured extra men into Harlem in riot-prevention strength, to scatter crowds and get the Muslims to shut down their mosque and their restaurant until the heat died down. To run the investigation, they drafted Joseph L. Coyle, a thick-set, sixty-one-year-old assistant chief inspector then in charge of all Manhattan North detective operations, and let him have pretty much what he wanted—let him borrow detectives from all over, for example, so that there were fifty or more working the case in the first hectic days.

"The genius in a case like this," one detective said, "is in making order out of total confusion." It began that afternoon and evening in the squadroom, a babel of cops questioning witnesses and sending a lot of them home and shoving the live ones along to Coyle and Cavallaro and then to Herbie Stern. A lot of them were scared. Some were scared speechless. The majority hadn't really seen much that was helpful—maybe they hit the deck or got knocked over or were looking at the smoke bomb or the shouting match when the shooting started—and were useless as witnesses except to supply the names of people they had come with or had recognized around them. Some mistrusted the police and accused them straight out of complicity in the assassination. "You know who did it—*you* did it. Fuckin' CIA. *You're* the people set him up." A few, as the detectives discovered later, told the radio and TV people outside the Audubon that they saw everything and recognized everybody and then got to the police station and didn't know anything. Even those who wanted to help gave confused and wildly contradictory stories. "You get everything," Keeley said. "You get it was four guys with beards, or it was a green man with long hair. We got stories that up to ten were involved. You have to weed out what's incredible and come up with a basic description of what happened."

Gradually, working all night, they began to piece together the picture. They found few solid witnesses—only three out of the first day's catch lasted to testify at the trial, and of those only one was central—but they did figure out the basic scenario for the assassination: the faked fight, the smoke bomb in the aisle, the guards drawn away from their posts, the gunmen slipping forward, the sudden burst of shots, the brazen dash out straight through the middle of the crowd. The chief medical examiner, Dr. Milton Helpern, a round, serene man who had done twelve thousand autopsies and witnessed fifty thousand, got the body after Sister Betty had identified it and went quickly to work, jotting as he did that the deceased was an *adult Negro male . . . well-nourished, well-developed, slender, muscular . . . 6 feet 3 and 178 pounds.* Helpern counted ten shotgun wounds and two bruises in a tidy circle on the chest, plus various bullet wounds of both legs, both hands and the chin—twenty-one wounds in all—and retrieved three bullets and nine shotgun slugs, three of which had to be chiseled out of the spine. Ballistics looked at these along with various other slugs and cartridges that had been retrieved from around the stage at the Audubon and determined that they had all come from three guns: a shotgun, a .45 and a 9-mm automatic, possibly a Luger. The detectives at that point were satisfied that they were looking for three gunmen. Ballistics matched the clip retrieved from Hayer's pocket to the cartridges found in the ballroom and to the .45 brought in by the FBI during the night. The lab at the same time undid the smoke bomb, dusted a piece of film inside and lifted Hayer's left thumbprint off it. These findings persuaded the police to a reasonable certainty that one of their three men was Talmadge Hayer.

But Hayer, by the end of the first day, was really all they had. The early editions of the Monday morning papers said that two suspects had been arrested, each account relating how Aronoff had got Hayer away from the mob and the *Times* going on to quote Hoy in colorful detail about how he had grabbed "a suspect" dashing out the door with Malcolm's people in hot pursuit. The confusion was quickly straightened out; it developed that both Hoy and Aronoff were talking about Hayer and that while Hoy had laid hands on him first, Aronoff—who had got him loose and who had rank and seniority on Hoy besides—was credited with the arrest. (This amused some of the detectives, and offended their sense of caste as well. "It was Hoy's collar," one of them told me.

"Anyway, what was a *sergeant* doing making arrests?") The papers corrected their stories between editions, but the folktale that a Second Suspect had been arrested was born that first evening and has nourished the CIA-cum-police conspiracy theory of the assassination ever since. The suspect, in this theory, was a secret police agent who participated in the murder; the fact that he was arrested and got into the papers at all was seen as a blunder of the White Power Structure—and the fact that he disappeared from print between editions was evidence of its sinister conspiratorial control of the press.

The police, of course, had their own working hypothesis for the case. They committed themselves within the first hour to the theory that it was as simple as it seemed—that the Black Muslims had murdered Malcolm and that the motive was his desertion and his competition with the Nation for souls and money. This theory seemed to them to flow logically out of their accumulated intelligence reports, plus Malcolm's own repeated public accusations, plus the common assumption of those witnesses who were talking and were not blaming the police themselves. The only flaw in it was that they had a man in custody and didn't know who in the hell he was—didn't even know his right name until they had fingerprinted him at the hospital and got a make from the FBI, which reported that he was Talmadge Hayer, Negro/male/22/of Paterson, N.J., with arrests in 1961 for disorderly conduct and in 1963 for possession of eighteen guns that had been stolen in a store burglary and had been discovered in his basement. They learned otherwise that he was married but still living with his mother and two kid sisters and that they didn't like him. "An animal," one cop said. "A real robot." There was nothing at that point to connect him directly with the Nation. The first stubborn riddle of the case was summed up eloquently on Hayer's admitting papers at Bellevue Hospital. In the box where it said "RELIGION," somebody had drawn in a question mark.

31. What the Brothers Did

The Messenger of Allah said he didn't know who Hayer was either. The old man invited the devil press in two relays to the mansion in South Side Chicago and met them in his sitting room, a great cavernous chamber with bay windows and white silk on the walls and see-through plastic covers on the furniture. He sat in an armchair, beige on beige, looking tiny and transparent and breakable as a china doll. Yes, he said, the breach between him and Malcolm had been "kind of bitter" for him, but he had believed that Allah would punish Malcolm for deserting—would chastise him and bring him back to the Nation on his knees. "Malcolm died of his own preaching," he said. "We are innocent of his death. We have never resorted to no such thing as violence." His public view of the murder was thus not unlike that of the *New York Times*, which found a kind of Mosaic justice in Malcolm's having advocated violence and died violently. Somebody asked him about Talmadge Hayer. "He is," Mr. Muhammad said firmly, "a stranger to us."

A few of the brothers accepted this. Most of them did not. They scattered immediately after the shooting, some wandering home, some drifting up to the Theresa. For a while, they just stood there on the corner of 125th and Seventh, catching the late reports on pocket transistor radios, staring blankly at the old gray building, and at one another. After a time, somebody went to the desk and got the key to Suite 128. They let themselves in and sat there for an hour or so. The telephone kept ringing, everybody wanting to know was it true about Brother Malcolm, and they answered sadly, yes, it was true. Among themselves, the talk was bitter and vengeful. Some of them spoke about getting their pieces and going out in the street and shooting the first man they saw selling *Muham-*

mad Speaks. Some made up hypothetical hit lists, with targets ranging from Captain Joseph to Mr. Muhammad himself. Little Leon 4X Ameer came in from Boston with his scars and his furies, predicting openly that the Messenger's days were numbered. The New York police picked up word that six men were en route to Chicago to get the old man; they relayed this intelligence to the Chicago police, and a heavy guard detail materialized outside the iron fence around the mansion.

There were two immediate problems for the brothers. One of these was how to respond to the official inquiry into the assassination. Some of them met to discuss this question one night early on in an apartment on the west fringe of Harlem, away from the Theresa with its traffic of strangers and its presumed taps and bugs. Some thought they ought to cooperate with the police—"get some *results,*" one argued. But the opposing view prevailed; the policy, to the extent that there was one, was that the white power structure—including the police—had been involved in killing Malcolm and that if anybody came around investigating, *you don't know nothing.* Not everybody abided by this policy. One man who was actively promoting the police-did-it theory in fact cooperated with them off the record; he hadn't seen anything himself but encouraged some of those who had to tell it to the cops.

Still, the policy of noncooperation, and the general suspicion and resentment of the police among Malcolm's people, hampered the investigation from the beginning. One detective tracked an eyewitness to Philadelphia and showed him a picture of Hayer; the eyewitness said positively yes, he was one of the killers. After the detective left, however, the witness called the Theresa, where the police still had a tap, and asked what to do. *Come up,* a man in Suite 128 said, obviously suspecting that somebody was listening in; *come on up here and we'll talk.* The man did, and shortly thereafter dropped out as a prospective witness. The incident, so it seemed to the police, was not an isolated one but part of a pattern. "Sometimes," said Keeley, "I think the man had more enemies in that room than friends." The assumption of the police was that if you loved Malcolm, you would cooperate with them.

The assumption of some of the brothers was that if you *really* loved him, you wouldn't.

The second urgent piece of business was how to respond to the murder itself. Some of Malcolm's people said cool it—there was nothing white folks would like better than to see them and the Muslims wipe one another out in a fratricidal war. But Malcolm was gone, and a lot of the brothers believed that they knew who took him off, and at least a few were past caring about the consequences of seeking revenge.

The Fruit of Islam met nearly until midnight Monday the twenty-second in Mosque No. 7, the top floor of an old four-story, red-brick building at 116th Street and Lenox Avenue, then locked up the place and went home. At around 2 A.M., three or four men nosed a station wagon to the curb around the block, out of sight of the token police guard standing watch on the front entrance on 116th Street. The building was sealed and dark, but its secret places—its back doors and alleys and fire escapes—would not have been a mystery to those of Malcolm's followers who had been in the Nation with him. Two of the men got to the roof of a connecting building fronting on Lenox, around the corner from the mosque entrance and the cops, and stole across to the mosque roof, lugging a shopping bag with all the makings of Molotov cocktails. They dropped down to the fire escape at the fourth-floor level. There was the sound of breaking glass. The men scrambled back up to the roof and over to the next building, where they dumped the shopping bag, some oily rags and a five-gallon gasoline can, and dashed downstairs and out.

There was a sudden, roaring *varoooom!* and windows were breaking and slashes of flame were leaping thirty feet high against the moonlit sky. *"Run!"* one of the cops yelled; he and his partner dashed out into the middle of the street in a shower of glass and turned in the alarm. People spilled out of bars and stood there in the icy night, watching the place go up. The flames dissolved the roof in a matter of minutes, engulfed the mosque and spread downward to the Gethsemane Church of God in Christ on the third floor. Part of the fourth-floor wall cascaded into the street, injuring five firemen; one of them was halfway up a hundred-foot ladder when a flying brick skulled him, and another was pinned under the debris. The police hit the riot button, bringing three hundred additional men into Harlem out of Brooklyn, Queens and the Bronx; nothing happened, but the extras stood by through the night just in case. The firemen labored two hours just getting the fire under something approximating control; they were still there, and the mosque was still smoldering, when dawn came to Harlem. A single wall of the fourth floor survived, its windows framing squares of sky and vagrant eddies of smoke. Ice hung from the building front where the firemen had doused it; the old place glittered in the winter sunlight like the ruin of a crystal palace.

The firing of the mosque was another embarrassment for the police, who could surely have guessed that the place would become a prime target in any blood feud between Malcolm's people and Mr. Muhammad's and who theoretically had it under watch. But it was a major break for the police as well—at least for those assigned to the murder case. With their taps, bugs and informers and a BOSS agent among the brothers, it could not have been difficult for them to work up a list of suspects in the fire-bombing. Yet no charges were ever filed and no arrests ever made. "Our main concern was the homicide," one man on the case told me vaguely. "The bombing only involved property. It wasn't pushed."

It wasn't pushed because, in a hard murder investigation, you use what you have to get what you need, and you don't blow your main case to make a couple or three arrests for arson. An arson charge can serve you better as a persuader—a legal blunt instrument that can get people talking and doesn't leave any marks. The authorities wanted suspects in the Malcolm X murder case more than they needed arrests in the mosque bombing; their choice was as simple and as pragmatic as that. One can only speculate as to what precisely passed between them and the brothers on their list of suspects. One can fairly note that, notwithstanding the we-don't-know-nothing policy, cooperation became freer and witnesses more plentiful after the mosque burned down.

32. The Second Man

The mosque bombing was the second break in the investigation. The first came when Detective Kilroy reminded his boss, Inspector Frederick Lussen, of the Benjamin Brown shooting in the Bronx—the case in which he had got his face mask creased making an arrest. Lussen passed this on to Joe Coyle, the man running the Malcolm X investigation, in a routine phone conversation the day after the shooting, and Coyle passed it down the line to his detectives. They got hold of Kilroy, went over the Bronx case with him and felt a rush of excitement at the obvious parallels: the defector who sets up a competitive mosque, the visitation by a group of Muslims, the exemplary shooting of the deserter in full view of his followers. Kilroy gave them the names of the suspects, among them Norman 3X Butler, the karate expert, and Thomas 15X Johnson, the man in whose apartment they found the rifle.

Kilroy's tip was not the only thing that nudged the detectives toward Butler and Johnson. They were already largely committed to the working theory that the Muslims had killed Malcolm and so had focused their attention on known Muslim "enforcers," which was to say the more muscular of the Fruit of Islam; they began a picture file of these men, a stack that grew during the investigation to perhaps thirty from Harlem, Brooklyn and the Bronx and a similar number from various New Jersey mosques. Butler and Johnson would have made this list anyway, and some of the first rough descriptions of the killers, furnished before the detectives knew about the Bronx case, turned out to fit the two of them rather well. The conference with Kilroy could be said to have pushed their photos to the top of the pile. After that, the eyewitness identifications began accumulating, and the net began to close.

But only slowly. The case was a sweaty one, "all go-and-get-'em," Keeley said, from the very beginning. Hardly anybody slept at all the first two or three nights, and after that you napped at the squad or Manhattan North when you could and got home long enough to shower and change clothes and just miss seeing the kids off to school. Coyle organized a squad of ten white and ten black detectives to work the case in its early stages. They all met for daily conferences, red-eyed and yawning, to compare notes and trade addresses and pick up assignments; then everybody scattered, questioning witnesses, meeting informers, begging, buying and badgering hard information where you could get it and names where you couldn't get anything else, until finally they knew probably 150 of the 300 or 400 people who had been at the Audubon and saw pretty nearly all of them. Radio and TV tapes helped them find and catch out witnesses who had talked at the scene but not at the stationhouse. *Life* bought up some photos one of the brothers had taken immediately after the shooting stopped. The pictures, when the police got hold of them, identified and placed still more witnesses. One of them showed a known Muslim, the man who had got into the hall wearing an FOI pin and was allowed to stay once he took it off. The camera caught him standing there staring at Malcolm's body. He looked as if he were laughing.

Others of these photos, including one that *Life* actually published, showed Gene Roberts crouched over Malcolm, giving him mouth-to-mouth resuscitation; there was a bullet-hole in the skirt of Roberts's suit coat, and a bulge—a gun?—in his pocket. "We all almost fainted when we saw that," said one of Roberts's superiors at BOSS. The detectives on the case had no idea who he was, BOSS being secretive by nature even among its brethren on the force. They showed the pictures to friendly witnesses and asked who the man was. "Brother Gene," somebody told them, and they ordered Roberts brought in. "No one gave him to us—we had to go and find him," one detective told me. "We really took him over the coals. I don't mean physically, but we were putting pressure on the bodyguards, and we put pressure on him. And then the next thing you know we get a phone call, and we found out who he was. So we couldn't put pressure on him any more." Some of the police were puzzled that the other brothers never figured Roberts out after that—never guessed why he seemed suddenly immune when they were being called in repeatedly. They were equally puzzled about how oddly fuzzy Roberts seemed to be about detail, given that he was a cop and had helped slow Hayer down; a few of them wondered if he hadn't got *too* close to Malcolm to keep his objectivity. In any case, nobody thought it worth breaking his cover to put him on as a witness at the trial. "When you got undercover people," Coyle told me, "you don't like to reveal 'em. You don't want to throw out the whale to catch a fish." They left Roberts alone to operate among the brothers and later to infiltrate the Panthers; the state never called him to testify,* and, so one detective told me, "nobody else from BOSS was ever brought forward" in the Malcolm X case.

The detectives thus were on their own, and slowly, laboriously, they began drawing the net tighter. There is always a chancy element in cases based heavily on eyewitnesses; detectives much prefer physical evidence even in the best circumstances. The circumstances in the Malcolm X investigation were very nearly the worst, given the bedlam at the scene and the enduring mistrust of the police afterward. "It was hard getting people who had recollections that didn't border on hysteria," Stern remembered. "Plus a lot of them were against the system and against whites. They were not accustomed to cooperating with the police or dis-

*Roberts finally did surface in December 1970 as the star police witness in the trial of thirteen Panthers charged with (and eventually acquitted of) conspiring to blow up various targets, including Macy's, Bloomingdale's, three other department stores, a commuter rail line and the Bronx Botanical Gardens. On cross-examination, Gerald Lefcourt, one of the Panther lawyers, asked him if he had been present during the assassination. Roberts said he had. "Did you help do it?" Lefcourt asked suddenly. "No, I did not," Roberts replied. ". . . Isn't it a fact that you helped murder Malcolm X?" Lefcourt pressed. "No, it isn't," Roberts answered. But he seemed to the Panther defense thereafter to change subtly as a witness. He went on to describe what he had seen at the Audubon; he included the observations that there had never been so few police outside the ballroom as that afternoon and that they had taken "what appeared to be twenty minutes" getting there afterward—both debatable observations that could only embarrass the police in the Malcolm X case and, by association, the prosecution in the Panther trial.

trict attorneys." Some responded to the conventional appeals to conscience ("Come on—for *Malcolm*") or to enlightened self-interest; others, out of fear or suspicion, did not. Several—one woman leftist particularly—gave what seemed to the detectives to be deliberately misleading accounts of what had happened. Others, full of vengeful anger at the Muslims, were almost too eager to help and so were almost equally useless. Muslims showed up for questioning with their lawyers, FOI lieutenants and tape recorders. Time disappeared in low-profit pursuits; Keeley negotiated a meeting with Betty Shabazz at Frank's Restaurant in Harlem—she insisted on neutral ground—and discovered that she leaned to the CIA theory and hadn't seen very much anyway. Potentially solid witnesses were confused looking at mug shots of suspects; photo identifications are always tricky, particularly in cases involving black people, who may look light in one picture, dark in another and medium in real life. But when descriptions began to overlap and identifications started focusing on particular men, the police felt more comfortable with their case and got ready to make their move.

The case on Butler was the stronger of the two from the beginning, and they moved against him first. Butler was six-feet-two and powerfully built, an utterly self-assured young man with an angular face and wide-set almond eyes and hair shorn almost to the scalp in the Muslim manner. He lived in a project in the Bronx with his wife and four children, the youngest an infant, the oldest five. He had done two Navy hitches and had finished high school in service but had worked only intermittently since, driving an ice cream truck, trying out as a Pinkerton guard and a private detective, once taking and passing the qualifying exam to be a policeman. (He flunked his personality screening; to regard white people as devils is in the eyes of the police not a religious principle but a defect of character.) At the time of the assassination, Butler had been out of work for six or eight weeks and was getting by on a $55-a-week government stipend while going to a trade school for the unskilled. He seemed nevertheless to be living rather well, with eight suits and four topcoats in his closet and a car outside.

This in itself excited the suspicion of the police, who associate even political and religious murders with money; Butler said he had bought the car and a lot of the clothes cheap from brother Muslims and did occasional odd jobs for them on the side. He had been a Muslim for just under two years and, like any new convert, wore his faith like armor against the world. Policemen tended to resent him in direct ratio to his cold superiority toward them. He had come out on $10,000 bond in the Benjamin Brown case with both legs painfully bruised by a blackjacking; they had been bothering him off and on ever since, and they became central to his alibi.

He was supposed to stay off them, so he said, and he was stretched out on the living-room couch in his pajamas, resting his legs and watching television, when the police came for him near midnight on the twenty-fifth, four days after the murder. The detectives were nervous about him after the karate chop he dealt Kilroy in the Brown case, so they assembled a raiding party of five or six and drove to the Bronx in two cars to take him. They stopped at a phone booth near Butler's project and had Kilroy, who knew him, call ahead blind to check if he was there. Then they went upstairs and rang the bell.

Butler's wife looked out through the peephole. "Who is it?" she asked.

"It's me, Detective Kilroy. I want to speak to Norman."

She opened the door. The detectives came crowding through, guns unholstered and at their sides—"I wasn't about to be Jack Dempsey," Keeley said—and there was Butler, lolling on the couch with the TV on, looking up and asking them, cool as can be, "What's it all about?"

The police, for tactical reasons, didn't want to arrest him there; Cavallaro told him they were working on the Malcolm X case and maybe he could help and would he mind coming back to the stationhouse with them. Butler said okay. He went into a bedroom, stripped and got into a blue pinstripe suit and a knit shirt. Two detectives followed and watched, "to make sure," one said, "that he didn't put on anything besides his clothes." As they started out, Butler reached into a closet and picked out a black-

and-white herringbone overcoat. A couple of the detectives looked at one another; some of their witnesses had said that one of the killers had on a coat that looked like that.

They put Butler in the back of the car and drove across to Manhattan, to the Three-Four Precinct. The brass was assembling when they arrived; somebody had sent a car for Herb Stern, and other cops had rounded up a couple or three of the eyewitnesses and parked them out of sight. The call went out all over Manhattan North for black detectives of about Butler's size and skin color for a line-up; the police are not always that fastidious, but this was a high-pressure case, they were dependent on eyewitness evidence and they weren't going to blow everything in the show-up room. When they had four or five men available, they put Butler into the room with them, let him pick his own spot and brought on their witnesses one by one to look at the lot of them through a pane of one-way glass. At least two picked Butler out that night, not the best witnesses but good enough to warrant holding him.

Various detectives questioned Butler over the next three or four hours, and so did Stern, none of them getting anywhere. Cavallaro tried taking him off to a little room by themselves and telling him, no bluster and no bullshit, "Look—you're being arrested for murdering Malcolm X. You've been identified. You want to tell me about it?" Butler wasn't playing. "That's ridiculous," he said. "I didn't kill him." The others had a try, less diplomatically, with no better results; the tougher the questioning, the deeper Butler sank behind that frozen Muslim mask. He told them he wasn't a man of violence, that Muslims didn't do things like that. They threw the Benjamin Brown case at him, but he denied that one, too. He told them about his legs; he could hardly get around, he said, and in fact he had been to see the doctor about them the very morning of the murder. Stern decided they had better get him photographed nude with his bruises showing, so they would have something to dispute him with if he used his injuries as an alibi. Butler was combative at first, quieter but no more communicative as the night stretched on. "He was arrogant," Stern said. "He gave you the Muslim cant." They finally quit trying; Stern sorted out the identifications, satisfied himself that there was probable cause to hold Butler and told the detectives: Book him.

At 3:30 A.M. Friday the twenty-sixth, Norman Butler/a.k.a. Norman 3X/Negro/male/26/The Bronx, N.Y., stood glowering in the tweed topcoat while Detective Cavallaro placed him formally under arrest for murder. Later that morning, he was taken downtown to criminal court, arraigned swiftly under heavy police guard, then delivered to the ancient city prison, the Tombs, to be held without bail until his trial. Butler accepted this, with a kind of opaque calm, as the will of Allah. The police command was palpably relieved. "The city is afraid and Harlem is afraid," one official told the papers. "Everyone asks what the police are doing. This is something we can show."

33. The Rites of Winter

Harlem was afraid because everybody said Harlem ought to be. Driving through, Ossie Davis said, you'd see kids out playing with hoops and shooting baskets like they always did. "There weren't even people walking around saying, *They killed Malcolm.*" Harlem was like it always was in February, a lot of people shivering through the winter and wishing for the warm times; some of them sorrowed for Malcolm and some didn't, and many of them felt a kind of unsurprise, because Malcolm was Malcolm and, anyway, a lot of men die young uptown. Still, the papers were full of voices prophesying war, and after the Harlem mosque burned, and another caught fire in San Francisco, the headlines, particularly in the evening papers, screamed that Harlem was on the brink of a blood bath. So Harlem was afraid, or at least civic Harlem. A backstage committee came together, Davis and Percy Sutton and some of the civil-rights crowd, with two major missions. One was to raise money to bury Malcolm and provide for Sister Betty and the children, since he had died broke, and three separate fund drives quickly got going. The other was to keep Harlem cool—to head off a full-blown vendetta, one participant said, "so there would be no excuse for the police to come in blasting and waste the citizens."

Harlem was swarming with police already, the regular garrisons reinforced by busloads of six-footers from the elite Tactical Patrol Force. The civic committee met almost nightly with the high police command to discuss ways of maintaining calm. The *Amsterdam News* ran a page-one appeal for peace, headlining it, "STEADY EDDIE!" James Farmer, who had been out of town working on a book, drove hurriedly back, called a press conference and said that Malcolm hadn't been murdered by the Muslims—that it was a political killing with international implications. "I wasn't sure precisely what I meant then," Farmer told me, "and various editorials jumped to various conclusions, depending upon the point of view of the papers. Some said I meant the Chinese Communists and some said I meant dope—that the campaign Malcolm was waging against drugs in Harlem had something to do with it. They were closer to the truth. The real reason for holding the press conference was to head off what at that point seemed just about inevitable—internecine warfare between Malcolm's boys and the Muslims. Malcolm's boys were going to seek reprisal by shooting Elijah Muhammad, and then somebody would get somebody else, and it could have been quite a war."

The funeral became the center of concern—the perfect symbolic target for anybody bent on keeping a civil war going. Malcolm's body had been placed in a zipper bag on Monday and sent uptown under guard to the Unity Funeral Home, where it was laid out in a $2,100 bronze coffin and covered with glass so Harlem could see him when it paid its last respects. By Muslim tradition, Malcolm ought to have been buried Monday, before the sun had set a second time on his body, but the funeral was delayed so that any of the African leaders he had met in his travels could attend. (None of them came, although a number sent condolences.) There were almost daily bomb threats against the funeral home and

Faith Temple Church of God in Christ, a made-over Harlem movie house that had been borrowed for the funeral. Police saturated both areas and took up posts on the roof of the funeral home when the body went on view on Tuesday evening. Harlem came out anyway. There were 350 people queued up in the freezing cold when the doors opened that night, and 22,000 filed past the coffin during the week. They came in out of the alleys and the stockrooms and the bootblack stands and Miss Anne's kitchen to say good-bye. Women wept and fainted. One night a black kid stood at the coffin and said he wanted to die with Brother Malcolm and raged at the police to shoot him; they moved him gently out.

Friday the twenty-sixth was God's birthday, the opening of the annual Savior's Day convention of the Nation of Islam at the Coliseum, a drafty old sports palace south of the Chicago business district. Some 2,500 of the Original People came in spite of the threats and counterthreats and the heavy police contingents and the ominously redoubled vigilance of the Fruit of Islam, searching everybody and prowling everywhere, even in the rafters high overhead. The place was only a third full; the crowds of "dead" brothers and sisters who usually came to look had been frightened away, which was a shame, because the elders of the Kingdom of Allah in the wilderness wanted everybody to witness Mr. Muhammad's power and glory and Malcolm's final degradation.

It was a grand moral theme grandly staged. They produced Philbert and Wilfred X to repudiate their brother one last time (". . . a man who was no good . . ."); they brought out the Messenger's stray son Wallace to repent of having left the church and beg the Original People to accept him back; they put Muhammad Ali down front to lead the cheering when two dozen of the Fruit marched to the stage in a moving square and parted to reveal the Messenger of Allah. "We did not want to kill Malcolm and we didn't try to," Mr. Muhammad said, his voice faint and breathless. "It was his foolishness, ignorance and his preachings that brought him to his death." He gasped on, Ali jumping in yelling *Yes sir!* or *Sweet words, Apostle!* and the crowd answering with cheers. "Where I'm standing, he stood. . . . In those days, he was a *light*, he was a *star* among his people, as long as he was with me. But he criticized the God who brought him salvation and liberation. I lifted him up and he came back preaching that we should not take the enemy as an enemy, which we knew him to be. . . . He tried to make war against me. I looked up at him and I laughed." He was hoarse and coughing and the people were yelling *Easy! Take it easy!* "If Malcolm had died a natural death, we would have given him a glorious burial; we would have stood over his body and prayed with tears of grief in our eyes. . . . But it's wrong to even stand beside the grave of a hypocrite. He turned his back on the man who taught him all he knew. It was me. Elijah Muhammad. Malcolm got what he was preaching." The crowd could hardly hear his small voice in the great cavernous hall, but they could tell where the sentences ended and they would say, *Sweet words! That's right! That's right!*

Saturday the twenty-seventh was the day they buried Malcolm X. Sheik Ahmed Hassoun had wrapped the body in a white winding sheet, and Sister Betty had made her private farewells on Friday night, after the crowds were gone. Then it was Saturday, everybody downtown terrified, and when first light broke on Harlem, the people were queuing up in the street and hanging out tenement windows and crowding onto fire escapes in the bitter cold just to witness and say good-bye. "I remember the *Times* saying the Apostle of Hate is dead, he only had two or three hundred followers," Dan Watts said, "and I remember going uptown, and it was fourteen degrees out, and those little old soul sisters were coming out of the subway and getting on line for a last look at Malcolm." A lot of them never got inside; there were more bomb threats, so the church closed off its basement, where the overflow crowd was to have been seated, and hung loudspeakers outside instead, and the street people—Malcolm's people—stood there with their hands in their pockets and their hats jammed down and their coat collars up around their ears, looking sad and listening.

The coffin lay on red velvet, with a single floral piece, a white star and crescent on a field of blood-red carnations, and a card that said, "TO EL-HAJJ MALIK, FROM BETTY." There were hundreds of policemen inside this time, eight of them surrounding the coffin, two—both black plainclothesmen—flanking Sister Betty. Ossie Davis delivered the eulogy, because he was eloquent and noncontroversial and because he loved Malcolm; he spoke of his old friend as "our manhood, our living black manhood" and "our own black shining prince," and people didn't cry—you don't weep for Muslims or for revolutionaries—but they were stirring and coughing; his rich voice cracked a little when he got to the part about Malcolm being gone forever. Afterward, they led Betty forward to kiss the glass; then they closed the coffin and loaded it onto a two-tone blue hearse, and two dozen cars followed it out to Ferncliff Cemetery for the last Muslim prayers at the grave. Some of the mourners plucked flowers from the top of the coffin, and some stood there staring at the little bronze plaque that said, "EL-HAJJ MALIK EL-SHABAZZ." At the end, the gravediggers moved up with their shovels. A half-dozen of the brothers got between them and the grave. "No white man is going to bury Malcolm," one of them said. A woman burst into tears and said no, don't let them throw dirt in Malcolm's face. James Hicks of the *Amsterdam News* interceded with the gravediggers. They were union men. "Shit," one of them said, "this is a dead man. We're supposed to bury him." Hicks stood there in the cold arguing. The undertaker told the brothers that the cars were going and they would be left behind. "We'll bury him first, man," one of them said. "We'll walk." They started throwing in dirt with their bare hands. The undertaker saw they meant it, and so did the gravediggers. They moved away, and the brothers picked up the shovels, and the last mourners stood watching them silently filling in Malcolm X's grave.

34. The Third Man

It really began coming together when Cary 2X Thomas decided to start talking. Thomas was a big, balding man, pushing thirty-five, an ex-junkie and ex-pusher who had kicked the heroin habit after coming under the spell of Malcolm and the Muslims. He had dropped out of high school in the eleventh grade and had done six stormy years in the Army, including one tour in Korea and several in the stockade, before they busted him out for hitting a noncom. He had worked only sporadically since, as a house painter, a floor waxer and a truck driver, and was fooling around with acting, playing the flute and writing—a drug memoir he called *Tragic Magic.* He had a wife and four kids, but they had split, and he hadn't seen them for a year. Thomas had joined the Nation and got his "X" in 1963, in Malcolm's last days as minister, and hung on till November 1964 before following him out and joining the Muslim Mosque, Inc. On the last day, he had been one of the bodyguards and had brought his .357 Magnum, a pistol that hits like a cannon, but he never got it out of his shoulder holster. He stood there transfixed through the shooting, he told the authorities, and then ignominiously ducked when everybody began running.

Only he was a long time telling it. The detectives could place him at the scene, thanks to the *Life* photos, and knew he was on the guard detail, but he was up-tight, scared of reprisals, and it was the beginning of March before they got anything good from him. When they did, it was really good: he handed them all three men, Hayer and Butler, who were already locked up, and Thomas 15X Johnson, who till then had been just out of reach. As Thomas told it to the police, and later to the grand jury, Malcolm had just gone on when Hayer popped up in the audience, drew a gun, turned on Butler, sitting beside him, and yelled, "What are you doing?

What are you doing in my pockets, man?" The bodyguards moved toward them. Butler backed away, out into the aisle. Johnson materialized out of somewhere, and while Hayer was scuffling with the guards, he and Butler moved forward toward the stage, crouching, as if they were running some well-charted football play. Thomas heard a loud report, maybe a shotgun or rifle; he saw Malcolm falling, and Butler leaning over the stage, and Johnson on one knee with his hand moving in short, straight jerks. And suddenly everybody was running, and chairs were crashing flat, and Hayer was running for the stairs, slipping and stumbling and grabbing.

It took the detectives two days getting this story together, and there were problems with it that had to be straightened out later; the state had some embarrassing moments at the trial when the defense discovered that Thomas had rearranged the suspects since his grand-jury appearance and that his trial testimony more nearly suited the emerging prosecution theory of what had happened. Still, it was the strongest account the police had to go on at the time. On Wednesday, March 3, Keeley, Confrey and a couple of other detectives took Thomas under wraps to the Bronx County Courthouse, where Johnson was due for an appearance in the Benjamin Brown shooting. Thomas looked at him and said that was the third man—the one who rushed the stage with Butler.

While Stern was talking to Thomas, the detectives shadowed Johnson and his wife as they left the courthouse, did a few errands and then went home. The four of them parked out front and waited until they got the go-ahead from Stern. They had just got out of their car when Johnson came walking down the steps from his place and asked them what they were doing in the neighborhood and did it have anything to do with him. Keeley said they would like him to come with them to Manhattan North. Johnson wanted to know what it was about. "We'd like to talk to you," Keeley said. Johnson got their permission to call his lawyer. They followed him inside. He dialed the attorney, Charles Beavers, spoke with him for a few moments, then hung up and told the police he wasn't to go anywhere unless they arrested him first.

"You're under arrest for the crime of homicide," Keeley told him. They put handcuffs on him, led him out to the car and drove back to Manhattan North.

Johnson rode in silence. He was a hefty man, five-feet-ten and thick-set, with a wide, square jaw and a thin mustache and a long, colorful rap sheet from his pre-Muslim days, when he had a $10 or $15 daily heroin habit and had run numbers and stolen to support it. Like Cary Thomas and dozens of others, he had come into the mosque during Malcolm's administration and had turned around, working as a house painter until a bout of rheumatic fever laid him up and threw him onto welfare and the occasional charity of the temple to feed his wife and five children. He told the detectives something about having been left with a heart condition, but they had no trouble getting together evidence of his basic robust health—a picture of him bodyguarding Muhammad Ali helped—and Johnson quit raising the issue by the time he got to trial. The police thought him a straightforward sort, all yes-sir, no-sir manners in the Muslim style, and almost pleasant compared to Butler. But Johnson was no more cooperative, cooperation in their terms meaning a willingness to confess everything. They tried questioning him for a while, till his lawyer got there, to no particular effect. It didn't matter, not with Thomas's evidence in; Stern gave the word, and at 3:15 P.M. March 3, ten days after the assassination, Thomas Johnson/a.k.a. Thomas 15X/Negro/male/30/The Bronx, N.Y., became the third and last man to be booked for the murder of Malcolm X.

A grand jury had been impaneled two days earlier, and that afternoon it began hearing witnesses. Cary Thomas went in early and told his story, but he was still shaky and frightened for his life, and the police were afraid to turn him loose—afraid he might get hurt or get scared and disappear. They couldn't afford to lose him, so they decided to put him on ice. They made a case that he be held under $50,000 bail as a material witness and, when he came out of the grand-jury room, deposited him among the alimony cheaters and white-collar miscreants in the civil jail. "We *had* to lock him up," one detective said. "He had no job, no means of support, no family with him, nothing to hold him, and we were afraid he'd wind up dead someplace. He got up-tight once he learned we were going to keep him. But he couldn't be out on the street. We got him his $3 a day—that's what the law allowed a material witness—and some of the detectives, Cavallaro and Taylor and Rushin, would take him out once a week to buy things or maybe go to a movie, and we'd bring him in once a week to talk to him."

Thomas stayed on ice for nearly a year. The grand jury sat for a week. On March 10, seventeen days after the event, it handed up an indictment charging that Talmadge Hayer, Norman Butler and Thomas Johnson "willfully, feloniously and of malice aforethought shot and killed Malcolm Little, a.k.a. Malcolm Shabazz, a.k.a. Malcolm X, with a shotgun and pistols." A lot of the cops had peeled off the case by then, but not Cavallaro or Confrey or Keeley or Taylor or Rushin, and not Herb Stern. For them, the investigation was only just beginning.

35. Two Matters for the Police

In March, there were cases of passing interest to the police in Harlem and Boston:

• On the night of March 1, while Percy Sutton was in Albany on legislative business, somebody took down the transom from his apartment and law office in Harlem, let himself inside, yanked out desk drawers, rummaged through files and left the place littered with paper. Sutton, in Albany, guessed that it had nothing to do with the Malcolm X case, and the police were disposed to agree: one official told the papers, "We're carrying it as a straight burglary." Among many missing items, when Sutton got his losses sorted out, were three affidavits that he had been holding for Malcolm. These had been dictated and signed by women who had worked as secretaries to the Honorable Elijah Muhammad.

- On the afternoon of March 13, a chambermaid let herself into Leon 4X Ameer's room at the Sherry Biltmore Hotel in Boston and found Ameer lying dead on the bed in his underwear. In February, Ameer had been trying to sell the papers the inside story of Malcolm's death. A Boston newspaperman, Jim Droney of the *Herald-Traveler,* visited him at the Sherry Biltmore and found him alone, broke—he was down to his last $1.07—and certain that the Muslims were going to come after him again because he "knew too much." Droney taped what he knew; it turned out to be another account of Malcolm's supposed treaty negotiations with the Ku Klux Klan on behalf of the Nation of Islam in 1961. The story didn't excite Droney, so he wrote later, but he pressed a ten on Ameer anyway, and left. On March 3, on the complaint of the local Muslim mosque, the authorities in New Haven issued a warrant for Ameer's arrest on a charge of having embezzled $500 when he quit as captain there. On March 12, the day before he died, Ameer is said to have appeared at a Socialist Workers meeting in Boston with a new inside story—that the government was responsible for Malcolm's death and that he would shortly produce tapes and documents of Malcolm's to prove it. "This may be the last time any of you will see me," he said. In conspiracy theories of assassinations, all deaths of connected persons are connected; Ameer's death has accordingly become a murder. The Suffolk County medical examiner, Richard Ford, said that there were no marks of violence on the body and that Ameer had died in a coma induced by an overdose of Doriden, a sleeping pill.

36. The Ones That Got Away

"Okay," said one of the detectives, "now you got three guys locked up, and all you have to do then is prove the case on each of them, plus prove the case of association between them." The arrests by this measure were only an event in the investigation, not the conclusion. Some of them spent a solid year on it. Keeley worked sixteen hours a day, seven days a week for seven straight weeks before he got his first day off. Cavallaro went off the chart at the 34th Squad for the duration and operated mostly out of the DA's office with Herb Stern, till Stern left to take a better job as Assistant U.S. Attorney in Newark and almost immediately began building a reputation as a racket-buster. A half-dozen detectives in all—two Irishmen, two Italians and two blacks in sometimes uneasy ethnic alliance—stuck with the case through the trial, and it was ten months from the last arrest till the trial even got started.

It was an intermittently dangerous assignment—"Some days," Keeley remembered, "we felt like we could be in the jackpot"—but mostly a tedious one, digging witnesses out of nowhere, questioning them three and four and five times before you got anything, tracking informers and buying information from them with good fellowship or a couple of drinks if you could or with cash out of your own pocket if you couldn't. "I put out maybe a thousand dollars for stoolies," one detective said. "A case like that can put you in the poorhouse." They all had to do a quick cram course on Malcolm and the Nation, and between that and spending a lot of time in those circles, a number of the cops—even the white cops—found themselves talking like Muslims. You got calls all night—Keeley had to tumble out of the sack once and go bail out one of his informers who had got himself in some kind of trouble—and when you didn't, you lost sleep anyway with the case spinning in your head. "My wife got sick and tired of hearing about the bloody thing," Keeley remembered; when you spend that much time on a case, it becomes all you have to talk about.

The easiest part was arriving at the working theory that the Muslims did it. Other hypotheses were kicking around—that Malcolm was the victim of a drug war, or a Maoist cell among his own followers, or, as some of the brothers argued, a CIA-police-establishment conspiracy—but the police took none of these seriously. Policemen tend instinctively to believe in Occam's Razor or at least a variation of it—the presumption that one looks not only for the least complicated but the basest explanation for a given set of facts. Neither the politics nor the theology of Malcolm's apostasy interested them much; they saw him quite simply as a casualty in what one of the investigators called "a black gang war with a smattering of religion and civil rights." The first rule in a homicide that doesn't solve itself instantly at the scene is to figure out who gained by it. The immediately obvious answer was the Muslims, and what they had to gain, as the police saw it, was the elimination of competition for money and power. "Malcolm," Keeley said, "was drawing off Black Muslims into the MMI and people who didn't buy the religion into the OAAU. He was cutting both sides of the cake. He would have busted the Black Muslim empire completely apart." The fact that the Nation as a whole is a peace-loving, law-abiding place did not impress the investigators. Their informers told them that the Muslims indeed had enforcers—a doom squad, some called it—and that they had actively stifled competition, as witness the beating of Leon 4X Ameer and the shooting of Benjamin Brown. The very audacity of the murder seemed to them to support this hypothesis: it suggested to the police not only that the killers were fanatics but that the killing was, as one put it, "like a lesson"—a message to Malcolm's heirs to get out of the Muslim business.

There was no trouble making Butler and Johnson fit this theory. They were proud and well-known Muslims; a central anomaly in the state's case, indeed, was the proposition that they could have got into the Audubon at all without being recognized and stopped, or at least watched, by some of the ex-Muslims on Malcolm's guard detail. The police concluded finally that the guards had been either incredibly sloppy or incompletely loyal; they were satisfied when they arrested the two men that they could place them inside the Audubon, and in the weeks that followed, more witnesses and more identifications came in against them.

The prize was still Cary Thomas, and the police pampered him, riding him around every Monday or Wednesday just for air, arranging for writing materials so he could work on *Tragic Magic*, getting permission for him to practice the flute in jail until the other inmates complained that he was doing his practicing at 3 and 4 A.M. He got up-tight a couple of times, once burning his mattress—he was placed under a formal charge of arson—and another day ripping off his shirt in the warden's office and bellowing, "Shoot me, motherfuckers! Kill me!" (Cavallaro came in that time and told Thomas, actor to actor, to run through that once again, only with a little more feeling; Thomas grinned, buttoned on his shirt and simmered down.) There was a momentary flap when the police decided that Muslims on the jail guard force might be getting to Thomas; Muslims actually qualify rather well for the work, being tough, clean and incorruptible by any of the normal jailhouse temptations, but the police, out of their own conspiratorialist outlook, regarded them as infiltrators and were unhappy having them anywhere near their star witness.

That scare blew over, too, and by then the police had come up with a supporting cast for Thomas anyway—had even discovered a prospective co-star in Charles X Blackwell, the brother who rode up to the Audubon with Malcolm the last day and had been a member of the guard detail. Blackwell mistrusted the police when they first found him shooting pool in a bar and grill in New Jersey, and he was worried for his family if he cooperated; he told the grand jury that he didn't know who had done the shooting. "He didn't believe we were actually trying to solve the case," Keeley said. "But I gave him the name of somebody we had talked to, and he checked this fellow and found out we were on the level, and after that he was great." After that, he placed all three men in the ballroom, Hayer and Butler with guns and Johnson ducking into the ladies' lounge after the shooting. Others materialized; the police found them, collected their stories, then jollied them along through the anxious months waiting for the trial by saying they might not be needed anyway and don't worry about it. They anticipated alibis from Butler and Johnson; Stern accordingly put both their wives on the stand before the grand jury to get their stories on the record early, and the detectives spent a good deal of investigative effort thereafter picking them apart.

Hayer presented an opposite problem. He had been caught at the scene, so there was no possibility of his alibiing himself, and the detectives had solid physical evidence—the .45 clip in his pocket and the thumbprint on the smoke bomb—to go with the eyewitness testimony against him. The puzzle was connecting Hayer, a kid nobody knew from Jersey, with Butler and Johnson, two Muslims everybody knew from the city. The law didn't require the state to prove a motive in court, but the realities of a complicated murder trial meant they would have to show a jury some reason for murder common to the three men. The key was identifying Hayer as a Black Muslim; the proof, for all the heavy surveillance the Nation was under, was surprisingly hard to come by.

Hayer denied that he was a Muslim. Mr. Muhammad said he was a perfect stranger. Keeley and Confrey slogged around Paterson talking to family and friends with minimal success (though they did find a poolroom proprietor who remembered Hayer and another man trying to sell him a *Muhammad Speaks* so aggressively that he finally called the cops). Cary Thomas told them that Hayer had been in the Nation, but it turned out on closer questioning that he thought he recalled seeing Hayer around the mosque with a Muslim crowd from Jersey City and couldn't really swear that he was a member. The best single piece of goods they found, Keeley told me, was a Muslim membership list with Hayer's name on it as Talmadge X. But it turned out that the Newark police had seized it from the local mosque without a warrant, which meant it couldn't legally be introduced at the trial; all the prosecution could do then was ask Hayer if it wasn't true that he had registered as a Muslim on September 23, 1962, and when he said no it wasn't, there was no way directly to contradict him. It was hard going, but they finally came up with a strong pair of hole cards—two photos of a group of young black men suited up for a karate demonstration in the Newark mosque, with Talmadge Hayer or his perfect double conspicuously among them.

At that point, they figured they had their case on the three principals. What troubled them—what troubles them still—was the ones that got away.

At the trial, for symmetry's sake, the state made the case that Hayer, Butler and Johnson by themselves murdered Malcolm and that nobody else was involved; nobody, that is, except whoever commissioned them to do it. None of the investigators believed this. Their guesses at the number of men actually involved in the execution ranged from four to six or seven—three guns, plus one or two people to create diversions and maybe get in the way of the bodyguards, plus one or two getaway drivers. "They weren't going to take the bus home," one detective told me dryly. They thought for a while that they had one of the wheel men, a black cabbie whose trip records showed that he had been in the rough area of the ballroom not long before the shooting and had checked into his garage in the Bronx, where Butler and Johnson lived, a half-hour later. There was at least one other entry between these, but the police were suspicious because the times were exact to the minute and the addresses to the building number; most drivers—including this one on most other days—round off the times and put down rough addresses. Keeley and Confrey clocked the ride from the ballroom to the garage, not pushing it and stopping for traffic lights, and got there inside the half-hour with minutes to spare. They questioned the cabbie but got nowhere; his trip sheet was his alibi, and there was no way to disprove it. The police guessed there was another car and another driver for Hayer. They had checked out parked cars for blocks around the Audubon and found neither his own car nor any other that couldn't be accounted for; this meant he was depending on somebody else to get him out. "I'm satisfied we had the three gunmen," one detective said years later. "I'm not satisfied that we had everybody involved."

Knowing that drove you crazy, Keeley said. So did the fact that they couldn't prove who gave the order. It was possible, of course, that a group of rank-and-file Muslims might have organized the assassination themselves—might have read in *Muhammad Speaks* about how Malcolm was the chief hypocrite and imagined that they could please the hierarchy by bringing in his head unbidden. This might have been particularly appealing to Muslims who had got into criminal trouble, as Hayer had in the Paterson gun-shop burglary and Butler and Johnson had in the Brown shooting, and so were, or ought to have been, in bad odor in their mosques. The investigators simply didn't believe this. For one thing, Butler and Johnson had remained active in the mosque since the Brown affair and seemed not to be out of favor at all. For another, rank-and-file Muslims are notable for many positive attributes of character, but autonomy is not one of them.

The police believe that the order to execute Malcolm originated at a point somewhere further up in the table of organization. The problem was evidence; there wasn't any—not the kind that would stand up in a court of law. One informer told them he had witnessed a meeting at which a local official had passed out the assignments, to Hayer, Butler and Johnson among others. The story was tantalizing but the source weak; they didn't think either the tale or the teller would hold up well under cross-examination. Another tipster told them that the Muslims had thrown a dinner at the Audubon on February 16, the Tuesday before the assassination, and that some people there had shown an interest in the locations of stairways and exit doors. Again, the story was suggestive, its viability as evidence limited. The prosecution, during its cross-examination of Butler, did contrive to get into the trial record the assertion that John Ali, the Muslims' national secretary, had come in from Chicago on February 19, checked into the Americana Hotel in midtown Manhattan and checked out on the evening of February 21, the day of the assassination. Butler said nobody had told him about that. The prosecutor, Vincent Dermody, asked him if he had had a conversation with Ali and Captain Joseph at the Muslim restaurant on the evening of the nineteenth. Butler said he had never had a conversation with Ali and didn't remember seeing him at the restaurant that evening, though he might have been there. Dermody worked the point for a couple of minutes for whatever effect it might have on the jury, then moved on to something else. There was no way for him to get by Butler's denial and no evidence that Ali's presence in town was anything more than coincidental.

The investigators heard a lot of names and ran down a lot of tips during the long inquiry, and none of them led to anything you could come into court with. "We were dealing with paid assassins," Stern said, "and they weren't giving anybody above them up. You can believe, feel, *know,* but that isn't legal proof." And that *really* drove you crazy: it meant to the investigators that they were closing the Malcolm X murder case without being able to say who had Malcolm X murdered.

37. The Judas Factor

The other thing the police suspected but could not prove was that somebody among Malcolm's people set him up for murder. They looked on the brothers with a mirror image of the mistrust the brothers felt toward them; each party believed that the other had to have been implicated for the assassination to have been brought off or even attempted. The principal evidence held out by Malcolm's people was the behavior of the police from their announced discovery of a bottle of gasoline inside Malcolm's burned-out house to their indifferent coverage of his last meeting despite the clear threat to his life. The principal evidence offered by the authorities was the sudden collapse of Malcolm's own security arrangements—the no-guns and no-search policies, the ease with which the assassins got in and got at Malcolm, the apparent paralysis of the bodyguards when the shooting started. But what each side mostly had was its suspicion of the other—a mutual paranoia so acute that what might have been happenstance or negligence was seen as complicity in murder.

"He was definitely set up for it," one of the investigators said, expressing a judgment common to nearly all of them. "To us, it was all so—*perfect.* Nobody would have walked in there to shoot him unless you know nobody has a gun and unless you know you've got one key man in your pocket. Generally, Malcolm's bodyguards carried guns, but this particular day he supposedly said no. Nobody was searched—that supposedly was from Malcolm, too. Somebody tells the duty captain that they don't want the policemen visible; he said *that* came from Malcolm X. Of course, Malcolm X was dead, and we can't question him. Normally there were at least four people on the stage with him, but this time, nobody. I think the word was given out to stay away. And how do these three guys get in? These were men who were known to Malcolm's followers; they shouldn't have even been in there, or if they were, they should have been searched. I mean, it all worked *too* smoothly. It was incredible that these things could have all happened in one day."

They could have, of course. Malcolm was in fact upset with some of the obtrusive security around him—the body searches, for example—and might perfectly consistently have said no guns and no police on the door as well. The empty stage could have been sad coincidence; no evidence to the contrary materialized. Hayer, assuming that he was a Muslim, was from New Jersey and would not have been easily identifiable by Malcolm's fellow émigrés from the Harlem temple. Butler and Johnson, assuming that they were at the Audubon, might have slipped in before the guard got set up or walked in past it afterward; it was common enough for Muslim waverers and backsliders to come to Malcolm's meetings and check out his teachings, as witness the FOI lieutenant who got to the front row unchallenged with his lapel pin on at Malcolm's last meeting. The disintegration of the guard under fire might have resulted from the combination of surprise, the cleverness of the diversionary tactics and the simple fact that Malcolm's protectors turned out in the end to have been overmatched amateurs. "I don't think he was set up," said a man from BOSS, the only police source I found who doubted the Judas theory. "I don't think they needed it."

Still, the police and their Left critics share a conspiratorialist view of events, and the men actively on the Malcolm X case never stopped suspecting treason. They got wind early on of the conflict between the political and religious factions in Malcolm's following;

members of each faction, as the police soon discovered, were suspicious of one another, and the investigators at various points leaned toward particular people on one side or the other as possible traitors. As they got deeper into the case, however, the detectives zeroed in on one man whom they suspected had betrayed Malcolm for cash—a motive that fit their understanding of human behavior more nearly than the debates among the brothers as to whether whites were devils or merely capitalist-imperialists. The man they focused on had a police record—"a professional hood," one detective said—and had suddenly come into money and clothes before the assassination, despite the fact that he was out of work. He was on guard duty the last day but, like several of the others, had been drawn off his post when the quarrel started in the audience. Afterward, so the police heard second hand, he told some of the brothers he had seen everything and knew everybody, but he vanished before the police got to him. At one point, Cavallaro's informers told him the man had gone South; Cavallaro sent a message to the appropriate police force asking them to pick the fellow up for questioning, but when they knocked on the front door, he got out the back window, B-movie style, and disappeared again. The detectives never did get to question him about Malcolm X; by the time they caught up with him, he was under arrest and on his way to prison in another, unrelated case, and the file on the murder of Malcolm X had been closed.

"We figured this guy might be the man on the inside who ostensibly defected to Malcolm but really remained loyal to the Black Muslims," one detective said. "Where else did he get the money?" In the end, they had nothing to go on but speculation and the habit of mind that made a black gang war of the conflict between Malcolm and the Muslims; if one is trying to solve a hit, as against an assassination, one automatically looks into the loyalty, and the purchase price, of the *capos* and the button men around the victim. "The murderers got cooperated with," one detective assured me. Everybody on the case believed this to be true, but they finally closed the books with that page missing, too.

38. Trial

It was political theater played by a criminal-court company. The judge was Charles Marks, an insuperably placid old man of seventy-one who had tried a lot of murder cases—a fourth of the men then on New York State's death row came out of his courtroom—and never had one reversed on appeal. The prosecutor, with Stern off the case, was Vincent J. Dermody, a short, gristly cop's son who had been around since Tom Dewey was District Attorney and was thought to be the best murder-trial man in the office. The co-stars for the defense were both traditional trial lawyers, William Chance, a large, theatrical black man who had known Malcolm casually around Harlem, and Peter L. F. Sabbatino, a tiny, peppery ancient of seventy-four who had come up out of Little Italy and in fifty years at the bar had defended more than three hundred people charged with killing other people, including eleven separate murder-one cases all active at the same time. ("I turned nine of 'em out," he remembered, "and the other two pleaded to reduced charges.") It was their theater and their play; Malcolm was gone, and the three defendants, wandering ashy out of ten sunless months in the Tombs into the bad light of the courtroom, were rarely more than objects in the proceedings.

Their day in court finally arrived on the morning of January 12, 1966, after all of the law's normal delays plus two extraordinary interruptions occasioned by the great East Coast blackout of 1965 and a city-wide transit strike that had begun with the new year. Attendants showed the three defendants and their six lawyers to a single table, an arrangement that had already provoked some controversy, since the chances for all of them rested importantly on dissociating Hayer, who had been caught at the scene but might not have been a Muslim, from Butler and Johnson, who were Muslims but might not have been at the scene. Sabbatino, representing Hayer, had asked a separate trial for his man, or, failing that, a separate table; Judge Marks said no, as he did to most of what the defense asked during the eight weeks of the trial. So the defendants had to make the point of their separateness as best they could sitting together, Hayer staring blankly dead ahead most of the time, Butler and Johnson conferring occasionally with one another but never with him.

The first seven days were passed picking a jury of mixed color (nine whites, three blacks) and caste (half white-collar, half working-class). On the eighth, before a gallery of Muslims on the defense side of the aisle and Malcolm's admirers on the prosecution side, Dermody briefly outlined the people's version of the events —Hayer and Butler stage a phony quarrel, Johnson slips forward in the confusion and shotguns Malcolm, Hayer and Butler follow close behind pumping pistol shots into the body, everybody runs and everybody but Hayer makes it out and away. This was a highly tailored scenario, and not all the details fit it, but, for a jury, it had the virtue of simplicity and the comfort of feeling that all the assassins were present and accounted for. Dermody did not need to prove why they did it, and so did not promise to. But, over the clamorous objections of the defense, he made the prosecution theory transparently clear by identifying all three defendants as "active members of the Black Muslim sect" and Malcolm as a former Black Muslim turned competitor.

The defense never did float a credible alternative hypothesis. They didn't even have a working list of eyewitnesses—the state wouldn't make its list available until the trial was half over—and they didn't have the cash for a wide-ranging investigation anyway; Sabbatino was on a modest retainer from Hayer's family, and the four black lawyers representing Butler and Johnson were all court-appointed at the statutory fee of $2,000 per man. Chance and Joseph Williams, co-counsel for Butler, were on to the faction fighting among Malcolm's followers and tried to exploit it for what it was worth as a possible alternate motive. Chance hoped to raise the CIA theory as well, out of one part suspicion and one part strategy, but was cut off before he got started. Sabbatino, defending an impossible case, improvised his own fanciful conspiracy theory as he went along. He started from the awkward fact that Hayer had been shot running out of the Audubon; he ended with the proposition that his man was "a bright young lad interested in social movements," nothing more, and that because he happened to get in the way of a bullet, he was made the fall guy for an assassination plot actually hatched by traitors among Malcolm's own bodyguards.

The state-conspiracy theory is the kind of defense one raises in a political trial—a trial, that is, in which one's prime objective is the political education of the audience. The principal defenders in the Malcolm X murder trial were criminal lawyers engaged in a criminal case, in which the point is to get one's client off. Constructing an alternative theory of the assassination was therefore secondary to developing alibis for Butler and Johnson and explaining how Hayer happened to be at the Audubon with a .45 clip in his pocket. Americans tend to overrate trials in any event—to equate arriving at verdicts with getting at The Truth. A trial is too narrow and formal, too *lawyerly* an instrument for that. The Malcolm X trial was not concerned, really, with why Malcolm died or even with who wanted him killed. It reduced the questions of his death and life to the single issue of whether three particular men had or had not pointed the guns and pulled the triggers, and in this restricted frame, as everybody agreed later, the state made and quite possibly won its case with its second witness.

39. Thomas

The first was a scene-setter, the civil engineer from the DA's office who had measured and diagramed the Audubon Ballroom. The second was Cary Thomas.

He came out of civil jail waxy and subdued; he answered a good many questions in monosyllables and a good many more in a voice so incongruously small that he constantly had to be reminded to speak up. But Thomas told his story compactly and well, and a long, grinding cross-examination never changed a word of it. He got to the Audubon around 2:20, he said, and saw "Thomas Fifteen"—Johnson—sitting in a back booth. He mentioned this to Reuben Francis, an officer of the guard that day, then took a booth of his own and was sitting there when Hayer stood up in the middle of the audience, a pistol in his hand, and yelled at Butler, beside him, "Man, what are you doing with your hand in my pocket?" Several bodyguards started toward them, leaving the stage open. Suddenly, Thomas heard a blast up front. He wheeled and saw a man at the foot of the podium, turning back toward the audience, with a sawed-off shotgun in his hand.

"And what was his name?" Dermody asked.

"Thomas 15X," Thomas replied.

"What was the next thing that happened?"

"Well, the next thing that happened was Hayer and Butler had ran to the front . . . and they started shooting in the area of the stage where Malcolm X's body was laying." He couldn't see the guns, but he could see their hands pumping and hear the shots, maybe ten or fifteen of them. "The audience seemed to run and break, and everybody was running . . . I crouched down behind a booth." He stayed there a minute or so, then pushed through the crowd to the stage and saw Malcolm. He looked unconscious. The killers were gone, but Thomas insisted that he had recognized them all—that he had known Butler and Johnson in "the Muhammad mosque" and had seen Hayer twice there and once in the Muslim restaurant.

In less than an afternoon, Thomas had set out the essentials of the people's case—had connected Hayer with the Muslims and identified all three defendants as the gunmen who got Malcolm. The defense, working in relays, spent three and a half days trying to take the story and the witness apart. They got out that Thomas had taken heroin for three years and pushed it for two until he was arrested in Boston for possession of narcotics in 1961. They spread his raucous Army record before the jury—a string of courts-martial for offenses ranging from missing formation to joy-riding in a Jeep, several stretches in the stockade, the eventual bad-conduct discharge. ("I had broken some rule—I don't remember now what it was," Thomas said, talking about one of these busts. "Was it a rule," Chance boomed, "or a jawbone?") They brought out that he had been picked up screaming drunk on wine in midtown one day in November 1963 and had been delivered to the Bellevue Hospital psychiatric ward running on about how he wanted to go back to Africa and how he hadn't killed Jesus; his gray-jacketed hospital folder showed that he had quieted down and was sent home after three or four days, but it made an excellent stage prop for the defenders. They discovered the arson case against Thomas—the indictment charging him with having burned his mattress in the jail. "Were you told," asked Chance, "that if you gave certain testimony in this case that someone would speak to someone in the arson case and make your life a little easier?"

"Never," Thomas shot back.

First Sabbatino, then Chance worked over Thomas's performance—or nonperformance—as a bodyguard the day Malcolm died. He surprised the prosecution by admitting that he had been carrying guns since he was fifteen and that he was packing his .357 Magnum on the twenty-first—both points he had neglected for eleven months to mention to the police or the DA's office. "When you saw Butler and Hayer going toward the stage," Sabbatino asked, ". . . your own arms were free?"

"Yes, my arms were free."

"Your hands were not tied?"

"Not tied."

"Your legs were free?"

"Free."

"And you still had a holster with a revolver?"

"Yes."

"Did you do anything with these two men going toward Malcolm X? Did you do anything with your gun to stop these two men?"

"No."

". . . You were there as a member of the security guard to protect Malcolm X, weren't you?"

"Yes."

"Or were you a fake protector?"

"I was just there."

"Or were you a part of any conspiracy?"

"I wasn't a part of anything."

"Against Malcolm X?"

"No, I wasn't."

Chance took over the next day.

". . . I remember seeing one man crawling across the floor with a baby under his arm," Thomas said.

"Right," said Chance. "Protecting the baby?"

"Sort of, I guess."

"While you with a pistol got under the table?"

"It was—at that time it was after the firing that I decided to take cover."

". . . There was great confusion, wasn't there?"

"Chaos."

"Through the midst of the chaos you were able to detect what certain persons were doing—is that correct?"

"Yes, sir, I hold myself together pretty good."

"Under the table?"

"I wasn't under the table."

Dermody ultimately bailed his witness out on this point; Thomas swore on redirect examination that he hadn't ducked until most of the shots had been fired and that he hadn't fired back because innocent men, women and children were all running around and he was afraid of hitting them. The defense lawyers made much of the fact that he had hesitated for an oddly long time before telling anybody—the police, the brothers, anybody—that he had seen everything and knew the killers. Dermody came to the rescue on this question, too. "I was afraid that I might be killed myself by saying anything [to the police]," Thomas said. Then why not to Malcolm's own people? "Number one, because I was afraid, and number two, I didn't know who I could tell it to. I didn't know who was who. . . . The organization was wide open and there were different members that came from other organizations and what-not . . . and—I was just afraid."

The bumpiest passage for Thomas came with the disclosure that he had told his story differently to the grand jury—an embarrassment that the defense got into the record and then let pass with curiously minimal questioning. His version at the trial was that Johnson reached the stage first with the shotgun, followed by Butler and Hayer dashing up the aisle to finish Malcolm off with pistols. Before the grand jury, however, he had made it Butler and Johnson rushing the stage together while Hayer hung back scuffling with the bodyguards, out of the shooting entirely. Since this version had only two of the three defendants shooting, and since Malcolm was hit by three guns, the implication was that an unidentified third gunman had got away. In Thomas's trial testimony, the names of the players remained the same, but the scenario had been streamlined to involve only three men doing everything, the diversions as well as the shooting, which was precisely the prosecution's theory of the case. Yet only Chance among the defenders taxed him with the discrepancies, and that briefly. "I was quite upset and nervous and I could have made [a] mistake," Thomas offered. ". . . I had a fear for my life."

"The fact was that you were unsure," Chance pressed. "Is that correct?"

"No, sir," Thomas said, and that essentially was that.

Through it all, he was even and consistent, and when Sabbatino finally let him go on the morning of his fifth day of testifying, the prosecution was well pleased. They were quite painfully aware of the differences between Thomas's grand-jury and trial testimony and the likelihood that the defense would exploit them. "We just waited to see how he'd stand up," said Gerald Ryan, a young assistant DA who helped Dermody with the case. "He stood up very well. He was good. He was cool. They tried to rattle him and they all got stung. They didn't do anything to Thomas." The defense knew it—knew that the prosecution had led with its best card and that they hadn't trumped it. "Thomas," one defense lawyer told me, "was—" He stopped, looking absently into the remains of a Chinese lunch between us, trying to think of the best word. *"Vindictive,"* he said at length. And tough? The lawyer dipped into a plate of fried noodles and nibbled at a couple of them. "Yeah," he agreed. "The toughest."

40. T

In a long trial, you have to have a sense of timing. It is wearing listening to people tell essentially the same story again and again, even if the story has to do with murder. Jurors drift into inattention, and one or two start nodding after lunch; attorneys draw squares and circles on their legal pads and catch up later from the minutes; some days, lawyers will tell you, even the defendants get bored. You try accordingly to ration your moments of drama—to space them out so that, when the going gets heavy, you bring everybody awake with a star performance, or a smart curtain line. Or, if you have got one available, a Mystery Witness.

The prosecution had T, but it held him back for a few days and put on some of its routine eyewitnesses, none of them so strong as Thomas but each putting new bits of evidence into the mosaic. Two of these were bodyguards who had been in the back when the shooting started and didn't see who killed Malcolm, but they both identified Hayer as one of the men who came down the aisle hurdling chairs and firing wildly immediately afterward. Another, a seventy-year-old Portuguese black from the Cape Verde islands, swore he had stood fast through the action ("I no was scared nothing") and had seen both Hayer and Butler squeezing off shots at Malcolm. A janitor who belonged to neither Malcolm's group nor the Muslims said he had sat right next to Butler in the audience and chatted with him "about the big crowd and it was a nice day for it"; he testified that Butler was one of the two men who put on the fake scuffle. Another nonaffiliated witness, a grade-school dropout then working as a porter in a Harlem saloon, placed Johnson in the hall and Hayer in the shooting; he said he remembered seeing both of them at various Muslim functions and in fact once watched Hayer quiet a disturbance at the Harlem mosque with a single well-placed karate chop. They were an odd-lot assortment out of the crowd and the defense tried with mixed luck to discredit them—to portray the janitor as a hard drinker, the old man as addled and dim-eyed, the porter as slow-witted and hard of hearing. The effort was valiant but its impact limited. The state was piling on eyewitnesses for their sheer cumulative effect on the jury; the gamble, apparently successful, was that their particular flaws would prove less memorable than their number and their composite memory of the events.

And then came T. T was thirty-one years old, a high-school dropout, a maintenance-of-way man in the subways, an orthodox Muslim and an early OAAU member; he was the brother who found the .45 automatic on the Audubon steps and had turned it over to the FBI later the night of the assassination. T had seen a lot of what happened, or said he had, but was terrified of telling it. "Just talking to him," Ryan remembered, "was like walking on eggshells." He came into court with his lawyer, who told Judge Marks with the jury out of the room that T's life had been threatened and that he would testify only if the courtroom was cleared of reporters and spectators; otherwise he would stand mute and take the consequences, presumably including a jail sentence for contempt. The defense lawyers were all on their feet at once, arguing heatedly that to hear him in closed court would deny the accused their right to a public trial and hopelessly prejudice their case. But Marks looked at his lawbooks during the lunch break and decided there was precedent for closing the court under the circumstances, or at least none against it. Sabbatino predicted an end to American liberty and a return to the star chamber; Marks sat him down and, before an empty courtroom, T took the stand.

He had been standing in the back of the ballroom, he said almost inaudibly, when a commotion started in the audience in front of him. "I just saw a group of men standing up and people started to scream. . . . Malcolm raised both his hands and asked people to keep their seats. . . . Then shots began ringing out. . . . The crowd began breaking up and people began throwing chairs." He saw three men running straight at him—spectators fleeing the room, he guessed—and close behind them two more men, one in a leather coat and the other in a salt-and-pepper tweed, both of them "running and turning and firing, shooting back toward the stage." T made a move. The man in the leather coat—Hayer—wheeled on him and leveled his pistol directly at him. "We both froze momentarily and I went after the other man which was spinning and hit the steps. . . . I hit him with a body block as he was spinning, and he fell down the flight of steps." T started down after the two of them, vaulting the top four or five steps. He saw the pistol lying there, snatched it up and tried to shoot. Nothing happened; T discovered only later, when he got the gun home, that the safety was on. He got as far as the door, where some of the crowd jostled him back inside, but he could see both the gunmen struggling with the crowd. One was Hayer. The other, T swore, was Norman Butler.

Chance pounced at this last. There was nothing in the FBI's report on its initial contact with T that night about Butler having been caught by the crowd, and no other witness before or after T remembered anything like that. "Did there come a time," Chance asked, "when you saw Butler being held by people outside?" T said yes. ". . . When you saw people pummeling Butler outside?" Yes, again. ". . . When you saw the police officers take Butler from those people that were outside?" Chance clearly was angling for another yes, which would have suggested to the jury that T was mixing up Butler with Hayer and so undercut both the identifications. It didn't work—T said "No, sir" this time—but his exclusive glimpse of Butler in the hands of the mob remained another loose end in the case; there was no corroborating testimony that Butler had been knocked downstairs or caught by the crowd and nothing to show how he could then have got away.

Sabbatino badgered T for a while, but he stuck with his story, and at the end Sabbatino was reduced to a last argumentative question about whether he wasn't demanding secrecy as a pretext for keeping anybody from hearing—and challenging—his story. Sometimes you help your cause with a question like that and sometimes you get stung. T stung. "The fact is," he said, "I fear for my life because I have been threatened." The question of who might have threatened him was left to the imagination of the jurors. It was not difficult, given the context of the case, to guess which way their imagination was likely to run.

41. Zeroing In

It was like prosecuting two cases in one courtroom at one time.

People v. *Hagan/Hayer* was easy: Hayer had been caught at the scene, which meant no alibi, and he had scattered enough hard physical evidence around to hang himself even if there hadn't been a single eyewitness to identify him. The prosecution filled the record with identifications anyway, but Hayer's ruin was achieved effectively without them; it took just seven witnesses over parts of four days to convict him of murder.

Two of the witnesses were ballistics-squad detectives, of whom one had collected a number of .45-caliber slugs and shells at the autopsy and at the scene and the other had examined these sweepings along with the recovered .45 automatic and the clip taken from Hayer's pocket. The tests showed that both the slugs retrieved from Malcolm's body and the cartridges in Hayer's clip had all come from the .45; this, barring some credible explanation to the contrary, put one of the murder weapons in Hayer's hands.

The defense had expected this evidence, and Hayer had worked up a story to cover it. But Dermody had held back the homemade flare as a little surprise; he left it out of his opening statement and sprung it on the defense piecemeal over two days. One of the brothers told of having seen the bomb flaming and smoking at around the time the shooting started. Keeley said he had found it later and turned it over to the police laboratory. One lab specialist said he had undone the bomb—it was made of broken-up safety matches and scraps of film balled up in handkerchiefs and stuffed into a sock—and had lifted two fingerprints from separate bits of film. Another detective said he had taken Hayer's prints at Bellevue Hospital. Still another closed the trap: he had found one of the prints useless but the other perfectly matched Hayer's left thumb on nine points of comparison. "Is there any question in your mind about that?" Dermody asked. "There is none whatsoever," the print man said. Ryan stole a glance at Sabbatino. "That print," he told me later, "really collapsed him."

But *People* v. *Butler and Johnson* was another, harder case. They had been picked up at home well after the fact, and their wives were standing by to alibi them. The state couldn't connect them with Hayer except by connecting Hayer with the Muslims; the evidence of this connection—at least that evidence that could be presented in court—was suggestive but considerably short of absolute proof. There was no real physical evidence against Butler and Johnson, as there was against Hayer; the Luger, which several witnesses placed in Butler's hand, had disappeared, and the shotgun had neither fingerprints nor a traceable history tying it to Johnson. What all of this meant was that the state's case against the two of them was only as persuasive as the testimony of its eyewitnesses—the composite recollections of seven men out of the crowd of several hundred present at the death of Malcolm X.

Cary Thomas had hurt both men, and T's testimony damaged Butler particularly; still, in an eyewitness case, more are better, and the state held out two of its best till it was two-thirds of the way through its presentation. The first of these was Fred Williams, the maintenance man from New Jersey who drove Malcolm to the

Audubon on the twenty-first; he had been to a few OAAU rallies before then but hadn't taken out a card until that very day. He was sitting in the audience, he testified, when the scuffle started somewhere behind him. He turned to look and saw two men, one in a tweed coat, hassling each other; the one in tweed, he said, was Butler. "The minister said, 'Will you straighten out everything, everything will be all right,' or something like that. . . . Then I hear a large bang. Come from up front. . . . This bang, and then I push my wife to the floor because everybody is hollering. . . . Then here come the second bang and a lot of other pistol shooting." He looked up at one point, he said, and saw Johnson down on one knee facing the back, with a shotgun in his hand; then he ducked again, hearing chairs collapse and people yelling and his wife crying under him. When the shooting stopped, he went toward the stage and found the Luger—he called it a "palooka"—and the shotgun.

The defense, still trying to construct a conspiracy of the palace guard, did what it could with the coincidence of Williams's having delivered Malcolm to the ballroom before the fact and having found the guns afterward and turned them over to the brothers rather than the police. One of Johnson's lawyers, Joseph Pinckney, did better getting Williams to admit that he hadn't been sure of the identification when the police first showed him Johnson's picture. This kind of confusion is common enough—a mug shot is never as satisfactory as seeing a suspect in the flesh—but it was a bit more substantial than the notion that Williams had joined some janissary plot against Malcolm on his first day in the OAAU.

Next came Charles X Blackwell, who had come over from Jersey with the Williamses that afternoon and whose testimony now finished what Cary Thomas had begun. Blackwell had just taken his post as a rostrum guard, he said, and was drawn far out of position when the scuffling began several rows back in the crowd. He heard a blast behind him and spun toward it. "I seen the minister grab the podium and then grabbed himself . . . I seen him fall." He heard more shots, he said, and as he turned back toward the audience, he saw the two men who had put on the fight come barreling down the aisle, shooting at the stage. One of them pointed a Luger at him and he hit the floor fast, but not before he got a good look at both men; one, he said, was Hayer and the other —the man with the Luger—Norman Butler. They got as far as the rostrum, then started back, firing wildly over the crowd. "I got up and gave chase after them. . . . I ran into a fellow that seemed very startled as I came toward him. . . . He turned and ran towards the ladies' lounge." This man, Blackwell said, was Thomas Johnson—and the ladies' lounge, as it happened, led to a back way out of the building.

The trouble with this account was that Blackwell, like Cary Thomas, had rearranged the men between his appearance before the grand jury and his testimony at the trial. As he told it to the grand jury, he had seen Butler and Hayer in the front row, not in the middle of the audience; another man he couldn't identify had started the scuffle further back. He heard a "pop" toward the rear —presumably the smoke bomb—and a volley of shots, but he was moving toward the scuffle and didn't see where they came from. Only afterward did he see Butler and Hayer making their mad dash for the exit and Johnson disappearing into the ladies' room. The implication of this version was that there had been at least four men involved, three with guns and a fourth to start the scuffle. Blackwell's testimony at the trial had not altered as to the identity of the principals, but, like Thomas's, his new version reduced the number of people actively involved to three—the three who happened to be in the courtroom on trial for murder.

Chance confronted him with the discrepancies.

"That's what I said," Blackwell conceded.

"And at the time you told them that, that was true, is that correct?"

"No, it wasn't true."

"When you told them that you did not see anyone fire a gun, you were lying, is that correct?"

"That's correct."

The admission hurt, and at the end of a day's hard cross-examination, Dermody once again had to rescue his witness. "When you said in the grand jury that [Butler and Hayer] were sitting in the front row," he asked, "were you lying or were you mistaken?"

"I was mistaken," Blackwell answered. ". . . Well, at that time that I said this I was lying because—mistaken—anyway, what happened, I was ashamed to say that I left my post, and when this brother had pointed the gun at me I had dropped on the floor. Actually, I should have tried to protect the minister."

And when he told the grand jury he hadn't seen anybody rush the stage shooting—was that a lie, too?

"That's right," Blackwell answered. ". . . I was ashamed . . . I felt very bad that I didn't even make any move to protect the minister."

Mostly, however, the defense went on pursuing its own mutiny theory of the case. Sabbatino nagged at the point that Blackwell had delivered the shotgun and the Luger from Williams to Reuben Francis instead of to the police, and Chance filled the record with the internal controversies between the political and the religious brothers. Blackwell was vague as to what this dissension had been about—"I did not go into the inside, the details of it"—but he was clear about his own elemental beef: "I was dissatisfied at the leadership that did not allow us to carry protection for our leader." Led by Chance, he mentioned two of Malcolm's lieutenants particularly as having been against packing guns. Chance asked if it wasn't true that Malcolm had finally decided that he wanted the brothers armed on the twenty-first and that these two lieutenants had persuaded him to delay it one week longer. Blackwell didn't know anything about that. Chance tried to develop the point that at one quarrelsome meeting during Malcolm's absence in Africa, the same two brothers had spoken against his position in the faction fighting, but Blackwell didn't know anything about that either.

A few more prosecution witnesses remained—Cavallaro, Keeley and some other policemen and one last spectator who could identify Hayer. But with Blackwell's testimony, and the laboratory evidence against Hayer, the state essentially had its case. It put on twenty-six witnesses in all, of whom twelve had been at the Audubon Ballroom on the afternoon of the twenty-first. Eight of these identified Hayer as one of the killers and two thought they remembered him from around the Black Muslim scene, visiting the Harlem temple, selling *Muhammad Speaks,* karate-chopping a troublemaker in the mosque. Six placed Butler at the Audubon and four put Johnson there. Two of the strongest witnesses—the only two who testified to having seen all three men—had changed their stories in detail between the grand-jury hearings in 1965 and the trial a year later, but both had stood up well under cross-examination in spite of the discrepancies. By the fifth week of the trial, the People had got their evidence essentially into the record and had begun winding down their presentation. A single piece of theatrics remained: on February 17, the twenty-sixth day in court, Vincent Dermody called Mrs. Betty Shabazz.

42. Betty

She hadn't seen much, really, and her own guess, as she had expressed it to the police, was that the Power Structure—the CIA, probably—had commissioned the killing even if Muslim hands carried it out. The single thin necessity for putting her on at all was that she had looked at the riddled body they brought out of the Audubon and had said yes, that was her husband. But it never hurts in a murder trial to display the widow and her bereavement to the jury, and so they brought her out, dressed all in black with a single strand of white pearls, to sit in straight-backed formality and tell what it was like being at the Audubon with her babies when the shooting started and Malcolm was falling and they couldn't even see what was happening.

Dermody asked her how long she had been married to The Deceased. "Seven years," she said, "and six weeks." He led her gently through the story—how she had brought the four girls, then six months to six years old, to the ballroom and had taken a booth down front and was trying to get them out of their snowsuits when Malcolm came on. "I heard someone, I saw someone stand. First I heard a voice. They said something to the effect of, 'Get your hands out of my pocket,' or 'Don't go in my pocket'—you know, very loud and demanding. . . ." Dermody asked her if this man was white or Negro, and she said, "Afro-American," but she hadn't seen him well enough to identify him.

She could hear Malcolm saying everything would be all right, and then "it was a lot of things happening all at once. There was chairs falling, people hollering . . . a succession of shots being fired. . . . My babies started crying, and they wanted to know if somebody was going to kill us . . . and I was trying to quiet them. Everyone had fallen to the floor, chairs were on the floor, people were crawling around, and I pushed them under a bench that had a back to it. . . . I covered the bench with my body, but one of them started crying they couldn't breathe and they couldn't see, so I turned around to try to quiet them, and when I turned back around I saw people crawling on the floor, I saw folded chairs on the floor, and I saw someone gasp, like—you know—and I looked towards the stage. I didn't see my husband. . . . When I looked and didn't see him, I ran—started running to the stage—but they wouldn't let me go." She finally struggled through; Malcolm was on his back, and she waited beside him until they came to get him. "And did you identify his dead body for the medical examiners?" Dermody asked. She said yes. "Thank you," Dermody said. "I have no further questions."

She had sat still through the questioning with her hands folded in her lap, telling the story with a quiet, abstract anger; when Dermody let her go, not a man among the defenders wanted to cross-examine her. She started out of the room, but when she got near the defense table, she stopped suddenly, her fists balling, and cried out, "They killed my husband! They killed him! They had no right to kill my husband." She started turning toward the defendants, but two court attendants got her by the arms and hurried her out, still saying they killed her husband. The lawyers flocked to the bench moving for a mistrial. "I watched her very carefully," Judge

Marks said. "She did not point to anyone." The lawyers protested, but Marks let it go with an admonition to the jury to disregard the outburst; the state plodded on with the last of its proof, and at the end of the next day, Dermody dismissed his wind-up witness and said, "Your honor, that is the People's case."

43. Hayer

His defense consisted of his wife, his brother, his half-sister and his half-sister's husband, all of whom said no, they never heard Tommy say anything about any Black Muslims, and his own injured innocence on the witness stand. Talmadge Hayer, leading off the three defendants, said he went to the Audubon on the afternoon of the twenty-first with no gun, no schemes, no grudge against Malcolm—nothing except his curiosity and this sudden urge to go to the bathroom practically as soon as he got inside the door. He was sitting there in a nickel booth when his eyes fell on a metal object, which turned out to be a clip of .45 cartridges. "I found it as I was sitting on the bowl there. It was down on one side of the toilet. I picked it up and looked at it. And out of curiosity —girls like dolls and boys like other things—I decided to keep it. I put it in my pocket." Then he went out in the big ballroom where everybody was and found a seat, and the next thing he knew Malcolm was out greeting the audience ("Hello, or whatever the words were he used") and then some people started a commotion behind him.

"I turned to see what was happening," he said. "And as I turned around, I could see some people moving—moving and standing, and as—then I heard a loud bang. . . . I thought—I thought maybe it was an argument between some people and somebody had shot somebody in the argument. So I ducked on the floor, and I heard more shots, sound like it was coming from the direction of the stage. And when it stopped I started to get out of the ballroom. I ran for the exit. I fell a couple of times. I fell over somebody as I was running, and as I was going out of the ballroom my leg went numb—I think I was shot. . . . My leg caved in under me. I hopped. I hopped all the way out to the exit . . . I slid down . . . and hit the bottom and fell on the floor . . . and I opened my eyes and I wasn't unconscious . . . so I crawled on my elbows and arms out the door. And when I went out the door a whole swab of people came out behind me and they were kicking at me and grabbing at me, saying 'Stop him, stop him, he killed—he killed Malcolm X. Stop him, stop him, he killed him, he killed him, he killed him.' " And suddenly a cop was there, and then a couple more, "and they were getting hit and I was getting hit," but they got him in a car and off to the precinct, and that was all he knew. He didn't know Butler. He didn't know Johnson. He didn't have a gun—a hat was the only thing he ever had in his hands. He couldn't imagine how his thumbprint got on that smoke bomb. "I didn't put it on there, if it's on there. I didn't put it on there."

It was a rushing, tumbling narrative that took less than half a day's telling. The trouble was that, in practically every important particular, Talmadge Hayer was lying.

Dermody, serene with his proof, hardly bothered with the story at all on cross-examination. What he really needed to do was not to prove Hayer's guilt out of his own mouth—there was evidence enough of that already—but to persuade the jury that he was a Black Muslim. To do so would buttress not only the case against Hayer himself, by suggesting his motive for murder, but the case against Butler and Johnson as well, by associating them with the one suspect caught at the scene. But Hayer, under questioning by Sabbatino, had denied everything the prosecution witnesses had said connecting him with the Nation—denied that he had ever been a member, or that he had sold anybody a *Muhammad Speaks,* or that he had ever karate-chopped anybody, or that he knew anything about karate at all.

This last was the perfect setup for Dermody's best evidence, but he held it back for the end and built to it with a few cat-and-mouse questions out of the file the detectives had put together on Hayer. He asked about the poolroom incident in Paterson, where the proprietor got annoyed with Hayer's sales pitch for *Muhammad Speaks* and sicced the police on him. Hayer said that had never happened. Dermody asked whether one of his sisters and three of his brothers weren't all Black Muslims. Hayer said no. Dermody popped his question as to whether Hayer himself hadn't registered at Mosque No. 25 in Newark in September 1962 under the name Talmadge X Hayer. "No, sir," said Hayer. Dermody rattled off names from a Newark membership roll, all of them adorned with X's and 3X's and 12X's. Hayer said he didn't know any of them.

During this series, Dermody began baiting his trap, collecting Hayer's denials that he had ever attended any Muslim meeting or that he even knew the Newark mosque existed. Then, with that sudden placid *politesse* of the cross-examiner who knows he has got a pair of aces in his pocket, he began drawing Hayer gradually in.

The incident of the karate chop: "You testified on direct examination that no such thing ever happened?"

"True," said Hayer.

"You also testified . . . that you have never studied or practiced karate, is that correct?"

"That's right."

"There is no question in your mind about that, is there?"

"No, sir."

". . . Let me ask you, Mr. Hayer, at any time in your lifetime did you ever take part in any kind of karate or judo or jiu-jitsu training?"

"No, sir."

Dermody came idling back to the prosecution table and slipped two photographs out of a folder—the two the detectives had scared up of the karate demonstration group at the Newark mosque. He handed one to Hayer.

"Do you see yourself in that photograph?"

"Somebody looks like me."

"My question is do you see yourself portrayed in that photograph?"

"No, sir."

Dermody, hot, pointed to a figure in the photo—a strong match for Hayer—and demanded that he look again.

Hayer studied it. "I don't think that's me," he said.

Dermody handed him the second picture and they repeated the catechism, the prosecutor asking again and again whether Hayer saw himself in the photo, Hayer granting only that "it favors me." Dermody finally asked in exasperation whether the pictures didn't show him "and other Black Muslims" who had put on a karate show in the Newark mosque. The prosecutor was by then only trying to get the provenance of his pictures before the jury; he knew what Hayer's answer would be—"No, sir."

A mistake in identity was possible, of course; people do have doubles, and photographs—even unaltered photographs—sometimes do lie. But Dermody, as it developed, had a third ace to play. The day after Hayer stood down, Assistant DA Jerry Ryan, accompanied by FBI agents and detectives of Manhattan North, drove over to Newark and hunted up the photographer, Franklin X Durant, a twenty-year-old newspaper wire-room employee who was himself a Muslim. They showed him the pictures. He said yes, he had taken them. They got him to come back to New York and tell it in court. As they crossed the state line in the Hudson River tunnel between New Jersey and New York, Ryan got out a blank subpoena and wrote it out in Durant's name just in case he changed his mind. He didn't; Dermody put him on that very morning. He testified that he had taken the photos at a Muslim bazaar at Mosque No. 25 in spring 1963 and that the man in question was indeed Hayer; he had even told Durant his name—"Talmadge." On cross-examination, he said that he didn't remember seeing Hayer in the mosque ever again and that he couldn't say of his own knowledge that all the men in the pictures were necessarily Black Muslims. But his testimony was enough to get the photos into evidence and thus to place Hayer dressed for karate, an art he claimed he had never practiced, inside Mosque

No. 25, a house of worship he said he hadn't known existed. The state was still short of proving conclusively that Hayer was a signed-up Muslim the day Malcolm died. But the photos and the photographer did place compelling evidence in the record that Hayer was lying when he said he had never been around the Muslims at all. And that hurt: to be caught lying once on so critical a subject was to create the suspicion that all one's answers on that subject were lies.

44. Butler

Had the Muslims actually been involved at all? Norman Butler's basic defense was his alibi, but his lawyers were trying to keep some alternative theory constantly before the jury, so they opened with Charles Kenyatta, then still Charles 37X Morris, and a long recitation about how Malcolm himself had got suspicious toward the end of some of the more politically inclined people among the brothers. Kenyatta said that Malcolm had assigned him specifically to watch some of these people on the twenty-first and that a lot of them were thickly involved with his security detail that afternoon. This line of questioning seemed aimed at establishing some internal Left plot against Malcolm, but Chance was cut off before he got very far, and Dermody, who had been well briefed on Kenyatta, wound up turning him to the state's own purposes. Kenyatta testified on cross that he had heard people in the Nation say that Malcolm was a hypocrite and should be killed. Dermody asked if the mosque had any "enforcers." Kenyatta said yes—they had a "hundred-man squad" to check out waverers and heretics.

"What do you mean by check them out?"

"By making visits to their homes."

"And to your knowledge would these enforcers if necessary resort to violence?"

"Some cases they would shake them up a little bit."

Dermody asked if Butler had been one of these enforcers in Kenyatta's day.

"Sir," Kenyatta answered, "he was a member of the hundred-man enforcing squad."

And Johnson, too?

"Yes, sir."

Butler himself in due course denied this—"We don't have anything like that whatsoever"—but his real problem was proving that he hadn't been at the Audubon that day. Putting on one's wife, or husband, as an alibi witness is a commonplace in trials in which the defendant has been arrested somewhere other than at the scene of the crime; their stories are authentic in *n* number of cases, but jurors tend to measure alibis against their expectations of how their own loved ones might act in similar circumstances and to discount them accordingly. Butler's wife, Theresa 7X, testified that he had gone out to see the doctor that morning—"His legs were all messed up . . . all bruised and cut and everything"—but had come home at about five minutes to 1 and never left after that. The murder was roughly at 3 o'clock. "Approximately after 3," she said, two of the sisters from the mosque—first Gloria 11X Wills, then Juanita 8X Gibbs—had telephoned with the news about Malcolm, and Butler had answered the phone both times. The defense produced both women; Mrs. Wills said she had heard the news from her mother-in-law at exactly 3:02 and phoned the Butlers at exactly 3:05; Mrs. Gibbs remembered only that her call was "before 3:30." Dermody dealt briskly with all of this by establishing that none of the three women had told any of it to the police; that Mrs. Wills couldn't possibly have phoned when she said she did, since the first news of the shooting didn't get on the air till 3:15 and then only on one station, and that Mrs. Butler herself had told the grand jury that there had been "a lot of calls, a lot of calls" that afternoon and that she couldn't remember what time they had come in.

The doctor, Kenneth Saslowe, appeared, too, and testified that yes, he had in fact seen Butler at Jacobi Hospital the morning of the twenty-first. Butler had been in a month before with infected wounds of both shins; this time, however, he complained only of pain in his right leg. Saslowe diagnosed the trouble as a superficial thrombophlebitis—an inflammation of the vein—and had given Butler an Ace bandage and some penicillin and advised him to go home and stay in bed. On cross, however, Dermody showed him the nude photo of Butler, and Saslowe noted that the *left* leg was discolored, too; he didn't remember having seen anything like that and hadn't noted it on his admission sheet. It developed further that Butler had come back on the twenty-fifth, four days after the assassination, with a new problem—a painfully swollen right ankle that looked like a possible fracture but turned out to be a tissue inflammation. Dermody asked if this could have resulted from Butler having been knocked down a flight of stairs. "Sure it could," Saslowe replied.

So it all came down to Butler's own credibility on the stand; his problem was that credibility sometimes gets mixed up with likability in a jury trial, and Butler under challenge, pitting that icy Muslim superiority of his against the devil's tricknological questioning, was not very likable. He did well enough while Chance was questioning him, beginning with the folkways of the Nation of Islam; yes, said Butler, you took orders, but you were "never, never, ever for the most part to be the aggressor," and you couldn't break the laws of the larger American society and still stay in the mosque. They proceeded quickly to the events of the twenty-first—the nonevents, as Butler told them. "My leg was quite sore"—the vein inflamed from his thigh to his big toe—"and at the instep . . . it was much too swollen for me to even put on my shoe correctly." He went to the hospital at around 9:15; some of the house staff "were wondering whether they should keep me there," but he told them he didn't want to stay, so he got his instructions and his medication and left. He stopped for "a very short time" at the Muslim restaurant—an odd detour given his aches and pains and the doctor's orders—and then went home, arriving around 1 o'clock. Chance asked if he had set foot in the Audubon Ballroom on the twenty-first. "Emphatically no," said

Butler. Or talked to anybody about killing Malcolm X? "Positively not." Or ever attended any of Malcolm's meetings? "Negative." Or fired any guns in the Audubon? "Absolutely no." Or run out of the ballroom after the shooting? "I couldn't run."

But when Dermody came at him, short and hot-pink and hectoring, you could see Butler go taut—see his eyes burn and his jaws work and his muscles bunch as if not only his own fate but the defense of all Islam against the infidel rested solely with him in that room at that moment. He was combative almost from Dermody's first questions about how he had managed to pay the bills and keep himself in clothes and a car on the $55 a week he was getting from the government for taking job training. "As a matter of fact, Mr. Butler," Dermody started, "weren't you being supported—"

"Negative," Butler interrupted.

"You haven't heard my question."

"I know what you're going to say. No."

"What was I going to ask you?"

"You were going to ask me was I supported by the mosque."

Dermody started again and Butler interrupted again.

"What was I going to ask you?" Dermody asked.

"Did I ever tell a detective that."

"You knew I was going to ask you that?"

"Certainly. I know what you're going to say before you say it."

He sassed and patronized and quibbled over words. He disputed the name Norman 3X Butler on the indictment: "Part of it is mine, part of it is yours." He instructed Dermody in the proper nomenclature of the faith: "Pardon me, I'm not a member of the 'Black Muslims.' . . . You wouldn't refer to a pear as an apple." He got Dermody shouting once with a conspicuously unresponsive answer, then asked him coldly, "Do you have a reason to yell at me?" He told Dermody that one of his questions was irrelevant, another senseless, another "really stupid," and that his star witness Cary Thomas was "obviously lying." Once, Dermody asked him a question he felt he had answered adequately before. "What did I just say?" said Butler. "I'm asking you, don't you ask me," Dermody bristled back. Another time, Dermody asked him something provocative, and Butler said, "I didn't do anything—you know it and everybody else knows it."

He yielded nothing important in his alibi under cross-examination, but his bickering with Dermody gave it rather too bellicose a tone: juries tend to like their innocence a little less outraged than that. Dermody fished out the admission that Butler had managed to get to other places—his job-training class, for example—despite his leg trouble. And on the twenty-first, he pressed—"Were you able to walk unassisted from your home, your apartment, down to the street and get into your car?"

"Hobbling," Butler said.

When he stopped off in Harlem on his way home from the hospital to pick up the papers and chat with Captain Joseph at the restaurant—had he been hobbling then, too?

"Well, that's the way I had to walk, wherever I went."

"You weren't using a cane, were you?"

"No, sir," Butler shot back. "That might be construed as a weapon."

Dermody didn't have any evidence to present implicating any of Butler's superiors in the Nation, but he did drop a couple of names into the questioning. He sprung his question about whether Butler had met with John Ali and Captain Joseph the Friday night before the assassination; Butler said no. He asked if Captain Joseph had denounced Malcolm as a hypocrite; Butler said he didn't remember, though he agreed that he had heard that word used around the mosque. Dermody asked if he had ever heard anyone there say that Malcolm should be killed. Butler said no—"They wouldn't have said it in my presence. That's against our law. No acts of violence unless attacked directly."

Dermody did draw out Butler's own biliously low regard for Malcolm. "Did you yourself regard Malcolm X as a hypocrite?" he asked. "I did," Butler replied. Dermody asked whether Malcolm hadn't attracted a lot of the believers away from the Nation. "I can say that I know of, maybe thirteen," Butler said. ". . . There might have been a couple of sisters. Say *fifteen*."

"And to your knowledge," Dermody went on, "was there any discussion among the brothers and sisters of Mosque No. 7 about the fact that people were leaving Mosque No. 7 and going with the now deceased?"

"We're a body," said Butler. "You take on and you excrete."

"You take on," said Dermody, delighted, "and you *what?*"

"Let off," Butler said.

". . . Excrete, is that the word?"

"We're a body. Everything that the body does, that's what we do—function. You take in and you let out."

"You used the word *excrete* before, didn't you?"

"I don't remember," Butler said.

Dermody held Butler on the stand for the better part of two days, and by the end of it, the prosecutor was like a fighter way ahead on points in the late rounds, dropping his guard and jutting his jaw and teasing his opponent to swing. He closed with the stock question about whether Butler wouldn't lie to protect himself. Butler made even that an insult to his religion and said angrily that Muslims don't lie; Dermody, for what seemed the hundredth time, got the answer stricken as unresponsive. When Butler stepped down at last, the state was rather well pleased and the defense dismayed, for reasons quite outside the narrow questions of evidence. Presenting a believable story is only half the battle in an alibi defense; the other half is making the jury want to believe it. Butler was too *Muslim* at a time when the Muslims were the objects of great public alarm. "He had no sympathy as a witness," one defense lawyer told me, choosing his words carefully. What he meant was that, sitting there, you could almost *feel* the jurors disliking him, and you could guess that when they got off by themselves, they would be looking a good deal less enthusiastically at Butler's alibi than at the holes in it.

45. Johnson

Thomas Johnson played the game rather better, but his alibi was not quite so tidily buttoned down as Butler's. His evidence began, actually, with one of Butler's witnesses, Ernest Greene, a twenty-one-year-old student who had been at the Audubon on the twenty-first and who said the man with the shotgun was stout and very dark and had a thick beard. Johnson had changed in jail—had dropped thirty pounds and shaved his mustache—but nothing in Greene's description fit him, before or after. The only thing was that, as Dermody brought out on cross, Greene had once been a Muslim himself and was testifying because Captain Joseph had asked him to. Johnson's wife, Etta X, said he had spent the whole day at home in his pajamas, and a Muslim neighbor couple, Edward 4X and Muriel Long, said they had come visiting separately some time after Malcolm was shot and found Johnson in. But their stories conflicted badly on which Long got there first and at what time. Mrs. Johnson said it was around 3:30 but had told the grand jury after 4; Long said it was "in between 3:30 and 4:30, something of that sort"; Mrs. Long said she got there probably "right after 5," because she worked at one of the midtown hotels till 4:30. None of the times proved anything, since nobody placed the Longs at Johnson's place before 3:30, and Johnson could have got home from the Audubon before then. Johnson himself wound up hedging on the time ("I don't watch the clock") and contradicting his wife a bit peevishly on several less critical details of her story. "My recollection," he said, "is she must be confused."

His recollection was that he had indeed stayed home all day, or at least till evening, when he got dressed and went out for ice cream. They had got up at 5 A.M., he said, for the day's first family prayer; afterward, he read the Qur'an for a while, rested a while more, then pottered around vacuuming the living room and getting lunch started while Etta, who had stayed up watching the late movie, slept on past noon. "Sometime that afternoon—it was before dark, I don't remember the hour—Brother Edward came up. . . . He asked me did I hear the news. At the same time, he had a black portable radio in his hand, and that's when I found out that Malcolm had been killed."

Dermody poked at the story and at the variances between it and what the alibi witnesses said; none of these was very consequential in itself, but even modest discrepancies, if there are enough of them, are helpful with a jury in an alibi case. Dermody spent time on Johnson's criminal past as well—his ten years as a junkie; his five convictions for the standard addict crimes, possession and theft; his gigs as a numbers runner and a lookout for a gambling room; his six months kicking heroin at the Federal narcotics hospital in Lexington, Kentucky. None of this was very consequential either, except as further testimony to the Nation's successes at turning addicts around; Johnson's police pedigree was that of a dropout, not an assassin, and was hardly worse than Malcolm's own. Still, a police record helps with a jury, too. "He's got quite a sheet," Dermody noted in his closing argument; the unspoken assumption is that a man with a sheet, no matter how banal, is presumptively a liar and probably guilty as charged.

Mostly, Dermody worked at the Muslim Connection. As he had with Butler, he made a mystery of Johnson's living in apparent comfort without a job; Johnson conceded that he had got a little help from the mosque, \$25 once and \$40 another time, but had been subsisting mainly on welfare. Dermody asked him at one point if he was obliged to take orders from Captain Joseph. Johnson said yes, "if it was within the realm." Dermody asked what realm. "Of our duties," Johnson answered. "Functioning of the mosque." Dermody asked if he had ever heard Captain Joseph call Malcolm a hypocrite. "No," said Johnson. " . . . I heard him say that Malcolm has *defected.* He left. Malcolm left on his own. He made clear that Malcolm left." Dermody asked if he had ever heard Captain Joseph say that Malcolm should be killed. Johnson answered quickly: "No, sir."

He held to his story through two days, and apart from the business of his record and the discrepancies in the alibi testimony, Dermody really managed only one palpable hit. "Let me ask you, Mr. Johnson," he asked midway into the first day's questioning, "in your lifetime did you ever have occasion to fire a shotgun?"

"Never."

". . . A rifle?"

"Never."

"Did you ever have occasion in your lifetime to ever handle any kind of gun?"

"I never handled any gun, any time in my life," Johnson answered firmly.

Dermody let the subject drop then and saved it for the end. He got back to it via the Benjamin Brown shooting, in which both Johnson and Butler had been arrested. Johnson conceded that he knew Brown and was aware that he had set up some sort of spin-off Muslim enterprise, though nothing you could properly call competitive with the Nation. "It's a *storefront,* first of all," Johnson said disdainfully. "I don't know of any *mosque.*" Dermody asked him straight out if he had shot Brown with a rifle. "No, sir," Johnson answered over a burst of protests from the defense table. "Definitely not."

Then Dermody pounced. "Mr. Johnson—did you ever have in your apartment a rifle?"

"Yes, sir, I had a rifle."

"Was it loaded?"

"I believe so. I'm not sure."

". . . Do you recall testifying yesterday, Mr. Johnson, that never in your lifetime had you handled a weapon of any kind?"

"No, sir, I don't recall that."

Dermody read him the exchange.

"Well," Johnson granted, "I must have said it if you are reading it from the paper."

"Did you lie yesterday when you were asked that question . . . ?"

"Why would I have to lie?" Johnson asked.

Dermody got that stricken.

"I took it home," Johnson said. "You mean *that* is handling it? I handled it, then. I took it home, I had it in my closet . . . I must have didn't understand you."

He wasn't very convincing. Dermody had caught him covering up on a tangential but still damaging issue; a jury could proceed easily from the premise that Johnson had lied about handling a gun to the judgment that he could as easily have lied about firing a gun at Malcolm. Dermody quickly wound up his cross-examination at that point. You learn a lot of things trying cases for twenty-five years, and one of the first is that you quit while you are ahead.

46. Confession

Sabbatino was practically the last one to know. He came into court a little late on a Monday morning in the midst of Butler's case, and there were all these whispered conferences going on, in the courtroom and the feeder pen where they bring the prisoners in and out and park them during recesses, and all of it was about Hayer. His own client. The judge knew, the colored lawyers all knew, the other defendants knew, and the DA's people knew or had guessed. *Son of a bitch.* Then Chance came to him for permission to talk to Hayer, in Sabbatino's presence of course, and they went out in the pen, where it developed that Hayer had been talking to everybody about going back on the stand and changing his testimony. Sabbatino didn't want to call him back, but at length he told Chance *you* do it, and Chance did. The afternoon session was an hour late getting started with all the delays, Sabbatino still asking for more time to talk to his client alone, but Judge Marks said no, and Hayer got back on the stand. The judge asked him if anyone had forced him to testify again. "No, sir," Hayer said, his voice a near-whisper. "I just want to tell the truth, that's all."

The new truth, he said, with Chance leading gently, was that he had just been backstairs telling Butler and Johnson "that I know they didn't have anything to do with the crime that was committed at the Audubon Ballroom February 21, that I did take part in it and that I know for a fact that they wasn't there, and I wanted this to be known to the jury and the court, the judge. I want to tell the truth." Chance asked him if he had killed Malcolm by himself; he said he hadn't, but when Chance asked him to identify his confederates, he said, "No, sir, I can't reveal that." The judge intervened and directed Hayer to name names. But Hayer, having just effectively sentenced himself to life imprisonment for murder, could hardly be budged by the threat of a few extra weeks or months in jail for contempt. He said no again—"I just want the truth to be known that Butler and Johnson didn't have anything to do with this crime, because I was there, I know what happened, I know the people that did take part in it."

The prosecution was not precisely surprised by this: they knew they had Hayer sewn up, and in the process of war-gaming their case they guessed that he might at some point cop out and try to clear the others. Still, now that it had happened, the whole case came down to Dermody's skill at cross-examination. He had to persuade the jury that the confession was a Muslim postlude to a Muslim plot—that Hayer's own cause was lost and that he had been persuaded or directed to take the fall for his two brother believers. It was that or blow the case, and Dermody came out slugging.

He wanted it on the record first that Hayer was in fact a murderer—not just that he was there but that he had spilled Malcolm's blood. "Tell us how you were involved," he said.

"I had a weapon and I—"

"What kind of a weapon did you have?"

"Forty-five."

". . . And did you fire that weapon at the deceased?"

"Yes, sir."

"How many shots did you fire?"

"Maybe four."

And later: "Did you fire right into his body?"

"I did."

But when Dermody pressed on into who had organized the murder, and why, Hayer shut up. "Give us the whole thing from the very beginning," Dermody said.

"No, sir."

"What's that?"

"No, sir . . ."

"Let me ask you this question, Mr. Hayer—did somebody ask you and others to shoot and kill Malcolm X?"

"Well, yes, sir."

"Do you know the name of that person who directed you to do it?"

"No, sir."

"Well, did you receive orders or instructions from that person?"

"No, sir. No, sir."

"You testified a few moments ago that you were told to do this by somebody, is that right?"

"I was offered some money for doing it from people that probably would have been revealed if Mr. Williams could have continued his interrogation."*

". . . You say you were offered some money?" Dermody pressed.

"Yes, sir."

"To kill Malcolm X?"

"Yes, sir."

"Did you ever *receive* any money for killing him?"

*Dermody got this answer stricken as unresponsive, and it remains another of the mysteries of the case. "Mr. Williams" presumably was Joseph Williams, who, along with Chance, was defending Butler. But Chance had been doing most of the interrogating; Williams questioned only a few witnesses and those mostly about details of evidence, not who might have organized the assassination. The only remotely suggestive questions were a few about the political/religious cleavage among Malcolm's own followers. One suspects from the pattern of Hayer's testimony that he seized on this because it was there, an available alternative to the Muslims-did-it theory, which he seemed extraordinarily eager to refute.

"No, sir."

". . . How much money were you offered to kill Malcolm X?"

"I don't—can't say. I won't say."

". . . When do you say you were first approached by anybody in connection with the assassination of Malcolm X?"

"Sometime in February, I guess . . . beginning of February."

"Who approached you?"

"I won't say."

"Where were you approached?"

"I won't say."

Hayer disputed the state's reconstruction of how the plot actually was carried out and substituted his own four-man version—a version that, coincidentally or not, was nearer to the ones Cary Thomas and Charles Blackwell had given before the grand jury. He denied that he had started the fake fight—"That was lies." Dermody asked him what was the truth. "Four people," he said. "Two people sitting in the front row, man with the shotgun—short dark man with the beard—sitting around the fourth row from the front, man in the back; one man [in the back] starts commotion, says 'Get your hand out of my pocket,' guards from the stage goes after this man, man with the shotgun shoots Malcolm, two men on the front row shoot pistols."

"And which of these men were you?"

"One of the men sitting on the front row."

". . . Did the other man sitting in the front row with you also have a pistol?"

"Yes . . . A Luger."

"Tell us the name of that man who had the German Luger."

"I will not."

"As a matter of fact, it was Norman Butler, wasn't it?"

"No, sir."

Hayer transparently had seized on Ernest Greene's description of the man with the shotgun, but when Dermody pressed him on it, he said that wasn't so. "The witness told the truth when he described this person with the shotgun, that's all, so since you have the description already—" He said the man who started the commotion was "about my size, height and complexion"—another point that conveniently suited the existing testimony. He wouldn't describe the man with the Luger at all, except to say during the first day's cross that he had been wearing a dark-brown three-quarter-length topcoat; the second day, this became a greenish-brown trench coat, whereupon Dermody guessed sardonically that, anyway, Hayer was sure it wasn't a gray tweed topcoat like Butler's. He hounded Hayer for names, but got nowhere. He asked whether they had rehearsed the assassination; Hayer said yes but wouldn't say when or where. Dermody asked about the smoke bomb; Hayer admitted this time that he had made it but not that he had thrown it—the man in the rear who kicked up the commotion had tossed the bomb, too. He wouldn't say whether there was a getaway car, or who supplied the guns, or any other details of the plot, except that the state witnesses had it all wrong. "It was quite impossible for the crime to have been committed the way those people said."

Dermody hectored him to say that the Muslims were involved, with no more success. "Let me ask you, Mr. Hayer," he said, "this person who approached you and the others to do this assassination —was this person, to your knowledge, a member of the Black Muslims?"

"No, he was not."

"Did this person tell you why he wanted to hire you and these others to assassinate Malcolm X?"

"No, sir."

His confederates—"Were any of them, to your knowledge, Black Muslims?"

"No, they weren't."

Dermody got out the karate pictures again. Hayer at first repeated his denial that he was in the photos, then abruptly changed his tack and said, "I won't say anything. I won't answer that." Dermody pushed first one, then the other at him. "I have nothing to say about that picture," Hayer said each time. Dermody asked if he remembered saying that he had never heard of Mosque No. 25 in Newark. "I have nothing to say about that," Hayer said. "I got up here in behalf of two people . . . to clear these two men, to tell the truth, they didn't have anything to do with this crime." Dermody and Marks both kept after him for names, but Hayer refused to give them.

"Why?" Dermody demanded.

"Because I don't want to tell on them."

"Or isn't it a fact that you can't give us the names of anybody else because the people who were involved with you, you know to be Johnson and Butler?"

"No, that's not a fact."

Hayer's Hayer was a man belatedly but honestly conscience-stricken, confessing first to his co-defendants and then to the court; Dermody's Hayer was a murderer drowning in evidence and trying, probably on instructions from his masters, to get two equally guilty brethren off the hook. Dermody poked and prodded and bullied and got all his arguments before the jury in the form of questions; and, finally, flushed and exasperated, he bore down on Hayer and demanded to know why he had got in the plot at all.

"What was your motive?"

"Money."

"Money?"

"Mm-hm."

"How much?"

"I won't say."

"Well, was it in the thousands?"

"I already answered the question."

"Was it for twelve pieces of silver?"

There was a wrangle over this—Dermody had deflated the price of betrayal by eighteen pieces of silver—but he finally said he meant "exactly what Judas got."

And Hayer said, "No, it wasn't for—" He hesitated. "No."

47. Judgment

Sabbatino was old school, short and natively combative, the kind who rocks on his heels and jabs with his forefinger and waves a fat green cigar around and talks to you about the weather or the ball scores as if you were a jury and he was summing up a close case. He came up the hard road; he learned language the way Malcolm did, out of a dictionary, a used Webster's he bought for 35 cents on Book Row when he was a kid, and naturally, being a kid, he looked up "whore" first, which led him to "prostitute" and "paramour" and "concubine" and the beginnings of a vocabulary of mixed earthiness and elegance. He once got locked up briefly, when he was eleven years old and somehow was swept up in a crap-game bust, so he knew what getting locked up was like. He was an Assistant DA in the twenties, so he knew what that was like, too; the last case he was assigned to prosecute was a jerry-built robbery charge, and he went to the judge and got it dismissed. His life since had been criminal law. He never liked lawbooks much —"They're full of judges rehashing the same crappy opinions"— or riffraff lawyers, the kind who take cases for $10 here and $25 there and plead everybody guilty just to get them out of the way. Sabbatino liked trials—liked the combat and the theater and the wind-up where it's up to you to stand alone in front of the jurors and convince them that they ought to let your guy off. One time he had a whole jury in tears—every last one of them wet-eyed and snuffling—and the only thing that spoiled the memory was that they went sadly out and came sadly back with a verdict of guilty.

So they let Sabbatino sum up last in the Malcolm X case, out of respect for his years and his gifts. Charles Beavers led off for Thomas Johnson, arguing that the whole case against his man was based on the shaky testimony of four eyewitnesses and the fact of his religious affiliation. "You've heard repeatedly and repeatedly the words Black Muslims, and the Black Muslims also have been on trial in this case." Next came Chance, large and smoldering, attacking the state's witnesses as old or shortsighted or ex-criminals or, in Cary Thomas's case, afflicted by "an impaired mentality." Chance denounced the Muslim theory as "totally absurd" and contended that Butler had only *seemed* fanatic on the stand; maybe he "spoke a little curt and sharp," but that was to be expected from an innocent man who had spent eleven months in jail and then had been put eye to eye with a man—Dermody—whom he considered his enemy. Chance's half-formed alternative hypothesis was that the police were at least "vicariously liable" for Malcolm's death. His evidence was that they had posted an officer inside the building, in walkie-talkie communication with a larger detail in the very hospital to which Malcolm's body was taken. "I submit to you that they either knew or expected trouble. And if the police officer had been standing in that ballroom with his uniform on instead of hidden in a back room, nobody would have assassinated Malcolm X."

And then came Sabbatino, pleading the cause of a man who was buried in evidence, and who had confessed on the stand, as if none of that had happened and Hayer was an eleven-year-old innocent swept up in a raid on the grownups' crap game. He paced. He rocked. He jabbed. He peered through his horn-rims. He talked on for two and a half hours, his voice high and husky. He created a marvelous conspiracy of the bodyguards, with Reuben Francis, the man charged with having shot Hayer, as "the arch conspirator of all."* Hayer a killer? Impossible. "This boy was not guilty of anything. This boy was an identification by gunshot by Reuben Francis and no other. And stooges of Reuben Francis took up a cry and began to shout, 'Killer!' " The .45 clip in his pocket? Sabbatino

*Francis, who had been freed on bail in the Hayer shooting and then rearrested during the Malcolm X trial for missing a court appearance in his own case, was never called by the state. Dermody did ask the judge to make him available to the defense in the Tombs. Marks agreed to, but the defense never called its "arch conspirator" either.

chose to ignore Hayer's confession on that point. ". . . As part of this conspiracy somebody put this clip in the toilet and watched who took it, and then when the assassination took place, made sure to divert the attention of the police to that individual. . . ." The witnesses? They were assassins or confederates of assassins. Only the thumbprint on the smoke bomb slowed him down. "Frankly," he said, "I have been worried about that. . . . How could it get there? Well, I am going to leave that problem to you." It sounded almost sweetly ingenuous; Sabbatino might have been asking them to help with a hard answer in the Sunday crossword puzzle.

At the end, he was going for the tears, rocking and jabbing and shouting and throwing everything at them. Here was Malcolm X, "a man who was changing his social philosophy for the betterment of his own kind, and these secret conspirators gunned him down . . . and they pick out my kid, who was gunned down, because he happened to have a clip, and they picked the other two boys because they are Muslims," and maybe Hayer said he did it, but maybe also that was "a noble Christian act on his part" to get the other two boys off. The other defenders winced at this: they naturally preferred it Hayer's way—that his clearing Butler and Johnson was the truth, not some act of charity. But Sabbatino plunged on. "We want no superior justice because these boys are colored, and we want no inferior justice. . . . Don't be impressed by what my client said on February 28. Don't condemn a Christian act. . . . There is no reason for this lad to do what he did excepting a high sense of Christian virtue, Christian charity. . . ."

It was fine and bravura, and in the end it came to nothing. Vincent Dermody wasn't going to win any Academy Awards, but he had his own way with juries—a tidy, square-cornered logic putting a case together and a direct, unadorned style of speaking that told jurors through the New York diction and the tabloid lingo that this is true; this is the way it *really* happened. He rehearsed the whole case from the beginning, witness by witness; he conceded their shortcomings where he had to—maybe the porter wasn't the brightest young man in the world and maybe the old man was foolish and shortsighted—but he moved relentlessly on through their accumulating identifications until it all looked whole and seamless and airtight. Cary Thomas—"What does he stand to gain or lose?" The janitor who said he sat next to Butler—"Is *he* one of the conspirators?" The mystery witness, T—why would he have come in at all when he feared for his life? Charles Blackwell—if he was a conspirator lying to frame somebody else, why didn't he sew it up tight and say he saw the shotgun in Johnson's hands? Ernest Greene, the kid who said the man with the shotgun was stout, black and bearded—"I guess," said Dermody, a study in sensibility outraged, "that's about the best description you could get and keep it away from the defendant Johnson."

It was, as Dermody told it, a choice between the defense theory—"some conspiracy that I haven't been able to figure out at all"—and the Muslim hypothesis; a choice, that is, between fantasy and logic. "We do not claim, we don't say we intend to prove or can prove . . . that Elijah Muhammad . . . had ordered the death of Malcolm X and designated these three defendants to be the killers. That is what we have been accused of trying to establish here, and that couldn't be any further from the truth." But based on the evidence, he went on, "I submit that these three defendants are members of the Black Muslim organization. And the evidence definitely indicates that these three defendants caused his death." The state had no obligation to go beyond this and prove why they wanted Malcolm dead, but, said Dermody, the brazenness of the act suggested the answer. "Ordinarily, if a person makes up his mind to kill somebody, he does it in secret. He doesn't want any witnesses available. It's done in the dead of night, secretly, quietly. But when you consider the evidence . . . whoever did it chose to do it in the presence of between 200 and 400 people in broad daylight in a public room. . . . Is it abusing your common sense to suggest that it was done deliberately in the presence of these people as an object lesson to Malcolm's followers that this is what can happen and what will happen?"

Dermody brushed aside the alibi testimony, Johnson's as too ragged—even Sabbatino called it "shaky" in his summation—and Butler's too pat. He scoffed at Hayer's first appearance ("before he becomes the Christian") and wrote off his second, all but the confession part, as the act of a man smothered by evidence; the photos tying him to the Muslims were, in Dermody's recapitulation, the last straw. "Is it abusing your common sense to suggest to you that . . . over that weekend sometime it was decided—by whom I cannot say—that since he was a dead duck, to use the vernacular, he should take the fall in this case, admit his guilt and try to bail out his two accomplices?" Christian charity? "It was a futile, desperate gesture on his part . . . an act of *criminal* charity."

He's cold, Sabbatino thought. *A machine.* Dermody, under the circumstances, might have felt flattered; he had argued his case as he had presented it, with a kind of mathematical inexorability, and he was going to be hard to beat. Judge Marks instructed the jurors the next morning. They went out after lunch, stayed out until 2 A.M. that night and most of the next day as well, a total of twenty hours and twenty minutes in all, before they filed back in with their verdicts. It hadn't been as close as their long time out of the courtroom made it seem; a lone woman, as it developed, had held out against the rest of them on each of the three defendants. It was 20 past midnight on March 11 when she finally gave in and they all stood in the box while the foreman, George Carter, small and bespectacled, announced the verdicts.

"Ladies and gentlemen of the jury," the clerk intoned, "as to the defendant . . . Talmadge Hayer . . . have you agreed upon a verdict?"

"Yes," Carter said, almost inaudibly.

"Will you please state your verdict?"

"Guilty."

"Of what?"

"Murder in the first degree."

"As to the defendant Norman Butler, have you agreed upon a verdict?"

"Yes."

"Please state your verdict."

"Murder in the first degree. Murder in the first degree."

"As to Thomas Johnson, have you agreed upon a verdict?"

"Yes."

"Will you please state your verdict?"

"Guilty."

"Of what?"

"Murder in the first degree."

Hayer stared at the jurors. Johnson looked blankly ahead. Butler said something almost to himself about it being the will of Allah. The lawyers started shoveling papers into their briefcases. In the gallery, John Keeley and Rocky Cavallaro got up and went home.

48. Inquest

One does not want Malcolm to have died shabbily. He was an authentic black hero, and a hero ought to have a glorious end, in combat, eye to eye with the real enemy. Instead, Malcolm X died in squalor, at the hands of black men and—so the official theory ran—as the casualty of a black tong war. For those who followed or admired him in life, and for that larger number who have helped beatify him since his death, the notion that his assassination should be so mean—so *banal*—has proven intolerable. The creation of the Malcolm legend has included the creation of a better death for him—a death in which black men may have been the immediate agents but in which the orders came from the establishment, or the white power structure, or Washington, or the police, or, most commonly, the CIA.

This state-conspiracy theory has become the orthodoxy to an astonishing degree among black intellectuals and black leaders of practically every shading of opinion. It is announced every bit as confidently by those who know nothing at all about the murder case—who are only vaguely aware, for example, that anybody was ever tried and convicted—as by those who followed the inquiry closely. There are a number of reasons why the theory has flowered so, despite the absence of anything but the most speculative sort of evidence supporting it. For one thing, it *is* an orthodoxy, and for blacks to challenge it is to risk all the normal sanctions against heresy. For another, the Nation of Islam, as one civil-rights radical put it wryly, is still there, and those few concerned blacks disposed to believe the Muslims guilty are almost universally indisposed to say so for attribution. For yet another, a state-conspiracy theory is politically useful to revolutionaries and has been actively promoted, with maximum surmise and minimal real investigation, by the sectarian Left. And for another still, black people have experienced state violence and state lies often enough to have earned a certain cynicism; one may come easily to believe in police-conspiracy theories when one's recent memories include the bloody police actions at Jackson State College, Attica prison and Fred Hampton's Black Panther crib in Chicago, to name three, and when one is oneself liable to the sudden and arbitrary attention of the police for no other reason than one's color. One black writer I interviewed had reason enough to credit the official version—a friend who had been at the Audubon on the twenty-first called him shortly afterward and said he had recognized the killers as Muslims—but still declared himself neutral as to whether the Nation or the CIA was the prime mover. "You have to remember," he said, smiling half-apologetically, "we come out of a terribly paranoid bag."

Yet one suspects that paranoia has less to do with it than some myth-making impulse deep in the black unconscious. The concept of murder as an existential absurdity is a luxury of the comfortable, which is to say the literate white middle class. Black people in the main cannot afford it. They have had few enough heroes all their own, and some of those, from Jack Johnson to Marcus Garvey to Adam Powell, have ended badly; it is now too costly for them, and too late in the day, to allow Malcolm to be cheapened by his death. The state-conspiracy theory is part of his monument. It is usually proposed this way:

Malcolm was harmless enough as long as he stayed in the Nation, preaching a narrow sectarian religion and holding back from the real action; he was watched and maligned by the authorities but was not actively molested. Once he quit, however, he became dangerous, beginning a promising black (or Left) revolutionary movement at home, stirring anti-American feeling in Africa, organizing a human-rights action against the United States in the United Nations. The CIA made a first attempt to kill him, by poison, in Cairo in July 1964 and was about to try again in Paris in February 1965; French counterintelligence learned of this, however, and he was barred from entering the country. The firebombing of Malcolm's home was surely not the work of the Muslims, who owned the place, and may in fact have been engineered by the state conspirators to help make Malcolm's death look like an event in his war with the Nation. Malcolm himself blamed the Muslims at first but in the end guessed at the government conspiracy against him.

The assassination itself, in this view, was ordered from Washington and carried out with the active connivance of the New York police. The police command, as part of their complicity, saw to it that Malcolm was left unprotected and that the Audubon was put under minimal guard; the two men inside with the walkie-talkie were stationed there so the department would be instantly informed when the murder had been carried out. Nobody was supposed to get caught. Hayer, a hired gun for the conspiracy, was arrested only because Malcolm's people shot him and got him first. A second suspect, probably a police agent, was seized by Patrolman Hoy, who hadn't been let in on the plot; this blunder was compounded when the papers learned of the arrest and reported it in their early editions. The agent/suspect vanished into the system, and the press was persuaded (or instructed) to forget about him. But Hayer could not be disposed of so easily and there had to be a trial. The authorities immediately announced that the Black Muslims were responsible; this was buttressed by the burning of the mosque, probably by agents, which further contributed to the popular impression that Malcolm was the casualty of a black cult war. (The conspirators may also have hoped that Malcolm's people would avenge him by killing Elijah Muhammad, thus silencing two inconvenient black men for the price of one.) In the investigation, Hayer was falsely linked with the Nation of Islam, and Butler and Johnson, both known Muslims who had already been arrested once for shooting a defector, were elected the fall guys and framed for a murder they had no part of. Leon 4X Ameer somehow caught on to the conspiracy and was about to reveal his evidence when he was strangled to death in his room. The show trial was put on; Butler and Johnson were convicted on false or unreliable eyewitness testimony, despite the fact that Hayer exonerated them; the case was closed and the true conspirators were safe.

My own research does not support this theory. My inquiry was limited by my resources, and no doubt also by my color, class, politics and a certain irremediable skepticism about conspiratorialist explanations of events where nonconspiratorialist explanations appear to be adequate. Within these limitations, I have spent a great deal of time over three years re-examining the record and interviewing people on both sides of the great divide between Malcolm's admirers and the police. (The Nation's denials that the Muslims had anything to do with the murder were already richly on the record.) I have tried to approach the question unsentimentally as to either Malcolm or the government. I began, for example, with the premise that the authorities in New York and Washington did consider him a dangerous man and that few tears were spilled in government at any level when he died. I found unsettled questions in the case and unsettling elements in the behavior of the police toward Malcolm during his lifetime—their constant and intrusive surveillance and their extraordinary detachment in the face of sound intelligence that his life was in imminent danger. But to proceed from a finding that the authorities trifled with Malcolm's civil liberties and were too casual about his life to a charge that they actually plotted his murder is a long step that requires substantial evidence and compelling logic. I found neither in sufficient quantity to discredit the official verdict—that is, that the plot against Malcolm was a Muslim plot, initiated by officially unidentified men at some officially undetermined level of authority in the Nation.

This is so even if one concedes for argument's sake that the state had sufficient motive for murdering Malcolm. My own judgment is that it did not—that its concern over Malcolm, while active, was considerably less than murderous. His activities in Africa and the United Nations were clear embarrassments to the government but embarrassments that could be handled, with money where moral suasion failed; it is worth remembering that Malcolm died pleased at having "internationalized" the black struggle but discouraged over his UN human-rights project, the first-priority business of his diplomacy. Neither was he building a revolutionary movement of great immediate menace to the state, though, given time and the help of some of those people who flocked to him only after his death, he might have. The authorities feared him in his day less as a revolutionary than as a rabble-rouser, at a point when the destructive potential of the ghetto street people was only just surfacing in the first of the Long Hot Summers. White power does contrive to take such men off the street, though not by some conspiratorial grand design and not ordinarily by murdering them; the case file from Garvey to the black radicals of the sixties and seventies—Robert Williams, Stokely Carmichael, H. Rap Brown, Eldridge Cleaver, Kathleen Cleaver, Huey P. Newton, Bobby Seale—suggests that the far more common sanctions are prison and/or exile. It does not diminish Malcolm to say that the state did not fear him enough to assassinate him; the government, one suspects, underestimated what was *really* subversive about him—not that he was inflaming the street people to burn Harlem or setting Africa against America or turning into a crypto-proto-Trotskyist but that he began transforming the consciousness of a whole new black generation.

Even if one accepts that the state was motivated to murder, one must concede the equal interest of elements of the Nation of Islam in seeing Malcolm dead. The Nation's own newspaper, *Muhammad Speaks,* called him the chief hypocrite and asserted flatly that he not only deserved to be killed but would have been if it were not the Muslim way to leave vengeance to Allah. It is true that the Muslims have not commonly buried their heretics. "They're quiet people, well behaved," Benjamin Goodman, who has never accepted the official theory, told me. "The best-behaved people I know. And they have too much to lose—they have businesses, they have women and children in the organization; they'd be risking all that. The Nation wouldn't have done it." Still, Leon Ameer was beaten and Benjamin Brown shot by men identified as Muslims, and we have Malcolm's own word that men he knew as Muslims made at least three or four attempts or direct threats on his life during his last year. There are possible alternative hypotheses for Malcolm's violent seizure in Cairo—food poisoning is the simplest—and his expulsion from France was most probably the result of French and French-African, not American, power politics. There are no credible alternative explanations for attempts or threats by Muslims, unless one accepts that the CIA or the police somehow engaged them in a murderous alliance of convenience with the devil. Malcolm himself, even in those last jangled days when he began suspecting a plot against him involving the Federal government, the police, the fire department and the press, did not stop believing that somebody in the Nation also wanted him dead for Muslim reasons—his competition for souls and his blasphemies against the Messenger of Allah. His list of suspects, which was never made available to the police, named only Muslims; Malcolm may have come to believe that somebody else had got control of them, but he never changed his mind about who would be pulling the trigger.

The real culpability of the police was not their involvement in some fantasy conspiracy against Malcolm but their cool disinterest toward the real one—a disinterest that in the end verged on outright negligence. If they had been plotting Malcolm's murder, with his feud with the Muslims as cover, they would surely have blamed the Nation for fire-bombing his home. Instead, with marvelous professional detachment, they invited the suspicion that Malcolm had fired the place himself—a line of suspicion that could only discredit the notion that a cult war with the Muslims was really going on and which pictured Malcolm instead as a paranoiac, or a publicity-seeker, or both. The police at that point were on to the gathering threat to Malcolm; their close surveillance of both sides in the vendetta had finally paid off with the discovery, or at least the strong guess, that his former brethren would shortly make an attempt on his life. Their response to this was to make pro forma offers of protection, in the full and, as it developed, accurate expectation that he could not accept them. The police did not seriously attempt to persuade him to accept protection or to force protection on him; they simply considered themselves absolved of blame for whatever happened. One tries to imagine them being so casual about a comparable threat to some other, more congenial spirit; the probability is that they would not have been.

This is not to say that the police could have saved Malcolm's life. It is true that one cannot enjoin an assassination from happening, and we have the bodies of John and Robert Kennedy as evidence that one man determined to take another's life can do so even under close security precautions. Even if he had accepted protection, Malcolm would not have wanted the protectors too close at one of his own rallies; it was one of his trusted lieutenants, indeed, who told the police that Malcolm wanted the normal sidewalk contingent placed somewhere less obtrusive on the twenty-first. This was done; one woman spectator, writing about the event later in the Baltimore *Afro-American,* reported having seen eight policemen and two police cars stationed around the Audubon when she first drove close, and none at all ten minutes later. The final deployment, given the basic decision, had its own logic: a token man at the door, two inside with a walkie-talkie as close to the main ballroom as they could get and still be out of sight, and the main force in the nearest public place, which happened to be the hospital. A large and conspicuous detail in the street would probably not have deterred the assassins anyway—the very soul of the act was its audacity—and might not have resulted in any more on-the-scene arrests, given the bedlam in the streets immediately after the shooting. But a bigger show of force at the scene might at least have contained more potential eyewitnesses, and a more activist show of concern for Malcolm's safety from the moment the threat became evident might conceivably have had some discouraging effect on the assassins. One cannot do more than guess what might have been had the police asserted a public interest in protecting Malcolm, whatever his politics, and with or without his cooperation. One can only wish that they had tried.

The Second Suspect remains a star player in most of the conspiracy theories—the "secret agent" who helped murder Malcolm, got caught by Patrolman Hoy, was packed off to the 34th Precinct and had to be dematerialized to cover his complicity in the plot. The one flaw in this is that the Second Suspect never existed; first Hoy, then Sergeant Aronoff and Patrolman Angelos all had hold of the same suspect, Talmadge Hayer, and the single collar got reported twice—a confusion of a sort familiar to every reporter who has ever covered a fast-breaking story. It is a trait of conspiratorialists to doubt everything in the establishment press except its mistakes, which are accepted on faith as the truth come accidentally to light; the mystery of the Second Suspect has accordingly survived and flourished since 1965 without benefit of serious inquiry.

The first suspect, Hayer, is anomaly enough for any state-conspiracy theory. There is reasonable ground to believe that he was or had been a Muslim, although the best single piece of evidence —the Newark membership list—was inadmissible in court. Even if one does not accept this, the alternative proposed by the conspiratorialists, that he was a hired gun for the CIA or some other state plot against Malcolm, is rather more difficult to credit. There is, for one thing, Hayer himself, a dropout from Jersey with a job in a machine shop and a bust for a kid-stuff gun burglary. ("Can you see the CIA employing *Hagan?*" said Herb Stern, who, like most people on the case, never stopped thinking of him by his wrong name. "A guy who sells Muslim papers in *Paterson?* That's not stupid—that's lunatic.") There is, for another, the high improbability that the CIA, having hired Hayer or anybody else, would have risked his getting caught by sending him out to dispatch Malcolm before several hundred witnesses and a troop of presumably loyal bodyguards. A religious murder might be transacted in such circumstances, as a lesson to the wayward in the faith. A political murder could (and one guesses would) have been done under less risky conditions—by sniper fire, say, or midnight ambush—and been blamed just as easily on the Muslims.

It is unlikelier still that the CIA, having hired a man who sold Muslim papers in Paterson and directed him to kill Malcolm in full public view, would then have suffered his survival to trial. It is said in the conspiracy literature that, because he was arrested, there *had* to be a trial. What "had to" happen is an infinitely plastic feature of assassination conspiracy theories, malleable to fit any circumstance; thus, Lee Harvey Oswald "had to be" shot and James Earl Ray "had to be" pleaded guilty, to silence them respectively about the plots against John Kennedy and Martin Luther King; thus in his turn, Hayer "had to be" tried—one guesses because he *was* tried. He didn't have to be tried at all, of course, not if one believes the state-conspiracy theory; a plot so malignant as to have murdered Malcolm and so comprehensive as to include the CIA and substantial elements of the New York police would much more likely have disposed of Hayer as well and hung the whole rap on certifiable Black Muslims who couldn't betray the real conspirators. The single hint in Hayer's courtroom confession as to who commissioned the murder—his reference to Williams's broken line of inquiry—seemed to point not at the CIA or the white power structure at all but at some fuzzy civil war among Malcolm's own people; this never got developed* and was not very persuasive in any case, given Hayer's palpable habit of incorporating whatever bits of testimony suited him into his own revised version of the events. One imagines that if Hayer were in fact the hireling of the CIA or any other non-Muslim conspiracy, and if he had somehow lived to take the stand, he (or at least his masters) would have been quite content—even eager—to see the Muslims take the blame. A Muslim or Muslim employee, on the other hand, would have done everything he could to clear them; that, of course, is precisely what Hayer tried to do.

One wonders, moreover, at a conspiracy in which one of the

*Dermody has been accused by the conspiratorialists of having deliberately cut Hayer off, presumably to suppress the truth; the charge ignores the fact that he demanded repeatedly thereafter that Hayer say straight out who hired him. I made an effort to interview Hayer in Attica prison about this among numerous other points. He sent out word that he would see me only with the assent of his new lawyer, Edward Bennett Williams. Williams declined, on the ancient and honorable tradition that the game is never over until the last appeal is exhausted. I find Williams's protectiveness perfectly reasonable, even admirable; still, it ought to be noted that it is the defense, not the state, that has foreclosed further inquiry into what the single confessed assassin might have to say about the crime.

assassins is allowed not only to live but to testify while a peripheral player, Leon 4X Ameer, must be murdered because he knows too much. Hayer might have exposed a conspiracy, or at least the middleman who approached him. Ameer's "new evidence," by contrast, materialized only after he had tried and failed to sell the media his old evidence, which was that Malcolm knew about the skeletons in the Nation's closet—its supposed romance with the Klan, for example—and that Muslims killed him to silence him. Ameer was alone, broke and wanted for embezzling Muslim funds in New Haven. When his body was found, the police noted a light froth around his mouth and guessed that he might have had an epileptic seizure. Since Ameer was not epileptic, his passing became first a "mystery death" and then a strangling. It was neither. He died of an overdose of a powerful sedative; the medical examiner's office put it down as accidental, a normal courtesy to the dead in barbiturate o.d. cases where there is no direct evidence of suicide.

There remain unsatisfying elements in the case as it was presented at trial. There is no evidence that the authorities "framed" anybody; my own belief, quite to the contrary, is that they conducted a conscientious investigation under extraordinarily difficult circumstances, the difficulties including not only the hysteria at the scene and the fears of many of the eyewitnesses but the active noncooperation of several of Malcolm's key people. The authorities, given this situation, did not always follow the police manual: they did not light the fire in the mosque, but there is ground for believing that they found out who did, and a somewhat greater degree of cooperation followed. Witnesses even then were hard to find; most hadn't seen anything helpful, and among those who had, descriptions varied wildly—a normal hazard in eyewitness cases, compounded in this one by the sheer chaos of the event. That only six eyewitnesses against Butler and four against Johnson were put on by the state is not in itself remarkable under these circumstances, nor is the fact that some of them made more credible witnesses than others. A frame-up, given the resources attributed to the supposed Malcolm murder conspiracy, would surely have been more artistic—might, for example, have included a dozen more, and more authoritative, eyewitnesses (no one could say finally who was and who wasn't at the rally) and might have found all the guns fairly oozing with the fingerprints of the accused. Instead, the prosecution took its chances with the relative handful of witnesses whose stories converged into a single, credible account; it is worth remembering that only one eyewitness who disputed any of the identifications offered himself to the defense during the investigation and trial, and his disinterest as a witness was compromised for the jury by his admission that he had gone to Captain Joseph with the story first.

There is, on the other hand, ground for believing that the case was tidied up for trial—that, since only three suspects had been arrested, the official scenario of the assassination was streamlined to include only three participants. Most of the detectives on the case believed that they had caught the three gunmen but that there was probably at least one more man in the room to help with the diversions and otherwise run interference for the killers. This squares with the version Hayer gave in his courtroom confession; one must make appropriate discounts against anything he said, given his vocation for perjury, but there was no obvious compelling reason for him to lie about this point. A four-man hypothesis also squares with the versions that the two star witnesses, Thomas and Blackwell, gave the grand jury; neither of them ever budged from his identifications of the principals, Hayer, Butler and Johnson, but their testimony at the trial rearranged them and in the process reduced the number involved to three—those three. Each offered reasons why he had told the story differently to the grand jury: Thomas his fear, Blackwell his shame at having left Malcolm undefended. It is fair also to note that their revised testimony accorded with the state's own cut-down, three-man-three-gun theory. The obvious profit in a tidying-up, if that is in fact what happened, was that the authorities would be spared the embarrassment of acknowledging that at least one member of the team that murdered Malcolm had got away and was—is—still at large. The cost was the creation of new loose ends —enough to nourish the conspiracy theory years after the event.

There are other puzzles in the state's case. The most difficult of these was how Butler and Johnson, both well-known Muslims and supposed Muslim enforcers at that, could have got past Malcolm's security guard so easily. Hayer would have been ideal for the assignment: he was, according to the state's case, a Muslim but an obscure New Jersey one whom Malcolm's people wouldn't necessarily recognize. But a lot of the brothers had come out of Mosque No. 7 and so presumably would have known Butler and Johnson on sight. The two might have been allowed in without a search like everybody else, Benjamin Goodman guessed, but they surely would have been watched—a fact that made them unlikely candidates for the job. The anomaly of this was of course not lost on the investigators; it is one of the sources of their suspicion that Malcolm was betrayed by some of his own men. Even if one does not put so sinister an interpretation on it, his security was curiously loose on the twenty-first. ("Talk about vigilance," Stern snorted, "*somebody* carried a shotgun in there.") Neither treason nor incompetence is a wholly satisfying explanation, but, so far as the state's case was concerned, no wholly satisfying explanation was required. Each man was identified, mostly by Malcolm's own people, as having been inside; therefore, said Stern, "they got in."

The make-up of the assassination team is nevertheless curious—two known Muslims and an out-of-the-way Jersey kid. The police could only offer that Butler and Johnson were in that line of work, as witness the Brown shooting, and that, as one put it, "maybe Hagan had a specialty." There was no ironclad evidence of Hayer's Muslim affiliation, not in court at any rate; the state had to rest its case on this point essentially on the spongy recollections of two witnesses plus the photographic evidence that Hayer had lied about never having set foot in the Newark mosque. (Hayer hardly helped himself with his sudden refusal to discuss the matter at all during his second appearance on the stand.) The Muslim connection itself no doubt hurt the defendants, tying them as it did to a group much maligned in the media and much feared in the larger society; the prosecution made no real effort in court to track the assassination up the Muslim chain of command, but it did keep the association constantly before the jurors.

Yet, with all the flaws, there was substantial evidence against the three men. Any lingering doubts about Hayer's guilt, reasonable or unreasonable, dissolved the afternoon he took the stand and confessed having fired at Malcolm's fallen body. Butler and Johnson were brought down by the multiple eyewitness identifications. A trial record is a bloodless thing; it can record a witness's testimony and reveal his inconsistencies, but it cannot recreate his real authority, which has to do with the chemistry between him and the jurors; in the end one can only note their verdict and surmise from it whose witnesses were the more persuasive. In the Malcolm X murder case, the state's were, inconsistencies and all. To acquit Butler and Johnson, one would have had to believe that all of them were lying or mistaken; the jury in the end chose to believe them. That the two men offered alibis was routine; Butler's was damaged by the mismatched patterns of his leg injuries before and after the event, Johnson's by the mazy contradictions in his alibi evidence. Neither was Hayer's effort to exonerate them finally persuasive. He tried perhaps too strenuously to shift the blame not only from them but from the Muslims; the jury decided he was lying.

None of this has satisfied the true disbelievers; their doubts long preceded the presentation of any evidence at all and will very likely survive anything. Those doubts were born the moment the police blamed the Muslims, in the first hour of the inquiry, and so made Malcolm a martyr to nothing nobler than the competition for the Islamic fringe of the black community. The doubters are probably right in arguing that the investigation leaped with undeliberate speed to this conclusion, to the exclusion of any other hypothesis. Other hypotheses were of course possible. I happen to doubt that the CIA theory was one of them; the CIA cannot possibly have committed all the villainies attributed to it, though it will remain open to suspicion, sometimes well founded and sometimes not, for just so long as it enjoys total secrecy and the ultimate irresponsibility that secrecy confers. Rational alternative hypotheses to either this or the Muslim theory were put forward by reasonable men; James Farmer still believes that the Syndicate may have iced Malcolm for his warring against narcotics in Harlem; Bayard Rustin, who doubts the involvement of the Muslim hierarchy, offers the additional possibilities that the murder was organized by followers of Malcolm's who feared that he was going soft on whitey or by disgraced Muslims who had been cast out of the Nation and who imagined they could get back in by taking the head of the chief hypocrite. The police, as it happened, were not striking out blindly (or conspiratorially) with the Muslim theory: the threat that BOSS had anticipated two weeks before was a Muslim threat, not a CIA or a Syndicate plot, and the investigators were quite literally following their own intelligence. Still, the judgment *looked* hasty, if nothing else, and the appearance of the thing has fed the suspicion that first the Muslims and then Butler and Johnson specifically were made the fall guys for somebody else.

There is, on the other hand, no particular reason to believe that keeping other lines of inquiry open would have led to any other conclusion. The gestalt of the investigation from the beginning, as one of the investigators put it, was that everybody *knew* it was the Muslims—not just policemen and prosecutors but Malcolm's people. *Everybody.* "They all knew what this was about," Stern said. We had met for a drink in Greenwich Village, Stern on his day off from trying former Mayor Hugh Addonizio of Newark for civic corruption. He was a *Mr. District Attorney* kind of prosecutor, young, bright, stylish and serious about his work; he was just three years out of law school when he took over the Malcolm X case but obviously precocious, and he looked authentically pained when we started talking conspiracy. "Look," he said. "Malcolm's own followers identified these guys, and they're hardly people who would ally themselves with the DA's office. Five years later they can spin this out of their minds, but his own people were the witnesses. This was not something that was spun out by me—I was just sitting there, and they were bringing in witnesses by the carload, and they all knew what it was." We kept coming back to it as more details floated into memory. "Can you see the CIA leaving a *shotgun* there?" he exclaimed once. And: "So-and-so"—he named one of the sisters who hadn't much cooperated with the investigators—"said on *television* that she recognized one of them." And: "I never talked to anybody outside my office. It was just myself and the detectives—I never spoke to *any* government person." He looked at me across the booth, wondering, I suppose, whether I was going to promote the CIA theory, too. He was at that point in his career being called antiwhite for having pushed the Addonizio case on the eve of Addonizio's re-election run against a black challenger, Kenneth Gibson, who ultimately won; he supposed that he would have been called antiblack if he had waited. "I guess," he said, smiling thinly, "you can't win."

49. The Case Is Closed

On April 14, 1966, they assembled once again before Judge Marks, the lawyers making their last futile arguments against the state's case. "I don't think," Sabbatino said, "that you have a solution here that history will support." But Marks said he thought the verdict amply justified by the evidence, and, one by one, the defendants were brought before him, first Hayer, then Butler, then Johnson; each stood mute as Marks intoned, in that carefully denatured language of the law, that they were to be confined to state prison for the period of their natural lives.

Edward Bennett Williams, the celebrated Washington lawyer, was retained "by friends and those closely related to the accused men," and an appeal was shortly taken. The central issue it raised was that T's testimony in closed court had deprived the three men of the public trial guaranteed them by the Constitution. On April 16, 1969, the New York Court of Appeals—the state's highest court—held unanimously that if a trial were otherwise open, a judge could close it during the testimony of a particular witness if this was done "for a good reason directly related to the management of the trial." Marks's decision in T's case stood this test, the court held; it found no other reversible error in the 3,600-page trial record and observed that the proof against all three defendants was "abundant." Williams had not abandoned hope when I spoke to him more than two years later, and his file on the assassination was in this sense still active. Nobody else's was. With the verdict and the appellate decision, the requirements of the law were satisfied, and so far as the People of the State of New York were concerned, the Malcolm X murder case was closed.

PART IV

Every Goodbye Ain't Gone

NEGROES:

We want to kill you, Yankee Captain.

DELANO:

Who could want to kill Amasa Delano?

—ROBERT LOWELL,
Benito Cereno

50. The Day Malcolm X Died

The day Malcolm X died, Bobby Seale, who would later be chairman of the Black Panther Party, broke six bricks in half and flung the halves at every white person he saw drive by. John Killens's teen-age daughter, who Malcolm used to say was tougher on white folks than he was, started crying and didn't quit for a month. The Mississippi Freedom Democratic Party stopped its state convention and said a prayer for his repose. Professer Lewis Michaux started composing one of his famous rhyming signs and soon had it out front of his bookstore at the Gateway to Harlem's Problems:

> MAN, IF YOU THINK BRO. MALCOLM IS DEAD,
> YOU ARE OUT OF YOUR COTTON PICKING HEAD,
> JUST GET UP OFF YOUR SLUMBERING BED,
> AND WATCH HIS FIGHTING SPIRIT SPREAD.
> EVERY SHUT EYE AIN'T SLEEP,
> EVERY GOODBYE AIN'T GONE.

But not everybody wept. The day Malcolm X died, Maya Angelou was in San Francisco, resting between Ghana and her commitment to the OAAU, and was visiting an aunt when a friend called and said, "Why'd you come back? These people are *crazy* —why else did they kill that man?" She hung up numbly, and after a while her brother came by for her. "He didn't even phone—he just came and said, 'Let's go.' I was pretty out of it. He took me into a bar and ordered a drink and said to someone, 'You see what just happened to Malcolm X?' And this guy said, 'Shit, you live by the sword, you die by the sword.' We went to another place and a guy said, 'Shit, man, he had it coming.' Today, if anybody—middle-class, boojie, *anybody*—said anything against Malcolm X, he'd be stoned. But that day my brother made me walk the gantlet through the Fillmore district [the San Francisco black quarter], and it was the same everywhere. My brother said, 'These are the people that man died for.' "

51. The Malcolm Legend

The transfiguration came about slowly, out of the traumata of the riots and the exhaustion of the movement and the final intractability of The Man, yet it *happened* suddenly; suddenly, people in ghetto storefronts and black student unions were saying "St. Malcolm" and meaning it. Little kids in Harlem and Hough and Watts wore gold Malcolm X sweatshirts and Malcolm X buttons that said, "OUR SHINING BLACK PRINCE." Black college students put on festivals on his birthday, and black public schools closed, or winked at absences, on his death day. A publicly funded college in Chicago was named after him, and another in California nearly was. A ghetto school in Philadelphia changed its name *de facto* from Benjamin Franklin to Malcolm X High, in defiance of local laws requiring heroes to be long and safely dead before their names get engraved over schoolhouse doors. There was a Malcolm X Democrat Club in Harlem, a Malcolm X Association in the military, a Malcolm X Center in nearly every inner city, a Malcolm X soul-food restaurant in New York with a menu full of pork specialties that Malcolm himself would have been forbidden by faith to go near. The Nebraska Historical Society authorized a marker near Malcolm's birthplace in Omaha. An assemblage of black community groups in Boston marched to the corner where Malcolm came too soon to manhood and christened it Malcolm X Square. A black woman officeholder in Washington waved away the Bible at her swearing-in and substituted a copy of the *Autobiography.* Malcolm's books sold in the hundreds of thousands and were required reading at dozens of universities; his recorded speeches became underground best-sellers with no promotion except word of mouth; his poster flowered everywhere, not the prophetic Malcolm of the last year but the pitiless finger-pointing Malcolm of the Black Muslims; two plays, a book of poems, even a ballet were done about him; two separate companies attempted movie biographies, with James Baldwin and Louis Lomax prominent among the relays of scriptwriters. Malcolm, to what surely would have been his own astonishment, had become a commercially tradable image. His name and face sold everything from bumper stickers to greeting cards; one white publisher spread his ghostly image over the jacket of a black writer's book with a single reference to him —a sentence that began, "Like Malcolm X, [Adam Clayton] Powell . . ."

Those who called him saint were not far off the mark: the process has been very like a beatification. It is telling that the volume of poems to Malcolm was the first work about him by black writers, and a book made up largely of eulogies by friends and acquaintances was the second; the more prosaic labor of defining what he actually stood for—collecting his speeches and analyzing his changing politics—was left almost exclusively to a white Trotskyist for a half-dozen years after Malcolm's death. Definition is for political leaders. One *celebrates* a saint; his theology is never quite so important as the legend of his life and martyrdom.

The sheer spread of the celebration would have astonished Malcolm, too. It has been joined by people who loved him when he was alive and people who were terrified of him; by nationalists and integrationists, black Marxists and black capitalists, Urban Leaguers and Black Panthers and street-gang kids with nothing but the dimmest apprehended sense that he was the *baddest;* even, *mirabile dictu,* by white folks. Whitney Young got a Malcolm X card one Christmas season from Imamu Amiri Baraka, then still LeRoi Jones; it was meant as a token of unity, which Malcolm would have approved, but the fact that a nationalist like Baraka chose his image and an assimilationist like Young showed it around with pleasure suggested how little of Malcolm was left except his blackness and his sainthood. "Lot of people now say they were his bosom buddy," one black writer told me. "You meet 'em all over —they'll say, 'I was his best friend,' or 'I was his mistress,' or 'Malcolm never pissed without consulting me first.' Course, it's very difficult for a corpse to defend himself." Or to exact commitments from those who swear fealty. It is one of the incongruities of Malcolm's sainthood that more than a million people have read his life but fewer than four hundred turned out for his last meeting. "Like Lenny Bruce," Dick Gregory said. "It's called *eulogizing.* A lot of people today swear they'd show up at the crucifixion and carry the cross. Well, the cross is in the street right now, and they not carrying it."

Malcolm's death, then, was in one sense a convenience: it meant that everybody could express devotion to him without cost and claim a piece of him without rebuttal. The tragedy of it—the private as against the public tragedy—was that his martyrdom should be part of the price he had to pay for the legitimacy he had always wanted. The assassination and the *Autobiography* were bracketing events in a year that irrevocably transformed our understanding of race in America—a year that shattered what lingered of our innocence and revealed to all of us, black and white, the furies just beneath the skin. It was the winter of Malcolm's death; the spring of the last of the grand civil-rights parades, from Selma to Montgomery, and the last of the great civil-rights victories, the Voting Rights Act of 1965; the summer when a place called Watts that nobody ever heard of before went up in flames and Martin Luther King got hooted out of the ruins and the ad hoc American majority for racial justice turned out to have been for racial justice in the South, not next door. When Malcolm's memoirs were published that autumn, America was only just getting ready to read him without the intervening scare image he and the media had created together. The book was a searing experience for whites but in the end a hopeful one: a satisfying life in which not only the hero but the enemy—white people—got redeemed. Blacks read it quite another way, as a record of white brutalities and Malcolm's triumph over them; one suspects that the last hazy passages about the brotherhood of men counted less than Malcolm's emancipation as a man—a victory of the soul so complete that, having achieved it, he didn't even need to hate whitey any more.

And now we have the Malcolm Legend, the man layered over by the myth, his gifts and flaws and passions and private ironies—his humanity—all smoothed flat and stylized, like the holy men burning coolly in a Byzantine icon. We have a Malcolm who was about to announce a program that would surely have achieved the liberation of the blacks; who had successfully begun building a revolutionary mass organization of the ghetto street people; who would shortly have converged with Martin Luther King in a mighty alliance of the black and maybe *all* the oppressed against poverty, racism and war; who was persuading black Africa to forget its distance from Harlem and its dependence on American aid and to embrace the struggle of black America as its own; who was at the very eve of bringing the United States into the dock at the United Nations and exposing its hypocrisies to the world; who was a danger to the state and finally was murdered by the state. The discouragements and disappointments have been forgotten. The promises made, or hinted at, in Africa and broken in UN Plaza. The debilitating and finally deadly war with the Nation of Islam. The wearying timidity of black leaders and black intellectuals, all but a few artists and writers, who jollied him in private *(You're saying all the things we can't)* but seldom dared stand with him where anyone white or bourgeois black might see. The rickety twin organizations, fragmenting from internal tensions and neglect, too frail in the end even to protect Malcolm's life, let alone carry out his dreams. The jangled last days, when, so some friends believed, he may have been beginning a nervous breakdown. A saint is memorialized for the miracles that happened, or might have, not those that failed; no saint can be defeated.

Malcolm's victories, as it happened, had to wait until history caught up with him. It was his mischance to have lived during the great romantic flowering of the civil-rights movement and to have died before it spent itself; he was playing "A White Man's Heaven Is a Black Man's Hell" on side-street jukeboxes while the massed chorus was singing, and almost believing, that they would overcome someday. Malcolm's rediscovery and beatification happened only with the disappointment of that dream—with the exhaustion of white will and black hopes and the gradual return to neglect, benign or malign as one prefers, as a national policy on race. It was then that Malcolm X could be celebrated, not for the brotherliness of the last days that so relieved liberal whites but for the defiant blackness of all his adult life. "Black history began with Malcolm X," Eldridge Cleaver once wrote. Hyperbole is another of the afflictions of being a saint; Malcolm himself would have been happy to count Nat Turner, say, and Frederick Douglass and Garvey and DuBois as part of his lineage. But Cleaver was, in another sense, right, if one dates one's history from the day one began writing it oneself. It was Martin Luther King who, in our generation, set black people in motion as the makers and not merely the victims of history. But the momentum was away from blackness and toward incorporation into a dream white America gone colorblind. The dream was ennobling but doomed. It was Malcolm's curse to see this before most of the rest of us; it was the beginning of his sainthood that when black Americans reached that point—when they arrived, that is to say, at their blackness—Malcolm was already there.

52. How John O. Killens Memorialized a Black Artist

"I had always thought of Malcolm as an artist," Killens said. "But an artist of the spoken word. I remember I was a writer-in-residence at Fisk University when he was killed—I had an appointment for the second semester and I came on February 1. On March 1, I spoke at a convocation, and I asked them to stand for a moment of silence for four departed black brethren. I named them slowly. 'Nat Cole . . . Sam Cooke . . . Lorraine Hansberry . . .' Half that faculty was white, but they all began getting up. '. . . And Malcolm X,' I said, and some of those people wound up squatting in mid-air."

53. Malcolm and Martin

"The sixties were defined by Martin Luther King and Malcolm X," said Ivanhoe Donaldson, a survivor of the SNCC campaigns of the early and middle years of the decade. They were almost precisely contemporaries, born black preachers' sons just four years apart, and each came into his ministry in the middle fifties, when the black revolt was only just beginning to stir into life. But they arrived from opposite directions, one out of the seminary and the other the penitentiary, and they stood at opposite poles in the national consciousness; they were Christian and Muslim, idealist and cynic, pacifist and warrior, color-blind and color-conscious, forgiving and incapable of forgiveness. The early years of the decade belonged to King—the years when the theater was the South, the issue Jim Crow and a national consensus for common decency still possible. Malcolm then was perceived as a demonic presence at the edges of our field of sight, a constant goad to King and the orthodox movement to be tougher, a constant warning to whites that unreasonable black men were waiting to move in if reason failed. Our vision was too Manichaean, too simply cast as a competition between the angel of darkness and the angel of light for possession of the black soul; what we missed in our innocence was the extent to which both of them, Malcolm and Martin, were talking about the same things—and to which both of them could set the pulse of black America racing.

Their identity of purpose was blurred for just so long as King and the mainstream movement he represented kept winning victories. King owned the popularity polls, which are the way we settle questions of success and failure. His majorities were always swollen past meaning; one searched King's poll ratings in vain for the dudes on the corners and the maids at the bus stops who grinned and waved at Malcolm on his rounds, or the strivers who sat watching him on TV in their front parlors and felt that little stab of empathy with his rage and guilt at their own comfort. They hung King's picture, but even then they heard Malcolm's voice, and came to see the two of them less as opposites than as halves in a yin-yang duality deep in the black soul. James Farmer was always struck by the fact that when he debated Malcolm before a black audience, they both got applauded, with apparently equal vigor: what counted really was not your particular politics but the fact that you were black and that you were fighting the way things were.

Malcolm's day came later, out of the ashes of the riots and the desperation they revealed in the black casbahs of the urban North; you could look at the pre-teen black kids in their Malcolm X sweatshirts, skittering in the ruins of a burnt-out street in Watts called Charcoal Alley No. 1, and almost see the Malcolm cult being born. King couldn't even go there; he attempted one peacemaking speech near the end of the rioting, was heckled mercilessly and shortly thereafter left town. His single effort at organizing a Northern ghetto against Northern-style problems failed in Chicago; one measure of his dislocation there was the fact that his Southern-bred field workers had neglected to pack for the Lake Michigan winter and had to send home for funds for thermal long johns. They knew the backwater towns and the wayside churches and the poverty of the cottonfields and the Catfish Rows. The streets were Malcolm's; he had lived there; he belonged. The destruction of the rioting would have appalled him, not because it was illegitimate but because it wasted black lives and spoiled neighborhoods where black people lived; still he would not have dissociated himself from it. It was the established leaders who addressed the street people as "you." To Malcolm, there was no such distance; they were always *you and me.*

His vision of events was street vision, cynical and mocking, sometimes even cruel, and it held him back from participation in the movement during his lifetime. He helped energize the established leaders, helped force them into a quickening militancy, but he wounded them, too. "With Malcolm," Roy Wilkins of the NAACP told me, "the only way you could judge things was whether you did the thing that was *manly,* no matter if it was suicidal or not. A prosecutor like Malcolm has to be able to put himself in the shoes of people who did the best they could under the circumstances." Malcolm couldn't. For all his sense of history, he had no sympathy for the heroes and heroines of that long middle passage in the black American past when the NAACP and the Urban League were all there was and you petitioned and sued and, yes, swallowed your pride and begged at the back door if you had to. Malcolm assumed that what was middle-class was venal and that what was polite was cowardly; he never got over that suspicion, even in his last year, when he was out of the sunless little Nation of Islam and trying his best to be ecumenical. The mainstream leaders neither forgot nor forgave what he said about them; even the radical kids, nearly to the end of Malcolm's life, rather wished that he would go away. The movement people reciprocated insult for insult, but their answer to him finally was that *they* had the bodies and the motion and the pulse of the times; *they* were out in the rush of history, where the real battles were fought and the real risks run, and he was not.

The older leaders never quit believing that, and neither did King, who more than any single man had set the forces of rebellion in motion. But the movement kids did cool off: they came into the sixties as King's children, and came out Malcolm's. The process of disenchantment was a broken one, not a revelation but a series of painful recognitions. It came out of too many knocks on the head and nights in jail, and too many funerals; out of the banner headlines when two white volunteers disappeared along with one black in Mississippi and the scanty shirttail stories when the searchers fished two mutilated black victims of another lynching out of a river; out of the gathering suspicion that the Federal government saw the events not as a moral struggle but as a contention of interests to be balanced; out of the political, social and sexual tensions between the Northern white kids who summered in the movement and the Southern black kids who would still be there when the whites went home; out of the great compromise at the 1964 Democratic Convention, when the necessity of re-electing Lyndon Johnson took precedence over the claims to justice of a little group of disfranchised black people from Mississippi; out of the creeping paralysis of the old liberal audience when the struggle moved North and got abrasive, and when ghettos started burning down; out of the discovery that "integration" was a delusive hope for the black poor in the backwater South and the inner-city North, since they didn't have the money to be mobile and, anyway, the liberals talking integration weren't talking about integrating with *them.* The movement hung on, but to the extent that its informing dreams were dying, it was dying, too. Milton Galamison, the integrationist whose school boycott Malcolm favored with a brief look-in in 1964, was arrested two years later for the ninth and last time in his civil-rights ministry; he remains an integrationist now, but he remembers a lady in Harlem watching him go off to the paddy wagon and saying there was nothing left to do but throw a brick through a window and run. "Which," Galamison said sadly, "was true."

It was roughly at that point, a year and more after Malcolm's death, that his path and the radical movement's crossed, and his real beatification began. He left his heirs little that was tangible—no viable organization, no systematic program, no one tidy body of thought. But he bequeathed them a legacy of words—the *Autobiography* and the speeches became the gospels of the new movement, along with Fanon and, later, Eldridge Cleaver—and a series of priorities. The beauty, and the worth, of blackness. The racism of white America. The legitimacy of defending oneself, by any means including violence. The irrelevance of integration for the black poor, and the self-loathing implied in begging for it. The futility of appeals to conscience in the conscienceless. The connection with Africa and the African past. The necessity of confronting power with power. The urgency of black control of the black community. It wasn't so much an ideology or a strategy for change as a style of thought; it came back to us beginning that summer of 1966 codified under a new name—Black Power—and now the sayings of Minister Malcolm have become the orthodoxies of an entire black generation.

Stokely Carmichael was Malcolm's spiritual descendant, though he ungenerously neglected to acknowledge the debt in his own book, *Black Power.* So were Rap Brown and Imamu Baraka and the Black Panthers and the insurgents who turned CORE from a mostly white integrationist group into an all-black nationalist organization in the space of a year or two. So were the ghetto militants, the kids in funky 'Fros and dashikis who came out of the remnants of the movement and the new poverty storefronts and set the angry tone of discourse about race in the late sixties and early seventies. So were the black students who seized all those buildings and called themselves Malcolm X Liberation Universities and hung out that raging poster, the eyes burning, the finger pointing, the lower lip curling back under the teeth beginning an "f"; the plain implication of the poster was *Fuck you,* and while he never would have used the language, Malcolm in those days would not have rejected the sentiment. Even some surviving integrationists, those who stayed in the movement, felt obliged to make their accommodations to the black revival—to start saying "black," and talk about *desegregation,* not integration, and reformulate their platforms around the question of power; even to make their small obeisances to the memory of Malcolm X.

There is a sport among Malcolm's admirers now, a nostalgic guessing game as to what cause, what ideology, what leaders or styles of leadership he would have identified with had he lived. In his own uncompleted search, he left bits of evidence enough for everybody of every tendency to claim a special affinity with him. Some of these claims are easily dismissed (Mecca broadened Malcolm but did not make him an integrationist) and some are less consequential than others: the bits of socialism in his late vocabulary, whatever they may have signaled about his thinking, are not an important source of his continuing influence in the black community since his death. One guesses that Malcolm would have been pleased with the emergence of Pan-Africanism as a major trend in black thought but would have been saddened at the collapse of direct diplomacy between the American and African black nations. (The most common explanation I heard for this last was that yes, Malcolm's work in Africa was terribly important, but nobody had the contacts to carry it on; neither did Malcolm, of course, until he went out and made them.) He would certainly have approved the impulse summed up in the new vogue phrase of the 1970s as "nation time"—the recognition that black America is a *de facto* nation within a nation and that black energies ought accordingly to be concentrated on its political, economic and social development independent of white beneficence and control. The Panthers believed themselves to be the true heirs; several of the party's national leaders were first turned on to the black revolt hearing Malcolm preach in the San Francisco Muslim mosque, and Bobby Seale once assured me that they had only carried Malcolm's politics to a higher level by picking up the gun, where he had merely spoken about it. Malcolm surely would have admired their nerve, their style, their ghetto roots and their rudimentary breakfast-for-children socialism; one imagines on the other hand that he would have been put off by their period of infatuation with what they called "revolutionary suicide," a formulation that rationalized their hopeless fire-fights with the police. He would have liked Carmichael for his heresies against his own nonviolent, integrationist past, and Rap Brown for that one wild kick-ass year when everybody white thought he might burn down America by himself, and Baraka for trying to move nationalism past the old breast-beating rhetoric into the hard labor of organizing a nation beginning in the Central Ward of Newark. But Malcolm wouldn't have been the exclusive property of any of them. Having once indentured his soul to a particular leader and a particular dogma, he would not have done so again. His imperative at the end of his life was his independence, his ideology the liberation of the blacks *by any means necessary.* The answer to the guessing game is that there is no single answer; Malcolm would have served no one, and would have applauded anyone honestly—sincerely—in the fight.

The grandest dream of all is the *entente noire* that might have been between Malcolm and Martin Luther King—the confluence of two great currents in contemporary black history in a single, irresistible revolutionary tide. One argues in vain that this is wishful thinking; the dream of power—even power irretrievably lost—is one of the few sustaining comforts of the powerless, and the dream of Martin and Malcolm coalescing is proposed by reasonable men not as a hope or a possibility but as a fact that was kept from happening. The argument is that, after Mecca, color alone was no longer decisive for Malcolm—that he was moving from a narrow politics of black against white to a subtler politics of the oppressed against the oppressor. King, too, had passed beyond the issues of race raised in his early campaigns to the broader problems of poverty amid affluence; he died organizing (some say *because* he was organizing) the multiracial Poor People's March to Washington and Resurrection City in 1968. The two men thus were converging in the struggle against racism and poverty, and in their precocious opposition to the war in Vietnam as well. Their intersecting views, and the deepening resistance of the white establishment, would surely have thrown them together, or so the dream runs; the possibilities, with King's global following and Malcolm's constituencies in the ghettos and in Africa, were limitless. Or would have been: the implication of the dream is that both men had to die to keep it from coming true.

It is a marvelously enspiriting vision; its flaw is that it was not going to happen. There was too much unhappy history between the two men, too many irreconcilable differences of politics and personality and soul. King's moral authority was that he asked black people to transcend their humanity; Malcolm proposed that they embrace it—that they reserve their love for one another and address white people as men have always addressed their enemies. Their goals had always been in the largest sense identical: the liberation of black people from their humiliation in white America. But the means for both of them had always been inextricably one with the end. King's politics was insistently multiracial, Malcolm's insistently black—black first even at the height of his brotherhood period. And King to the end kept his absolute commitment to nonviolence. To Malcolm, any means necessary did not include nonviolent means, not so long as the larger society was violent. He considered nonviolence beggarly, and he was too proud to beg. Resurrection City, hunkered up on the grass amid the monuments and cherry trees of Washington that late spring and summer of 1968, offended white people and frightened them but was in the end still a supplication; one tries in vain to picture Malcolm waiting among the Poor People in the A-frame shacks, hoping by the reproach of their presence to move the government to action.

That was King's thing, not Malcolm's. King's politics to the end was demonstrative; it depended on pageantry and on the existence of an audience that could be moved by pageants; it worked as long as the King/Connor dialectic worked—the confrontation of petitioner and bully before the world. When the dialectic got blurry—when the petitioners got pushy, and the villains were not cops but liberal institutions, and the distance between the players and the audience narrowed—demonstrative politics quit working.

Malcolm had never believed in it anyway—had never credited the audience with enough conscience to do anything more than scatter a few token rewards among a few "acceptable" Negroes. The politics he thought might move us was the politics of the whirlwind and the storm; Malcolm did not incite the riots, or even welcome them, but he saw them coming and saw where they were coming from, and he thought them more authentic than prayer and parading as demonstrations of black grievance. He was right for a time, as King had been; the riots brought about the judgment of a blue-ribbon commission that we are a racist society and forced some palliative spending in the ghettos. But the dialectic of rioting ultimately failed, too, once the rest of society discovered that riots occur in the black quarter and can be contained there with sophisticated police deployment and advanced weapons technology. King, of course, was against rioting from the beginning; Malcolm was, too, in his way, but on the narrow pragmatic ground that one does not burn one's own house or spill one's own blood unilaterally.

The distance between utility and morality—between Malcolm's proposition that ends justify means and King's that means and ends are one—was a vast one; the distance between the street and the seminary, between the necessities of the flesh and the imperatives of conscience, between the American reality and the American Dream. The two men saw one another across this distance, the brother on the corner and the Nobel laureate, each proud and accustomed to command. It was one measure of their separation that they patronized each other; Malcolm, at his most mannerly, said that King probably meant well sending women and children out to conquer an armed enemy with love; King, a close associate told me once, responded to Malcolm pastorally rather than politically, as if he were a soul struggling against a darkness that King had already mastered. Malcolm did look in on King's Selma campaign, and King's people did think of him dimly as somebody who might be "valuable" to them if and when they got their crusade going in the North. But the evidence suggesting that this might have led to a real alliance remains insufficient. King's people regarded Malcolm as a problem for the Selma campaign, not an asset to it, and Malcolm's pride would have demanded some larger role in a coalition than the possibility that he might be valuable to King. One need not imagine a partnership between them to honor their memory properly: it is enough that each of them was there and that each struggled according to his lights toward a more just America. History favored King while they both lived; it is King to whom we build monuments now. But somewhere since their deaths, or perhaps in them, the times ran past King and his improbable dream and caught up with Malcolm X. Harry Edwards, the black athletes' organizer, mourned both men but, like many of his generation, felt the larger debt to Malcolm. "It wasn't so much that he led in action as that he inspired action in others, even beyond the grave," Edwards said. "I suspect that won't be so true of Martin Luther King. He's dead."

54. What Became of the Lost-Found Nation of Islam

"You know more about Malcolm X than I do now," the Messenger of Allah told a visitor some months after Malcolm's death. "I don't know nothing about what he had set up. I didn't even know he had an organization." Mr. Muhammad's comfort, as it developed, was well founded. Malcolm's death, whether or not it was intended as an object lesson to his followers, functioned as one. The brothers scattered afterward, some out of discretion, some in despair. Most dropped out of the movement. A few went to Ghana, because Malcolm had made connections and been happy there, and stayed until Nkrumah fell; one was thereupon run out at the point of a submachine gun. One got caught in a stickup and was sentenced to a Southern chain gang; another, charged with a routine homicide, wounded two cops coming to take him and wound up in the pen in New York. The organizations had never been more than vehicles for Malcolm and were not strong enough to survive him. His half-sister, Ella Collins, took over the OAAU herself, announcing that this was Malcolm's wish expressed to her, and bought it a town house in a handsome block in Harlem called Strivers' Row. The sign was still up when I visited, and a full-length life-size photo of Malcolm hung in the parlor, a heart-stopping ghost in the shadows; but the OAAU's active membership had dwindled to a handful, and its most visible activities in Harlem were the annual commemorations of Malcolm's birth and death.

The Nation of Islam, by contrast, was built for survival. There were dire predictions about its future when Malcolm left, and again when he died, but it has endured and even grown in a contained way; it remains a refuge from the stresses of the world, and men and women continue to seek it, some of them doubting that the Nation was involved in Malcolm's death, some accepting that it was. The little Messenger reigned on in Chicago, where the tithes of the faithful were building a new $500,000 residence for him and only modestly less grand homes (at $350,000 each) for four of his sons and hierarchs. The Nation's interest in the return to the East diminished as its holdings in the wilderness grew. Its businesses prospered and expanded; it bought up large parcels of farmland in the Midwest and South and urban real estate in Chicago; it advertised regularly in *Muhammad Speaks* for all the personnel normally required by modern conglomerated big business, from secretaries to supermarket managers to jet pilots. The burnt-out New York mosque was rebuilt and topped off elegantly with a dome, which wowed Harlem almost past caring that a white contractor put it up. The ground-floor bookshop was probably the only one uptown where you couldn't find a copy of the *Autobiography,* Malcolm by then having been erased from the history of the Original People. The mosque, far from folding, prospered under its new management. The minister, Louis Farrakhan, who once wrote in *Muhammad Speaks* that Malcolm was worthy of death, achieved the legitimacy that Malcolm had always wanted for himself and the Nation; where Malcolm existed at the far edge of respect, Farrakhan spoke at high-school commencements and collected civic awards from the fraternal order of black policemen.

In the early 1970s, the peace of the Original People was disturbed by a new but hauntingly reminiscent series of insurgencies among some of the younger brothers, who had grown restless over the isolation and the *embourgeoisement* of the Nation; the rebels continued in their allegiance to Mr. Muhammad but complained about the diversion of tithes into executive salaries and creature comforts for the Messenger's court. The ensuing internal struggles were bitter and at intervals bloody; there was an attempt on the life of the Messenger's son-in-law, Raymond Sharrieff, and while the Nation continued to remind everybody that its people are forbidden to own guns, the police attributed at least seven deaths to the dissidence, some on each side. But these rumblings, too, quieted, at least so far as the world outside was permitted to know, and the serenity of the Last Messenger of Allah remained inviolate. "There is some little splinter group," he said, "that sometimes wants to go out for themselves and be big boys and so they take such chances sometimes and try to do something, and they stub their toes and they have to go back home and bandage them up. By that time we're back where we was."

The succession to Mr. Muhammad's throne could be schismatic, even violent; yet one imagines that the Nation, having endured more than forty years in the wilderness, will endure the transfer of power, too. Malcolm bequeathed his organization nothing but dreams, and dreams were not sufficient to keep it going after his death. But Mr. Muhammad will leave his a rich and diversified empire with a book value of $74 million; his heirs apparent are men of affairs, and one guesses that a certain sense of the common good will lead them to compose, or suppress, their differences.

55. The Malcolm Legacy

What Malcolm left his heirs was at once less tangible and more durable than wealth, or organization, or a formal 1-2-3 agenda for the salvation of black America. It does not diminish him at all to say that none of these were his particular gifts for leadership—that he had no interest in fund-raising, and too little time and concentration for the hard labor of organizing or writing a program. Neither can his contributions be measured by the conventional standards of success or failure, as King's could, say, or Roy Wilkins's or Whitney Young's. "Malcolm," said Bayard Rustin, who rather liked him across their enormous political differences, "has to be seen over and above the pull and tug of struggle for concrete objectives. King had to be measured by his victories. But what King did, what the NAACP did, what the March on Washington did, what Whitney Young did, what Roy Wilkins did, all that was for the benefit of the Southern Negro. There were no obtainable, immediate results for the Northern ghettoized black, whose housing is getting worse; who is unable to find work; whose schools are deteriorating; who sees constantly more rats and roaches and more garbage in the streets. He, because he is human, must find victory somewhere, and he finds his victory within. He needed Malcolm, who brought him an internal victory, precisely because the external victory was beyond his reach. What can bring satisfaction is the feeling that he is black, he is a man, he is internally free. King had to win victories in the real world. Malcolm's were the kind you can create yourself."

Malcolm's victories, that is to say, were private victories; and yet they were no less consequential for having been won in the soul instead of that world of legislation and negotiation and compromise—the world of affairs—that most of us think of as real. He was a force for the liberation of black people, both by the example of his triumph over the degradation of his own young manhood and by the furious war he waged on the myths and manners and polite hypocrisies of race in America. That he contributed to the education of some few whites in the process was a fact largely lost to him —the Malcolm explosion began after his death and the publication of the *Autobiography*—and was of secondary concern in any case. What interested Malcolm first was the decolonization of the black mind—the wakening of a proud, bold, impolite new consciousness of color and everything color means in white America. In his lifetime, he was called irresponsible, which pleased him; an extremist, which didn't bother him, given the justice of his cause; an apostle of hate and violence, which injured his pride and mistook his real purpose. He has passed now from one kind of caricature to another, to a kind of plaster sainthood, which does him honor, no doubt, but not justice. He was a man of human vices as well as human strengths; he could be demagogic on a platform and ruthless in a fight; he was profligate with his time and his rhetoric, at the expense of other requirements of leadership. He was not a saint, really; neither was he a strategist or a seminal thinker or even a major leader, if one defines leadership in the narrow sense of having a large and organized following under one's proximate control. Malcolm X was something more important than any of these things. He was a prophet.

He could be, as prophets often are, unreasonable; he could stretch, color, heighten, rearrange, distort and grossly oversimplify the truth; he could contradict himself from speech to speech, or sentence to sentence; he could even be wrong. In his lifetime, moreover, he was a prophet widely dishonored in his own country, which is to say black America—dishonored not only by his enemies but by those of his celebrants who discovered and announced the depth of their feeling for him only after he was dead. It was white America that forced him to the far margin of respect, but black Americans left him there, with his few score followers and that vast silent sympathy he felt but could never utilize. There are traces of guilt in some of the breast-beating over Malcolm now;

some of the cult are children who were too young to have known him alive, but some are grownups for whom he was a discomfort in life, like an unhappy memory or an unquiet conscience. Malcolm would have traded the poems and the eulogies for commitments when they still counted for him—when his ministry and even his life depended on them. He didn't get them then, but that is the way with prophets, too; they live in their scriptures and their heirs.

What was prophetic in Malcolm's ministry was a way of seeing. Marcus Garvey anticipated some of it, and Elijah Muhammad taught him a lot of it. But Malcolm transmuted it and combined it with an intuitive genius for modern communications—he was the first of the media revolutionaries—and it was he in catalytic chemistry with his times who really began the difficult passage from Negro to black consciousness. Semantics was Malcolm's hang-up: he placed enormous importance, probably too much, on terminology, as though by redrawing the map one actually could alter the territory. He argued that the name "Negro" was itself a prison—that it disconnected black people from their land and their history and turned them into denatured, deracinated objects rather than men. It was, he said, as if "you and I didn't exist before we came over here to America; or if we did exist, we must have been on such a savage level, or low level, that there was no record of our having existed anywhere." Now, when the name "black" is common to everybody from the Republic of New Africa to the *New York Times,* it is easy to forget how revolutionary Malcolm's argument was only a few years ago. Even the Muslims then shrank from their blackness in sad little ways—said "the East," not "Africa," and resented being called *Black* Muslims and lived almost a parody of the American white petit-bourgeois life style. It was a conscious political act in those days to call oneself black, a breach with settled habit—not even Malcolm always remembered to say "so-called Negro"—and an affirmation of a word and a color that had been a humiliation in the past. Now, almost everybody does it; it is regarded as a sign of regressive politics or advancing age to call oneself "Negro"; "black" has become the word of habit, and while it has not altered the material condition of the people who wear it, it is at least the beginning of an altered perception of oneself and one's world.

The old perception was the suspicion that the world—the white world—must surely be right; that the condition of black people was somehow a judgment upon them. The core of the Malcolm legacy was that, having been there, he understood the final degradation of self-hatred. "We hated our head, we hated the shape of our nose—we wanted one of those long, *dog*-like noses, you know. Yeah. We hated the color of our skin. We hated the blood of Africa that was in our veins. And in hating our features and our skin and our blood, why, we had to end up hating ourselves. . . . Our color became to us a chain. We felt that it was holding us back. Our color became to us like a prison which we felt was keeping us confined . . . and it became hateful to us. It made us feel inferior. It made us feel inadequate. It made us feel helpless. And when we fell victims to this feeling of inadequacy or inferiority or helplessness, we turned to somebody else to show us the way." The single, central object of Malcolm's ministry was to reverse that—to reveal to black people their own beauty and worth and competence to find their own way. The point was self-esteem, an assertion of size and place and what Martin Luther King called *somebodyness*. Everything else in his politics was an elaboration of this inner purpose. The fallacy of the Malcolm myth is that it requires one to believe that Malcolm really was going to organize the unorganized, and bring the UN down on America, and make the revolution. The fact is that the success or failure of his particular enterprises was almost beside the point. He was dealing, as he recognized himself, in symbolic action; he was attempting the liberation of black men by altering the terms in which they thought and the scale by which they measured themselves.

"Malcolm was the first of the contemporary black revolutionaries," C. Eric Lincoln said. He was a revolutionary without an army, or an ideology, or any clear sense of how the revolution was to be waged and what it would do if it won. Malcolm, instead, was a revolutionary of the spirit, which is the most subversive sort of all; he was interested less in overthrowing institutions than in undermining the assumptions on which our institutions have run. His genius was not policy but polemic. He brought the case for the prosecution; he said the things that black people had been afraid to say, even to think, for all those years; he got it all out in the open, the secrets and the guilts and the hypocrisies that underlay the public mythology of the melting pot. A lot of it got lost in his scare image, in which he was not wholly blameless, and a lot more in the *ad hominem* attacks against him: we have progressed as a civilization from murdering the bearers of bad news to describing them in our wire-service dispatches and six o'clock newscasts as "controversial." But he forced us to respond to him even then—forced white people to examine their consciences and black people to confront their color—and to that extent he won. It was heretical when Malcolm called America a racist society, but a mostly white, entirely middle-class Presidential commission affirmed it a scant three years after his death, and now it has become a commonplace. The keepers of America's public conscience are its city editors, and their threshold of boredom is low; you can't make the papers calling America racist any more.

It wasn't news to black people even then: their excitement at Malcolm was not so much over the message as over his audacity in delivering it. "He was the first to talk about the size of the elephant on my toe," Dick Gregory said. It was a white elephant. Malcolm's view of the world got subtler in his last year, and the harsh blacks and whites of his politics took on shadings of gray. But the beginning of his appeal was that he identified white people as the devil, and his continuing authority was that he never quit thinking of whites in the large as the enemy. "I don't judge a man because of his color," he said late in his life. "I get suspicious around a lot of [white people] and cautious around a lot of them—from experience. Not because of their color, but because of what experience has taught me concerning their overall behavior toward us." For white people who sentimentalize the Malcolm of those last days—who imagine that he was becoming a liberal or an integrationist or an ecumenical Marxist revolutionary—it is instructive to listen to his taped and recorded speeches before black audiences. It is the shots at whitey, not the apologetic little asides about brotherhood, that evoke the startled, happy cries and the thunderclaps of applause. Malcolm may have come to regard this as a prison at the end, but it was a prison he constructed for himself, and he had either to inhabit it or to find a whole new audience. The point of Malcolm, the root of his continuing influence, is that he knew the enemy. It is not the letters from Mecca or the little fragments of dialectic that the kids around the black student unions and the Harlem poverty storefronts quote at one another; it is the "Message to the Grass Roots," from Malcolm's last months as a Black Muslim, when whites were still the undifferentiated enemy and the proper objective of the black revolution was not integration but land.

That Malcolm could convey the depths of black rage to white people with civility and even charm—that he could call you and your kind devils conversationally with nothing personal about it—was not really paradoxical. Hatred, for him, was abstract, a point of principle; he responded to particular white people as politely, or as belligerently, as they behaved toward him. At some point in his life, feeling hate became a necessity for him no longer; he still enjoyed outraging white people, but his main purpose was to let us know that hatred existed and, more important still, to demonstrate to black people that they would not be struck dead for expressing it—that they could even make whitey shiver in his boots a little. King appealed to their higher instincts, Malcolm to their viscera; he asked them not to sublimate their resentments but to recognize and express them, to turn their hatreds outward against the enemy instead of inward against themselves. "He was a kind of alter ego for people who were too vulnerable and too insecure to say what they really felt regarding our situation in America," Eric Lincoln said. "He wanted them to understand the inconsistencies between what the white man said and what the white man did, and to prove by these inconsistencies that there was no magic in being white. He was trying to strip the white man of his mystique, and that made him a demagogue for most white people."

It made him an authentic folk hero for blacks, and it was they to whom Malcolm primarily addressed himself. His supreme gift to them was that he loved them; that he believed in their beauty and their possibilities and tried to make them believe, too. He recognized the inner despair of Harlem in its dropouts, its welfare lines, its muscat drunks, its terrifying rates of addiction and crime; he knew that white people made Harlem, but he understood that only black people and black pride could save it. The restoration of that pride, that ruined *amour-propre*, was his mission. He made substantial contributions to what is now orthodox Black Thought —the stresses on land, power, community control, national identity, Pan-Africanism, the right to self-defense—and his utterances on these subjects are invoked today as priests invoke God and revolutionaries invoke Lenin. But his more important legacy was his example, his bearing, his affirmation of blackness—his understanding that one is paralyzed for just so long as one believes one cannot move.

His politics was his blackness. To see him in conventional terms is to judge him a failure, since most of the formal tasks he set himself never got done; his victories were the victories of an evangelist, not a general or a politician. The real meaning of his diplomacy was not whether he would have won or lost in the UN but that he found his own connection with the larger nonwhite community beyond America and wanted to share it—to make black Americans feel the exhilaration of being part of the ascendant majority of the world. His insistence on reading black history was full of exaggerations and chauvinisms, most of which he recognized and laid on anyway; to be dissociated from one's past, he said, was to believe "that we were always this way." His real objection to integration was the standard of worth it implied; it suggested that there was something ennobling in being around whites, and it demanded that blacks make themselves "acceptable" to whites as the price of admission. Land was the metaphor for his nationalism nearly to the end of his public life, but his larger purpose was making an ethnic group—a *community*—out of a scattered and atomized population of the grandsons and granddaughters of incompletely emancipated slaves. Even his veiled appeals to armed violence had less to do with guns than with manhood. "I don't believe we're going to overcome [by] singing," he said. "If you're going to get yourself a .45 and start singing 'We Shall Overcome,' I'm with you." What Malcolm got was a tear-gas pen, and that only in the desperation of his last hunted days; he talked about .45s because he wanted all of us, black and white, to understand that the .45 may be the legitimate last resort of people for whom there is no other redress.

Because the message was for those of us who are white, too; Malcolm belonged to black people, but the second purpose of his ministry was to let white people know exactly how rough it could get. The message was that we could neither define nor control the black leadership by inviting those who most closely resembled us to the White House; that we were deluding ourselves no less than black people with the fiction of integration, when it took a small army to put one black man in the University of Mississippi and when the sprawl of suburbia attested to the distance even liberal whites wanted to put between themselves and ordinary blacks; that our insistence that blacks address us nonviolently was incongruent with our own violent history, from Lexington and Concord to Seoul and Saigon; that the ruin white America had visited on the blacks was about to be returned to us, out of the explosive anger of our inner cities; that maybe a lot of black people imitated us, and maybe some even loved us, but in the back alleys of our consciousness, there were people who hated us in direct proportion as we despised them; that, yes, there were black men and women who would rejoice in our death. Malcolm, much as he scoffed at the notion of the odds against so small and frail a minority, did not seriously believe that the death of The Man could be achieved and would probably have shrunk from the bloodletting; he only wanted us to confront the reality that, in some fraction of the black American nation, the wish was there and that parades and pageants and marches on Washington were not an adequate surrogate experience. We called him irresponsible for saying so; he left us Watts and Newark and Detroit as his evidence. We protested that we were making progress; he responded by quoting to us what Lumumba told the King of Belgium—*We can never forget these scars.*

He spoke to whites, that is, as a man of pride; a man trying to waken both the colonists and the colonized out of the habits of mind of the colony. And now we live in the America Malcolm was warning us against. Riots have become a normal condition of our urban native quarters; we may flatter ourselves that they have ended when it is only that we have got bored with reading about them. A good deal of desegregation has been transacted in the South with minimal "integration" anywhere; we live more irrevocably than ever in two distant and mutually paranoid Americas, the one anticipating genocide, the other the black revenge. The policy of the Presidency of the United States has returned to "separate but equal" under the guise of opposition to school busing. The series of events of the sixties that we identified as the Second Reconstruction threatens now to collapse as the first did, in the exhaustion of will before the stubbornness of the opposition and the complexity of the task. Liberals have embraced other, more grateful minorities; the young have rushed on to other, more romantic causes. White intellectual fashion has shifted from the condition of the blacks to the complaints of white Middle America; it is stylishly "tough-minded" once again, as it was in the late nineteenth century, to discuss the possible genetic inferiority of black people as though they were not sentient human beings or were not in the room. *(The servant sees the master, but the master does not see the servant.)* Black intellectual fashion has retreated into the myths and shibboleths of "nationhood"; it is a garrison state of mind, suspicious and isolationist, heavy with the rhetoric of revolution. White people are terrified of black crime; black people catch the brunt of it, and of the casual violence of the police as well. And somewhere a piece of the American Dream has got lost. It is that part that had to do with the melting pot; for the great mass of black people, it simply has not worked out.

In the last month of his life, Malcolm did one of those radio talk shows on which he squandered so much of his ministry; he was then in the full flowering of what we imagined to be his brotherhood period, and a woman caller took him up on it—asked him whether, if white people held out their hands to him, he would take them in the same generous spirit. And Malcolm flared in his blackness. "I don't think that *I* should be asked whether if whites hold out their hands to me, will I take *their* hand. You're putting the burden on me. I should think you'd ask white society to do something *meaningful.*" It was no more possible to buy Malcolm with kindness than it was with money or promises; America's hand, in any case, did not go out, not in Malcolm's lifetime, and Malcolm did not believe in unrequited love. And so he lived out his days at that desperate outer edge of the nation's life where salvationists compete for the souls of the damned with strange gods and bitter gospels, and sometimes with guns. America's complicity in his death was that when he tried to move back from that margin, there was no place for him to go. We are the smaller as a nation for having consigned him there. We are the less as a people for having lost him.

56. The Death of Malcolm X

Charles Kenyatta lives at that margin still, and is trying to keep the flame. "I walked with Malcolm," he said. "I walked with him when nobody else would. When the leaders denied him—wouldn't be seen with him on the streets. I felt I really knew who Malcolm were. He didn't know who he were himself. He was almost like a Christ child—see, he was in the East at the age of thirty-nine, and Martin Luther King was in the West at the age of thirty-nine. I thought that was interesting—almost like Islam and

Christianity was battling. And now you hear everybody saying 'Malcolm, Malcolm, Malcolm,' but they selling a lot of woof tickets. They really make the white man think they're going to do things when they're not." Kenyatta tried in his way; he took Jomo Kenyatta's name, because Malcolm had met and liked him, and organized a Harlem Mau Mau, because Malcolm had said in a lot of speeches that that ought to be done. The Mau Mau was never much more than Kenyatta speaking from a stepladder at 125th and Seventh with a grown-out 'Fro and a Bible folded around a machete and a few young followers, and once he got shot by somebody else who lives on the margin; when I saw him, a fragment of bullet was still lodged inoperably in his coronary artery, but he planned to be out on the ladder again when the weather turned nice, because Malcolm would have wanted that, too.

One day not long after they buried Malcolm, Kenyatta went back out to be at his grave. "Black peoples," he said, "do not take care of their dead. You can go to any graveyard and find it rundown—overrun by weeds and everything. People who can't look out for the dead certainly can't look out for the living." Malcolm's grave was just like all the others. Kenyatta looked at the weeds and leaves and litter, and an old black saying came into his mind: *The dead know what the living is doing but the living do not know what the dead is doing.* He glanced at the marker that said EL-HAJJ MALIK EL-SHABAZZ. Then he bent over and began pulling up weeds.

Notes on Sources

This book is intended as an original work of biography. I have tried therefore to avoid duplicating material readily available elsewhere. My primary sources have been previously unpublished interviews with Malcolm, including my own and several others that have been made available to me; my nearly one hundred interviews with friends and associates of Malcolm's and with others whose lives intersected with his; several additional interviews conducted for me by *Newsweek* colleagues in Europe and Africa; perhaps thirty hours of tape recordings of Malcolm's speeches, interviews, debates, radio and television appearances; various unpublished notes and memoranda assembled by Helen Dudar and colleagues for a New York *Post* series on Malcolm and the Muslims; various unpublished reporting in the files of *Newsweek*; and the generously shared recollections of a number of colleagues who covered Malcolm, the Muslims and what used to be known as the race beat.

Still, there is a large and growing literature about Malcolm; I read most of it in my three and a half years working on this project; I have drawn directly on some of it, and, in a larger sense, this book, like any other, is the sum of all the influences on it. One begins with *The Autobiography of Malcolm X* (Grove Press, 1965), which is an authentic American classic not only for itself but for a particularly affecting afterword—a memoir of Malcolm by his collaborator, Alex Haley. I have drawn minimally on the *Autobiography* as a direct source, on the theory that my book ought not to duplicate it even where it overlaps; even so, it has been an important influence. The only other full-length biography is the late Louis Lomax's *To Kill a Black Man* (Holloway House, 1968), actually a joint treatment of Malcolm and Martin Luther King; it has passages of interesting gossip—Lomax was one of the best-wired men I ever met—but is essentially a paperback quickie, with all the normal vices of that form. George Breitman's *The Last Year of Malcolm X* (Merit Publishers, 1967) is an ingeniously done Marxist analysis, purporting to show that

Malcolm was evolving into a prosocialist, anticapitalist revolutionary particularly friendly with the Trotskyist Socialist Workers Party. My own feeling is that the book is too narrow and schematic a treatment of Malcolm's lively and free-running intelligence; it has, in any case, caused his family and friends some pain. (In the course of our several conversations as to why she would not sit for an interview for this book, Malcolm's widow, Mrs. Betty Shabazz, said little that was substantive but did tell me firmly, "Malcolm was *not* a socialist.") *Malcolm X: The Man and His Times* (Macmillan, 1969) is a selection of pieces about Malcolm and speeches by him, edited by a distinguished black scholar, John Henrik Clarke. The pieces, with a few exceptions, tend to the abstract and elegiac; I found the book most interesting for its selection of speeches and interviews and for one marvelous (though misdated) taped conversation between Malcolm and two FBI agents. *From The Dead Level: Malcolm X and Me* (Random House, 1972), an interesting memoir of Malcolm by a cousin-in-law, Hakim Jamal, appeared after this book was completed.

A large number of Malcolm's speeches are available in print and on LP records. The most valuable collections are one edited by Benjamin Goodman, *The End of White World Supremacy* (Merlin House, 1971), drawn from Malcolm's last year in the Nation of Islam, and two edited by Breitman, *Malcolm X Speaks* (Merit Publishers, 1965) and *By Any Means Necessary* (Pathfinder Press, 1970), both consisting of speeches, interviews and papers drawn almost exclusively from the year between his break with the Nation and his death. Several speeches are also available in pamphlet form; most of these duplicate selections in the two Breitman anthologies, but *Malcolm X on Afro-American History* (Pathfinder Press, 1967 and 1970) is an excellent additional sample of the Malcolm style. *The Speeches of Malcolm X at Harvard* (William Morrow, 1968) is another useful anthology, though a long introductory essay by the editor, Archie Epps, rather engulfs the three speech texts. Lomax appended a sampling of Malcolm's Muslim speeches, plus an important interview from the suspension period, to his *When the Word Is Given . . .* (World, 1963). A partial text of Malcolm's 1964 speech at the University of Ghana appears in *Where To, Black Man?* (Quadrangle, 1967), by Ed Smith, a sometime Peace Corpsman who was there.

The recorded speeches have unfortunately not had the wide circulation they deserve; they are staples in black and Left bookshops and on some campuses but are relatively scarce elsewhere. By far the best is the *Message to the Grass Roots* (Afro-American Broadcasting Co., 1965), the brilliant late Muslim speech that remains Malcolm's most quotable and most quoted; a transcription is available in *Malcolm X Speaks*, but, like most of Malcolm's talks, it is immeasurably better in the listening than in the reading. The runner-up is *Ballots or Bullets* (First Amendment Records), a version of Malcolm's standard road speech in the period immediately after his break with the Nation. Among the others are *Malcolm X Speaking* (Ethnic Records); *Malcolm X Speaks Again* (Twenty Grand Records); *Malcolm X Talks to Young People* (Douglas International), a recording of his chat with a group of young civil-rights volunteers from Mississippi in December 1964; and *Malcolm X: The Last Message* (Discos Hablando, undated), which was not quite the last, actually, but close enough—the sad, wandering Detroit speech the night after Malcolm's home was fire-bombed. The radio and TV stations I canvassed had by and large not saved tapes or transcripts of Malcolm's frequent talk-show appearances, but a number of his followers taped them at home, and some of these were made available to me. I am also greatly indebted to my friend Claude Lewis for a tape of an enormously moving interview with Malcolm in his doom-haunted last days.

The best published interviews, apart from those anthologized in the collections mentioned above, are in Kenneth Clark, *The Negro Protest* (Beacon, 1963), a TV conversation from Malcolm's later Muslim years; *Playboy Interviews* (Playboy Press, 1967), a 1963 talk with Haley, who became Malcolm's collaborator; Robert Penn Warren, *Who Speaks for the Negro?* (Random House, 1965); and Pierre Berton, *Voices from the Sixties* (Doubleday, 1967), the early 1965 interview on Canadian TV during which Malcolm announced, among other accesses of fraternal feeling, that intermarriage was all right with him. The cream of the journalism about Malcolm during his lifetime includes various articles by Helen Dudar in the New York *Post*, especially her April 1964 series, "The Muslims and Black Nationalism," from which Malcolm said he had learned things he hadn't known before; intermittent spot-news pieces by M. S. Handler in the *New York Times*, 1963–65, especially on the break, the letters from Mecca and the UN project; a series by Tom Topor in the Bergen (N.J.) *Record* in June 1964; late interviews with Theodore Jones in the *New York Times*, February 22, 1965, with Marlene Nadle in the *Village Voice*, February 25, 1965, and with Gordon Parks in *Life*, March 5, 1965; profiles by Joseph T. Friscia in *Saga*, July 1962, and by Hans J. Massaquoi in *Ebony*, October 1965. There are interesting spot pieces by George Plimpton on Malcolm's visit to the Muhammad Ali fight camp, in *Harper's Magazine*, June 1964; by Abram V. Martin on his visit to Nigeria, in the *New Leader*, June 22, 1964; by *Jet* on his look-in on the Selma campaign, March 11, 1965; by the editors of *Ramparts* on the CIA's involvement in financing James Farmer's post-Malcolm tour of Africa, June 1969. Malcolm's treatment in the New York daily press, with the exceptions noted above and a few others, was on the whole ragged. Only the Trotskyist newspaper, *The Militant*, and Harlem's weekly, the *Amsterdam News*, covered him regularly and attentively. *Muhammad Speaks* did, too, for a time, mainly while Malcolm himself was editing it; he slid from its columns thereafter until the break, then re-emerged as "the chief hypocrite" with more space in some issues than he ever got when he was the Nation's pre-eminent public spokesman.

Malcolm is a principal player in the literature about the Black Muslims, most of which was written before the break; it is regrettable that scholarship and journalism have lost interest in the Nation since the departure of its most charismatic single leader. The best of the Muslim books is still C. Eric Lincoln's seminal *The*

Black Muslims in America (Beacon, 1961). E. U. Essien-Udom's *Black Nationalism* (University of Chicago, 1962) profited from his apparently freer access to the life of the little Nation, but Lincoln's work is full enough in detail and is enriched not only by Lincoln's intelligence but by his black American perspective. Lomax's Muslim book is a lighter-weight treatment, useful mostly for its selection of Malcolm's speeches. There is considerable journalism about the Nation; the most distinguished single piece is Morroe Berger's "The Black Muslims," in *Horizon*, Winter 1964, though a number of other interesting appraisals have appeared, in *Life* (by Gordon Parks), *The Reporter* (by Nat Hentoff), the New York *Herald Tribune* (by Robert Bird), *Trans-action, Newsweek, Time* and the *Saturday Evening Post* among others. All Muslimologists are in debt to Erdmann D. Beynon, who discovered the Nation twenty years ahead of anybody else and described it in *The American Journal of Sociology* for May 1938. Among Mr. Muhammad's own books, the most important are *The Supreme Wisdom* (The University of Islam, undated), intended principally for use within the movement, and *Message to the Blackman in America* (Muhammad Mosque of Islam No. 2, 1965), made up mostly of occasional pieces and cuttings from speeches and radio sermons. Bernard Cushmeer's *This Is the One: Messenger Elijah Muhammad, We Need Not Look For Another!* (Truth Publications, 1971) is an extended answer by a true believer to Mr. Muhammad's critics, including, almost as an afterthought, Malcolm X. *Muhammad Speaks* is the best continuing source of information about the Nation, although in recent years it has tended to focus less and less on news of the Original People and more and more on the world outside. Howard M. Brotz's excellent *The Black Jews of Harlem* deals only briefly with the Nation but is helpful in illuminating the impulses underlying it. The best published sources on Marcus Garvey, who was a spiritual ancestor to both Mr. Muhammad and Malcolm, include Garvey's own *Philosophy and Opinions of Marcus Garvey*, first published in 1923 and 1925 and now available in an Atheneum paperback; his widow Amy Jacques-Garvey's *Garvey and Garveyism* (A. Jacques-Garvey, 1963); E. D. Cronon's *Black Moses* (University of Wisconsin, 1955); and Theodore G. Vincent's *Black Power and the Garvey Movement* (Ramparts, undated).

Much of the literature about Malcolm since his death tends to be eulogy; some of it is eloquent (my own feeling is that Ossie Davis's brilliant funeral oration rather retired the trophy), but its utility is limited. There are, however, interesting chapters, sections or thoughts about Malcolm in Eldridge Cleaver's *Soul on Ice* (McGraw-Hill, 1968) and *Eldridge Cleaver: Post-Prison Writings and Speeches* (Random House, 1969); in LeRoi Jones's *Home: Social Essays* (William Morrow, 1966); in I. F. Stone's *In a Time of Torment* (Random House, 1967); in *Anyplace But Here* (Hill & Wang, 1966), by Arna Bontemps and Jack Conroy; in James Farmer's *Freedom—When?* (Random House, 1965); in Albert B. Cleage, Jr.'s *The Black Messiah* (Sheed and Ward, 1968); in Leslie Alexander Lacy's *The Rise and Fall of a Proper Negro* (Macmillan, 1970) and "African Responses to Malcolm X," anthologized in *Black Fire* (William Morrow, 1968), edited by LeRoi Jones and Larry Neal; in Bobby Seale's *Seize the Time* (Random House, 1970); in Calvin Hernton's *White Papers for White Americans* (Doubleday, 1966); in Michael Abdul Malik's *From Michael de Freitas to Michael X* (André Deutsch Ltd., 1968); in Floyd Barbour, editor, *The Black Power Revolt* (Extending Horizons, 1968); and in Brother Imari, *War in America: The Malcolm X Doctrine* (The Malcolm X Society, 1968). In the journals, the noteworthy posthumous appraisals include John Illo's "The Rhetoric of Malcolm X," in *Columbia University Forum*, Spring 1966; Barrett John Mandel's "The Didactic Achievement of Malcolm X's Autobiography," in *Afro-American Studies*, March 1972; and Robert Penn Warren's "Malcolm X: Mission and Meaning," in the *Yale Review*, December 1966. An interesting exchange between Cleage and Breitman is available in pamphlet form as *Myths About Malcolm X* (Merit Publishers, 1968).

There has been no serious reporting on Malcolm's death and the ensuing investigation and trial, except for what appeared in the daily and weekly press at the time. Beyond these accounts, the single useful source on paper is *People v. Thomas Hagan et al.*, the 3,600-page record of the trial. The *Autobiography* and a piece by one of the brothers, Earl Grant, in *Malcolm X: The Man and His Times* both contain detailed and helpful accounts of Malcolm's last week, but neither is very strong on the assassination itself. The principal conspiratorialist treatments are Eric Norden's "The Murder of Malcolm X," in *The Realist*, February 1967, and *The Assassination of Malcolm X* (Merit, 1969), a selection of articles from *The Militant* by Breitman and Herman Porter. Breitman-Porter is the soberer, Norden the more fanciful; both are wanting in objective reporting and both accordingly are stuck with the fictitious Second Suspect as the major single piece of "evidence" of a state conspiracy.

My major single source has been my interviews, conducted between late 1968 and early 1972. These are clearly identified in the text. I regret that some quoted material is not attributed to interviewees by name. The blind quote is one of the vices of our journalism. But much of my reporting was done in two highly suspicious communities, the ghetto and the police department; it therefore became necessary to accept some material—more than I would have liked in more relaxed circumstances—on a not-for-attribution basis.

More detailed citations follow:

Page

PART I. Matters of Color

3. Malcolm

9 *America's problem is* us: Recording, *Message to the Grass Roots;* also in Breitman, ed., *Malcolm X Speaks* (hereafter *MXS*), p. 4.
Your father isn't here . . . : Breitman, ed., *By Any Means Necessary* (hereafter *BAMN*), p. 123.
11 *I'm not going to sit . . . :MXS,* p. 26.
13 *Like Samson, I am ready . . . :* Lomax, *When the Word Is Given . . . :* p. 207.
14 *This is the thing . . . :* Claude Lewis interview, December 1964.
When a man is hanging . . . : Debate with Bayard Rustin, Community Church, New York, January 1962.
16 *You don't stick a knife . . . :* Panel discussion on WNDT-TV, New York, 1963.
17 *He got the peace prize . . . :* Claude Lewis interview.
18 *. . . was created by them and by me . . . :* Marlene Nadle interview, *Village Voice.*
22 *During slavery, there were two kinds . . . :* Bayard Rustin debate.
24 *When I speak . . .* : Recording, *Ballots or Bullets.*
Anything that's paradoxical . . . : Claude Lewis interview.
25 *The servant sees the master. . .* : A stock turn of Malcolm's; I heard it from him in an interview in August 1962.

4. Malcolm Descending

The discussion of Malcolm's early years here and in the sections immediately following is influenced by the *Autobiography* but not drawn from it except where directly indicated. Among my major sources were my own interviews and brief correspondence with Malcolm. I am also indebted to the New York *Post,* Kenneth Clark, *Playboy, Ebony* and *Saga* interviews listed above.
27 Garvey quotation: *I asked, "Where . . ." : Philosophy and Opinions,* II, p. 126.
28 Garvey quotation: *After my enemies are satisfied . . . : Ibid.*, pp. 238–39.
29 *They didn't have too many Negro doctors . . .* : Claude Lewis interview.
31 *The cops in Harlem . . .* : Interviews with Al Ellenberg, New York *Post,* March–April 1964.
32 *Things were getting too hot . . . : Ibid.*
The cops caught us . . . : Ibid.
The judge told me . . . : Ibid.

Page

5. The Devil in the Flesh

33 *Them. White people are the devil . . . :* The *Autobiography*, Grove paperback edition, p. 159.

6. Allah in Paradise Valley

The material on Muslim doctrine comes largely from my own interviews with Muslims and former Muslims over a dozen years and my readings in the word according to Messenger Muhammad. The Lincoln and Essien-Udom studies both contain excellent longer synopses.

36 Mr. Muhammad quotation: *Who are you . . . : Message to the Blackman in America*, p. 17.

7. The History of the End of the World

41 Baldwin quotation: . . . *no more indigestible than . . . : The Fire Next Time*, p. 64.

44 *In that quiet of death . . . :* Brecht-Weill, *The Threepenny Opera*, Marc Blitzstein translation.

8. Malcolm Redux

46 *The Honorable Elijah Muhammad teaches us . . . :* Panel discussion on Radio Station WOR, New York, October 1962.

48 *I am not the author . . . :* Fragment of a radio tape; I was unable to ascertain the show or the station, though the date appears from internal evidence to be mid-1962.

9. Harlem

53 Nationalist speaker quotation: *Why, with all the hell you caught . . . :* Tape recording lent me by Charles Kenyatta.

55 Malcolm's housing and expense-account arrangements with the Nation are detailed in *Muhammad's Temple of Islam Inc.* v *Malcolm X Little*, the record of the eviction suit.

10. The Parable of Hinton Johnson

Other versions of the Hinton Johnson story appear in the *Autobiography*, in

Page

Benjamin Goodman's introduction to *The End of White World Supremacy* and in Lomax's books, *When the Word Is Given . . .* and *To Kill a Black Man.*

59 Some of Goodman's background appeared in the Helen Dudar series in the *Post.*

63 *Anybody who's effective . . . : The Barry Gray Show,* Radio Station WMCA, New York, April 11, 1964.

64 *People don't need to sign up . . . :* Claude Lewis interview.

12. Strangers in a Strange Land

66 *What you don't realize . . . :* Radio discussion on *Program PM,* WINS, New York, June 13, 1963.

67 *These aren't white people . . . :* Goodman, ed., *The End of White World Supremacy,* p. 57.

Historically, I think . . . : 1963 WNDT television panel.

We don't think that any whites . . . : Ibid.

68 *How can anybody ask us . . . :* Goodman, ed., *The End of White World Supremacy,* pp. 79–80.

69 *You can't solve a problem . . . : The Barry Gray Show,* Radio Station WMCA, New York, September 30, 1962.

Before Negroes came here . . . : 1962 Bayard Rustin debate.

70 *The only way we could be made slaves . . . :* Speech in the Boston mosque, 1961.

Usually the criminal . . . : 1962 Bayard Rustin debate.

71 *When you begin to think . . . : The Barry Gray Show,* Radio Station WMCA, New York, March 1963.

If you'll notice, whenever I refer to America . . . . 1962 Bayard Rustin debate.

. . . founded by white Europeans . . . : Program PM, WINS, 1963.

The founding fathers . . . : 1961 Boston mosque speech.

You got a gorilla on your back . . . : A Harlem street rally, summer 1962.

72 *They want your wife . . . :* 1962 Bayard Rustin debate.

If all of the token integration . . . : Taped radio program, spring or summer 1963.

73 *The man who tosses worms . . . : Playboy Interviews,* p. 39.

After the black man who is seeking . . . : Program PM, WINS, 1963.

. . . this little passive-resistance . . . : Listening Post, Radio Station WBAS, Philadelphia, autumn 1963.

Page

74 *They controlled you . . . :* Recording, *Message to the Grass Roots;* also in *MXS,* p. 13.

75 *Dr. King is an Uncle Tom . . . : Program PM,* WINS, 1963.
Martin Luther King's primary concern . . . : Ibid.
Once we accept ourselves . . . : Ibid.
Clean yourself up . . . : 1962 Harlem street rally.

76 *The whites came here . . . : Program PM,* WINS, 1963.
In this country, it seems to be all right . . . : The Barry Gray Show, WMCA, March 1963.

78 *The sheep isn't running away . . . : Program PM,* WINS, 1963.
You never call Chinatown . . . : Ibid.
Here in the 137th Psalm . . . : 1961 Boston mosque speech.

13. We Are a World

The material on the Muslim life comes, again, largely from my own interviewing, 1961 to date, and from other primary sources; Lincoln and Essien-Udom remain the premier Muslimologists.

14. Waiting for Allah

93 *The Messenger has seen God . . . :* Lomax, *When the Word Is Given . . .* pp. 209–10.

96 *Uh—sir—one little black man . . . :* WOR panel, October 1962.
Up to now, we haven't been involved . . . : 1962 Bayard Rustin debate.
We believe that God is angry . . . : Ibid.

99 *I would like to announce a very beautiful thing . . . :* This quotation about the plane crash was taped and widely reproduced in the press.
Sir, just as America thanked God . . . : WOR panel, October 1962.

100 I am indebted to my *Newsweek* colleagues Joseph B. Cumming, Jr. and Karl Fleming for much of what I know about Birmingham and the Southern movement of the early sixties; they covered it bravely and brilliantly, and occasionally took me along.

106 *The Black Muslim movement has nothing within its mechanism . . . :* Claude Lewis interview.

16. Paradise Lost

Gladys Towles Root's office kindly supplied me with copies of the complaints and other papers in the paternity suit.

Page

113 Malcolm's account of his confrontation with Mr. Muhammad is in the *Autobiography,* pp. 298–99.
In the Bible, a righteous prophet . . . : Muhammad Speaks, July 31, 1964.

114 *I told [Joseph] and the secretary . . . : Muhammad's Temple of Islam Inc.* v. *Malcolm X Little,* p. 201; the quotations immediately following appear at p. 218.

115 *I believed in him as a man . . . :* Incomplete tape of a radio discussion of early 1965.

116 *You don't catch hell . . . :* Recording, *Message to the Grass Roots;* also in *MXS,* p. 4.

117 *Once they excluded the white man . . . : Ibid.* (and in *MXS,* p. 5).
Same man . . . : Ibid. (and in *MXS,* p. 6).
Was no love lost . . . : Ibid. (and in *MXS,* p. 7).
These Negroes aren't asking for no nation . . . : Ibid. (and in *MXS,* p. 9).
They acted like . . . : Ibid. (and in *MXS,* p. 17).
. . . you sit there . . . : Ibid. (and in *MXS,* p. 12).

118 The text of the Manhattan Center speech appears in Goodman, ed., *The End of White World Supremacy.*
So this statement was taken . . . : The Barry Gray Show, WMCA, April 11, 1964.

119 *The Honorable Elijah Muhammad told me himself . . . : Muhammad's Temple of Islam Inc.* v. *Malcolm X Little,* p. 181.
He told me that because of the climate . . . : Ibid., p. 182.

PART II. The Hour of the Knife

121 *Brother, it is now or never . . . :* Quoted by Leslie Alexander Lacy in his piece in the Jones-Neal anthology, *Black Fire,* p. 23.

17. At the Edge of the Grave

123 *. . . something in nature had failed . . . :* The *Autobiography,* p. 304.

124 *It's just as if you had cut off . . . : When the Word Is Given . . . ,* p. 177.

125 The account of the secret hearing and the suspension is based importantly on Malcolm's testimony in *Muhammad's Temple of Islam Inc.* v. *Malcolm X Little,* particularly at pp. 149–50, 159–60, 178–79 and 201–5. My interview of March 13, 1964, and Helen Dudar's of March 27 were also particularly helpful.

131 *I could have remained quiet . . . :* Helen Dudar interview, March 27, 1964.

Page

132 The March 8 press release and the March 11 wire to Muhammad were both distributed by Malcolm to the media.
It's hard to make a rooster stop . . . : Gertrude Samuels, "Feud Within the Black Muslims," *New York Times Magazine,* March 22, 1964.

18. A Declaration of Independence

133 *Because 1964 threatens . . . :* Statement distributed by Malcolm to the press and read by him at his March 12 press conference; also, with the following, in *MXS,* pp. 20–22.
. . . complete separation . . . : Ibid.
134 *I do not pretend to be . . . : Ibid.*
As of this minute . . . : Ibid.
There can be no black-white unity . . . : Ibid.
It is legal and lawful . . . : Ibid.
The subsequent quotations are from my own notes at the press conference.
137 *I don't know whether you'd say . . . : The Barry Gray Show,* WMCA, April 11, 1964.
138 *Graham has an evangelical gospel . . . :* Helen Dudar interview, March 27, 1964.
145 *The only way to uncover . . . : Ibid.*
146 *The same as they are Christian . . . :* Recording, *Ballots or Bullets.*
148 *We have to be realistic . . . :* A Harlem rally, March 29, 1964.
Millions of so-called Negroes . . . : Ibid.
One hand will wash . . . : The Barry Gray Show, WMCA, April 11, 1964.
That's what black nationalism is . . . : Ibid.
149 *The political philosophy of black nationalism . . . : Ibid.*
Woolworth didn't start out big . . . : Recording, *Ballots or Bullets.*
. . . a man who doesn't even look like us . . . : Ibid.
150 *It will eliminate the need . . . : Ibid.*
He'll never *collect . . . : The Barry Gray Show,* WMCA, April 11, 1964.
151 *. . . smiling and wagging his tail . . . : MXS,* p. 56.
You today are in the hands . . . : Recording, *Ballots or Bullets.*
They'll lynch you in Texas . . . : Ibid.
And at the same time . . . : The Barry Gray Show, WMCA, April 11, 1964.
You put them first . . . : Recording, *Ballots or Bullets.*
152 *Any minority group . . . :* Harlem rally, March 29, 1964.
153 *They haven't never had a bloodless revolution . . . :* Recording, *Ballots or Bullets.*
What do we care about odds? . . . : Ibid.

Page

154 *They put some guerrilla action on him . . . : Ibid.*
The Negroes should not wait . . . : Gertrude Samuels in the *New York Times Magazine.*
I wasn't advocating that Negroes . . . : The Barry Gray Show, WMCA, April 11, 1964.

157 *We're not Americans . . . :* Harlem rally, March 29, 1964.
When you are begging for civil rights . . . : The Barry Gray Show, April 11, 1964.

158 *Here he is standing up . . . :* Recording, *Ballots or Bullets.*
. . . doesn't beg. He doesn't thank you . . . : MXS, p. 52.

159 *They're fed up . . . :* Recording, *Ballots or Bullets.*

20. A Pilgrim's Progress

162 *We're not going to stand up . . . : BAMN,* p. 25.

166 *I think that the pilgrimage . . . :* The quotations about Mecca, continuing through . . . *he means more than color,* are from *The Barry Gray Show,* Station WMCA, New York, July 8, 1964.

168 *. . . some of this earth's most powerful kings . . . :* The quotations from the Mecca letter, continuing through . . . *the older generation of American whites to turn with them,* are from M. S. Handler,, "Malcolm X Pleased by Whites' Attitude on Trip to Mecca," *New York Times,* May 8, 1964.

21. The Child Has Come Home

There are published accounts of Malcolm's visit to Ghana in the Leslie Lacy works cited above and in Ed Smith, *Where To, Black Man?;* my version is based mostly on interviews with others Malcolm met there. John Williams and E. U. Essien-Udom were helpful on Malcolm's visit to Nigeria; so was the *New Leader* report cited above. A partial transcript of the Ghana speech appears in Smith's *Where To, Black Man?* My colleague Mary Doris interviewed Preston King for me; I am grateful to her, and to Peter Webb of *Newsweek* for helping locate him.

22. The Return

183 *. . . a new regard by the public . . . :* The *Autobiography,* p. 375.

184 *You have to walk in . . . : BAMN,* p. 100.

Page

185 *. . . sentence anyone who has not . . . :* Clarke, ed., *Malcolm X: The Man and His Times,* p. 303.

I'm not saying all of them . . . : BAMN, p. 54.

The exchange with Warren is from *Who Speaks for the Negro?,* p. 261.

188 *Any time you lay a few Klansmen out . . . : BAMN,* p. 102.

They've been pretending . . . : Topor series in the Bergen *Record.*

190 The OAAU statement is appended to Breitman's *The Last Year of Malcolm X* (and is also on file at the Schomburg Collection in Harlem).

23. The Far Side of the Rubicon

191 *It was* mine . . . : Claude Lewis interview.

192 *. . . shrewd hypocritical move . . . : Muhammad Speaks,* September 11, 1964.

The Majied cartoon appeared in the issue of April 10, 1964.

. . . the number one hypocrite . . . : Muhammad Speaks, July 3, 1964.

195 The material on the trial is based on interviews and on *Muhammad's Temple of Islam Inc.* v *Malcolm X Little,* especially Malcolm's testimony, pp. 127–228; he did not get to The Subject until page 201.

202 *They've got all the machinery . . . : BAMN,* pp. 66–67.

204 *Right now, things are pretty hot . . . : Ibid.,* p. 103.

25. The Second Time Around

208 The quotations from the OAU memorandum are from *MXS,* pp. 74 and 75. Copies of the 1963 and 1964 OAU resolutions on race in America are available in *Organization of African Unity: Assembly of Heads of State and Government, Resolutions and Decisions of Ordinary and Extra-Ordinary Sessions.*

210 *For twelve long years . . . :* The quotations from the Mecca letter, continuing through . . . *human beings are obligated to correct,* are from M. S. Handler, "Malcolm Rejects Racist Doctrine," *New York Times,* October 4, 1964.

212 Handler's piece on the government's concern—"Malcolm X Seeks U.N. Negro Debate"—appeared on August 13, 1964.

26. By Any Means Necessary

All quotations not otherwise attributed are from the Claude Lewis interview of December 1964.

223 *It is important for you to know . . . :* Recording, *Malcolm X Speaks to Young People;* also in *MXS,* p. 151.

Page

225 *. . . just one human being marrying . . . :* Berton, *Voices of the Sixties,* p. 39.

226 *When I got back . . . : MXS,* p. 179.
We heard you changed . . . : Nadle *Village Voice* interview.
I haven't changed . . . : Ibid.

227 *I'm not blanketly condemning . . . : MXS,* pp. 100–1.
We must make them see . . . : Nadle *Village Voice* interview.
. . . or a real threat of it . . . : Ibid.
Nobody who's looking . . . : MXS, p. 142.

230 A report by William Cook to *Newsweek* was helpful on Malcolm's visit to Selma; other accounts are in *Jet,* March 11, 1965, and in Coretta King, *My Life with Martin Luther King, Jr.,* at p. 259 of the Avon paperback edition.

233 Louis Lomax published the rumors of a Malcolm–Nkrumah–Ben Bella axis in *To Kill a Black Man.*

234 *You show me a capitalist . . . : MXS,* p. 129.
Instead of you running downtown . . . : Ibid.

235 *Is it good for black people? . . . :* The exchange on socialism is reported by Lacy in *Black Fire,* p. 31.

236 *I am the man . . . : MXS,* p. 213.

27. Coming Apart

242 *They won't let me . . . :* Haley's epilogue to the *Autobiography,* p. 424.

243 *. . . the best teacher I left behind . . . : BAMN,* p. 112.

244 *You can make the Muslim Mosque . . . : Ibid.*
No organization meets . . . : Claude Lewis interview.

247 *. . . playing with fire . . . : Muhammad Speaks,* September 11, 1964.
. . . an international hobo . . . : Muhammad Speaks, December 4, 1964.
Only those who wish to be led to hell . . . : Ibid.

248 *. . . the chief hypocrite of them all . . . : Muhammad Speaks,* January 15, 1965.
It begins with their feeling . . . : Ibid.

249 An account of the Ameer beating, written by Jim Droney, appears in the Boston *Herald Traveler,* February 24, 1965.
An account of the Brown shooting, written by Alvin Davis, appears in the New York *Post,* February 26, 1965.

250 An account of the Los Angeles visit, by Edward Bradley as told to Louis Lomax, was circulated by the North American Newspaper Alliance and widely published after Malcolm's death.

254 My account of the reasons for Malcolm's exclusion from France is based on unpublished reporting in *Newsweek's* files. I am grateful to the London *Daily Express* for allowing me access to their morgue files.

Page

28. The Malcolm File

The material is drawn largely from interviews with law-enforcement sources. Anthony V. Bouza's "The Operations of a Police Intelligence Unit," an unpublished master's thesis at the Baruch School of Business and Public Administration, City College of New York, 1968, is an excellent survey of the activities and methods of the Bureau of Special Services.

29. The Hour of the Gun

264 *. . . which, when they come to light . . . :* Recording, *Malcolm X: The Last Message;* also appears, in slightly different form, in *MXS,* p. 193.
I'm not a racist . . . : Ibid.

266 The Jones interview quotations are from Theodore Jones, "Malcolm X Knew He Was a 'Marked Man,'" *New York Times,* February 22, 1965.
The Parks interview quotations are from Gordon Parks, "'I Was a Zombie Then—Like All Muslims I Was Hypnotized,'" *Life,* March 5, 1965.
My account of the assassination is drawn from interviews with Malcolm's followers and law-enforcement sources, plus the minutes of *People* v. *Hagan.*

PART III. A Detective Story

My principal sources on the investigation and trial were interviews with police, prosecutors, defense lawyers and friends and admirers of Malcolm's; the trial record of *People* v. *Hagan;* and press accounts, principally in the *New York Times, Post, Herald Tribune* and *Daily News.*

32. The Second Man

295*n* Lefcourt's cross-examination of Roberts appears in the trial record of *People* v. *Shakur et al.*, pp. 5723–36. The Roberts photo appeared in *Life,* March 5, 1965.

35. Two Matters for the Police

308 Droney's account of his visit with Ameer appeared in the Boston *Herald Traveler,* March 25 and 26, 1965.

Page

48. Inquest

The major conspiratorialist works in print are Norden's *Realist* piece and the Breitman-Porter pamphlet mentioned above. The more influential source, however, is simple word-of-mouth within the black community—at least the black leadership and intellectual community.

PART IV. Every Goodbye Ain't Gone

54. What Became of the Lost-Found Nation of Islam

392 Mr. Muhammad quotation: *You know more . . . :* from an unpublished *Newsweek* interview, July 8, 1965.

394 Mr. Muhammad quotation: *There is some little splinter group . . . : Newsweek,* January 31, 1972.

55. The Malcolm Legacy

397 *. . . you and I didn't exist . . . :* A Harlem speech of December 1964 or January 1965.

398 *We hated our head . . . :* Recording, *Malcolm X: The Last Message;* also, in slightly different form, in *MXS,* p. 185.

399 *I don't judge a man . . . : BAMN,* p. 152.

401 *. . . that we were always this way . . . : Malcolm X on Afro-American History,* p. 4.

402 *I don't believe we're going to overcome . . . : MXS,* p. 143.

403 *We can never forget . . . : BAMN,* p. 64.

404 *I don't think that* I *should be asked . . . :* Fragmentary tape of a radio broadcast of late January or early February 1965.

Index

73 10 9 8 7 6 5 4 3 2 1